# PRAISE FOR RONAN FARROW'S
# CATCH AND KILL

## LIES, SPIES, AND A CONSPIRACY TO PROTECT PREDATORS

One of the Best Books of the Year
*Time*, NPR, *Washington Post, Bloomberg News,*
*Chicago Tribune,* Chicago Public Library, *Fortune,*
*Los Angeles Times, E! News, The Telegraph,* Apple,
*Kirkus Reviews, Library Journal*

IndieBound #1 Bestseller
*USA Today* Bestseller
*New York Times* Bestseller
*Wall Street Journal* Bestseller
Los Angeles Times Book Prize Finalist
Finalist for the National Book Critics Circle Award in
Autobiography

"The connections between presidents, media moguls, and spies described in *Catch and Kill* are stranger than fiction. As a novel, it would be a page-turner. As a reported piece of nonfiction, it's terrifying."
—Eliana Dockterman, *Time*

"At the heart of every great noir is a conspiracy of evil that imbues the initial crime uncovered by the hero with a weightier resonance than was immediately obvious. So it goes with *Catch and Kill.*"
—Elizabeth Bruenig, *Washington Post*

"Meticulous and devastating...part *All the President's Men*, part spy thriller."  —Associated Press

"The year's best spy thriller is stranger—and more horrifying—than fiction...Farrow weaves a breathless narrative as compelling as it is disturbing...bracingly exposes the rot that's persisted across elite American institutions for decades."
  —David Canfield, *Entertainment Weekly*

"*Catch and Kill* is an important, frightening book...It's also a propulsive, cinematic page-turner."  —Erin Keane, *Salon*

"Darkly funny and poignant...a winning account of how it feels to be at the center of the biggest story in the world. It is also, of course, a breathtakingly dogged piece of reporting, in the face of extraordinary opposition."  —Emma Brockes, *The Guardian*

"Absorbing...The behavior documented in *Catch and Kill* is obviously and profoundly distressing...But there are some hopeful threads, too."  —Jennifer Szalai, *New York Times*

"Must read: *Catch and Kill,* by Ronan Farrow. How #sexualabuse stories got suppressed, and how deep-diving, fact-gathering reporting blew the lid off, despite threats, intimidation, and cronymongering at the top. Chilling!"  —Margaret Atwood

"Reads like a thriller...The reveal in *Catch and Kill* is not that there are corrupt people; it's that corrupt people are in control of our media, politics, and entertainment and that, in fact, many of them remain in control."  —Rebecca Traister, *The Cut*

"*Catch and Kill* is exhaustively reported . . . and compulsively read-able, with nearly every page revealing a provocative detail about a household name in media or entertainment."

— EJ Dickson, *Rolling Stone*

"Read this book . . . Farrow's greatest success was to listen, believe, and act, even at his own peril."

— Maria L. La Ganga, *Los Angeles Times*

"Part memoir, part spy thriller, the book is an engrossing account of the dark arts employed by the powerful to suppress their stock-piled bad behavior as well as the cover-up culture that pervades executive suites — many of them at Farrow's former employer, NBC News."                    — Marisa Guthrie, *Hollywood Reporter*

"Historically this book is going to have lasting importance as a viv-idly detailed, in-the-trenches account of the epic effort it took to try to bring down just a piece of the wall of patriarchy that has kept women exploited and oppressed in the media industry and American life forever."                    — David Zurawik, *Baltimore Sun*

"Exceptionally well written, well plotted . . . Reads like a movie."

— Josh Marshall, Talking
Points Memo

"This is an urgent, significant book."

— *Kirkus Reviews* (starred review)

"Explosive."                    — Kate Aurthur, *Variety*

"*Catch and Kill* weaves together months of reporting to reveal explosive allegations that play out like a terrifying spy thriller."

—Kate Storey, *Esquire*

"A measured but damning portrait of that failure at NBC, which he ties to a pattern of harassment and abuse within the network."

—Annalisa Quinn, NPR.org

"Befitting a Farrow story, *Catch and Kill* is chockablock with scoops and revelations."

—Paul Farhi, *Washington Post*

"Ronan Farrow has entered the pantheon of great investigative reporters. With meticulous research and endless revelations, he exposes a system of abuses and cover ups—a system that for too long has been protected. This is an invaluable book."

—David Grann, author of *Killers of the Flower Moon*

"Ronan Farrow's reporting has changed how we understand sexual predation by very, very powerful men in this country and how we understand the vast resources they can bring even on powerful institutions to shield themselves from accountability—and that's worth talking about anywhere, anytime."

—Rachel Maddow, *The Rachel Maddow Show*

"It is the kind of journalism that you want to do as a journalist. That everyone who works in the business should want to facilitate."

—Chris Hayes, *All In with Chris Hayes*

"*Catch and Kill* reads like a thriller, prime to be adapted for the screen."

—Sophie McBain, *New Statesman*

"The book no one can stop talking about."   —K.W. Colyard, *Bustle*

"One can only marvel at Farrow's courage, his resilience and moral fiber. It's one thing to tilt at windmills, it's another to tilt at a human power saw."   —Stephen Galloway, *Hollywood Reporter*

"Riveting and often shocking...*Catch and Kill* has gone off like a hand grenade in the world of New York media...Compelling."
   —*Sunday Times* (UK)

"The book is full of plot and drama...This is a story about a ruling class of men who protect one another—and about the courage of women who speak up."   —Abraham Gutman, *Philadelphia Inquirer*

"An engrossing, emotive, often drily funny binge...A humdinger of a story...A nuanced appreciation of how women are smeared and discredited...Combines righteous anger, gossip, and comedy."
   —*The Times* (UK)

"Ronan is the kind of journalist that activists like myself rely on...His care and compassion for the stories survivors entrusted him with shows in how diligently he investigated each claim. After all of the work he has done to carry their stories forward, I am excited for the world to read this book."   —Tarana Burke

"*Catch and Kill* is proof that Ronan Farrow is the best kind of reporter: thorough, honest, and compassionate...It digs deep, and Farrow is never afraid to tell the truth no matter where the sparks may fly."   —James Patterson

"Combines the intricate reporting of *All the President's Men* with Kafkaesque atmosphere to reveal troubling collusion between the media and the powerful interests they cover. This is a crackerjack journalistic thriller."              —*Publishers Weekly*

"*Catch and Kill* is a rip-roaring account of the years spent chasing the Weinstein story and its spin-offs. It's a deep dive into the world of US media, Hollywood pay-outs, Donald Trump's eccentric ways, spies, and spineless editors. And is it gripping…dripping with jaw-dropping revelations and moments of astonishing pathos."
              —Harriet Alexander, *The Telegraph* (UK)

"*Catch and Kill* is literally jaw-dropping—a shocking, meticulous record of the vast machinery with which moral bankruptcy protects itself, and of the arsenal of weapons available to colossally powerful men whose careers depend on silencing those seeking accountability and truth…This book reveals damningly widespread corruption, complacency, and cowardice, and against it, the blazing courage of the women who spoke out—it's a blueprint of a hideous world, and a foundational building block of a new one."
              —Jia Tolentino, author of *Trick Mirror*

"We've been reading about sex scandals beginning with Harvey Weinstein, but only Ronan Farrow, who reported them, tells us how women's voices were discredited and suppressed for so long. *Catch and Kill* reads like a great detective novel, and could lead to a safer and more just future."              —Gloria Steinem

# CATCH AND KILL

## LIES, SPIES, AND A CONSPIRACY TO PROTECT PREDATORS

# RONAN FARROW

Back Bay Books
Little, Brown and Company
New York Boston London

Back Bay Books / Little, Brown and Company
Hachette Book Group
1290 Avenue of the Americas, New York, NY 10104
littlebrown.com

Originally published in hardcover by Little, Brown and Company, October 2019
First Back Bay trade paperback edition, June 2020

Back Bay Books is an imprint of Little, Brown and Company, a division of Hachette Book Group, Inc. The Back Bay Books name and logo are trademarks of Hachette Book Group, Inc.

The Hachette Speakers Bureau provides a wide range of authors for speaking events. To find out more, go to hachettespeakersbureau.com or call (866) 376-6591.

Interior illustrations © 2019 by Dylan Farrow

ISBN 978-0-316-48663-7 (hc) / 978-0-316-48664-4 (tpb) /
978-0-316-45413-1 (large print) / 978-0-316-49734-3 (international ed)

Cataloging-in-publication data is available at the Library of Congress.

2 2020

LSC-C

Printed in the United States of America

# *CONTENTS*

# PART IV
# SLEEPER

# PART V
## SEVERANCE

*For Jonathan*

# AUTHOR'S NOTE

*C*atch and Kill is based on two years of reporting. It draws on interviews with more than two hundred sources, as well as hundreds of pages of contracts, emails, and texts, and dozens of hours of audio. It was subjected to the same standard of fact-checking as the *New Yorker* stories on which it is based.

All of the dialogue in the book is drawn directly from contemporaneous accounts and records. Because this is a story about surveillance, third parties often witnessed or surreptitiously recorded conversations, and I was sometimes able to obtain their testimonials and records. I adhered to legal and ethical standards when creating my own recordings.

Most of the sources you will meet in these pages have allowed me to use their full names. Some, however, remain unable to do so due to fear of legal reprisal or because of threats to their physical safety. In those instances, the code names used for the sources during the reporting process have been used here. I reached out to all of the key figures in *Catch and Kill* prior to publication, to offer them an opportunity to respond to any allegations being made about them. If they agreed to speak, the narrative reflects their responses. If they did not, a good faith effort was made to include existing public statements.

For the written material quoted throughout the book, the original language, including spelling and copy errors, has been retained.

*Catch and Kill* takes place between 2016 and 2020. It contains descriptions of sexual violence that some readers may find upsetting or traumatic.

# PROLOGUE

*T*he two men sat in a corner at Nargis Cafe, an Uzbek and Russian restaurant in Sheepshead Bay, Brooklyn. It was late 2016, and cold. The place was done up with tchotchkes from the steppes and ceramic depictions of peasant life: grandmas in babushkas, farmers with sheep.

One of the men was Russian, the other Ukrainian, but this was a distinction without a difference: both were children of the disintegrating Soviet Union. They looked to be in their mid-thirties. Roman Khaykin, the Russian, was short and thin and bald, with a quarrelsome snub nose and dark eyes. Everything else about him was pale: eyebrows barely there, face bloodless, bald scalp slick and shining. He was originally from Kislovodsk, which literally translates to "sour waters." His eyes darted around the room, ever suspicious.

Igor Ostrovskiy, the Ukrainian, was taller and a little fat. He had curly hair that got unruly when he let it grow. He and his family had fled to the United States in the early nineties. Like Khaykin, he was always looking for an angle. He was also curious, meddlesome. During high school, he'd suspected that several classmates were selling stolen credit card numbers, probed until he proved it, then helped law enforcement disrupt the operation.

Khaykin and Ostrovskiy spoke in accented English enlivened with native idioms—"Krasavchik!" Khaykin would say, a word derived from "handsome" but in practice serving as praise for talent or a job well done. Both men were in the business of subterfuge and surveillance. When Ostrovskiy had found himself between private investigation jobs in 2011, he'd googled "Russian private investigators" and emailed Khaykin cold to ask for work. Khaykin had liked Ostrovskiy's chutzpah and started hiring him for surveillance jobs. Then they'd argued about Khaykin's methods and drifted apart.

As plates of kebab arrived, Khaykin explained how far he'd been pushing the envelope since they'd last worked together. A new and shadowy client had come into the picture, an enterprise he wouldn't name that was utilizing him as a subcontractor. He was doing big business. "I'm into some cool shit," he said. "Some dark stuff." He'd adopted some new methods, too. He could get bank records and unauthorized credit reports. He had ways of obtaining a phone's geolocation data to track unsuspecting targets. He described how much the phone hijinks cost: a few thousand dollars for the usual approach to the problem, with cheaper options for gullible marks and more expensive ones for those who proved elusive. Khaykin said he'd already used the tactic successfully, in a case where one family member had hired him to find another.

Ostrovskiy figured Khaykin was full of shit. But Ostrovskiy needed the work. And Khaykin, it turned out, needed more manpower to serve his mysterious new patron.

Before parting ways, Ostrovskiy asked about the phone tracking again. "Isn't that illegal?" he wondered.

"Ehhhh," said Khaykin.

On a tiled wall nearby, a blue-and-white evil eye hung on a string, watching.

# PART I: POISON VALLEY

# CHAPTER 1:

# *TAPE*

"**W**hat do you mean it's not airing tomorrow?" My words drifted over the emptying newsroom on the fourth floor of 30 Rockefeller Plaza, inside the Comcast building, which had once been the GE building, which had once been the RCA building. On the other end of the line, Rich McHugh, my producer at NBC News, was talking over what sounded like the bombing of Dresden but was in fact the natural soundscape of a household with two sets of young twins. "They just called, they're — no, Izzy, you have to share — Jackie, please don't bite her — Daddy's on the phone —"

"But it's the strongest story in the series," I said. "Maybe not the best TV, but the best underlying *story* —"

"They say we've gotta move it. It's *fakakt*," he said, missing the last syllable. (McHugh had this habit of trying out Yiddish words. It never went well.)

Airing a series of back-to-back investigative spots like the one McHugh and I were about to launch required choreography. Each of the stories was long, consuming days in the network's edit rooms. Rescheduling one was a big deal. "Move it to when?" I asked.

On the other end of the line, there was a muffled crash and several successive shrieks of laughter. "I gotta call you back," he said.

McHugh was a TV veteran who had worked at Fox and MSNBC and, for the better part of a decade, *Good Morning America*. He was barrel-chested, with ginger hair and a ruddy complexion, and wore a lot of gingham work shirts. He had a plainspoken, laconic quality that cut through the passive-aggressive patter of corporate bureaucracy. "He looks like a farmer," the investigative unit boss who had first put us together the previous year had said. "For that matter, he talks like a farmer. You two make no sense together."

"Why the assignment, then?" I'd asked.

"You'll be good for one another," he'd replied, with a shrug.

McHugh had seemed skeptical. I didn't love talking about my family background, but most people were familiar with it: my mother, Mia Farrow, was an actress; my father, Woody Allen, a director. My childhood had been plastered across the tabloids after he was accused of sexual assault by my seven-year-old sister, Dylan, and began a sexual relationship with another one of my sisters, Soon-Yi, eventually marrying her. There had been a few headlines again when I started college at an unusually young age and when I headed off to Afghanistan and Pakistan as a junior State Department official. In 2013, I'd started a four-year deal with NBCUniversal, anchoring a midday show on its cable news channel, MSNBC, for the first year of it. I'd dreamed of making the show serious and fact-driven, and by the end, was proud of how I'd used the inauspicious time slot for taped investigative stories. The show got some bad reviews at the start, good reviews at the end, and few viewers throughout. Its cancellation was little-noticed; for years after, chipper acquaintances would bound up at parties and tell me that they loved the show and still watched it every day. "That's so nice of you to say," I'd tell them.

I'd moved over to the network to work as an investigative

correspondent. As far as Rich McHugh was concerned, I was a young lightweight with a famous name, looking for something to do because my contract lasted longer than my TV show. This is where I should say the skepticism was mutual, but I just want everyone to like me.

Working with a producer on the road meant a lot of time together on flights and in rental cars. On our first few shoots together, the silence would yawn between us as highway guardrails flashed by, or I'd fill it with too much talk about myself, eliciting the occasional grunt.

But the pairing was starting to yield strong stories for my *Today* show investigative series and for *Nightly News*, as well as a reluctant mutual respect. McHugh was as smart as anyone I'd met in the news business and a sharp editor of scripts. And we both loved a tough story.

After McHugh's call, I looked at the cable headlines on one of the newsroom's televisions, then texted him: "They're scared of sexual assault?" The story we were being asked to reschedule was about colleges botching sexual assault investigations on campus. We'd talked to both victims and alleged perpetrators, who were sometimes in tears, and sometimes had their faces obscured in shadow. It was the sort of report that, in the 8:00 a.m. time slot for which it was destined, would require Matt Lauer to furrow his brow, express earnest concern, and then transition to a segment about celebrity skin care.

McHugh wrote back: "Yes. All Trump and then sex assault."

❖

It was a Sunday evening in early October 2016. The preceding Friday, the *Washington Post* had published an article demurely titled "Trump Recorded Having Extremely Lewd Conversation About

Women in 2005." There was a video accompanying the article, the kind you used to call "not safe for work." In a soliloquy captured by the celebrity news program *Access Hollywood*, Donald Trump held forth about grabbing women "by the pussy." "I did try and fuck her. She was married," he had said. "She's now got the big phony tits and everything."

Trump's interlocutor had been Billy Bush, the host of *Access Hollywood*. Bush was a small man with good hair. You could place him near any celebrity and he would produce a steady stream of forgettable but occasionally weird red-carpet banter. "How do you feel about your butt?" he once asked Jennifer Lopez. And when she, visibly uncomfortable, replied, "Are you kidding me? You did not just ask me that," he said brightly, "I did!"

And so, as Trump described his exploits, Bush chirped and snickered in assent. "Yes! The Donald has scored!"

*Access Hollywood* was an NBCUniversal property. After the *Washington Post* broke the story that Friday, NBC platforms raced their own versions on air. When *Access* broadcast the tape, it excised some of Bush's more piquant remarks. Some critics asked when NBC executives became aware of the tape and whether they deliberately sat on it. Leaked accounts presented differing timelines. On "background" calls to reporters, some NBC executives said the story just hadn't been ready, that it had required further legal review. (Of one such call, a *Washington Post* writer observed tartly: "The executive was unaware of any specific legal issue raised by airing an eleven-year-old recording of a presidential candidate who was apparently aware at the time that he was being recorded by a TV program.") Two NBCUniversal lawyers, Kim Harris and Susan Weiner, had reviewed the tape and signed off on its release, but NBC had hesitated, and lost one of the most important election stories in a generation.

There was another problem: the *Today* show had just brought

Billy Bush into its cast of hosts. Not two months earlier, they'd aired a "Get to Know Billy" video, complete with footage of him getting his chest hair waxed on air.

McHugh and I had been editing and legally vetting our series for weeks. But the trouble was apparent the moment I began promoting the series on social media. "Come to watch the #BillyBush apology, stay to watch #RonanFarrow explain to him why an apology is necessary," one viewer tweeted.

"Of *course* they moved sexual assault," I texted McHugh an hour later. "Billy Bush must be apologizing for the pussy grab convo right within spitting distance of our airtime."

Billy Bush did not apologize that day. As I waited in the wings at Studio 1A the next morning, looking over my script, Savannah Guthrie announced: "Pending further review of the matter, NBC News has suspended Billy Bush, the host of *Today*'s third hour, for his role in that conversation with Donald Trump." And then it was onward and upward to cooking, and more caffeinated laughter — and my story on Adderall abuse on college campuses, which had been rushed in to replace the one about sexual assault.

◆

The years before the release of the *Access Hollywood* tape had seen the reemergence of sexual assault allegations against the comedian Bill Cosby. In July of 2016, the former Fox News personality Gretchen Carlson had filed a sexual harassment suit against the head of that network, Roger Ailes. Soon after the tape was released, women in at least fifteen cities staged sit-ins and marches at Trump buildings, chanting about emancipation, carrying signs with reappropriated "pussy" imagery: cats, howling or arching, emblazoned with "PUSSY GRABS BACK." Four women publicly claimed that Trump had groped or kissed them without consent in much the fashion he'd described as routine to Billy Bush. The Trump campaign denounced them as fabulists. A hashtag, popularized by the commentator Liz Plank, solicited explanations of why #WomenDontReport. "A (female) criminal attorney said because I'd done a sex scene in a film I would never win against the studio head," the actress Rose McGowan tweeted. "Because it's been an open secret in Hollywood/Media & they shamed me while adulating my rapist," she added. "It is time for some goddamned honesty in this world."

# CHAPTER 2:

# *BITE*

Since the establishment of the first studios, few movie executives had been as dominant, or as domineering, as the one to whom McGowan was referring. Harvey Weinstein cofounded the production-and-distribution companies Miramax and the Weinstein Company, helping to reinvent the model for independent films with movies like *Sex, Lies, and Videotape*; *Pulp Fiction*; and *Shakespeare in Love*. His movies had earned more than three hundred Oscar nominations, and at the annual awards ceremonies he had been thanked more than almost anyone else in movie history, ranking just below Steven Spielberg and several places above God. At times, even this seemed a fine distinction: Meryl Streep had once jokingly referred to Weinstein *as* God.

Weinstein was six feet tall and big. His face was lopsided, one small eye in a habitual squint. He often wore oversize tee shirts over drooping jeans that gave him a billowing profile. The son of a diamond cutter, Weinstein was raised in Queens. As a teenager he and his younger brother, Bob, had snuck off to see *The 400 Blows* at an arthouse theater, hoping it was a "sex movie." Instead, they stumbled into François Truffaut and a burgeoning love of highbrow cinema.

Weinstein enrolled at the State University of New York at Buffalo partly because the city had multiple movie theaters. When he was eighteen, he and a friend named Corky Burger produced a column for the student newspaper, the *Spectrum*, featuring a character they called "Denny the Hustler," who menaced women into submission. "'Denny the Hustler' did not take no for an answer," the column read. "His whole approach employs a psychology of command, or in layman's terms—'Look, baby, I'm probably the best-looking and most exciting person you'll ever want to meet—and if you refuse to dance with me, I'll probably crack this bottle of Schmidt's over your skull.'"

Weinstein dropped out of college to start a business with his brother, Bob, and Burger, at first under the banner of Harvey and Corky Productions, which specialized in concert promotion. But at a Buffalo theater he acquired, Weinstein also screened the independent and foreign films he'd come to love. Eventually, he and Bob Weinstein started Miramax, named after their parents, Miriam and Max, and began acquiring small foreign films. Weinstein turned out to have a flair for making the movies into events. They received awards, like the surprise Palme d'Or win at Cannes for *Sex, Lies, and Videotape*. In the early nineties, Disney acquired Miramax. Weinstein spent a decade as the goose that laid egg after golden egg. And in the 2000s, when the relationship with Disney faltered and the brothers started a new enterprise, the Weinstein Company, they quickly raised hundreds of millions of dollars in funding. Weinstein hadn't quite recaptured his glory days, but did win back-to-back Best Picture Oscars for *The King's Speech* in 2010 and *The Artist* in 2011. Over the course of his ascent, he married his assistant, got a divorce, and later wed an aspiring actress he'd begun casting in small roles.

Weinstein was famous for his bullying, even threatening, style of doing business. He was deimatic, capable of expanding to frighten, like a blowfish inflating itself. He'd draw up to rivals or underlings, nose-to-nose, red-faced. "I was sitting at my desk one day and thought we were hit by an earthquake," Donna Gigliotti, who shared an Oscar with Weinstein for producing *Shakespeare in Love*, once told a reporter. "The wall just shook. I stood up. I learned that he had flung a marble ashtray at the wall." And then there were stories, mostly whispers, of a darker kind of violence against women, and of efforts to keep his victims quiet. Every few years, a reporter, alerted to the rumors, would sniff around, to see if the smoke might lead to fire.

For Weinstein, the months before the 2016 presidential election looked like business as usual. There he was, at a cocktail party for William J. Bratton, the former New York City police commissioner. There he was, laughing with Jay-Z, announcing a film and television deal with the rapper. And there he was, deepening his long-standing ties to the Democratic Party politicians for whom he had long been a major fund-raiser.

All year, he'd been part of the brain trust around Hillary Clinton. "I'm probably telling you what you know already, but that needs to be silenced," he emailed Clinton's staff, about messaging from Bernie Sanders's competing campaign to Latino and African American voters. "This article gives you everything I discussed with you yesterday," he said in another message, sending a column critical of Sanders and pressing for negative campaigning. "About to forward some creative. Took your idea and ran," Clinton's campaign manager responded. By the end of the year, Weinstein had raised hundreds of thousands of dollars for Clinton.

A few days after McGowan's tweets that October, Weinstein was at the St. James Theatre in New York City for a lavish fund-raiser he'd co-produced for Clinton, which put a further $2 million in her campaign's coffers. The musician Sara Bareilles sat bathed in purple light and sang: "your history of silence won't do you any good / Did you think it would? / Let your words be anything but empty / Why don't you tell them the truth?" — which seems too on the nose to be true, but that's what happened.

Weinstein's influence had dwindled somewhat in the preceding years, but it was still sufficient to sustain public embrace from the elites. As the latest awards season kicked off that fall, a *Hollywood Reporter* movie critic, Stephen Galloway, ran an article headlined "Harvey Weinstein, the Comeback Kid," with the subhead, "There are a lot of reasons to root for him, especially now."

❖

Around the same time, Weinstein sent an email to his lawyers, including David Boies, the high-profile attorney who had represented Al Gore in the 2000 presidential election dispute and argued for marriage equality before the U.S. Supreme Court. Boies had represented Weinstein for years. He was in his late seventies by then, still trim, with a face that had creased, with age, into something kind and approachable. "The Black Cube Group from Israel contacted me through Ehud Barak," Weinstein wrote. "They r strategists and say your firm have used them. Gmail me when u get a chance."

Barak was the former prime minister of Israel and chief of the General Staff of the Israeli military. Black Cube, the enterprise he'd recommended to Weinstein, was run largely by former officers of Mossad and other Israeli intelligence agencies. It had branches in Tel

Aviv, London, and Paris, and offered its clients the skills of operatives "highly experienced and trained in Israel's elite military and governmental intelligence units," according to its literature.

Later that month, Boies's firm and Black Cube signed a confidential contract, and Boies's colleagues wired 100,000 U.S. dollars for an initial period of work. In the documents around the assignment, Weinstein's identity was often concealed. He was referred to as "the end client" or "Mr. X." Naming Weinstein, an operative from Black Cube wrote, "will make him extremely angry."

Weinstein seemed excited about the work. During a meeting in late November, he pressed Black Cube to keep going. More money was wired, and the agency put in motion aggressive operations referred to as "Phase 2A" and "Phase 2B."

◆

Soon after, a reporter named Ben Wallace got a call from a number he didn't recognize, with a UK country code. Wallace was in his late forties, and wore narrow, professorial glasses. He had published, a few years earlier, *The Billionaire's Vinegar*, a history of the world's most expensive bottle of wine. More recently, he'd been writing for *New York* magazine, where he'd spent the preceding weeks talking to people about the rumors swirling around Weinstein.

"You can call me Anna," said the voice on the other end of the line, in a refined European accent. After graduating from college, Wallace had lived in the Czech Republic and Hungary for a few years. He had a good ear for accents, but he couldn't quite place this one. He guessed she might be German.

"I received your number through a friend," the woman continued, explaining that she knew he was working on a story about the entertainment industry. Wallace tried to think of what friend could have made such an introduction. Not many people knew about his assignment.

"I might have something that might be of importance for you," she continued. When Wallace pressed her for more information, she was coy. The information she had was sensitive, she said. She needed to see him. He hesitated for a moment. Then he thought, What's the harm? He was looking for a break in the story. Maybe she'd be it.

The following Monday morning, Wallace sat in a coffee shop in SoHo and tried to get a read on the mystery woman. She looked to be in her mid-thirties, with long blond hair, dark eyes, high cheekbones, and a Roman nose. She wore Converse Chucks and gold jewelry. Anna said she wasn't comfortable giving her real name yet. Frightened, she was grappling with whether to come forward. Wallace had been picking up on this theme in his exchanges with other sources. He told her she could take her time.

For their next meeting, not long after, she chose a hotel bar in the same neighborhood. When Wallace arrived, she smiled at him invitingly, even seductively. She had already ordered a glass of wine. "I won't bite," she said, patting the seat next to her. "Come sit next to me." Wallace said he had a cold and ordered tea. If they were going to work together, he told her, he needed to know more. At this, Anna broke down, her face twisting in anguish. She seemed to hold back tears as she began to describe her experiences with Weinstein. That she'd gone through something intimate and upsetting was clear, but she was cagey about details. She wanted to learn more before she answered all of Wallace's questions. She asked what had motivated him to take on the assignment and what kind of impact he sought. As he replied, Anna leaned in, conspicuously extending her wrist toward him.

For Wallace, working on the story was becoming a strange,

charged experience. There was a level of noise, of keen outside interest, to which he was unaccustomed. He was hearing from other journalists, even: Seth Freedman, an Englishman who'd written for the
*Guardian*, got in touch soon after, suggesting he'd heard the rumors
about what Wallace was working on and wanted to help.

## CHAPTER 3:

# *DIRT*

In the first week of November 2016, just before the election, Dylan Howard, editor in chief of the *National Enquirer*, issued an unusual order to a member of his staff. "I need to get everything out of the safe," he said. "And then we need to get a shredder down there." Howard was from southeastern Australia. He had a troll-doll tuft of ginger hair over a round face, and wore Coke-bottle glasses and loud ties. That day, he appeared to be in a panic. The *Wall Street Journal* had just called the *Enquirer* for comment about a story involving Howard and David Pecker, the CEO of the *Enquirer*'s parent company, American Media Inc. The story alleged that AMI had taken on a sensitive assignment at Donald Trump's behest, chasing a lead with the objective not of publishing it, but of making it go away.

The staffer opened the safe, removed a set of documents, and tried to wrest it shut. Later, reporters would discuss the safe like it was the warehouse where they stored the Ark of the Covenant in *Indiana Jones*, but it was small and cheap and old. It sat in an office that had belonged, for years, to the magazine's veteran executive editor, Barry Levine. It had a tendency to get jammed.

It took several tries and a FaceTime video call to the staffer's significant other for advice to get the safe properly closed. Later that day, one employee said, a disposal crew collected and carried away a larger than customary volume of refuse. A Trump-related document from the safe, along with others in the *Enquirer*'s possession, had been shredded.

In June 2016, Howard had compiled a list of the dirt about Trump accumulated in AMI's archives, dating back decades. After the election, Trump's lawyer Michael Cohen requested all the tabloid empire's materials about the new president. There was an internal debate: some were starting to realize that surrendering it all would create a legally problematic paper trail, and resisted. Nevertheless, Howard and senior staff ordered the reporting material that wasn't already in the small safe exhumed from storage bins in Florida and sent to AMI headquarters. When the reporting material arrived, it was placed first in the little safe and then, as the political temperature around the magazine's relationship with the president turned white-hot, in a bigger one in the office of human resources head Daniel Rotstein. (The HR offices of the *Enquirer*'s parent company, one person familiar with the company cracked with mock surprise, were not, in fact, in a strip bar.) It was only later, when one of the employees who had been skeptical started getting jumpy and went to check, that they found something amiss: the list of Trump dirt didn't match up with the physical files. Some of the material had gone missing. Howard began swearing to colleagues that nothing had ever been destroyed, an assertion he maintains to this day.

In one sense, destroying documents would be consistent with a baseline of malfeasance that had, for years, defined the *Enquirer* and its parent company. "We are always at the edge of what's legally permissible," a senior AMI staffer told me. "It's very exciting." Illicitly obtaining medical records was one standard maneuver. At major hospitals, the *Enquirer* cultivated moles. One such mole, who had spirited the records of Britney Spears, Farrah Fawcett, and others out of UCLA Medical Center, ultimately pleaded guilty to a felony charge.

AMI routinely engaged in what employee after employee called "blackmail"—withholding the publication of damaging information in exchange for tips or exclusives. And the employees whispered about an even darker side of AMI's operations, including a network of subcontractors who were sometimes paid through creative channels to avoid scrutiny, and who sometimes relied on tactics that were hands-on and intrusive.

In another sense, however, something new seemed to be happening in AMI's offices in Manhattan's Financial District. Pecker had known Donald Trump for decades. When a reporter said to Pecker, after the election, that criticism of Trump was not synonymous with criticism of AMI, he'd replied, "To me it is. The guy's a personal friend of mine." Over the years, the two had enjoyed an alliance, to their mutual benefit. Pecker, a graying former accountant from the Bronx with a broad mustache, got proximity to power and Trump's many perquisites. "Pecker got to fly on his private jet," said Maxine Page, who worked at AMI on and off from 2002 to 2012, including as an executive editor at one of the company's websites. Howard, too, enjoyed Trump's favors. On the eve of the 2017 inauguration, he sent excited texts to friends and colleagues, with pictures of his access to the festivities.

The fruit of the relationship, for Trump, was more consequential. Another former editor, Jerry George, estimated that Pecker killed perhaps ten fully reported stories about Trump, and nixed many more potential leads during George's twenty-eight years at the *Enquirer*.

As Trump mounted his run for office, the alliance appeared to deepen and change. Suddenly, the *Enquirer* was formally endorsing Trump, and it and other AMI outlets were blaring sycophantic headlines. "DON'T MESS WITH DONALD TRUMP!" one issue of the *Globe* declared. "HOW TRUMP WILL WIN!" added the *Enquirer*. When the *Enquirer* tallied the "Twisted Secrets of the Candidates!," the tabloid's revelation about Trump was: "he has greater support and popularity than even he's admitted to!" Screaming covers about Hillary Clinton's supposed treachery and flagging health became a mainstay. "'SOCIOPATH' HILLARY CLINTON'S SECRET PSYCH FILES EXPOSED!" they howled, and "HILLARY: CORRUPT! RACIST! CRIMINAL!" The exclamation points made the headlines look like budget musical titles. A favorite subplot was Clinton's impending death. (She miraculously defied the tabloid's prognoses and kept right on almost-dying all the way through the election.) Not long before voters went to the polls, Howard had colleagues pull a stack of the covers for Pecker to present to Trump.

During the campaign, Trump associates, including Michael Cohen, called Pecker and Howard. A series of covers about Trump's competitor in the Republican primary, Ted Cruz, which chronicled a wild conspiracy theory about Cruz's father being linked to the assassination of JFK, were planted by another Trump associate, the political consultant Roger Stone. Howard even made contact with Alex Jones, a maniacal radio personality whose conspiracy theories had helped lift Trump's candidacy, and later appeared on Jones's show. And sometimes, AMI staffers were told not merely to kill unflattering leads about the magazine's favored candidate but to seek out information and lock it up tight in the company's vaults. "This is fucking nonsense," one of them later told me. "The operation became like Pravda."

◆

The pact with Trump wasn't the only alliance Howard and Pecker nurtured. In 2015, AMI had struck a production deal with Harvey Weinstein. Nominally, the deal empowered AMI, amid declining circulation numbers, to spin off its Radar Online website into a television show. But the relationship had another dimension. That year, Howard and Weinstein drew close. When a model went to the police with a claim that Weinstein had groped her, Howard told his staff to stop reporting on the matter—and then, later, explored buying the rights to the model's story, in exchange for her signing a nondisclosure agreement. When the actress Ashley Judd claimed a studio head had sexually harassed her, almost but not quite identifying Weinstein, AMI reporters were asked to pursue negative items about her going to rehab. After McGowan's claim surfaced, one colleague of Howard's remembered him saying, "I want dirt on that bitch."

In late 2016, the relationship deepened. In one email, Howard proudly forwarded to Weinstein the latest handiwork of one of AMI's subcontractors: a secret recording of a woman whom the subcontractor had enticed to make statements damaging to McGowan. "I have something AMAZING," Howard wrote. The woman had "laid into Rose pretty hard."

"This is the killer," Weinstein replied. "Especially if my fingerprints r not on this."

"They are not," Howard wrote. "And the conversation—between you and I—is RECORDED." In another email, Howard sent a list of other contacts to be targeted in a similar manner. "Let's discuss next steps on each," he wrote.

The *National Enquirer* was a tabloid sewer, a place to which much of America's ugly gossip eventually flowed. When stories were abandoned or successfully buried at the behest of AMI's friends in high places, they came to rest in the *Enquirer*'s archives, in what some staff called "kill files." As his collaboration with Weinstein deepened, Howard had been scrutinizing this historical repository. One day that fall, colleagues recalled, he requested that a specific file be pulled, related to an anchor at a TV network.

# CHAPTER 4:

# *BUTTON*

**M**att Lauer sat with his legs crossed just so: right knee over left, with a slight lean forward, allowing his right hand to grip the top of the same shin. Even in casual conversation, he looked as if he might effortlessly throw to a commercial break. When I tried to emulate Lauer's relaxed-yet-composed seating position on air, I just looked like someone new to yoga.

It was December 2016. We were in Lauer's office on the third floor of 30 Rockefeller Plaza. He sat behind his glass-topped desk. I was on the couch opposite. On shelves and credenzas, Emmys loomed. Lauer had worked his way up from local television in West Virginia to his current position as one of the most prominent and popular figures in network television. NBC paid him in excess of $20 million a year and ferried him by helicopter to and from his house in the Hamptons.

"It's really good stuff," Lauer was saying, of the most recent story in my investigative series. He had his hair buzzed close, which suited him, and tufty salt-and-pepper facial hair, which suited him less. "That leaking nuclear plant, where was it—"

"Washington State," I said.

"Washington State. That's right. And that government guy sweating bullets." He shook his head, chuckled.

The story was about the Hanford nuclear facility, where the United States government had buried several Olympic swimming pools' worth of nuclear waste left over from the Manhattan Project. Workers were getting sprayed with that waste with alarming frequency.

"That's what we need more of on the show," he said. We'd talked a lot about his belief in serious investigative reporting. "Plays well on set. And it rates," he continued. "What have you got coming up?"

I glanced at the sheaf of papers I'd brought with me. "There's one on Dow and Shell seeding California farmlands with toxic chemicals." Lauer nodded appreciatively, sliding on horn-rimmed glasses and turning to his monitor. Emails scrolled by, reflected in the lenses. "There's a series on addiction, one on truck safety reforms being blocked by lobbyists," I continued. "And one about sexual harassment in Hollywood."

His eyes snapped back to me. I wasn't sure which story had caught his attention.

"It's for a series about undercovered stories in Hollywood," I said. "Pedophilia, racism, harassment..."

Lauer was wearing a neatly tailored suit with a gray windowpane motif and a striped navy tie. He smoothed it down and shifted his attention back to me. "They sound terrific." He was eyeing me appraisingly. "Where do you see yourself in a few years?" he asked.

It had been nearly two years since MSNBC euthanized my cable program. "Ronan Farrow Goes from Anchor's Desk to Cubicle," a recent Page Six headline had offered. Turns out, my desk was in the background shot of MSNBC's daytime news coverage. There I was, typing behind Tamron Hall and on the phone behind Ali Velshi. I was proud of the work I was doing for *Today*. But I was struggling to find a niche. I considered everything, even radio. That fall, I met with Sirius XM Satellite Radio. Melissa Lonner, a vice president there, had departed *Today* a few years earlier. Trying to sound bullish, I told her that I figured *Today* would be a better platform for investigative reporting than cable anyway. "Yes," Lonner said, with a tight smile. "I loved it there." But the truth was, my future felt uncertain, and it meant a lot to me that Lauer was giving me this time.

I thought about his question about the future and said, "I'd like to get back to anchoring at some point."

"I know, I know," he said. "That's what you *think* you want." I opened my mouth. He cut me off. "You're searching for something." He slid his glasses off, inspected them. "Maybe you'll find it. But you're going to have to figure out yourself. What you really care about." He smiled. "You excited for next week?"

I was scheduled to fill in when he and the other anchors departed for the Christmas holiday.

"I am!" I said.

"Remember, you're the new guy on set. Interaction is everything. Write your Orange Room tags with bait for conversation." The Orange Room was the part of *Today* where we aired slideshows of Facebook posts, for some reason. "Personalize the scripts. If it were me, you'd mention my kids. You get the idea." I scribbled a few notes, thanked him, and began to leave.

As I reached the door, he said wryly, "Don't let us down. I'll be watching."

"You want this closed?" I asked.

"I've got it," he said. He pushed a button on his desk. The door swung shut.

◆

Not long after, I sent a copy of *The Teenage Brain: A Neuroscientist's Survival Guide to Raising Adolescents and Young Adults* to Lauer's house in the Hamptons. On air, I followed his advice in earnest. I stood in the *Today* show plaza and spread holiday cheer, breath clouding in front of me. I sat on the semicircular couch in Studio 1A with the other pinch hitters for intros and outros, and gripped my shin, and looked not much like Matt Lauer at all.

One morning, we closed out the show with a reel of outtakes and bloopers from the preceding year. We'd all seen the video: when we'd aired it once before, and then again at the show's nondenominational holiday party. When the tape began to play and the studio lights dimmed, most of the team wandered off or checked their phones. There was just one senior *Today* employee who remained in front of the monitor, transfixed. She was one of the hardest-working people I'd encountered in television. She'd worked her way up from local news to her role that day.

"I don't envy you," I said. "Having to watch this over and over."

"No," she said, still fixed on the screen. "I love this. This was my dream job." I was startled to see tears in her eyes.

◆

A few weeks after my conversation with Matt Lauer, around the corner in the NBC News executive suite, I sat opposite the executive in charge of the *Today* show, Noah Oppenheim. That day, the views of Rockefeller Plaza from his corner office were obscured by fog and drizzle. I was flanked by McHugh and Jackie Levin, the senior producer overseeing our next investigative miniseries, the one I'd told Lauer about, on Hollywood. "So, what have you got?" asked

Oppenheim, leaning back on a couch, and I prepared to give him an update.

Oppenheim, like Lauer, supported hard news. When he was tapped to run *Today*, he'd come to see me before he even had a desk, and told me to deal with only him, not the other executives at the show. He'd put me on the *Today* show more frequently and greenlit my increasingly ambitious investigations. When *Ronan Farrow Daily* became *Ronan Farrow Rarely*, it was Oppenheim who arranged to have me stay at the network and continue my *Today* show series. Oppenheim was in his late thirties, with affable, boyish features and body language that seemed forever in a slouch, waiting for you to lean in before he did. He had a quality I lacked and envied, which was this: he was insouciant, laid-back, cool. He was a doe-eyed stoner whose mellow seemed impossible to harsh. We'd laughed about his stories of getting high and ordering entire Thai delivery menus and we'd planned to spend a night in with edibles at some point.

Oppenheim was smart, with an Ivy League pedigree. Early in the 2000 presidential campaign, MSNBC personality Chris Matthews and his executive producer, Phil Griffin, who would go on to run that cable channel, encountered a snowstorm during a commute from New Hampshire back to New York and stopped off at Harvard. That night, Griffin and a colleague found Oppenheim, a senior who wrote for the *Harvard Crimson*, drunk in a corner. They ended up offering to put him on TV. "They stopped off at Harvard Square and started talking to some undergraduate girls at a bar," Oppenheim later told a reporter. "They followed them to a late-night party at the newspaper building and one picked up a copy of the paper and read an article I'd written about the presidential race."

That chance encounter with Oppenheim eventually led him from conservative punditry to producing on MSNBC, and then to a senior producer role on *Today*. But he always had wider ambitions. He co-authored a series of self-help books called *The Intellectual Devotional* ("Impress your friends by explaining Plato's Cave allegory, pepper your cocktail party conversation with opera terms," read the jacket copy) and boasted that Steven Spielberg had given them out as holiday gifts, "so now I can die happy." In 2008, he left the network and moved his family to Santa Monica to pursue a career in Hollywood. Referring to journalism, he said, "I had an amazing experience through my 20s doing that but had always loved the movie business, and movies, and drama." He worked briefly for the media heiress Elisabeth Murdoch's reality television empire, then transitioned to screenwriting. "I did that," he said of reality TV, "then got antsy because it still wasn't getting me to my real love: scripted drama."

Oppenheim had enjoyed a charmed ascent in each of his careers. He sent his first screenplay, *Jackie*, a morose biopic about the days between Kennedy's assassination and funeral, to a studio executive who had been a friend at Harvard. "Less than a week later, I find myself sitting with Steven Spielberg in his office on the Universal lot," he later recalled. The movie, which featured a lot of dialogue-free long shots of the woman in question pacing around with tear-streaked mascara, had been embraced by critics and, I was finding, less so by the public. "What was that movie he did again?" McHugh had said as we walked over to the meeting.

"*Jackie*."

"Oof."

Oppenheim had also co-written an adaptation of the young adult postapocalyptic adventure *The Maze Runner*, which made money, and a sequel to the *Divergent* series, which did not.

The years between Oppenheim's departure from Rockefeller Plaza and his return had been challenging for *Today*. The anchor Ann Curry, beloved by audiences and not beloved by Matt Lauer, had been fired. Ratings slipped behind the competition, the more caf-feinated *Good Morning America*. The stakes for NBC were high: *Today* was worth half a billion dollars in advertising revenue a year. In 2015, NBC brought Oppenheim back to *Today* to perform a rescue operation.

◆

In June 2016, I'd gotten a green light from Oppenheim on a series I had dubbed, in the exaggerated manner of morning television, *The Dark Side of Hollywood?*, but getting support on specific topics had presented some difficulty. The earliest pitch I sent to the brass focused on allegations of sexual misconduct with minors, including the ones ultimately reported in the *Atlantic* about director Bryan Singer, which he has long denied, as well as claims about pedophilia raised by the actor Corey Feldman. An interview with Feldman had been secured: *Today's* head of booking, Matt Zimmerman, had cut a deal whereby the former child star would perform a song and stay on to answer my questions. But Zimmerman had later called to say Oppenheim considered the pedophilia angle "too dark," and we'd scrapped the plan.

The stories I proposed as replacements presented their own obsta-cles. Levin, the senior producer, told McHugh and me that a story about celebrities performing for dictators, referencing Jennifer Lopez's seven-figure gig for Gurbanguly Berdymukhamedov, totalitarian leader of Turkmenistan, was a nonstarter in light of the network's relationship with Lopez. No one seemed to even want to acknowl-edge a story I proposed about racial discrimination in Hollywood. Oppenheim finally said, with a chuckle, "Look, I'm 'woke' or what-ever, I just don't think our viewers want to see Will Smith complain about how hard he has it."

Network television is a commercial medium. Conversations about the palatability of stories are commonplace. You pick your battles, and none of these were battles worth picking. We'd set aside the Hollywood series for a few months, reviving it late in the year, with an eye toward airing it around Oscar season early the next year.

◆

As we sat in Oppenheim's office that January, we mulled more potential topics, including a pitch about plastic surgery. Then I returned to one of my proposals that seemed to have withstood the development conversations so far: a story about the Hollywood "casting couch" — performers being harassed or propositioned for transactional sex at work. "We've been making steady progress," I said. I'd already begun talking to a few actresses who claimed to have stories.

"You should look at Rose McGowan, she tweeted something about a studio head," Oppenheim said.

"I hadn't seen that," I replied. I pulled out my phone and loaded a *Variety* article. The actress's tweets slid by under my thumb. "Maybe she'll talk," I said. "I'll look into it."

Oppenheim shrugged hopefully.

# CHAPTER 5:

# *KANDAHAR*

*A* few days later, Harvey Weinstein was in Los Angeles, meeting with operatives from Black Cube. The operatives reported that they had been making headway, encircling agreed-upon targets. Weinstein's lawyers had quickly covered the last payment, for Phase 2A, but they had been sitting on an invoice for Phase 2B for more than a month. It took several tense exchanges before another payment was delivered and the next, more intense, riskier stage of the operation began.

Our reporting at NBC was growing more intense, too. Over the course of January, the Hollywood series took shape. I had begun to report out a story on rigged awards campaigns, along with one about sexist hiring practices behind the camera and another about Chinese influence on American blockbusters. (The adversaries in *Red Dawn* turned North Korean in postproduction; doctors in Beijing saved *Iron Man* while sipping Yili brand milk.)

The sexual harassment story was proving to be a booking challenge. One actress after another backed out, often after involving prominent publicists. "It's just not a topic we want to talk about," went the responses. But the calls were kicking up dust, and Harvey Weinstein's name was coming up in our research again and again.

One producer, Dede Nickerson, arrived at 30 Rock for an interview about the China story. We sat in a bland conference room that you've seen on a hundred *Dateline*s, beautified with a potted plant and colored lights. Afterward, as McHugh and the crew broke down our equipment and Nickerson strode off to the nearest elevator bank, I trailed after her.

"I meant to ask one more thing," I said, catching up to her. "We're doing a story about sexual harassment in the industry. You used to work for Harvey Weinstein, right?"

Nickerson's smile slackened.

"I'm sorry," she said. "I can't help you."

We'd reached the elevators.

"Sure, okay. If there's anyone you think I should talk to—"

"I have a flight to catch," she said. As she got in the elevator, she paused and added, "Just . . . be careful."

A few days later, I hunched over a desk in one of the glass cubes set aside for private calls on the margins of the newsroom, dialing Rose McGowan, whom I'd reached over Twitter. We'd met once before, in 2010, when I was working at the State Department. Pentagon officials had announced she was visiting and asked if I'd join them for lunch, like they were looking for a language specialist and figured I spoke fluent actress. McGowan had met the officials on a recent USO tour. In pictures, there she was, at Kandahar Air Field or in Kabul, in neon, low-cut tees and skinny jeans, long hair blowing in the wind. "I looked like a stylized bombshell," she'd later recall. McGowan was a charismatic screen presence, exuding a quick wit and an acid sense of humor in a series of early performances—*The Doom Generation, Jawbreaker, Scream*—that made her an indie film darling. But in recent years the parts had been fewer and schlockier. When we met, her last lead appearance had been in *Planet Terror*, a B-movie homage directed by her then-boyfriend Robert Rodriguez, in which she played a stripper named Cherry Darling with a machine gun for a leg.

At that lunch in 2010, McGowan and I hit it off. She whispered quotes from the film *Anchorman*, and I served them back. She knew I'd grown up in a Hollywood family. She talked about acting—the fun roles, and the sexist or exploitative ones, which was most of them. She made it plain that she was tiring of the business and its oppressively narrow view of women. The next day, she emailed: "Whatever I can do in the future, I will make myself available. Please do not hesitate to ask."

In 2017, McGowan picked up my call from the newsroom. Her counterculture streak was still evident. She told me Roy Price, the head of Amazon's nascent movie and television studio, had greenlit a surrealistic show she was creating about a cult. She forecast a battle over the patriarchal power structures in Hollywood and beyond. "Nobody's covered what Hillary losing means to women," she said. "The war against women is real. This is ground zero." She talked, unflinchingly and far more specifically than in her tweets, about her allegation that Weinstein had raped her.

"Would you name him on camera?" I asked.

"I'll think about it," she said. She was working on a book, and weighing how much to reveal in its pages. But she was open to beginning the process of telling the story before then, too.

The media, McGowan said, had rejected her, and she had rejected the media.

"So why talk to me?" I asked.

"Because you've lived it," she said. "I saw what you wrote."

About a year earlier, the *Hollywood Reporter* had put out a laudatory profile of my father, Woody Allen, with only a glancing mention of the allegations of sexual abuse leveled against him by my sister Dylan. The magazine faced intense criticism for the piece, and Janice Min, the *Hollywood Reporter*'s editor, decided to face it directly, asking me to write about whether there was merit to the backlash.

The truth is, I'd spent most of my life avoiding my sister's allegation—and not just publicly. I did not want to be defined by my parents, or by the worst years of my mother's life, of my sister's life, of my childhood. Mia Farrow is one of the great actors of her generation, and a wonderful mom who sacrificed greatly for her kids. And yet so much of her talent and reputation was consumed by the men in her life, and I took from that a desire to stand on my own, to be known best for my work, whatever it might be. That left what happened in my childhood home frozen in amber, in ancient tabloid coverage and permanent doubt—unresolved, unresolvable.

So I decided to interview my sister about what happened, in detail, for the first time. And I dove into the court records and any other documents I could find. By the account Dylan gave when she was seven years old and has repeated precisely ever since, Allen took her to a crawl space in our family's home in Connecticut and penetrated her with a finger. She'd already complained to a therapist about Allen touching her inappropriately. (The therapist, hired by Allen, did not disclose the complaints until later, in court.) Immediately before the alleged assault, a babysitter had seen Allen with his face in Dylan's lap. When a pediatrician finally did report the allegation to the authorities, Allen hired what one of his lawyers estimated to be ten or more private detectives through a network of attorneys and subcontractors. They trailed law enforcement officials, looking for evidence of drinking or gambling problems. A prosecutor in Connecticut, Frank Maco, later described a "campaign to disrupt the investigators," and colleagues said he was rattled. Maco dropped the effort to charge Allen, attributing the decision to his desire to spare Dylan the trauma of trial, taking pains to state that he'd had "probable cause" to proceed.

I told Min I would write an op-ed. I made no claim to be an impartial arbiter of my sister's story—I cared about her and supported her. But I argued that her claim fell into a category of credible sexual abuse allegations that were too often ignored by both the Hollywood trade outlets and the wider news media. "That kind of silence isn't just wrong. It's dangerous," I wrote. "It sends a message to victims that it's not worth the anguish of coming forward. It sends a message about who we are as a society, what we'll overlook, who we'll ignore, who matters and who doesn't." I hoped it would be my one and only statement on the matter.

"I was asked to say something. I did," I told McGowan, trying to get off the subject. "That's the end of it."

She laughed bitterly. "There's no end to it."

◆

I wasn't the only journalist trying to get to McGowan. Seth Freedman, the same English writer for the *Guardian* who'd called Ben Wallace offering to help with his reporting, had been emailing HarperCollins, the publisher of McGowan's book. Freedman was persistent, reaching out repeatedly to express support and lobby for an interview. When he got on the phone with Lacy Lynch, a literary agent advising McGowan, he was vague about his reporting. He said he was working with a group of journalists on a story about Hollywood. He wouldn't say whether there was a specific publication attached. But Lynch told McGowan she thought the writer was benign, and that it seemed like an interesting opportunity.

Not long after my conversation with McGowan, she and Freedman were on the phone. He told her he was outside the farm his family owned in the English countryside, speaking quietly to avoid waking anyone. "What did you want to talk to me about?" McGowan asked.

"We're looking to do a snapshot of what life is like in 2016/17 for people in Hollywood," he explained. He broached McGowan's sharp criticism of Donald Trump, suggesting that there might be an opportunity for "a kind of spinoff piece," about her activism. It sounded like a lot of resources were being put into his efforts. He repeatedly mentioned other, unnamed journalists who were helping him gather information.

McGowan had seen more than her share of betrayal and abuse, and she was usually guarded. But Freedman was warm, candid, even confessional. Several times, he referenced his wife and their growing family. Slowly, McGowan warmed to him, talked about her life story, at one point cried. As she heaved off plates of armor, he grew more specific. "Obviously everything we say is off the record, but I've spoken to people who've worked at, you know, say, Miramax, who've told me 'I'm NDA'd' and they can't talk about anything that's happened to them but they're desperate to say 'X person abused me or X person made my life hell.'"

"My book is gonna address a lot of these things," McGowan said.

Freedman seemed very interested in her book, and what she planned to say in it. "How can you get the publisher to publish it?" he asked, referring to her allegation.

"I actually have a signed document," she said. "A signed document from the time of the attack."

But what would the consequences be, he wondered, if she said too much? "Most people I talk to in Hollywood, they say, you know, I'm not allowed to talk about it on record," he said.

"Because they're all too scared," McGowan replied.

"And if they do say it," Freedman continued, "then they'll never work again or they'll never—" But he didn't get to say what else. McGowan was talkative by now, on to her next point.

One, two, three times, Freedman wondered who in the media she planned to talk to before the book, and how much she planned to tell them. "Who would your ideal platform be right now to tell that message?" he asked. "Does that mean you keep the name out of the press because you would suffer," he said, alluding again to those consequences, "if you put the name out there and then someone came back at you?"

"I don't know. I'll see how I feel," McGowan said.

Freedman sounded full of empathy, an ally. "So," he asked, "what would make you kind of call it quits?"

## CHAPTER 6:

# *CONTINENTAL*

"They have been fighting for years on this," I said. A week after my call with McGowan, I sat at the anchor's table in Studio 1A, *Today* show cameras rolling. I'd just wrapped a segment on the battle between safety advocates and the trucking industry over whether to require side guards on tractor-trailers, to stop cars from slipping under them. The safety advocates said the move would save lives. The lobbyists said it would be too expensive. "Ronan, great job," Matt Lauer said, and turned briskly to the next segment. "Really strong," he added, as he filed off set during the next commercial break, production assistants swarming, handing him his coat, gloves, script pages. "And good engagement afterwards, got people talking."

"Thanks," I said. He stepped closer.

"Hey, how are those other stories coming along?"

I wasn't sure which ones he meant. "There's the big one on the contaminated California farmlands. I think you'll find it interesting."

"Sure, sure," he said. There was a beat of silence.

"And I'll be on around the Oscars for the Hollywood one I mentioned," I tried, tentative.

He frowned a little. Then his smile snapped back on. "Great," he said, clapping me on the back. Over his shoulder as he walked toward the exit, he added: "Anything you need, you come to me, okay?"

I watched him step into the cold air of the plaza, a burst of shrieks from the fans sounding as he passed through the revolving door.

◆

It was early February 2017. McHugh and I were ensconced in meetings with the network's legal and standards departments as they scrutinized every element of the upcoming Hollywood stories. Editorial oversight fell to an NBC veteran named Richard Greenberg, who had recently been appointed interim head of the network's investigative unit. Greenberg wore crumpled tweeds and reading glasses. He had spent nearly seventeen years at NBC, ten of them as a *Dateline* producer, several more vetting pieces for the standards department. He was quiet, bureaucratic. But he also professed strong moral convictions. In his *Dateline* producer's blog, he called sexual abusers "perverts" and "monsters." After working with Chris Hansen of *To Catch a Predator* on a story in a Cambodian brothel, Greenberg wrote: "often, when I lie awake in bed at night, I am haunted by the faces of the girls we saw who were not rescued and who are still being violated." The lawyer vetting the series was a Harvard Law alumnus named Steve Chung, who was studiously serious.

That week in February, McHugh and I sat with Greenberg in his office near the fourth-floor newsroom and outlined our shooting schedule for the following week, including some interviews to be conducted with the subjects obscured in shadow, as was frequent practice in my investigative work and so many *Dateline* stories Greenberg had worked on. He nodded approvingly. "And you've talked all this through with Chung?" he asked. I had. Greenberg then swiveled to his computer monitor and pulled up a browser. "I just want to double-check—"

He typed in both of my parents' names and Weinstein's. "Good idea," I said. "Hadn't thought of that." The results were what we'd expected: like most studio heads, Weinstein had touched movies both of my parents worked on. He'd distributed several Woody Allen movies in the nineties, and, more recently, a few my mother appeared in during the 2000s. Movie distribution tends to be an arm's length business: I'd never heard Weinstein's name from either of them.

"Looks good," Greenberg said, after scrolling through several articles. "Just double-checking to make sure there's no secret axe to grind there. Clearly not."

"Other than caring about the issue, no," I said. I'd liked Weinstein the one time I'd met him, at an event hosted by the CBS News anchor Charlie Rose.

A few days later, I sat in a Santa Monica hotel room. Dennis Rice, a veteran marketing executive, perspired heavily. Studio lights with cube-shaped shades threw him into shadow. Initially, we had planned only to discuss the story on rigged awards campaigns. Then I'd asked him about his time as Harvey Weinstein's president of marketing at Miramax in the late '90s and early 2000s, and he'd grown nervous. "You have no idea how tough this gets for me if I say anything," he told me. But Rice sensed there was an opportunity to help with something important, and agreed to come back for the follow-on interview in front of the harsh lights.

"There was money available in the event that there was an indiscretion that needed to be taken care of," he said of his time at Miramax.

"What kinds of indiscretions?" I asked.

"Bullying, physical abuse, sexual harassment."

He said he'd witnessed, firsthand, his boss "inappropriately touching" young women, and regretted not saying more. "They were paid off," he said of the women. "They were encouraged to not make this a big deal, otherwise their career may end." He said he knew of specific cases of retaliation and, when the cameras stopped rolling, glanced around and said, "Find Rosanna Arquette." The actress had come to prominence with her leading role in *Desperately Seeking Susan*. In *Pulp Fiction*, which Weinstein distributed, she'd had a small but memorable part as the heavily pierced wife of a drug dealer. "I don't know," Rice said, wiping the accumulated sweat from his forehead. "Maybe she'll talk."

Reviewing the footage later, I rewound to an exchange about the culture around Weinstein and hit Play again.

"And for all of the people around this man who saw this sort of thing going on," I asked, "did anyone speak up against it?"

"No," he said.

That evening and in the days that followed, I worked the phones. I was assembling a growing list of women, often actresses and models but sometimes producers or assistants, who were rumored to have voiced complaints about Weinstein. Certain names kept recurring, like McGowan's, and that of an Italian actress and director, Asia Argento.

I called back Nickerson, the producer who'd been hesitant to talk about Weinstein before.

"I'm so tired of what happens to women in this industry. I want to help, I do," she said. "I saw things. And then they paid me off and I signed a piece of paper."

"What did you see?"

A pause. "He couldn't control himself. It's who he is. He's a predator."

"And you can speak to having witnessed that?"

"Yes."

She agreed to go on camera, too. Sitting in shadow at the Encino estate where she was staying, she independently recalled a pattern of predation eerily similar to the one described by Rice.

"I think that happened all the time, the groping," she said in the interview. "This wasn't a one-off. This wasn't a period of time. This was ongoing predatorial behavior towards women—whether they consented or not." She said that it was almost ludicrously embedded in the corporate culture; that there was essentially a pimp on company payroll with only the thinnest job description to cover for his role procuring women for their boss.

"Was it common knowledge that he was being, to use a term you used, 'predatory' around women?" I asked.

"Absolutely," she said. "Everybody knew."

"FYI, that story is evolving into a pretty serious reporting job on HW," I texted Oppenheim. "Both execs are naming him on cam, but one is asking me not to show actual footage of him saying the name," I wrote, referring to Rice. "People are pretty freaked out about reprisals." Oppenheim wrote back: "I can imagine."

◆

The more people I called, the more Rice and Nickerson's claims were borne out. I was also looking for defenses of Weinstein. But those I found rang hollow. Nickerson had named a producer whom she believed to be a victim. I finally tracked her down in Australia, where she'd gone to start a new life. When she told me that she had nothing to say about Weinstein, there was strain and sadness in her voice that suggested I'd placed her in a difficult situation.

A conversation with Donna Gigliotti, the *Shakespeare in Love* producer, went much the same way.

"I mean, have I heard things? Maybe. But have I seen things?" she asked.

"What did you hear?"

An exasperated sigh, as if the question were ludicrous.

"The man is not a saint. Trust me, there is no love lost between us. But he isn't guilty of anything worse than what a million other men in this business do."

"Are you saying there's not a story there?"

"I'm *saying*," Gigliotti said, "that your time is better spent elsewhere. Others have looked at this, you know. They all come up empty."

I did not know. But soon enough I was encountering references to other outlets that had circled the story. Two years earlier, a *New York* magazine writer, Jennifer Senior, had tweeted: "At some pt, all the women who've been afraid to speak out abt Harvey Weinstein are gonna have to hold hands and jump." And then later: "It's a despicable open secret." The comments had generated a few blog items, then faded away. I sent her a message asking to talk. "I wasn't reporting on it," she told me. "David Carr, my office spouse when he was at NYMag, did a feature about him and came back with story after story about what a pig he was." Carr, the essayist and media reporter, who died in 2015, had recounted to Senior anecdotes about Weinstein flashing and groping women, but never got enough to render them publishable. "Lots of people have been trying to get this story," Senior told me, and wished me luck, like she was encouraging Don Quixote about a windmill.

I called other people close to Carr who added something else: he had become paranoid while working on the story. His widow, Jill Rooney Carr, told me that her husband believed that he was being surveilled, though he didn't know by whom. "He thought he was being followed," she recalled. Other than that, Carr appeared to have taken his secrets to the grave.

After the interviews with Rice and Nickerson, I met with a friend who worked as an assistant to a prominent NBCUniversal executive and who passed me contact information for another round of potential sources. "My question is," she texted, "would Today run something like this? Seems kind of heavy for them."

"Noah, the new head of the show," I wrote back, "he'll champion it."

The next week, on the morning of February 14, Igor Ostrovskiy, the pudgy Ukrainian who'd met with Roman Khaykin, the bald Russian, at Nargis Cafe, sat in a hotel lobby in Midtown Manhattan. Khaykin had dispatched him there, on one of the jobs for the mysterious new client. Ostrovskiy pretended to be engrossed in his phone, while discreetly capturing video of a graying middle-aged man in a trench coat shaking hands with a tall, dark man in a suit. Then he followed the two men to the hotel restaurant and sat at a table nearby.

The last few days had been busy with these assignments in fancy hotel lobbies and restaurants, surveilling meetings between operatives sent by the mysterious client and what appeared to be unsuspecting marks. Ostrovskiy's task was "countersurveillance": he was supposed to make sure the client's operatives weren't followed.

That day in the hotel restaurant, Ostrovskiy texted a picture of the proceedings to Khaykin, then ordered a continental breakfast. The food was a perk of the assignment. "Enjoy yourself," his boss had said. "Have a nice meal." As juice and rolls arrived, Ostrovskiy strained to hear the conversation at the next table. The men had accents he couldn't quite place. Eastern European, maybe. He overheard snatches of dialogue about far-flung locations: Cyprus; a bank in Luxembourg; something about men in Russia.

Mostly, Ostrovskiy spent his days hunting collectors of worker's compensation with fake limps or trying to catch straying spouses violating their prenuptial agreements. The suited operatives involved in these new assignments, some of whom seemed to have a military bearing, were something else. He swiped through the footage of the men and wondered who it was he was watching, and for whom.

# CHAPTER 7:

# *PHANTOMS*

*I* was in a car, threading my way through West Hollywood toward my next shoot, when the announcement came over the wires: Noah Oppenheim had been promoted to president of NBC News. He was taking on a slate of make-or-break projects alongside his boss, Andy Lack, who oversaw both NBC News and MSNBC. Their first order of business: launching Megyn Kelly, the former Fox News anchor, in a new role at NBC. Several positive profiles highlighted Oppenheim's Ivy League luster and screenwriting career and rapid ascent through the cutthroat world of television. Oppenheim's and Lack's predecessors had both been women. Deborah Turness, who preceded Oppenheim, was described in lightly sexist profiles as having "rock-chick swagger," which as far as I could tell just meant she sometimes chose to wear pants. Patricia Fili-Krushel, whom Lack replaced, was an executive with a background in human resources and daytime television. The chain of command was now all male, all white: Noah Oppenheim, and above him Andy Lack, and above *him* Steve Burke, the CEO of NBCUniversal, and Brian Roberts, the CEO of its parent company, Comcast. "I am pretty, pretty, pretty into this announcement. Congrats, my friend!" I texted Oppenheim, sucking

up a little but also sincerely meaning it. "Hah — thanks," he wrote
back.

I flicked through my contacts, hovered over my sister Dylan's
name, then called her for the first time in months. "I'm headed into
an interview," I told her. "It's with a well-known actress. She's accusing a very powerful person of a very serious crime."

In family photographs, Dylan, two and a half years my senior,
often sheltered behind me: there we were, in Huggies on the ugly
brown couch in the living room; before my first kindergarten play,
her in a rabbit onesie, knuckles mid-noogie, grinding into my head;
in front of various tourist attractions, laughing, usually hugging.

I was surprised she'd picked up. She usually didn't keep her cell
on her. In frank moments, she'd confessed that ringing phones made
her heart race. Men's voices on the other end of the line, especially,
were a challenge. She'd never held a job that involved lots of phone
calls. Dylan was a talented writer and visual artist. Her work was
rooted in worlds as far from this one as she could manage. As kids,
we'd invented an elaborate fantasy kingdom, populated with pewter
figurines of dragons and fairies. Fantasy remained her escape. She
wrote hundreds of pages of minutely described fiction and painted
faraway landscapes. These sat in drawers. When I suggested that she
build a portfolio or submit a manuscript, she'd freeze, get defensive.
I didn't understand, she'd say.

On the phone that day in February, she paused. "And you want
my advice?" she asked, eventually. Her allegation, and the questions
that swirled between us as to whether I'd done enough, soon enough,
to acknowledge it, had introduced a space between us that hadn't
been there in the childhood photos.

"Yes, I want your advice," I said.

"Well, this is the worst part. The considering. The waiting for the
story. But once you put your voice out there, it gets a lot easier." She

sighed. "Just tell her to hang tough. It's like ripping off a Band-Aid."
I thanked her. Another pause. "If you get this," she said, "don't let it
go, okay?"

Rose McGowan lived in the quintessential movie star's house: a
stack of tan midcentury modern boxes tucked into a grove of cypress
trees high in the Hollywood Hills. Outside, there was a wide terrace
with a hot tub overlooking a sweep of Los Angeles. Inside, it was
staged as if for resale: no family photos, just art. By the front door
there was a salvaged neon sign in the shape of a bowler hat that read
"THE DERBY: LADIES ENTRANCE." Just beyond, atop a set of stairs to
the living room, there was a painting of a woman in a cage, engulfed
in light. By a white brick fireplace in the living room, a bronze model
of McGowan's character from *Planet Terror* aimed its machine-
gun leg.

The woman who sat opposite me was not the one I'd met seven
years before. McGowan looked tired, a hard tension across her face.
She wore a loose beige sweater and little makeup. Her head was
shaved, military-style. She'd mostly abandoned acting in favor of
music, sometimes accompanied by surreal performance-art footage
of herself. She'd tried her hand at directing, with a short film, *Dawn*,
that screened at Sundance in 2014. In the film, a repressed teenage
girl circa 1961 is lured by two young men into a secluded area,
brained with a rock, then shot dead.

McGowan had a rough childhood. She'd grown up in the Children
of God cult in the Italian countryside, where women had been harsh
and men brutal—one, she later told me, sliced a wart off her finger,
without warning, at age four, leaving her stunned and bleeding. For a
period of time, as a teenager, she was homeless. When she made it in

Hollywood, she thought she had put the risk of exploitation behind her. She told me that shortly before Weinstein assaulted her, during the Sundance Film Festival in 1997, she'd turned to a camera crew following her and said, "I think my life is finally getting easier."

In the living room, as cameras rolled, she described how her business manager set the meeting where the alleged assault happened and how it had been abruptly moved from a hotel restaurant to a hotel suite. She recalled the routine first hour with the man she then considered only her boss, and his praise for her performance in one film he'd produced, *Scream*, and in another she was still working on, *Phantoms*. Then she relived the part that still visibly shook her. "On the way out, it turned into not a meeting," she said. "It all happens very fast and very slow. I think any survivor can tell you that . . . all of a sudden, your life is like ninety degrees in the other direction. It's — it's a shock to the system. And your brain is trying to keep up with what's going on. All of a sudden, you have no clothes on." McGowan tried to stay composed. "I started to cry. And I didn't know what was happening," she recalled. "And I'm very small. This person's very big. So do that math."

"Was this a sexual assault?" I asked.

"Yes," she said simply.

"Was this a rape?"

"Yes."

McGowan said she contacted a criminal attorney and considered pressing charges. The attorney told her to shut up. "I'd done a sex scene," she remembered the lawyer pointing out. "No one was ever gonna believe me." McGowan decided not to press charges, and brokered a financial settlement instead, signing away her right to sue Weinstein. "That was very painful," she said. "I thought $100,000 was a lot of money at the time because I was a kid." She considered it, on his part, "an admission of guilt."

McGowan described a system—of assistants and managers and industry power brokers—that she furiously accused of complicity. She said staffers averted their eyes as she walked into the meeting, and out of it. "They wouldn't look at me," she said. "They looked down, these men. They wouldn't look at me in the eyes." And she remembered her costar in *Phantoms*, Ben Affleck, seeing her visibly distraught immediately after the incident, and hearing where she'd just come from, and replying, "God damn it, I told him to stop doing this."

McGowan believed she'd been "blacklisted" after the incident. "I barely worked in movies ever again. And I was on a great trajectory. And then when I did do another movie—it got sold to him for distribution," she said, referring to *Planet Terror*.

For any survivor, memories haunt. For those with high-profile perpetrators, there's an added quality of inescapability. "I would open the newspaper," McGowan told me. "And there's Gwyneth Paltrow giving him [an] award." He was "omnipresent." And then there were the red carpets and press junkets where she'd have to pose with him, smiling. "I just left my body again," she said. "I pasted the smile on my face." The first time she saw him again after the alleged assault, she threw up in a trash can.

On camera, McGowan wasn't yet saying Weinstein's name. She was steeling herself, getting ready. But she referred to him during the interview again and again, urging viewers to "connect the dots."

"Did Harvey Weinstein rape you?" I asked. The room went pindrop silent. McGowan paused.

"I've never liked that name," she said. "I have a hard time saying it."

Off camera, she'd already used his name with me. Partly, she'd said, her concern was making sure she had a news organization that would go all the way with the story if she exposed herself to legal jeopardy. I was frank with her: this would be a delicate legal process at NBC. I'd need to be armed with every detail she could give me.

"Have the lawyers watch this," she said.

"Oh, they will be," I said, with a grim laugh.

"Watch it," she said, looking into the camera, tears in her eyes. "Not just read it. And I hope they're brave, too. Because I tell you what, it's happened to their daughter, their mother, their sister."

## CHAPTER 8:

# *GUN*

"The Rose interview is shocking," I texted Oppenheim.

"Wow," he replied.

"Felt like a bomb going off. Plus two Miramax execs on cam saying they saw pattern of sexual harassment. This'll be fun for legal."

"Geez," he wrote. "It sure will be."

As we finished our shooting for the Hollywood stories, McHugh and I traded calls with Greenberg, the head of the investigative unit, and Chung, the attorney. By then, I'd spoken to two people on McGowan's management team with whom she'd raised her complaint immediately after the meeting with Weinstein. If she was lying, she'd been doing so since that day in 1997.

"She does sound a little . . . flighty," Greenberg said.

McHugh and I were back in the same hotel in Santa Monica, on a sunny day, preparing to interview a Chinese filmmaker. "Well, that's why we line up a lot of corroboration," I told Greenberg. "And she said she'll give us the contract she has with Weinstein —"

"Careful about that," Greenberg said.

"What do you mean?" McHugh asked.

"I don't know that we can be interfering with contracts," Green-berg said. "Let's just be careful if those are being handed over."

McHugh looked frustrated. "We should run this," he said. "It's explosive. It's news."

"I just don't see it being ready in time for this series," Greenberg replied. The stories were due to run a week later, just before the Oscars.

"I think I can get other women to talk in time for air," I said.

"Give it the time it needs," Greenberg said. "The other stories can go now, and you can expand the reporting here." I got along well with the network's legal and standards staff. I defended my stories in a, shall we say, caffeinated way. But I was a lawyer myself, and I admired the old-fashioned care that went into producing a piece for programs like *Nightly News*. NBC was a serious place that valued the truth, an institution that had leapt from radio, to broadcast, to cable, to the internet — that mattered when it was one of three networks half a century ago and, in our fractured and fractious era, mattered still. As long as we were using the time to strengthen the reporting, I didn't mind a delay.

"Okay," I said. "We'll hold it."

◆

The reporting expanded like an inkblot. The day after the shoot with McGowan, we were at the offices of the *Hollywood Reporter* for an interview with their journalist on the awards beat, Scott Feinberg. Harvey Weinstein was inescapable in that conversation, too: he had essentially invented the modern Oscar campaign. Weinstein ran his campaigns like guerrilla wars. A Miramax publicist once ghost-wrote an op-ed praising the company's movie *Gangs of New York* and passed it off as the work of Robert Wise, the director of *The Sound of Music*, who was, at the time, eighty-eight. Weinstein orchestrated an elaborate smear campaign against rival film *A Beautiful Mind*, planting press items claiming the protagonist, mathematician John Nash, was gay (and, when that didn't work, that he was anti-Semitic). When *Pulp Fiction* lost a Best Picture Oscar to *Forrest Gump*, he'd publicly threatened to arrive on director Robert Zemeckis's lawn and "get medieval."

Before leaving the *Hollywood Reporter*, I met its new editor, Matt Belloni. I'd heard rumors that Janice Min, his predecessor who persuaded me to write the op-ed about the need for tougher coverage of sexual assault allegations, had pursued the Weinstein allegations for years. When I asked whether the outlet had come up with anything, Belloni shook his head. "No one will talk."

But he did have ideas about industry figures who might know of other women with allegations. He suggested I call Gavin Polone, the former agent and manager—a "Ferrari-driving tenpercenter," as *Variety* had described him. He'd since become a successful producer, and developed a reputation as a firebrand. In 2014, he'd written a column for the *Hollywood Reporter* entitled "Bill Cosby and Hollywood's Culture of Payoffs, Rape and Secrecy." In it, he'd referenced a set of allegations against an unnamed studio head who "used his power and money to keep it all quiet." He accused journalists of avoiding the story because they were "afraid of being sued and more afraid of losing advertising." No one, it seemed, had taken him up on the challenge.

Polone had appeared as an occasional commentator on my MSNBC show. By the end of the day, I was on the phone with him. "It needs to be exposed," he told me. He'd heard about a number of allegations against Weinstein. Some he'd heard directly from accusers, others he'd become aware of secondhand. "The most egregious example, the holy grail of this story, is Annabella Sciorra," he said. "This wasn't harassment. It was rape." I asked him to see if the women who'd told their stories to him would talk to me. He promised he would.

"One more thing," he said, after I thanked him for his time. "Watch your back. This guy, the people protecting him. They've got a lot at stake."

"I'm being careful."

"You don't understand. I'm saying be ready, in case. I'm saying get a gun."

I laughed. He didn't.

❖

Sources were scared. Many refused to talk. But others seemed willing. I reached the agent of an English actress who McGowan and others had suggested might have a complaint. "She told me the story in detail, as soon as we started working together," the agent told me. "He took out his penis and chased her around a desk during the shoot. He jumped on top of her, he pinned her down, but she got away." I asked if the actress would talk. "She was very open about it at the time," the agent replied. "I don't see why not." A day later, he called back with her phone number and email address: she'd be happy to discuss sitting for an interview.

An agent who worked with Rosanna Arquette appeared to know what the request was about immediately. "Hard topic for her," that agent said. "But I know she cares about the issue. I'm sure she'll talk."

I had reached Annabella Sciorra on Twitter. I told her it was about something sensitive. She seemed apprehensive, a little guarded. But we set a time for a call.

I was also chasing the only allegation against Weinstein that had entered the criminal justice system. In March 2015, Ambra Batti-lana Gutierrez, a Filipina-Italian model and onetime finalist in the Miss Italy pageant, had emerged from a meeting with Weinstein at his Tribeca offices and gone straight to the police to claim she'd been groped. New York law enforcement had brought Weinstein in for questioning. The tabloids set about fevered coverage.

Then something curious happened: the items about Weinstein were replaced with derogatory ones about Gutierrez. The tabloids reported that, in 2010, when Gutierrez was a young contestant in the Miss Italy pageant, she had attended a "Bunga Bunga" party hosted by Silvio Berlusconi, who was then the Italian prime minister, where he was accused of having sex with prostitutes. The items claimed that Gutierrez herself was a hooker, with wealthy sugar daddies back in Italy. The day after the alleged incident, she'd attended *Finding Neverland*, a Broadway musical Weinstein produced, the *Daily Mail* observed. Later, she'd demanded a movie role, Page Six reported. Gutierrez said she'd never been a prostitute, that she'd been brought to Berlusconi's party as a professional obligation and extricated her-self as soon as its seedier dimensions became apparent, and that she'd made no demand for a movie role. But her denials were printed as an afterthought, or not at all. The pictures of Gutierrez shifted: there she was, day after day, in lingerie and bikinis. Increasingly, the tab-loids seemed to suggest that she was the predator, ensnaring Wein-stein with her feminine wiles. And then, all at once, the charges went away. So did Ambra Gutierrez.

But the name of a lawyer who represented Gutierrez had made it into public reports, and lawyers have phones. "I'm not at liberty to talk about that," he told me. "Okay," I said, having paid just enough attention in law school and more than enough in real life to know an allusion to a nondisclosure agreement when I ran into one. "But can you pass on a message?"

Gutierrez texted almost immediately. "Hello, my lawyer said you wanted to contact me. Just wanted to ask about what," she wrote.

"I'm a reporter with NBC News, and this is for a Today show story I am working on. I think it's probably easiest to talk through on the phone, if you're comfortable with that," I replied.

"Could you be a little more precise on what is about 'I am working on'?" she wrote.

Ambra Gutierrez, it was immediately apparent, was no fool.

"It involves a claim being made by another individual — and potentially several of them — that may have some similarities to the one you brought, in the NYPD investigation in 2015. It could be a great service to others with claims if I could talk to you."

She agreed to meet the next day.

Before meeting with Gutierrez, I started methodically calling people who'd been involved in the case. One of my contacts in the district attorney's office called to say staff there had found Gutierrez credible. "There were . . . certain things presented about her past," the contact said.

"What kind of things?"

"I can't get into that. But none of it made anyone here think she was lying. And I heard we had some evidence."

"What kind of evidence?"

"I don't know exactly."

"Can you look into it?"

"Sure. And I'll just hand in my resignation right after."

CHAPTER 9:

# *MINIONS*

**W**hen I arrived at Gramercy Tavern, Gutierrez was already sitting in a back corner, ramrod straight and perfectly still. "I'm always early," she said. That wasn't the half of it. She was, I came to find, a formidably organized and strategic person. Gutierrez was born in Turin, Italy. She'd grown up watching her Italian father, whom she described as a "Dr. Jekyll–and–Mr. Hyde person," beat her Filipina mother. When Gutierrez tried to intervene, she was beaten as well. As an adolescent, she became the caretaker, supporting her mother and distracting her younger brother from the violence. She had an exaggerated beauty, like an anime character: vanishingly slender with improbably large eyes. That day at the restaurant, she seemed nervous. "I want to help," she said, a tremor in her Italian accent. "It's just I'm in difficult situation." It was only when I said that another woman had gone on camera with a complaint about Weinstein, and that still more were considering doing so, that she began to tell her story.

In March 2015, Gutierrez's modeling agent had invited her to a reception at Radio City Music Hall for *New York Spring Spectacular*, a show that Weinstein produced. As usual, Weinstein had rallied industry friends to support the show. He'd talked to Steve Burke, the CEO of NBCUniversal, and Burke had agreed to provide costumes of characters from the ubiquitous *Minions* franchise. At the reception, Weinstein stared at Gutierrez openly across the room. He approached and said hello, telling her and her agent several times that she looked like the actress Mila Kunis. After the event, Gutierrez's modeling agency emailed her to say that Weinstein wanted to set up a business meeting as soon as possible.

Gutierrez arrived at Weinstein's office in Tribeca early the next evening with her modeling portfolio. As she and Weinstein sat on a couch reviewing the portfolio, he began staring at her breasts, asking if they were real. Gutierrez said that Weinstein then lunged at her, groping her breasts and attempting to put a hand up her skirt while she protested. He finally backed off and told her that his assistant would give her tickets to *Finding Neverland* later that night. He said he would meet her at the show.

Gutierrez was twenty-two at the time. "Because of trauma in my past," she told me, "being touched for me was something that was very big." After the encounter with Weinstein, she remembered shaking, stopping by a bathroom, and beginning to weep. She caught a cab to her agent's office and cried there, too. Then she and the agent went to the nearest police station. She remembered arriving, and telling the officers Weinstein's name, and one saying, "Again?"

Weinstein telephoned her later that evening, annoyed that she hadn't come to the show. She picked up the call while sitting with investigators from the Special Victims Division, who listened in and devised a plan: Gutierrez would agree to see the show the following day and then meet with Weinstein. She would wear a wire and attempt to extract a confession.

"It was a scary decision, of course," she said. "And of course I had a sleepless night." Anyone asked to do something risky to expose something important has to balance a complicated mix of self-interested and altruistic incentives. Sometimes, in some stories, the two coincide. But in this story, there was almost no upside. Gutierrez faced legal and professional annihilation. She wanted only to stop Weinstein from doing it again. "Everyone told me the guy could close all the doors for me," she said. "I was willing to risk this for the fact that this guy should not have done this to anyone anymore."

The following day, Gutierrez met Weinstein at the Tribeca Grand Hotel's Church Bar, a plush room with golden stars and clouds stenciled on its blue walls. A team of undercover officers kept watch. Weinstein was flattering. He said, again and again, how beautiful she was. He told her he'd help her get acting jobs, if she would just be his friend, and named several other prominent actresses for whom, he said, he had done the same. The accent would need work, of course, but he said he could arrange lessons.

Weinstein excused himself to go to the restroom, then returned, demanding with sudden urgency that they go up to his penthouse suite. He said he wanted to take a shower. Gutierrez, frightened that he would touch her again or discover that she was wearing a wire, resisted. Undeterred, he tried to bring her upstairs repeatedly. The first time, she used a tactic the officers had suggested, leaving behind a jacket and insisting they go back downstairs for it. The second time, one of the undercover officers, posing as a TMZ photographer, started peppering Weinstein with questions, sending him to complain to hotel staff. Gutierrez kept trying, and failing, to extricate herself. Finally, Weinstein got her upstairs, leading her toward his room. By this time, they'd lost the undercover officers. Adding to her problems, her phone, which officers had instructed her to keep on and recording in her purse as a backup, was running out of power.

With increasing belligerence, Weinstein demanded that she go into the room. Gutierrez, terrified, pleaded and tried to draw away. In the course of the interaction, Weinstein copped to groping her the previous day: a full, dramatic confession, caught on tape. She kept pleading, and he finally relented, and they went downstairs. Officers, no longer concealing their identities, approached Weinstein and said the police wanted to speak to him.

Had he been charged, Weinstein could have faced a count of sexual abuse in the third degree, a misdemeanor punishable by up to three months in jail. "We had so much proof of everything," Gutierrez told me. "Everyone was telling me, 'Congratulations, we stopped a monster.'" But then the tabloids began to publish their stories about Gutierrez's supposed past as a prostitute. And the office of Manhattan district attorney Cyrus Vance Jr. began to raise the same points. When Martha Bashford, the head of Vance's Sex Crimes Unit, questioned Gutierrez, she grilled her about Berlusconi and her personal sexual history with unusual hostility, according to two law enforcement sources. The district attorney's press office later told the *New York Times* that the questioning was "a normal, typical interview" intended to anticipate questions that would be raised in a cross-examination. The law enforcement sources disagreed. "They went at her like they were Weinstein's defense attorneys," one of them told me. "It was weird," Gutierrez recalled of the questioning. "I'm, like, 'What is the connection? I don't understand. Just listen to the proof.'"

On April 10, 2015, two weeks after Gutierrez reported Weinstein to the police, the district attorney's office announced that it wasn't going to press charges. It released a brief statement: "This case was taken seriously from the outset, with a thorough investigation conducted by our Sex Crimes Unit. After analyzing the available evidence, including multiple interviews with both parties, a criminal charge is not supported."

The NYPD was incensed by the decision—so much so that the

department's Special Victims Division launched an internal review of the last ten criminal complaints in Manhattan stemming from similar allegations of groping or forcible touching. "They didn't have a quarter of the evidence we had," still another law enforcement source said of the other cases. "There were no controlled meets, and only rarely controlled calls." Yet, that source said, "all of them resulted in arrests." The public had never learned of the damning evidence Vance possessed.

Law enforcement officials began to whisper that the DA's office had behaved strangely. Vance's staff had been receiving new information about Gutierrez's past on a regular basis, and hadn't been disclosing where it was coming from. It was, one official told me, as if Weinstein had infiltrated Vance's office personally.

◆

At the time of the Gutierrez incident, Weinstein's legal team was stacked with political influence. Former New York mayor Rudolph Giuliani was closely involved. "Rudy was always in the office after the Ambra thing," one Weinstein Company employee recalled. "He still had his mind then." Giuliani worked so many hours on the Gutierrez matter that a spat arose afterward over billing. These fights over invoices were a leitmotif in Weinstein's business dealings.

Several members of Weinstein's legal team made donations to Vance's campaigns. One attorney, Elkan Abramowitz, was a partner at the firm that formerly employed Vance, and had contributed $26,450 to Vance's campaigns since 2008. I recognized Abramowitz's name. When my sister reiterated her claim that Woody Allen sexually assaulted her, Allen dispatched Abramowitz to the morning shows to smile affably and deny the allegations. That history made my feelings about Abramowitz less personal, not more. This wasn't about any one victim; this, for Abramowitz and many other lawyers, was a cottage industry.

David Boies had also worked on the Gutierrez imbroglio, and also kept the Manhattan district attorney close. He'd been a longtime donor. He would give $10,000 to Vance's reelection campaign in the months following the decision not to press charges.

◆

After that decision, Gutierrez was shaken, then worried about her future. "I couldn't sleep, I couldn't eat," she told me. As Weinstein leaned on his tabloid contacts to drum up items portraying Gutierrez as a hustler, she felt like history was repeating. She believed that the stories from Italy about her having worked as a prostitute were a product of her having testified in the corruption case against Berlusconi. She told me Berlusconi had used his power to smear her. "They said that I was a Bunga Bunga girl, that I was having affairs with sugar daddies," she said. "Anyone who knows me knows those things are completely fake." Slut shaming, it seemed, was a universal language. Several tabloid editors later told me they regretted their coverage of Gutierrez, and felt it laid uncomfortably bare Weinstein's transactional relationships in their industry.

Weinstein particularly exploited his bond with Pecker and Howard at the *National Enquirer.* Weinstein's employees recalled an uptick in calls from him to Pecker. Howard ordered his staff to stand down on reporting about Gutierrez's claim, then inquired about purchasing her story in order to bury it. And then there was the item the *Enquirer* ultimately ran, claiming, apparently based on its own entreaties to Gutierrez, that she was flogging the story on the open market.

It was as if "just because I am a lingerie model or whatever, I had to be in the wrong," Gutierrez said. "I had people telling me, 'Maybe it was how you dressed.'" (She had dressed in professional office attire to meet Weinstein, with thick tights because of the cold weather.) Her reputation was curdling. "My work depends on image, and my image was destroyed," she said. Casting calls evaporated. Paparazzi laid siege to her apartment. Her brother called from Italy to say reporters had found him at work.

When attorneys Gutierrez consulted urged her to accept a settlement, she at first resisted. But her resolve began to crack. "I didn't want to make my family suffer anymore," she said. "I was twenty-two years old. I knew if he could move the press in this way, I couldn't fight him." On the morning of April 20, 2015, Gutierrez sat in a law firm office in Midtown Manhattan with a voluminous legal agreement and a pen in front of her. In exchange for a million-dollar payment, she would agree to never again talk publicly about Weinstein or the effort to charge him. "I didn't even understand almost what I was doing with all those papers," she told me. "I was really disoriented. My English was very bad. All of the words in that agreement were super-difficult to understand. I guess even now I can't really comprehend everything." Across the table, Weinstein's attorney from Giuliani's firm, Daniel S. Connolly, was trembling visibly as Gutierrez picked up the pen. "I saw him shaking and I realized how big this was. But then I thought I needed to support my mom and brother and how my life was being destroyed, and I did it," she told me.

"The moment I did it, I really felt it was wrong." She knew people would judge her for taking the money. "A lot of people are not empathetic," she said. "They don't put themselves in the situation." After the contract was signed, Gutierrez became depressed and developed an eating disorder. Eventually, her brother, who was concerned, came to the United States. "He knew I was really bad," she said. He took her to Italy and then the Philippines "to start again." She told me, "I was completely destroyed."

# CHAPTER 10:

# *MAMA*

*T*wo years later, Gutierrez shut her eyes at the memory. "Do you have the document?" I asked. She opened her eyes, stared at me. "I promise you," I said, "I will only use anything I learn here today in a way you're comfortable with. Even if it means giving up the story." She picked up a white iPhone, began clicking and scrolling. She pushed the phone across to me, letting me read the million-dollar nondisclosure agreement.

The document was eighteen pages long. It was signed, on the last page, by Gutierrez and Weinstein. The lawyers involved in drafting it must have been so convinced of its enforceability that they never considered the possibility of it emerging. The contract ordered the destruction of all copies of audio recordings of Weinstein admitting to the groping. Gutierrez agreed to give her phone and any other devices that might have contained evidence to Kroll, a private-security firm retained by Weinstein. She also agreed to surrender the passwords to her email accounts and other forms of digital communication that could have been used to spirit out copies. "The Weinstein confidentiality agreement is perhaps the most usurious one I have seen in decades of practice," one attorney who represented

Gutierrez later told me. A sworn statement, pre-signed by Gutierrez, was attached to the agreement, to be released in the event of any breach. It stated that the behavior Weinstein admitted to in the recording never happened.

I looked up from the agreement, and the reporter's notebook in which I'd been transcribing notes as quickly as I could. "Ambra. Are all the copies of the tape destroyed?"

Gutierrez folded her hands in her lap and looked at them.

❖

A moment later, I was walking fast out of the restaurant and toward the subway, dialing Rich McHugh. I told him the story. "It's real," I said. "And there's audio of him admitting to it."

I texted Noah Oppenheim. "I'm now in touch with five women with HW allegations, FYI. I just met with a model who wore a wire for an NYPD investigation in 2015. She's going to play me the recordings. She wants to talk but she took a payout with an NDA — she showed me the document. It's legit. Signed by HW, a million dollars." When he replied hours later, he asked only, "Who's your producer on this?" then fell silent.

Back at 30 Rockefeller Plaza, McHugh and I sat opposite Rich Greenberg in his office on the fourth floor. "It's quite a story," Greenberg said, leaning back in his mesh office chair.

"I mean, it's huge," said McHugh. "He admits to a crime."

Greenberg swiveled toward his monitor.

"Let's see here . . . ," he said, typing Gutierrez's name into Google and switching over to the Images tab. He scrolled through a few pictures of Gutierrez sprawling seductively in lingerie and said, "Not bad."

"We're close to a big piece of evidence here," I said, impatient. "She says she'll play the audio for me."

"Well, let's see about that," Greenberg said.

"And there's the contract," McHugh added.

"That part's complicated," Greenberg said. "We can't be making her breach contract."

"We're not making her do anything," I replied.

Later that afternoon, I called Chung, the NBC lawyer. "Theoretically, someone could say we induced her to violate the contract. But that tort is weird. There are a lot of conflicting interpretations of what's required to prove it. Some say you need to demonstrate the defendant had the sole purpose of violating the contract, which obviously isn't your objective," he said. "I'm sure Rich is just being careful."

I had tried Jonathan a few times over the course of the afternoon but only got through as I ducked out of Rockefeller Plaza at sunset. "Six calls!" he said. "I thought it was an emergency!" He was stepping out of a meeting. "Five!" I countered. We'd met shortly after he left his job as a presidential speechwriter. In the years we'd been together, he'd drifted, creating a short-lived sitcom and tweeting a lot. A couple of months earlier, he and his friends had started a media company focused on podcasts on the West Coast. It had taken off faster than anyone predicted. His trips to New York had become shorter and less frequent.

"I'm checking," he was saying.

"Do it," I replied. I waited thirty seconds. "Jonathan!"

"Sorry! Forgot you were there." This happened more than you'd think. These days, our relationship consisted almost exclusively of endless calls. Occasionally, he'd try to pause me, forgetting I wasn't a podcast.

My phone pinged. I looked down to see a string of twenty or

thirty Instagram message alerts. They came from an account with no profile photo. They read, over and over, "I'm watching you, I'm watching you, I'm watching you." I swiped them away. Strange messages were an occupational hazard of being on television.

"The crazies love me," I said to Jonathan, and read him the messages.

"He thinks he loves you, but wait until he experiences dating you."

"What does that mean?"

"It means I love you?"

"Does it?"

"Just working on my vows for the ceremony. On the moon. In our gravity boots."

This was a running joke. Jonathan's mother wanted grandchildren, and not in the age of lunar bases.

"*This* conversation again?" I said, playing along.

"Just get someone at NBC to take a look at the threats. Take it seriously, please."

◆

After that first meeting with Gutierrez, I followed up again with the same contact in the district attorney's office. "It's weird," the contact said. "The recording. It's referenced in the case files. But I don't think we have it." This seemed improbable. The DA's office would, according to standard procedure, have retained any evidence, in case the investigation was ever reopened. I said "thank you" and chalked it up to an insufficiently thorough search.

A week after our first conversation, I met with Gutierrez again, at a basement noodle place near Union Square. She'd arrived from a casting call, in full hair and makeup. It was like conducting an interview in a shampoo commercial. She talked about Berlusconi's corrupt media empire, and how she'd marshaled the strength to help expose him. With each conversation we had, she sounded more like she was ready to do it again.

Earlier in the day, she'd sent me a picture of an ancient MacBook and explained that she'd lost the charging cable. I had found a cable of the right vintage and, as we talked, the laptop charged on a nearby chair. I kept glancing over at it nervously. Finally I asked, as nonchalantly as possible, if she thought it had enough juice. The restaurant was noisy, so we left and walked around the corner to a Barnes & Noble. She opened the laptop again. Glancing from one side to the other, she navigated through a series of subfolders, past modeling photos and innocuous-looking Word documents.

"Before the order to give all my phone, my computer," she said, as she delved deeper into her hard drive, "I sent recording to myself, to all my emails." She'd agreed to give Kroll the passwords to all those accounts, and knew they'd find any she didn't disclose. But, in order to buy herself a brief window of opportunity, she'd told them she couldn't recall one password. Then, as Kroll wiped the other accounts, one by one, she'd logged into the one for which she was supposedly recovering the password, forwarded the audio to a temporary "burner" email, then cleared her sent mail. Finally, she downloaded the files to this old laptop, which she stuffed in the back of a closet. "I was not sure it works," she said. "It was like —" She made a gasping noise and held her breath, as if bracing for the worst. But Kroll didn't come knocking, and the laptop collected dust, uncharged, for two years.

On the screen in front of her, Gutierrez came to a folder labeled "Mama." Inside were audio files titled Mama1, Mama2, and Mama3: the recordings she'd had to frantically start each time her phone issued a push alert about its dwindling battery life during the police sting. She passed me a pair of headphones, and I listened. It was all there: the promises of career advancement, the list of other actresses he had helped, the encounter with the officer Weinstein thought was a TMZ photographer. In the recording, Gutierrez's panic was palpable. "I don't want to," she said, standing in the hallway outside his room, refusing to go farther as Weinstein's tone turned menacing. "I want to leave," she added. "I want to go downstairs." At one point, she asked him why he had groped her breasts the day before.

"Oh, please, I'm sorry, just come on in," Weinstein replied. "I'm used to that. Come on. Please."

"You're used to that?" Gutierrez asked, incredulous.

"Yes," Weinstein said. He added, "I won't do it again."

After almost two minutes of back-and-forth in the hallway, he finally agreed to return to the bar.

Weinstein wheedled and menaced and bullied and didn't take no for an answer. But more than that, it was a smoking gun. It was inarguable. There he was, admitting not just to a crime but to a pattern. *"I'm used to that."*

"Ambra," I said, slipping off the headphones. "We need to make this public."

I produced a USB drive from my pocket and slid it toward her across the countertop.

"I can't tell you what to do," I said. "The decision is yours."

"I know that," she replied. She closed her eyes, seemed to sway for a moment. "I will," she said. "But not yet."

## CHAPTER 11:

# *BLOOM*

*T*he second meeting with Gutierrez made me late for drinks with a former assistant to Phil Griffin, my old boss at MSNBC. "This is the most important story I've ever been on," I texted her. "If I am late it's because I have absolutely no choice." After journalism, drama and being late were my great passions.

"No worries hope it's going well," she replied tolerantly.

I was still apologizing when I arrived at the little French bistro where we'd agreed to meet. When I asked how Griffin was, she said it was funny I should mention it—that he'd asked after me, too.

Griffin was the one who took a chance on me and brought me inside NBC. He was a talented producer who'd worked his way up through roles at CNN and, later, the *Today* show and *Nightly News*. At CNN, he'd focused on sports. He was passionate about baseball, and gracious about my incomprehension during his impassioned monologues about it. He talked about a lifelong dream of working for the New York Mets, and you got the sense he was only mostly joking. At the helm of MSNBC, he'd overseen the cable channel's periods of greatest success, and survived its brutal low points. Griffin was the son of a Macy's executive and grew up in wealthy suburbs outside New York City and Toledo. Trim and bald and excitable, he had the carefree bearing of a man who'd mostly gotten his way.

In the two years since my show was canceled, our contact had been limited to cordial office run-ins. I wondered if the former assistant was just being polite with the comment about Griffin mentioning me, and why I'd be on his radar if he had.

❖

Harvey Weinstein had been calling Boies, his attorney, about Rose McGowan since shortly after she tweeted the previous fall. But it wasn't until that spring that Weinstein mentioned NBC.

"I've heard they're doing a story," Weinstein said. He wanted to know if Boies had heard anything. Boies said he hadn't. Within days, Weinstein was on the phone again, repeating the question.

By the second call with Boies, Weinstein seemed unsatisfied with the lawyer's answers. "I know people at NBC," Weinstein reminded Boies. "I'm gonna find out about it."

Weinstein had been apprehensively calling his attorneys about news outlets pursuing troublesome stories for years. But there was something different this time: he began telling people around him that he was getting information directly from NBC. Soon, he was relating claims about exactly how much the network had—and the name of the reporter who was working on the story.

❖

Over the following weeks, I kept meeting with Gutierrez at the Union Square Barnes & Noble. She told me she'd meet with me and Greenberg and NBC's legal department to play them the audio and show them the contract. But she was still grappling with whether to actually hand over the evidence.

After one of the meetings, I hesitated again before calling my sister Dylan. "So, you need my advice again," she said, a teasing note in her voice.

I explained the situation: a source, a tape, a contract. Everyone I spoke with was a potential informant who might relay information back to Weinstein. If I ever fully assembled the story, I'd be laying out the reporting for him and seeking comment. But for now, I was vulnerable, and warnings from sources about Weinstein's tactics had put me on edge. "Who do I turn to on this?" I asked her. "Who do I trust?"

She thought for a moment. "You should call Lisa Bloom."

Lisa Bloom was the kind of lawyer who also plays one on television, but she appeared to use the platform to defend not just her clients but also the ideal of protecting survivors of sexual violence who confronted the rich and powerful. She had written and spoken repeatedly in defense of my sister, when few others did. "You, your sister and mother have comported yourself with grace and dignity through the storm, empowering sexual abuse survivors everywhere," she'd written to me once. "The very least I could do was to speak out about Dylan's obvious credibility."

Bloom had appeared often on my show, representing accusers of Bill O'Reilly and of Bill Cosby. "Rich and powerful people get a pass. I see this every day in my own practice," she said in one segment about Cosby. "I represent many victims of wealthy and successful predators. The first thing they do is go on the attack against the victim, try to dredge up anything from her life that they can find to embarrass her." She'd seen how "women are smeared, or they are threatened that they will be smeared."

When Bloom picked up, I offered to keep our conversation off the record. She waved this away. "Please," she said. She had a warm voice with a slight rasp. "Most of the time, I'll *want* to comment, you know that."

"Thanks," I said. "But I'd appreciate your confidence, anyway."

"Of course," she said.

"I know we're not under attorney-client privilege, but as a fellow lawyer, I trust you. If I ask you about a sensitive story, do you feel comfortable promising not to mention it to anyone until it comes out?"

"Absolutely," she said.

I said I was working on a story involving heavy-duty nondisclosure agreements and asked her view of their enforceability. She said the agreements usually held up: that they often stipulated financially devastating liquidated damages as a penalty for breach, and contained arbitration clauses that allowed them to be enforced secretly, rather than in court. (Curiously, Gutierrez's otherwise draconian agreement had lacked such an arbitration clause.)

Some entities, like Fox News, had of late declined to enforce the nondisclosure agreements signed by former employees with sexual harassment complaints. Bloom said it all depended on who was doing the enforcing.

"It would help if I knew who this was about, Ronan." She said this very slowly.

"And you promise I have your word this will be kept in confidence?"

"You have my word," she said.

"It's about Harvey Weinstein."

I was standing in my apartment, looking out at a wall of

warehouse-style windows. Through one, a sliver of a ballet studio was visible. A leotard-clad back strained in and out of frame.

"I'm going to go to him for comment if it progresses to that point," I continued. "But in the meantime it's important, for these women, that it not get back to his people."

Another pause. Then Lisa Bloom said, "I understand completely."

Gutierrez and McGowan had both said they needed attorneys. As a reporter, I had to maintain distance from sources' legal cases. I'd told both that I couldn't give legal advice or directly recommend lawyers. But I could point them to publicly available information about experts in the field. I asked Bloom for advice on attorneys with experience in cases involving nondisclosure agreements. McGowan would later reach out to one of them.

◆

Harvey Weinstein's standard approach to getting people on the phone was to bark their names at the assistants stationed in the anteroom outside his office. Not long after the calls with Boies about NBC, he shouted two new names: "Get me Andy Lack, now," he said. "And Phil Griffin."

When Weinstein reached Lack, the studio head and the network head exchanged brief pleasantries. But Weinstein, sounding anxious, got to the point quickly. "Hey," he said, "your boy Ronan is doing a story on me. About the nineties and stuff."

My name seemed to register only dimly. Lack suggested Weinstein try Griffin, my old boss at MSNBC. To this, Weinstein launched into an argument about his innocence and the folly of the story.

"Andy, it was the nineties. You know? Did I go out with an assistant or two that I shouldn't have, did I sleep with one or two of them, sure."

Lack said nothing to this.

"It was the nineties, Andy," Weinstein repeated. This seemed, for Weinstein, an important point of exculpation. And then, with a note of menace: "We all did that."

There was a pause before Andy Lack said, "Harvey, say no more. We'll look into it."

❖

It was evening when Bloom called again. I was heading home, emerging from a subway stop. "How's it going?!" she asked. "I was thinking. You know, I actually know David Boies a little. And— and even Harvey a little."

"You didn't mention this to anyone, did you?" I asked Bloom.

"Of course I didn't! I'm just, you know, I had this idea I could maybe help connect you to them."

"Lisa, this is very sensitive, and very early. I promise you, I'll get in touch with him when the time comes. Just please, don't say anything yet. You gave your word."

"I just think it's worth considering," she said.

"I'll let you know if things develop further," I replied.

I was passing by St. Paul the Apostle, the fortress-like Gothic Revival church near my apartment. I looked up, then hurried out of its shadow.

"I'm here if you need anything, okay?" Bloom said. "Anything at all."

# CHAPTER 12:

# *FUNNY*

That week, McHugh and I sat in Greenberg's office, updating him on the conversations with Gutierrez. I told him about her offer to meet with our legal department and show them the evidence. "Let's get this scheduled, before she gets cold feet," I said.

Greenberg wouldn't commit to the meeting. He said we needed the audio in hand, not just played for us. I agreed but said Gutierrez was getting closer to sharing it and argued that the meeting with NBC might help persuade her. Greenberg again raised his concern that looking at contracts might incur liability. "You need to be running all of this by legal," he said. He kept fiddling with a pen in front of him on the desk.

I was reminding him that I'd run every step of the reporting by legal when the phone on his desk rang. He looked at the caller ID, paused.

"It's Harvey Weinstein," Greenberg said. "He called earlier today." McHugh and I looked at each other. This was news to us. Greenberg said Weinstein had pressed for details about the story. He'd led with flattery, saying he was a fan of mine, a fan of the network. Then he'd turned to saber-rattling.

"He mentioned he's retained some lawyers, " Greenberg said.

He flipped through some notes in front of him.

"David Boies?" I asked.

"He mentioned Boies, but there was someone else as well. Here it is, Charles Harder." Harder was the pitbull attorney who, in an invasion of privacy case bankrolled by the billionaire Peter Thiel, had recently prevailed in shutting down the gossip news site *Gawker*.

"I told him we couldn't discuss specifics, of course," Greenberg continued. "We do this by the book. Let him call all he wants."

❖

Our reporting was in limbo. Gutierrez was still deliberating about handing over the audio. Rosanna Arquette's agent had stopped returning my calls. The English actress confirmed the story her agent had told me, then got cold feet and fell silent. Ashley Judd, whose comments about an unnamed studio executive had featured echoes of McGowan's and Gutierrez's claims—a meeting moved from a hotel restaurant to a hotel room, a request that she watch him take a shower—hadn't responded to my inquiries.

One afternoon that March, I found a quiet stretch of cubicles vacated for renovations and called Annabella Sciorra. In the preceding weeks, others had mentioned she might have a story. Sciorra, who was raised in Brooklyn by Italian parents, had made a name for herself in movies like *The Hand That Rocks the Cradle* and later received an Emmy nomination for a guest role on *The Sopranos*. She had a reputation for playing steely, tough characters, but when she picked up the phone, her voice sounded small and tired. "It was so strange hearing from you," she said of my Twitter inquiry that had prompted the call. "I wasn't sure what it was about. But I'm an MSNBC viewer, you know, so I was happy to talk."

I told her I was working on a story about allegations of sexual harassment against Harvey Weinstein, and that two people had suggested she might have something to say.

"Oh, that," she said, managing a tinny laugh. "It's weird, I've heard that before. Who told you that?"

I told her I couldn't reveal other sources without their permission. "It could help a lot of people, if you do know anything," I said. "Even if you can only talk anonymously."

On the other end of the call, Sciorra was in her living room in Brooklyn, staring out at the East River. She hesitated, then said, "No. Nothing happened." Another thin laugh. "I don't know. I guess I just wasn't his type." I thanked her and told her to call me if she remembered anything. "I wish I could help," she replied. "I'm sorry."

Early that April, I sat at my desk and looked at a text that had just come in. "Hey...," it read. "It's Matthew Hiltzik have a quick question for you." Hiltzik was a prominent publicist. He was a reliable choice for news personalities and had, for years, handled Katie Couric's communications. When I'd despaired at the flood of tabloid items about me and my family several years earlier, I'd briefly retained his services at MSNBC's suggestion, and he'd been compassionate. Hiltzik was an equal-opportunity spin doctor. He was closely entwined with both the Clinton and Trump families. Ivanka Trump was a client of his firm, and two of his underlings, Hope Hicks and Josh Raffel, had found roles in Trump's White House.

Soon, Hiltzik was calling. "Hey, how are you doing?" he said brightly. There was a hum of voices in the background, like he was stepping out of a party. "I'm at this event," he explained. "Hillary's speaking."

Hiltzik never called without a reason. I stayed vague about how I was. "Juggling a few shoots," I told him. "Dealing with a book deadline." I'd been spending my nights furiously assembling a long-gestating book about the declining role of diplomacy in America's foreign policy.

"So it sounds like your other stories are on the back burner a little," Hiltzik was saying. "Like I said, Hillary's here, and Harvey's here, who I've worked with over the years."

I said nothing.

"He just walked in, actually," Hiltzik continued. "He said to me, 'Who's this Ronan guy? He's asking questions about me? Is he investigating me?'"

"Are you representing him?" I asked.

"Not exactly. We have a long relationship. He knows I know you, I said I'd do him a little favor. I told him, 'Look, calm down, Harvey, Ronan is a good guy.' I said you and I would have a little chat."

"I investigate a lot of leads and I really can't talk about any of them until they're ready to go."

"Is this for NBC?" Hiltzik asked.

"I mean — I'm an investigative correspondent at NBC."

"Is this about Rose McGowan?" he pressed. "Because he says he can clear that up." Choosing my words carefully, I told him I always welcomed information. There was muffled shouting in the background. "He's so funny," Hiltzik said. "He's saying all kinds of" — he paused for effect — "*funny* things."

Two hours later, Hiltzik texted, "He is sort of hilarious. Gave your message. He asked me to call u back." Then Hiltzik was on the phone again, saying of Weinstein, "He doesn't always have a normal reaction," and, "He's agitated. He's upset."

"I'm sorry to hear that," I said.

"At times people can be aggressive and try to mess with him by suggesting there's even a story here. He says the same stories keep coming back, and the conclusion is always that it's not true, or not true to the degree people think." He mentioned that *The New Yorker* and *New York* magazine had pursued the story. One of the reporters had "just called everyone in Harvey's world. It freaked him out." Weinstein had "gotten more sensitive about it."

"What does 'sensitive' mean?" I asked.

"He's older now. He's mellowed a bit. I don't think he's going to be taking action immediately, but—"

"Taking action?" I said.

"Well, he's not dumb. He's going to do something. Look, you have your book to finish, right? So this is on the back burner for you," he said. I glanced at the notes I'd been taking throughout the call. My eyebrows went up when I saw it: Hiltzik had let slip a small but useful lead.

Applause sounded on Hiltzik's end of the line. "What event are you at?" I asked.

Hiltzik explained that Hillary Clinton had finished a greenroom conversation with Weinstein, her old friend and fund-raiser, then stepped onstage to give a speech at Women in the World.

I texted Greenberg about Hiltzik immediately. The next day, Greenberg called. He led with strained small talk about my foreign policy book that suggested he was ramping up to something. Then, he said, "By the way, I met with Noah today, and you know—we were talking about ten different things, it wasn't that we met about this topic, but he asked about your favorite story." He chuckled. "I told him there's smoke but I don't know that there's fire. We don't really have a smoking gun. I said, 'Noah, if you ask me right now, you know, I don't think we have it.'"

I reminded him that I'd heard audio of Weinstein admitting to an assault and seen his signature on a million-dollar nondisclosure agreement. I pressed on whether we could schedule that meeting between Gutierrez and our lawyers. "It's not in the news. I don't think there's any rush here," Greenberg said. "I think where we stand now is, we give it a rest."

"What does 'give it a rest' mean?" I asked.

"You know, just—just keep it on the back burner," Greenberg said. *That phrase again*, I thought. "Ronan, you have so many promising things going on. You've got a lot of stories in progress, the series is doing well. You know, you don't have to necessarily focus on this."

A few minutes later, I was on the phone with McHugh. He was as puzzled as I was. "This feels like somebody called them," he said. "You hear from Hiltzik and Harvey, then this? It doesn't feel like a coincidence."

"I'm sure they got calls, and I'm sure they're standing up to them. Noah will back this."

"Well, our immediate boss doesn't want you reporting. You're gonna have to decide if you go along with that."

"We'll bring them more evidence, they'll come around," I said.

But when McHugh told Greenberg he was setting aside an afternoon to make calls on the Weinstein story, Greenberg said, simply, "I think that can wait." The situation was creating a Catch-22. We needed more evidence, but continuing to gather it openly was, suddenly, a liability. "What happens when we need to shoot more interviews?" McHugh asked.

"We're in fantastic shape here," Alan Berger, of Creative Artists Agency — CAA — was saying. The San Andreas fault could split open and Los Angeles could slip right into the Pacific and agents would still be running around reassuring clients how fantastic everything was. "Your *Nightly* story about the prisons. Phew!" Berger continued. He had a warm, avuncular voice, with an accent that knew its way around the Long Island Expressway. He was regarded in the business as a steady dealmaker.

"You know your contract's up this fall."

"I know," I said. I was in my apartment. In the ballet studio across the street, someone was buffing the floor. As the Weinstein story expanded, it crowded out other reporting and career considerations. I'd missed so many deadlines on my foreign policy book that my publisher had finally given up and canceled it, that very week.

"They love you there," Berger said, of NBC. "Noah loves you. Everyone sees a bigger role for you."

"Well, I'm working on some stories that are making things a little —"

"A little what, Ronan?"

"I can't talk about it, Alan. Just let me know if anything seems weird."

"Ronan, you're killing me," Berger said, laughing. "Just keep doing what you're doing. And don't piss anyone off."

## CHAPTER 13:

# *DICK*

*I* flipped through my notes from the call with Hiltzik and looked at his comment about *New York* and *The New Yorker* magazines. At *New York*, Carr, with his suspicions of surveillance and intimidation, had chased the story, but that was in the early 2000s. Something in Hiltzik's observation about Weinstein's sensitivity suggested someone else had tried more recently.

I sent another message to Jennifer Senior, the writer who'd worked with Carr. "Can you find out if anyone else at *New York* was working on the story we discussed, potentially more recently than David?" I asked. "I keep hearing that this might have been the case."

"Yr right," she wrote back. "Just looked at my email. But I feel uncomfortable, in this case, saying who." The attempt at the story, it seemed, had ended poorly. I asked her to pass on a message to the mystery writer.

At *The New Yorker*, Ken Auletta, a writer known for his thorough appraisals of business and media executives, had profiled Weinstein in 2002. Entitled "Beauty and the Beast," the piece made no explicit mention of sexual predation, but dwelled on Weinstein's brutality. He was, Auletta wrote, "spectacularly coarse, and even threatening."

And there was a curious, overheated passage that hinted that there was more to the story. Auletta noted that Weinstein's business partners "feel 'raped' — a word often invoked by those dealing with him." I sent a message to an acquaintance who worked at *The New Yorker* and asked for Auletta's email address.

Auletta was seventy-five. He grew up on Coney Island, raised by a Jewish mother and an Italian father. There was something elegant and old-world about his carriage and speech. And he was a careful, experienced reporter. "Of course, there was more to it than we were able to print," he told me when I called him, from an empty office near the investigative newsroom. Back in 2002, Auletta had pursued the claims that Weinstein was preying on women, and even asked about the allegations in an on-the-record interview. The two had been sitting in Weinstein's Tribeca offices. Weinstein stood up, face red, and shouted at Auletta, "Are you trying to get my fucking wife to divorce me?" Auletta stood, too, "fully prepared to beat the shit out of him." But then Weinstein crumpled, sitting back down and beginning to sob. "He basically said to me, 'Look I don't always behave well, but I love my wife.'" Weinstein hadn't denied the allegations.

Auletta hadn't been able to secure an on-the-record claim like McGowan's, or a piece of hard evidence like Gutierrez's tape and contract. But he had spoken to Zelda Perkins, an employee of Miramax in London who, alongside a colleague named Rowena Chiu, was involved in a joint sexual harassment settlement with Weinstein. Though Perkins had been too frightened to go on the record, Auletta was able to use her account as leverage, compelling Weinstein to concede there had been some kind of settlement in London with her and Chiu.

Weinstein even presented to *The New Yorker* the voided check used in the transaction, to establish that it had been underwritten not by Miramax's parent company, Disney, but with private money from an account belonging to Weinstein's brother, Bob.

But the checks had been shown to him off the record. When the brothers, along with David Boies, met with Auletta and *New Yorker* editor David Remnick, Weinstein had provided none of the further information they'd hoped might render the claims publishable. He'd evinced only furious denials and a barely checked temper.

Years later, Auletta's frustration was still palpable. He was like a homicide detective kept awake at night by the case that got away. "I had a fixation," he told me. By the end of his reporting, he said, "I came to believe that he's a predator, a serial rapist, and to see exposing him as a public service." He had tried reviving the story twice over the years, most recently after the Gutierrez incident. But he'd gotten no traction. "If you have any chance of succeeding where I failed," he told me, "keep at it."

❖

Rose McGowan had stayed in touch, urging us to come shoot more with her. She mentioned, in our conversations, that she was finding more support. Lacy Lynch, the literary agent who had passed along the inquiry from Seth Freedman, the empathetic former *Guardian* writer, was also forwarding other expressions of solidarity. The day I spoke to Auletta, one such email arrived, from Reuben Capital Partners, a London-based wealth management firm seeking to enlist McGowan in a charitable project called Women in Focus. The firm was planning a gala dinner at the end of the year and hoped McGowan would give a keynote speech: "We have taken a keen interest in the work Ms Rose McGowan does for the advocacy of women's rights and we believe that the ideals she strives towards align closely with those upheld by our new initiative."

"I think it sounds good," Lynch wrote to McGowan. "Would love to set up a call to learn more."

The email from Reuben Capital Partners was signed by Diana Filip, deputy head of sustainable and responsible investments.

◆

The following morning, an email that I obtained many months later appeared in Harvey Weinstein's private Gmail account. "RF Info," the subject line read. "LEGALLY PRIVILEGED."

"Harvey," the email read, "Here is a rough overview of the info I have compiled so far on Ronan Farrow." Several dozen exhibits were attached. In a section of the email titled "persons of interest that Farrow is following" was a list of some accusers I'd found, and some I hadn't. The email noted that McHugh and I had followed, on social media, a cluster of McGowan's associates around the date of our interview, "out of the blue," and speculated that I'd gotten her to talk. It observed that I was "a fan" of Lisa Bloom, appearing to assess her level of access to me. And it described my attempts to get in touch with Judd, Sciorra, and Arquette. The email analyzed the likelihood that each of them would talk. It flagged any public statements the women had made about sexual violence as a warning sign.

A section titled "Farrow Employment" contained an exhaustive list of coworkers who might provide access or information. There were the obvious on-air investigative correspondents with whom I'd worked, like Cynthia McFadden and Stephanie Gosk. But the list also included coworkers who wouldn't be publicly identifiable, like an NBC intern whose desk was adjacent to mine.

A biographical section appeared to search for pressure points. It noted what it described as "family drama," stirred by "his sister Dylan Farrow in her accusations of rape against their father Woody Allen." The topic I'd spent years trying to outrun was coming back to haunt me.

The email was sent by Sara Ness, a private investigator at a firm called PSOPS. Jack Palladino and Sandra Sutherland, a husband-and-wife team, operated the firm. A rare profile of the two in *People* magazine compared them to Nick and Nora Charles, the detective couple from *The Thin Man*, minus the glamour. During the 1992 presidential campaign, Bill Clinton hired Palladino to "discredit stories about women claiming to have had relationships with the Arkansas governor," per the *Washington Post*. By the late nineties, Palladino had earned the nickname "the President's Dick." He said he never broke the law. But, he proudly noted, "I go right to the boundaries of the envelope."

"Jack is overseas, but I have kept him up to speed on this investigation and will confer with him this week on the issues/potential strategies you and I discussed yesterday," Ness wrote Weinstein that day in April. She promised that a fuller and more formal dossier was forthcoming. The message made two things clear: that the research was meant to complement a larger effort, involving players other than Palladino's firm; and that the dossier was just an opening salvo.

❖

Rich McHugh and I kept raising the idea of doing further reporting on the Weinstein story, and Greenberg kept telling us to focus on other things. Greenberg was our boss. The conversations were becoming awkward. But after the call with Auletta, it was becoming clear that we had secured more hard evidence than anyone had before, about a story that had stayed buried for decades.

"What do we do?" I asked McHugh. We were huddled on the margins of the newsroom.

"I don't know," he replied. "I think if you go to Greenberg — he told you to put the story on the back burner..."

"He didn't order us to stop," I said, wearily. "He said we could meet again about it."

"Okay," McHugh said, skeptical.

"But maybe it's strategic to be armed with as much as possible before that meeting," I conceded.

"That's my inclination," he said. "Let's just get on with it."

We agreed to shore up our reporting. We'd return with a bullet-proof body of evidence, and ask for forgiveness, not permission. Calls could be done quietly. But we debated how to keep our on-camera interviews going without running afoul of Greenberg.

◆

The next day, McHugh motioned me over to his computer. "We have a green light on shooting for, what, three, four stories?" We were working on several about addiction, and the one about Dow Chemical and Shell seeding California farmlands with toxic waste. "You think you can schedule these Weinstein interviews around those shoots?" he asked.

"Well, yeah. But they'd be marked as Weinstein interviews anyway," I said.

"Not necessarily," he said. "We add interviews that come up suddenly onto existing travel all the time. And we can label them anything we want."

There were limits to how much we could hide the work. The subject of any new interviews would still be revealed on detailed expense reports. But we could avoid calling attention to the matter with leadership.

On his monitor, McHugh navigated to a networked drive on an NBC server. He scrolled through a list of directories containing our stories. Then he took the Weinstein files out of a folder titled "MEDIA MOGUL" and dropped them into a different one. I looked at the screen and laughed. The folder he'd chosen, named after the California waste story, was labeled "POISON VALLEY."

# PART II: WHITE WHALE

## CHAPTER 14:

# *ROOKIE*

*T*he men sat at Harvey Weinstein's usual table near the kitchen in the back of the Tribeca Grill. It was April 24. Weinstein was there, and Dylan Howard, of the *National Enquirer*, and an operative from Black Cube. The operative looked young, with dark hair and a heavy accent.

Lanny Davis walked in and surveyed the room. Davis was by then in his early seventies, a thin man with graying hair and bags under his eyes. He was raised in Jersey City, his father a dentist, his mother a manager in the dental office. At Yale Law School, Davis had become friends with Hillary Rodham and, later, Bill Clinton. After a failed run for Congress and a few years of legal practice, he'd spun this friendship into a professional role as their most ardent defender in times of scandal and political peril.

Then Davis cashed in, taking on jobs that earned him $1 million to lobby his way around Equatorial Guinea's human rights abuses, or $100,000 a month to downplay a patently rigged election in Ivory Coast. If a passenger disappeared and left a smear of blood on the deck of your cruise ship, or the President criticized your football team's racist name, Davis was there. Trying to get ahold of Davis later on, I asked Jonathan, "Who would have Lanny Davis's number?" He replied, "I don't know, Pol Pot?"

Weinstein—who had met Davis at an event honoring Hillary Clinton and knew of the crisis manager's familiarity with the sexual misconduct allegations against Bill Clinton—had called that spring to enlist him.

At the Tribeca Grill that morning, Davis said they couldn't talk in front of the Black Cube operative if Weinstein wanted to maintain attorney-client privilege. "I can't talk in front of people who aren't attorneys," Davis said. "If I'm subpoenaed, I have to tell if someone else is in the room."

Weinstein seemed annoyed by this.

"Oh, yes, you can," he said. "You can maintain privilege if he works for me." This was an oversimplification of the law. But Weinstein was insistent, and Davis relented.

Weinstein ranted. McGowan, he said, was crazy, a liar. He wanted to discredit all the women making what he described as false claims about him.

"My advice is don't do that," Davis told Weinstein. "Even if you think you're right."

Weinstein began to bellow. "Why? Why? Why? Why?"

"Because it looks awful," Davis said.

Dylan Howard grinned, which he did a lot. The man from Black Cube did not. A few hours after the meeting at the Tribeca Grill, Dr. Avi Yanus, Black Cube's director and CFO, sent an email to Weinstein's attorneys at Boies Schiller Flexner, calling the meeting "productive." He wrote that Weinstein had agreed to a ten-week extension of Black Cube's operation on his behalf. An invoice was attached. The email continued: "We are committed as ever to bring you with game-changing intelligence in this case, and to successfully reach all of our main objectives."

I scoured Auletta's old profile of Weinstein for sources that might lead me to the two settlements in London, calling one after another. Donna Gigliotti, the *Shakespeare in Love* producer, had discouraged me when we first spoke. But when I called her again, she revealed more. "There are documents out there," she said. "Where he's never admitting guilt, but large sums of money are paid. You need those documents. But the victims are never allowed to keep them." I asked her if she meant, for example, documents related to two women with complaints in London. "If you find them," she said, "maybe I can talk. Until then, I'm afraid I can't." She did, however, give me the names of several other former employees who had been in the London offices in the same era and might help.

I thanked her. She was not optimistic. "Nothing's stopping Harvey," she told me. "He will squash this story."

Celebrities hurried out of SUVs, bowed their heads into heavy rain, and filed into *Time* magazine's annual gala dinner celebrating its "100 most influential people" list. I was not on the list. I was, however, soaked.

"I'm an aquarium," I said, walking into the Time Warner Center. "I'm the plot of *Chinatown*."

My mother shrugged. "Wet's always in. It's classic."

The event was heavy on television news figures. I blundered through awkward conversations with them. Megyn Kelly, tony and sequined and charismatic in a way that made you feel you were the only person in the room, mentioned her forthcoming NBC show. I congratulated her, then said I was sorry about "the Twitter thing." I quickly realized my gaffe. Kelly had departed Fox News tailed by supercut videos of her saying things that were, depending on whom you asked, either clumsy or malicious about people of color. "The Twitter thing" was that I'd called a comment of hers racist. A tendon stood out on Kelly's neck. "I made a lot of mistakes when I was at your point in my career, too," she said, smiling tightly. "You're kind of a rookie reporter."

I stalked off, moistly, to find a bathroom or a drink or anything but more conversation, and instead found Andy Lack. As we shook hands, he looked at me like he was processing something. Lack had tufts of graying hair and an affable but appraising smile. At almost seventy, he had enjoyed an eclectic career, with a through line of creative showmanship. Like Oppenheim, he'd dreamed of Hollywood. He'd studied acting at Boston University and, after graduating, landed roles in a Broadway production of *Inquest*, a play about Julius and Ethel Rosenberg, and in a few commercials. "He was charming, charismatic," one person close to Lack later told me. "His background in theater makes him a unique creative mind." At CBS News in the eighties, his signature achievement was *West 57th*, an edgy and stylish spin on the classic newsmagazine format. During his first stint as an NBC News executive in the nineties, he'd been credited with a turnaround in a time of disarray and declining ratings. Positions at Sony Music and Bloomberg Television had followed. In 2015, NBC had brought him back to right the ship again.

Lack was still giving me that searching look.

"Ronan," I said quickly.

"Yes," he said, finally, as if dredging something heavy up from the bottom of a deep body of water. "Yes, of course."

He said Oppenheim talked about me a lot. I thanked him for getting behind investigative stories. I reached for a personal connection. My brother had recently purchased Lack's home in Bronxville, New York.

"Apparently you left behind a giant safe they still haven't drilled open," I said.

Lack laughed. "That's true. There is an old safe." He said the safe had preceded him, and he hadn't opened it, either. He shrugged. "Sometimes it's better to leave things be."

◆

The room began to thin, guests filtering into an adjacent amphitheater for dinner. I found my mother, headed in the same direction. Oppenheim approached us. "That's Noah," I whispered to my mother. "Tell him you liked *Jackie*."

"But I didn't like *Jackie*," she said.

I shot her a withering look.

They said their hellos and then Oppenheim pulled me aside.

"So Harvey's here," he said. "He's sitting with me at dinner."

I stared at him. I'd been keeping him apprised of every element of the reporting. "You do know I've heard a recording of him admitting to a sexual assault," I said.

Oppenheim raised both hands in a defensive gesture. "I believe you!" he said.

"It's not about *believing* . . . ," I trailed off. "Don't mention anything, obviously."

"Of course," he said.

A moment later, I watched as Oppenheim stood at the entrance to the amphitheater, talking to a hulking figure in a baggy black tuxedo. Harvey Weinstein was recovering from knee surgery, leaning on a cane.

◆

The first week of May, Black Cube called Weinstein with a promising update. "We informed the client that following our intense efforts, we scheduled a meeting in LA next week, which we believe will lead to the disclosure of high quality intelligence and hard evidence for the purposes of our work," Yanus, the Black Cube director, wrote to Weinstein's lawyers at Boies Schiller. This new phase of the project would require a new cash injection as well. A few days later, on May 12, Christopher Boies, David Boies's son and a partner at his firm, oversaw the wiring of another $50,000 to Black Cube.

In the preceding days, Lynch, the agent advising Rose McGowan, had brokered the proposed introduction between McGowan and Diana Filip of Reuben Capital Partners, who had reached out to enlist McGowan in her Women in Focus campaign.

"Rose, it's a great pleasure to connect with you," Filip wrote.

"It is my great pleasure to connect with you as well," McGowan replied.

The day Boies Schiller's latest payment appeared in Black Cube's account, Filip and McGowan finally met face-to-face, at the Belvedere, the airy, pastel-colored Mediterranean restaurant at the Peninsula hotel in Beverly Hills. Filip had high cheekbones, a prominent nose, and dirty-blond hair. She had an elegant accent McGowan couldn't place. McGowan was skeptical of strangers. But Filip seemed to know everything about her, and, more than that, to understand her. The actress let her guard down, just a little.

# CHAPTER 15:

# *STATIC*

*J*ennifer Senior made good on her promise and introduced me to Ben Wallace, the *New York* magazine writer behind that publication's most recent attempt at the Weinstein story. One afternoon that May, I called him as I left Rockefeller Plaza. Wallace told me how frustrating the assignment had been. Anything he learned seemed immediately, inexplicably, to get back to Weinstein. "Everyone was a double agent," Wallace told me.

This seemed to be especially true of several sources who had offered to help. He'd suspected that Anna, the European woman who told him she had a story about Weinstein, was hiding something. Some of her questions had felt strange. Anna wanted to know not just how many other sources he was working with but who they were. The information she seemed bent on extracting was out of proportion to what she was giving. At times, she appeared to press him to make statements that betrayed bias. At the hotel bar, when she eventually broke down and recounted her story about Weinstein, it was mild and generalized. She said she and Weinstein had an affair that ended poorly. She wanted revenge. The performance had a soap-operatic quality. As she dangled her wrist in front of him, Wallace had a prickly suspicion that she might be secretly recording. He told Anna that he sympathized but considered consensual affairs to be Weinstein's own business. Then he left the hotel bar and stopped taking her calls.

Wallace had the same feeling that something was off when he received the email from Seth Freedman, the former writer for the *Guardian* who wanted to help. Freedman wrote that he was "working with a group of international journalists on a large story about the film industry, giving a sense of the present-day culture of Hollywood and other film capitals." He claimed to have "come across a great deal of information that we can't include in our pieces, which might be of use to you. I would be very happy to share it with you if you are interested." But after several conversations with Freedman, Wallace still hadn't gotten any meaningful information out of him. "He was pumping me for what I had heard and learned," Wallace recalled. Suspicious, he cut ties there, too.

Weinstein's associates started calling *New York* magazine, sometimes threatening to deliver unspecified personal information about Wallace. Weinstein demanded a meeting between his legal team, investigators from Kroll, and the magazine. The intention, Wallace assumed, was to "come in with dossiers slagging various women and me." The magazine declined the meeting. In January of 2017, after three months of reporting, Wallace and his editor, Adam Moss, decided to stand down. "At a certain point," Wallace told me, "the magazine just couldn't afford to spend indefinite time."

The experience had clearly put him on edge. As Weinstein and his team began calling *New York* with an uncanny knowledge of his leads, Wallace purchased a paper shredder and destroyed his notes. "I was more paranoid than ever before," he told me. "There was much more static and distraction than I've encountered on any other story."

Wallace hadn't gotten any sources on the record or discovered dispositive documents or recordings. But he had assembled a list of women with allegations. He rattled off a few names I had heard myself, including that of Asia Argento, the Italian actress whom several former Weinstein colleagues had suggested I find. There were also a few sources he had gotten to speak on background, telling their full stories but with their identities obscured — including a former assistant who had been harassed by Weinstein and complained to HR at his company.

"Please," I said. "Just ask her if she'd talk."

◆

In the glass that separated the investigative bullpen and the fourth-floor studio, I sometimes caught glimpses of my reflection. That spring, I'd filled out a little, and gotten some color from all the shooting in Los Angeles. There was a feeling of momentum around McHugh and me and our little investigative series. We were receiving the kind of television journalism awards you never hear of in the outside world and enthusiastic appraisals in outlets that cover media. The head of communications at NBC News, Mark Kornblau, had also worked at the State Department during my time there. Over coffee as I transitioned from my role at MSNBC to the network, and in our encounters since, he'd been supportive. Kornblau and his team nurtured the positive coverage, giving quotes or allowing me to do so.

The mood seemed to extend to others. An NBC veteran named David Corvo stopped me in the hall. Corvo was the executive producer of *Dateline*. A small, animated man with a bushy beard, he'd been working at NBC since the mid-nineties. He was close with Lack. "Let's get together," Corvo said. "You're doing exactly the kind of stories we want."

◆

It was early evening when Ambra Gutierrez and I sat down at a quiet restaurant in the theater district called Brazil Brazil. I'd spent the previous month trying to find another way to obtain the recording. Police sources told me that they believed Gutierrez. They were convinced they'd had the evidence they needed to charge Weinstein, despite the DA's decision not to. But none of the conversations had gotten me any closer to the recording.

With Gutierrez, I had tried on for size every possible approach that might allow her to pass me her copy. What if she left and went to the bathroom, and I just happened to have access to the computer? No, she said. She stood to lose too much. She was worried about her brother. "I have to get him here, from Philippines," she said. Gutierrez was sounding increasingly skittish.

It was Jonathan who, the night before, had suggested another feint toward plausible deniability.

"What if you record her recording. Literally hold a microphone to a speaker. You make something new. She never transfers anything."

"What does that do?"

"It just feels like a step removed, no files ever change hands. Forget it. It's dumb."

"Wait, it might be good."

"It's so good."

I laughed.

Besides, I didn't have a better idea. In the restaurant with Gutierrez, I leaned in and made the last-ditch proposal. "There's no digital paper trail. There's no flash drive to uncover. And I have a file that didn't come from your hard drive."

She drew a deep breath. I sat back, watching her, thinking there was no way on earth this would work.

"Maybe," she said. She pulled the old MacBook from her bag. "Okay, maybe is worth a try."

I felt a wash of adrenaline. We both knew the cover would be thin. She was taking a risk.

I thanked her. She nodded and opened the laptop, and I pulled out my phone.

"Wait," she said. "We have problem."

The old MacBook, it came to pass, had no working speakers. I leaned in again, speaking fast. "Ambra, if I go get us an external speaker, will you be here when I get back?"

She glanced around, gave me an uncertain look.

"Just give me twenty minutes," I said.

I sprinted from the restaurant and into the crush of West Forty-Sixth Street. Where to go? There would probably be a place with electronics among the small tourist shops that sell "I Love New York" hats on Broadway, but I didn't know exactly where to look. I took out my phone, found the nearest big-box electronics store. It was farther, but a surer thing. I shoved through the pre-theater crowd, got to the corner, waved a hand frantically at oncoming cabs.

By the time I limped into the store, I was drenched in sweat. I hurried down an escalator and all but screeched to a halt in front of a shelf of what looked like several thousand speakers.

"Hi, can I help you?" a clerk asked.

"I need a speaker," I gasped.

"Well, sir, we've got you covered," he said brightly. "We've got your Bluetooth, your Wi-Fi, your USB. You looking for something Alexa-activated? This one's got a little LED light show." I stared at him crazily. Fifteen minutes later I was running back into the restaurant, four different overpriced speakers jangling against one another. Gutierrez was still there. She shot me a nervous smile.

In a garden behind the restaurant, I unboxed one of the speakers.

The Bluetooth on the old Mac, mercifully, worked. We agreed that she would play the middle of the three files: anything that replicated the breaks between sections would betray that it had derived from her phone copy rather than the presumably unbroken one taken from her police wire. She drew a deep breath and said, "I hope the other girls get justice." We huddled over the laptop. She hit Play and I captured two minutes of a terrified woman struggling to get away from a hotel suite, and a brutal man not taking no for an answer. "Just come on in," I heard him say again. "I'm used to that."

❖

I needed advice. The next day, I knocked on Tom Brokaw's office door on the fifth floor of 30 Rock. In my earliest months at NBC, Brokaw had approached me as we stood on line for coffee at a shop in the building's basement concourse. He'd seen my show, he said. He thought I was trying to do something smarter than usual for the format.

"Thank you, sir," I'd said. "Means a lot coming from you."

"Tom, please," he'd responded. "We're not headmaster and head boy here."

He accepted my invitations to appear on air with me more often than he had to, and his commentary was always eloquent and full of historical insight.

Brokaw was in his late seventies then. A few years earlier, he'd been diagnosed with blood cancer. That day in May, he pottered around his office, showed me pictures of Meredith, his wife of more than fifty years, and told a few stories about old Hollywood.

"So what can I do for you?" he said finally.

I told him I was working on a sensitive story, and that I was concerned that it wasn't being elevated in the way it needed to be. I mentioned Greenberg's "back burner" comments.

"I know Noah will get behind it," I said. "I'm just worried about interference before it gets there."

"Well, you have to stick to your guns, Ronan," he said. "If you back down, you'll fuck your credibility." I laughed. Brokaw said he thought it was a good idea to shore up all the additional leads I could before taking it back to the powers that be. He said he'd call Andy Lack and Noah Oppenheim when I did so.

"Who's it about, by the way?" he said finally.

I hesitated for a moment then told him it was Weinstein. The warmth drained out of the room. "I see," he said. "Well, I have to disclose, Ronan, that Harvey Weinstein is a friend."

The two had connected when Brokaw was soliciting advice on a documentary about veterans, he said. Weinstein had been good to him.

*Shit*, I thought. *Is anyone not friends with this guy?*

"I assume I can still count on your confidence," I said to Brokaw.

"You can," he said. He showed me out of the office, seeming troubled.

As I stepped out, my phone rang. It was Lisa Bloom. "Hey!" she said brightly, and then proceeded to make small talk about a model she was representing who had been a victim of revenge porn. "We should get together and talk," Bloom said. "I could get you an interview with her."

"Sure," I said, distracted.

"By the way, are you still working on that story about NDAs?"

Bloom had said she was acquainted with Weinstein and his team — and, sure, she was attentive to her brand, and didn't hate a press conference — but she had moral fiber I felt I could trust.

Besides, she was a lawyer. Respecting confidences was the bedrock of our profession.

"I am," I said, after a beat.

"So it's going forward," she said.

"I — I'm working on it."

"Have you seen any of the nondisclosure agreements?"

I paused again. "I'm aware of some specific agreements, yes."

"How many women are you talking to? Can you tell me who they are?" she asked. "I may be able to help get you information, if you can share who you're talking to."

"I can't talk about specific sources," I said. "But there's a group, and it's growing. And if you have any advice on what I should be doing to insulate them from liability, I welcome it."

"Absolutely," she said.

When I checked my phone after we hung up, I saw I'd missed another volley of Instagram messages from the same mysterious handle. This time, the final message was a photograph of a pistol. One of the messages read, "Sometimes you have to hurt the things you love." I took a handful of screenshots and made a note to myself to find out whom to talk to at NBC about security.

CHAPTER 16:

# F.O.H.

*T*he next time my phone chimed, it was happier news. Ben Wallace, from *New York* magazine, was following up. The former assistant he hadn't quite managed to get on the record would talk to me.

The following week, in the closing days of May, I walked into the lobby of a Beverly Hills hotel. I hadn't looked up what the source looked like, but I recognized her quickly. She was slender and blond and striking. She cracked a nervous grin. "Hey!" she said. "I'm Emily."

Emily Nestor was in her late twenties and held law and business degrees from Pepperdine. She was working for a tech startup but seemed to be searching for something more purposeful. She talked about wanting to work in education, maybe something with underprivileged kids. A few years earlier, she'd harbored ambitions in the film business, hoping to produce and perhaps someday run a studio. But an experience she'd had as a temporary assistant had shaken her belief in the business. The casual, practiced nature of the harassment had made her worry it was a pattern. And the response when she reported it had left her disillusioned.

I laid out what we had: McGowan and Gutierrez named in the

story, and the audio, and the growing number of executives on camera. I was transparent about how precarious it all was, too.

Nestor still looked scared as she told me she'd think about it. She was frightened of retaliation. But I could tell that she was too fierce in her convictions to shy away.

A few days later, she was in. She'd go on camera, though she wanted to be unnamed and in shadow to start out, then see how she felt about going further. And she had evidence: messages from Irwin Reiter, a senior executive who had worked for Weinstein for almost three decades, acknowledging the incident and alluding to its being part of a pattern of predation inside the company. A third woman, and more hard evidence: it felt like the threshold we'd been waiting for.

"Once we bring him this," I told McHugh, "Noah will make sure it gets on air. He'll have to."

Back home in New York, at a gala dinner at the Museum of the Moving Image, New York media elites assembled to honor Lester Holt and Roy Price, the head of Amazon Studios. Jeffrey Tambor, the actor, who was at the time appearing in Amazon's *Transparent*, toasted Price. Noah Oppenheim did the honors for Holt, praising his unflinching coverage of tough stories. Then he returned to his seat at NBC's table alongside David Corvo, the *Dateline* producer. Nearby, at Amazon's table, Harvey Weinstein applauded.

◆

Not long after, Nestor, McHugh, and I sat in a hotel room overlooking a glittering marina in Santa Monica. We were still tiptoeing around our shoots on the story, making the case bulletproof before we triggered a conversation with our bosses. We had set the date for Nestor's interview around the margins of a trip to California's Central Valley for the pollutants story.

As we backlit her and her face deepened into shadow, Nestor said she anticipated a "personal and vengeful" response from Weinstein when he saw the story. In December 2014, when she was twenty-five, Nestor had worked as a temporary front desk assistant at the Weinstein Company in Los Angeles. She was overqualified, but took the job on a lark to get a firsthand view of the entertainment industry. On her first day, Nestor said, two employees told her that she was Weinstein's "type" physically. When Weinstein arrived at the office, he made comments about her appearance, referring to her as "the pretty girl." He asked how old she was, and then sent his assistants out of the room and made her write down her telephone number.

Weinstein told her to meet him for drinks that night. Nestor invented an excuse. When he insisted, she suggested an early-morning coffee the next day, assuming that he wouldn't accept. He told her to meet him at the Peninsula hotel, one of his favorite haunts. Friends in the entertainment industry and employees in the company had by then warned her about Weinstein's reputation. "I dressed very frumpy," she recalled.

At the meeting, Weinstein offered her career help, then began to boast about his sexual liaisons with other women, including famous actresses. "He said, 'You know, we could have a lot of fun,'" Nestor recalled. "'I could put you in my London office, and you could work there and you could be my girlfriend.'" She declined. He asked to hold her hand; she said no. She recalled Weinstein remarking, "Oh, the girls always say no. You know, 'No, no.' And then they have a beer or two and then they're throwing themselves at me." In a tone that Nestor described as "very weirdly proud," Weinstein added "that he'd never had to do anything like Bill Cosby." She assumed that he meant he'd never drugged a woman. "Textbook sexual harassment" was how Nestor described Weinstein's behavior. She recalled refusing his advances at least a dozen times. " 'No' did not mean 'no' to him," she said.

Throughout the meeting, Weinstein interrupted their conversation to yell into his cell phone, screaming at, of all people, *Today* show management, enraged that they'd canceled a segment with Amy Adams, a star in the Weinstein movie *Big Eyes*, when she refused to answer questions about a recent hack targeting Sony executives. Afterward, Weinstein told Nestor to keep an eye on the news cycle, which he promised would be spun in his favor and against NBC. Later in the day, items critical of NBC's role in the spat surfaced as promised. Weinstein stopped by Nestor's desk to make sure that she'd seen them.

Nestor found the ferocity with which Weinstein moved to intimidate a news organization unsettling. By that point, she recalled, "I was very afraid of him. And I knew how well-connected he was. And how if I pissed him off then I could never have a career in that industry." Still, she told a friend about the incident, and he alerted the company's office of human resources. Nestor had a conversation with company officials about the matter but didn't pursue it further after they told her that Weinstein would be informed of anything she told them. Later, employee after employee would tell me the human resources office at the company was a sham, a place where complaints went to die.

Irwin Reiter, the Weinstein Company's executive vice president of accounting and financial reporting, had reached out to Nestor via LinkedIn. "We view this very seriously and I personally am very sorry your first day was like this," Reiter wrote. "Also if there are further unwanted advances, please let us know." In late 2016, just before the presidential election, he'd reached out again, writing, "All this Trump stuff made me think of you." He described Nestor's experience as part of Weinstein's serial misconduct. "I've fought him about mistreatment of women 3 weeks before the incident with you. I even wrote him an email that got me labelled by him as sex police," he wrote. "The fight I had with him about you was epic. I told him if you were my daughter he would have not made out so well." Nestor gave me the messages and, eventually, permission to air them.

Nestor left after completing her temporary placement, feeling traumatized. "I actually decided not to go into entertainment because of this incident," she told me. Behind her, the sun was setting over the marina. "Is this the way the world works?" she wondered. "That men get away with this?"

◈

As McHugh and I sweated our way through interviews with toxicologists, local officials, and residents exposed to toxic waste in the Central Valley, the number of Miramax and Weinstein Company sources willing to talk grew. At a bar in West Hollywood, I met with one former employee who'd worked with Weinstein closely. She said that Weinstein's predation had become enmeshed with his professional life. He would ask her to join for the beginning of meetings with young women that, in many cases, had already been moved from day to night and from hotel lobbies to hotel rooms. She said that Weinstein's conduct was brazen. During a meeting with a model, he'd demanded, "Tell her how good of a boyfriend I am." She said that when she refused to join the meetings with women, Weinstein would sometimes fly into a terrifying rage. Once, they'd been in a limo, and he'd opened the door and slammed it shut again and again, face contorted and beet-red, shouting, "Fuck you! You were my cover!"

Weinstein had assistants keep track of the women. The former employee had them all filed under the same label in her phone:

"F.O.H.," which stood for "Friend of Harvey." "He's been systematically doing this for a very long time," she told me.

She took out an iPhone and navigated to a sentence she'd jotted down in her Notes app a few years earlier. It was something Weinstein whispered — to himself, as far as she could tell — after one of his many shouting sprees. It so unnerved her that she pulled out her phone and tapped it into a memo, word for word: "There are things I've done that nobody knows."

That former employee put me on the trail of a handful of others. As June turned into July, they began to go on camera. "There was a large volume of these types of meetings that Harvey would have with aspiring actresses and models," a former executive named Abby Ex told me, her face in shadow, as cameras rolled in a Beverly Hills hotel room. "He would have them late at night, usually at hotel bars or in hotel rooms. And, in order to make these women feel more comfortable, he would ask a female executive or assistant to start those meetings with him." She said she refused Weinstein's demands that she join such meetings, but watched some of them play out, and witnessed, first-hand, a wider pattern of physical and verbal abuse.

Ex told me that her lawyer advised her that she could be liable for hundreds of thousands of dollars in damages for violating the non-disclosure agreement attached to her employment contract. But, she said, "I believe this is more important than keeping a confidentiality agreement."

◆

After the interviews, I arrived back at Jonathan's place and sat at his kitchen table, poring over transcripts. He padded out in a science-themed tee shirt with an astronaut on it.

"Did you eat?" he asked.

"No," I replied, still staring at the screen.

"Let's go somewhere healthy or disgusting."

"Can't," I said. It occurred to me that it had been a while since we'd done anything together. I took off my glasses, rubbed my eyes. "Sorry. I'm a lot to deal with right now, I know."

He took a seat at the table next to me. "Yeah, all of our conversations are about sexual harassment now. It's a blast."

My phone pinged. It was a text notification. Type "Yes" to receive weather alerts, it said. I stared at it, confused. This was Los Angeles, weather didn't exist here.

"You're texting!" Jonathan was saying. "Hope he's worth it! Hope he's worth saying goodbye to all of this!"

"Definitely," I said, and swiped the message away.

## CHAPTER 17:

# *666*

*A*s Harvey Weinstein's former employees talked to me, Harvey Weinstein talked to Black Cube. On June 6, its operatives met with Weinstein and his lawyers at Boies Schiller in New York and delivered an exuberant update. After the meeting, Yanus, the director, checked in with Christopher Boies. "It's been a great pleasure meeting with you and your client today and to present you with our final report," Yanus wrote. "We have been able to successfully achieve the project's objectives and meet all three success fee clauses…the most important of which is to identify who stands behind the negative campaign against the client." He attached an invoice for $600,000. The contract with Black Cube stipulated that the "success fees" Yanus mentioned be paid in the event that Weinstein used the fruit of Black Cube's labors in litigation or in the media; or should Black Cube "succeed in putting a stop to the negative campaign" against Weinstein; or should its operatives discover the "individual or entity behind" that campaign.

A week later, Yanus checked in again: "Good morning Chris, I was wondering if you could give us an update about the status of the payment." This didn't get a response, either. On June 18, Weinstein met with Black Cube in London and, by Yanus's description in a peevish email sent to Boies shortly afterward, "thoroughly reviewed our findings again and discussed possible future steps to support your client's case, who has again spoken very highly of our work."

As Weinstein sat on the invoice, his rapport with Black Cube strained. Yanus would call and delicately say, "You haven't paid us." On a good day, Weinstein would feign ignorance, and get the Weinstein Company's general counsel on the line. "I didn't know that," he'd shout at his company's lawyer. "Get them paid!" But mostly Weinstein would just shout at Black Cube. "Why am I paying you? You're supposed to be on this!" he'd say.

Things came to a head in conversations in late June. Weinstein questioned if Black Cube's work might have broken the law, leaving him exposed to problems down the road. He insisted that the operation "hasn't solved his problem completely," as a summary email sent by the working-level project manager under Yanus explained. Weinstein reminded Black Cube that "other intelligence firms are involved in solving this crisis—and BC is only one piece of a much larger puzzle."

Finally, in early July, Boies and Black Cube signed a revised agreement. Weinstein agreed to pay a $190,000 settlement to square away the unpleasantness about the success fees. And Black Cube signed on to a new schedule of work, through November of that year, with a new, more targeted set of goals.

Internally, privately, the project manager conceded that his operatives "came short-handed on certain issues." In the contentious conversations with Weinstein, they'd promised to do more. They could still solve the problem. They just had to get more aggressive.

❖

Each time McHugh and I acknowledged to our bosses at NBC that we were still keeping an eye on the Weinstein story, a new round of warnings about our lack of productivity on other fronts surfaced. Soon McHugh was getting new assignments to work with other correspondents. Steve Chung, the NBC lawyer who had tempered Greenberg's hesitations about viewing nondisclosure agreements with, at least, a concession that there were shades of gray in the case law that might permit a news organization to do so, called to say he was departing the company. "You'll be in good hands with the rest of the legal team," he said.

There were signs that we were at risk of getting scooped. As I made a last, desperate attempt to get to Ashley Judd, I called the *New York Times* columnist Nicholas Kristof, who had worked on a documentary that featured both me and Judd. I had great respect for Kristof, who wrote about difficult human rights issues. I thought if anyone had a chance of persuading Judd to talk, it would be him.

When I told him I was working on a story about the kinds of women's rights and human rights issues Judd cared about, he said immediately, "The person this story is about, does his name begin with an *H?*" When I said yes, Kristof fell silent for a moment and then replied, speaking slowly: "I'm not at liberty to continue this conversation." He got off the phone quickly.

McHugh and I figured the only possible explanation was a competing *New York Times* story. I was glad to learn we weren't alone, but anxious to keep moving. When we told Greenberg, he seemed happy, too, but for different reasons. "Sometimes," he said, "it's best to let someone else go first."

◆

There were signs that not all of the reporting would hold indefinitely. For months, Rose McGowan had been all-in. In messages since our interview, she'd written, "I can give you more" and "This needs to be a nighttime special. Or a long form morning piece. You need to come film more I think."

But that July, her patience seemed to waver. "I've thought about it and I've decided I don't want to go forward with the NBC piece," she told me. My stomach lurched. She wasn't the only woman named in the story, but her interview was significant. I asked her to hear out what I'd uncovered before she made a decision. We agreed to meet again.

I made the trek to her house in the Hollywood Hills one more time. She came to the door wearing a tee shirt, face makeup-free. She looked tired. As we sat in her kitchen and she made coffee, McGowan told me she'd already begun to experience the costs of speaking out. She said she'd told Price, the Amazon Studios head, that Weinstein had raped her. Not long after, her deal with the studio was terminated.

Meanwhile, she suspected she was being followed. She didn't know whom she could trust. I asked if she had friends and family around. McGowan shrugged. She said she had some support. She and Diana Filip, the wealth manager with the women's rights project, had been drawing close. And there had been other supportive journalists, like Freedman, the former writer for the *Guardian*.

McGowan told me she'd grown leery of NBC, uncomfortable with the delays, concerned about — she paused here — things she'd heard about the people there. I asked her what she meant and she shook her head and said only, "I just don't want to be morning TV fodder." I said that wasn't the plan; that I did stories for *Nightly News* as well, that this was the kind of story that would go everywhere, not just in the morning.

I told McGowan there were good people at NBC, like Oppenheim, who had a career as a screenwriter and wouldn't feel bound by the traditional reticence of network news. But I said I needed to bring him everything, in the strongest shape it could be, and for that, I needed her. Then I told McGowan about what we had. I said I'd encountered others with stories about Weinstein — not just rumor or innuendo — and that they'd agreed to speak, partly because they knew she'd come forward. At this, her eyes filled with tears. "I've felt alone for such a long time," she said.

McGowan said she'd been thinking a lot, writing music. She and I had bonded, the first time we met, over songs we'd written. In her house that day, we each played a few demos. As one of hers called "Lonely House" played, she shut her eyes and listened to herself sing:

I stand for mind
For women who can't
And men too scared
To beat that beast
To watch him drown

McGowan regained her nerve. She told me we could air the interview. She said she'd go on camera again, naming Weinstein more explicitly. And she volunteered, before then, to get on the phone with NBC's legal department and make it clear to them that she'd named him on the record.

A few minutes later, I was on the phone with Oppenheim's assistant. I told her I'd had a break in the story and would be flying back on a red-eye to see him the next day. I'd take any opening he had on his calendar.

"We have it," McHugh said. "The clock is ticking."

◆

In New York the next morning, I took a winding staircase down into the basement underneath a Bank of America. It was a rare old-fashioned vault, with a circular door with bolts around its periphery, and, inside, a corridor of safe-deposit boxes. A bank manager pulled out a shallow metal box. It was numbered "666."

We stared at the numbers for a moment.

"You know what," he said, "I'm gonna find us something else."

In a less ominous box, I placed a list of our dozens of sources, and transcripts of the conversations with them, and a description of the patterns of predation and settlements. I included a flash drive containing the audio from the police sting. On top, I left the note of a person who was tired and genuinely unsure what was paranoid and what was practical anymore but, anyway, here it is:

If you're reading this, it's because I can't make this information public myself. This is the blueprint to assembling a story that could bring a serial predator to justice. Multiple reporters who have attempted to break this story have faced intimidation and threats. I have already received threatening calls from intermediaries. Noah Oppenheim at NBC News should be able to access the associated video footage. Should anything happen to me, please make sure this information is released.

# CHAPTER 18:

# *QUIDDITCH*

**N**oah Oppenheim seemed speechless. I'd handed him a printed list of the reporting elements. "Wow," he said. "This is a lot to digest." It was July 12. Outside of Oppenheim's office window, sunlight fell across Rockefeller Plaza. I explained that we had layers of hard evidence and credible sources. Some even knew Oppenheim. Abby Ex, one of the former executives who'd gone on camera, had recruited him to do an uncredited punch-up on the script for the Ryan Reynolds vehicle *Selfless*.

"We're going to take it to Greenberg, run it through the normal channels," I said quickly. "I just wanted you to be aware."

He lifted the top page again, looked at the one underneath. "Of course I'll defer to Rich, but—" He put the paper down on his lap, sighed. "We're going to have to make some decisions."

"Decisions?" I said.

"Like, is this really worth it?"

He was sitting on a beige couch. On a wall next to him, an array of screens flickered, news tickers racing by. Nearby, a framed diptych showed a game of Quidditch, rendered in brown and green Magic Marker and signed by Oppenheim's eight-year-old son.

"It's a big story," I said. "It's a prominent guy, admitting to serious misconduct, on tape."

"Well, first of all," he said, "I don't know if that's, you know, a crime."

"It's a misdemeanor," I said. "It's months in jail, potentially."

"Okay, okay," he said. "But we've gotta decide if it's newsworthy."

I stared at him.

"Look," he said. "You know who Harvey Weinstein is. I know who Harvey Weinstein is. But I'm in the industry. I don't know that normal Americans do."

"Roger Ailes wasn't a household name, either," I pointed out. "Weinstein's more famous than that. And it's a system, you know — it's bigger than him."

"I get it," he said. "I'm just saying we're going to have to make the case to the lawyers that this is worth it. There's gonna be a lot thrown at us if we do this." From Wallace's paranoiac recollections, I knew that much was true.

On my way out, I thanked him and said, "And if an 'accident' befalls me . . ."

He laughed, tapped the paper I'd handed him. "I'll make sure this gets out."

"Thanks. Oh, and don't do *Selfless 2*."

"I don't know," he deadpanned. "I might need career options after this."

That afternoon, I received another volley of strange Instagram messages, with another image of a gun. I sent a text to Oppenheim's assistant, Anna. "Hey, don't want to elevate this to Noah's level," I wrote, "but do we have a good security person at NBC I could talk to?" I was dealing with some "stalker issues." Things that felt "a little more alarming than the usual."

She told me she'd look into it.

❖

A few hours later, I got another call from Matthew Hiltzik, the public relations operative. "Just catching up with people," he said perkily. "You were on my list." Hiltzik had texted a few times since his last call, suggesting we get a meal, asking for updates. It was an uncharacteristic level of interest. On the phone that day, I told him I was still on book deadline and working on several NBC stories.

"So you're still on the Harvey story?"

I looked into the studio nearby. Behind glass frosted with peacock logos, a midday anchor silently mouthed headlines. "I'm working on a few stories," I repeated.

"Alright!" he said, laughing a little. "I'm here to give you information whenever you need it. And I think it's really good that you're busy with other things."

❖

I got home that evening a little on edge. In the elevator, I started at a greeting from the boyish neighbor the superintendent always said kind of looked like me. Soon after, Jonathan called from a Bank of America on the West Coast, where he was finalizing the paperwork that made him a co-owner of the safe-deposit box I'd just filled. "Don't. Lose. The key," I told him. As we spoke, there was a soft "ping": another automated message about weather updates. I swiped it away.

As I got into bed, a text from Lisa Bloom came in. "Hey Ronan are you still writing about NDAs? I have a new issue on my Kardashian case (you may have heard I rep Blac Chyna and K family is raising NDA issue). Anyway I'm coming to NYC tomorrow to do The View. Coffee/lunch Thursday or Friday?"

I pushed the phone away and failed to sleep.

McHugh and I had agreed to meet Greenberg at 8:30 a.m. I was at my cubicle, exhausted, when McHugh arrived.

"You look awful," he said.

"Thanks, nice to see you, too."

A few minutes later we were in Greenberg's cramped office. "You have a lot," he said, paging through the same printed list of elements I'd handed Oppenheim the day before. Then he looked up and asked, "Can I hear the tape?"

I slid my phone onto the desk in front of him and hit Play, and we listened as Weinstein said, again, that he was used to that.

As Greenberg listened, a determined smile spread across his lips. "Fuck it, let him sue," he said, when the audio was done. "If this airs, he's toast."

We said we were going to proceed with on-camera interviews with a few more sources from Weinstein's company and draft both a script and a written story for the web. Greenberg, still seeming a little excited, told us to prepare for a meeting with the legal department. McHugh and I left Greenberg's office feeling triumphant.

Later, Anna, Oppenheim's assistant, followed up about the stalkers. "Passing this along to HR, they deal with this for talent," she wrote. "Unfortunately these things happen more often than you think." HR, in turn, put me in touch with Thomas McFadden, a grizzled ex-cop. "Pretty typical stuff," he said, scrolling through my phone in his tiny office. "Seen it a million times."

"I bet," I said.

"We'll look into it," he said. "Mostly, we figure out who's hassling you, maybe we give 'em a little call, they stop what they're doing. Once in a blue moon maybe we call up our friends in law enforcement."

"Thanks," I said. "I feel like there's maybe other things happening than just the crazies. Weird spam texts, this sense like—"

"Like you're being followed?"

I laughed. "Well...," I said.

He leaned back, seemed to chew this over. Then he eyed me sympathetically. "You're under a lot of pressure. Leave it to me and get some rest."

All that month, McGowan and her new friend, Diana Filip of Reuben Capital Partners, exchanged emails and calls. Whatever coast McGowan was on, Filip always seemed to be there. A few days after my meeting with Oppenheim, they had a girls' night out, at the Peninsula in New York. Prompted by Filip's gentle questioning, McGowan spoke frankly about her efforts to go public with her rape allegation. She even revealed that she'd been talking to a reporter from NBC News. All the while, Filip sat close, listening intently, sympathy etched on her face.

The same day, Sara Ness, the investigator at Jack Palladino's firm in San Francisco, sent another email to Harvey Weinstein. It contained another, more detailed dossier. Across fifteen pages, the investigators exhaustively retraced my steps in the preceding months, identifying many of my sources. The dossier concluded that I'd been in touch with Sciorra, who "HW confirmed" was "a potential adverse source."

The list of reporters, too, had expanded: the dossier mentioned Kim Masters, the pugnacious writer from the *Hollywood Reporter,* and Nicholas Kristof, and Ben Wallace. It concluded that Wallace was "possibly helping to direct Farrow." There was a final new area of focus: a writer for the *New York Times* named Jodi Kantor.

The dossier identified several of Weinstein's double agents, who had spoken to me, then reported back to him on my activities. The producer in Australia with the strain in her voice was one of them. She had "alerted HW to Farrow's contact," the document said. "Did not offer any negative info about HW to Farrow."

And there were other, more veiled references to collaborators. The dossier noted that someone identified only as "LB" had been involved in Weinstein's effort to ferret out information, quietly talking to at least one lawyer an accuser consulted.

"Investigation is continuing," the dossier concluded.

❖

We kept encountering sources who threw us off the scent or reported back to Weinstein. But we were also finding more and more who were willing to stand up to him. A former assistant who had been assigned to Weinstein part-time during his trips to London, and told me he'd sexually harassed her, initially felt talking wasn't worth the risk of retribution. Her fears deepened as Weinstein's associates began calling her "quite ferociously," after twenty years of radio silence. "It's very unsettling," she told me. "He is on your tail." But, paradoxically, the calls had made her want to help. "I didn't want to talk," she said. "But then, hearing from him, it made me angry. Angry that he still thinks he can silence people."

The part-time assistant also knew about Zelda Perkins, the woman who had spoken with Auletta, and about the joint sexual harassment settlement Perkins had secured alongside her colleague Rowena Chiu. So did Katrina Wolfe, a former assistant at Miramax who later became an executive. Wolfe went on camera that month, with her face in shadow. "While working at Miramax I became directly aware of two female employees of the company who had accused Harvey Weinstein of sexual assault, and whose cases were settled," Wolfe told me. It wasn't hearsay: she'd directly witnessed the planning and execution of the transaction.

One night in 1998, Weinstein had barreled into the office, looking for Steve Hutensky, a Miramax lawyer dubbed "the Cleaner-Upper" among Weinstein's underlings. For forty-five minutes, the two men had huddled, Weinstein's anxious voice audible to staffers nearby. Afterward, Hutensky had ordered assistants to pull the personnel files of Perkins, who was then an assistant to Donna Gigliotti, the *Shakespeare in Love* producer, and Chiu.

In the following days and weeks, Weinstein exchanged frantic calls with his advisors, including elite New York lawyer Herb Wachtell. (When I was a law student, Wachtell's firm was the holy grail of summer associateships. I'd been devastated, in the way only students can be, when it rejected my application. I had to slum it at Davis Polk, like an ambulance chaser or President Grover Cleveland.) Wachtell and Hutensky had sought an English lawyer for Weinstein — Hutensky requested "the best criminal defense attorney in England"—and then Weinstein had gotten on a Concorde flight to London to deal with the problem personally.

I was edging closer to rendering the London settlements reportable.

❖

The circle of on-camera interviews kept widening. A few days after the interview with Wolfe, I conducted another with a former assistant and producer at the Weinstein Company. He made it clear that the pattern of harassment complaints hadn't stopped after the nineties. In more recent years, he'd been tasked with bringing young women into the honeypot meetings described by the other former employees. Some of the women seemed "not aware of the nature of those meetings" and "were definitely scared," he said.

He was also sometimes troubled by the aftermath of such meetings. "You'd see women who would come out of the room and all of a sudden there would be a giant need to—I don't wanna say handle the situation, but make sure they felt that they were rewarded or compensated professionally for what had just happened," he recalled. "And those women seemed pretty freaked out." Weinstein, he said, was "predatory," and "above the law that applies to most of us and should apply to all of us."

We shot the interview at the Four Seasons in Beverly Hills, with McHugh and me and a freelance shooter named Jean-Bernard Rutagarama crammed into a small room alongside our lights and tripods and cameras.

◆

That month, Black Cube circulated the latest version of a list of names. A project manager reviewed the list at Black Cube's satellite office in London—half a floor in a glass tower on Ropemaker Street, where the art on the walls featured silhouetted operatives looming over bustling cityscapes. Then the project manager forwarded the list to a network of contacts around the world.

The list contained many of the same names—and in some cases, the same language—from the dossiers generated by Jack Palladino's firm. But the research had grown deeper, too. Now, secondary sources who had corroborated McGowan's or Nestor's or Gutierrez's stories were also targets.

As the summer wore on, the list grew, with highlights appearing in yellow and then red to indicate urgency. Some of the names on it were spun out into separate profiles. Soon after the interview at the Four Seasons, one such profile, marked "JB Rutagarama," landed in the same in-boxes. A subhead explained, "Relevance: Cameraman that is working with Ronan Farrow and Rich McHugh on the HW report." The profile covered Rutagarama's upbringing in Rwanda and explored "ways to approach him." Its formatting was distinctive, with headers in blue italic Times New Roman and English-as-a-second-language malapropisms.

Among the contacts to whom the Black Cube project manager sent the list, and the profile of Rutagarama, was Seth Freedman, the former writer for the *Guardian*.

# CHAPTER 19:

# *SPIRAL*

*T*hat July, I called back Auletta and told him I had more information about the settlements in London. I asked if there was anything else he could show me to help shore up my reporting. To my surprise, he said, "Actually, yes." He'd given all his reporters' notebooks, printed documents, and tapes to the New York Public Library. The collection remained closed to the public. But he said I could take a look.

The Auletta files were housed in the Reading Room for Rare Books and Manuscripts, beyond the great hall. It was a dim chamber with sealed glass shelves and rows of low desks that glowed under reading lights. The library possessed more than sixty large cardboard boxes of Auletta's papers all told. McHugh and I signed in and a librarian brought out the boxes.

McHugh and I each took a box and began sifting through the contents. Auletta didn't have nearly as much as we did. But he had grasped at essential pieces of the puzzle. It was strange, seeing notes from fifteen years earlier that covered such similar ground. Even then, Auletta was encountering abandoned reporting jobs. On one page of notes, he had scrawled in doctor-illegible blue cursive: "David Carr: believes sexual harassment."

❖

In Auletta's spiral-bound reporter's notebooks, I found clues that led me to other clues, and which synced up with my emerging picture of what had happened between Weinstein and the two assistants in London.

In the late nineties, Perkins had started working as an assistant to Gigliotti. In practice, this meant working for Weinstein much of the time. "From my very first time left alone with Harvey," she told me later, "I had to deal with him being present either in his underpants or totally naked." He'd try to pull her into bed. Perkins was petite and blond and looked younger than her years. But she also had a sharp personality and was, even then, defiantly assertive. Weinstein never succeeded in his physical advances. The unending fusillade of attempts, though, exhausted her. And soon, he was wearing her down in other ways. Like so many of Weinstein's former employees, she found herself cast as a facilitator of sexual liaisons with aspiring actresses and models. "We had to bring girls to him," she said. "Though I wasn't aware of it at first, I was a honeypot." Weinstein would ask her to buy condoms for him and clean up after hotel-room meetings with the young women.

It was 1998 when Perkins got the green light to hire an assistant of her own, something she hoped would put some distance between her and Weinstein. She warned candidates for the job that Weinstein would make sexual advances. She even rejected "very overtly attractive" applicants, "because I knew he'd never leave them alone. It would never stop." In the end, she chose Chiu, a "prodigiously bright"

Oxford graduate, who would overcome paralyzing fears of retaliation and make her name public only years later.

At the Hotel Excelsior during the Venice Film Festival in September 1998, Chiu emerged from a meeting with Weinstein in his hotel room, shaking and crying, saying he had pushed her against a bed and attempted to assault her. Perkins confronted Weinstein, interrupting a lunch meeting with a prominent director on the hotel terrace. "He stood there and he lied and lied and lied," Perkins recalled. "I said, 'Harvey, you are lying,' and he said, 'I'm not lying; I swear on the lives of my children.'"

Chiu was, Perkins said, "shocked and in a traumatized state," and too frightened to go to the police. The difficulty of reporting the allegation was deepened by their location at the time, Venice's Lido island. "I didn't know who I would go to," Perkins recalled. "The security guard in the hotel?"

Perkins did what she could to ensure that Chiu was kept away from Weinstein for the remainder of the trip. After returning to England, Perkins notified Gigliotti, who gave her a referral to an employment attorney. Eventually, Perkins and Chiu sent notice that they were resigning from Miramax and pursuing legal action.

Their departure from the company set in motion the frenetic meetings at Miramax that Wolfe had described to me. Weinstein and other executives called Perkins again and again. The night she resigned, she received seventeen calls of "increasing desperation" from them. In the messages, Weinstein veered between pleading and menacing. "Please, please, please, please, please, please call me. I'm begging you," he said in one message.

Perkins and Chiu hired lawyers from the London-based firm Simons Muirhead & Burton. Perkins initially pushed back on accepting what she called "blood money" and inquired about going to the police, or to Disney, Miramax's parent company. But the attorneys seemed intent on foreclosing any outcome except a settlement and a nondisclosure agreement. In the end, she and Chiu accepted a settlement of two hundred fifty thousand pounds, to be evenly split between them. Weinstein's brother, Bob, cut the check to the women's law firm, obscuring the transaction from Disney and distancing it from Harvey.

In an exhausting four-day negotiation process, Perkins prevailed in adding provisions to the contract that she hoped would change Weinstein's behavior. The agreement mandated the appointment of three "handlers," one an attorney, to respond to sexual harassment allegations at Miramax. The company was obligated to provide proof that Weinstein was receiving counseling for three years or "as long as his therapist deems necessary." The agreement also required Miramax to report Weinstein's behavior to Disney and fire him if a subsequent sexual harassment settlement was reached in the following two years.

The company implemented the human resources changes, but other parts of the agreement were not enforced. Perkins pressed for months, then gave up. "I was exhausted. I was humiliated. I couldn't work in the industry in the UK because the stories that were going around about what had happened made it impossible," she recalled. In the end, she moved to Central America. She'd had enough. "Money and power enabled, and the legal system has enabled," she eventually told me. "Ultimately, the reason Harvey Weinstein followed the route he did is because he was allowed to, and that's our fault. As a culture that's our fault."

Auletta hadn't captured all of the details of the story, but he'd gotten the bones of it right. I looked at his meticulously organized notes and felt, for a moment, emotional about the dusty boxes and the old secrets they held. I wanted badly to believe that news didn't die, even when it was beaten back for so many years.

❖

As I finished both our script for television and a 6,000-word written story for the NBC News website, the ghosts of reporting attempts past seemed to gather. In late July, I finally called Janice Min, the former *Hollywood Reporter* editor. She was fierce in her belief that the story was real, and doubtful as to whether it would ever break. Min had come to the *Hollywood Reporter* from *Us Weekly*, but her roots were as a crime journalist for the *Reporter Dispatch* in New York. "We all knew it was true," she told me. "But we never got it over the finish line. Everyone was always too afraid to talk." She said she'd connect me with Kim Masters, the writer who'd worked on the story during Min's time at the magazine.

"It's an impossible story," Min said, before we got off the phone that day. "It's the white whale of journalism."

"White Whale," McHugh texted later that day. "Great frickin' title."

Masters was invariably described as a veteran media journalist, which she joked was a euphemistic way to call her old. She'd worked as a staff writer for the *Washington Post* and a contributor for *Vanity Fair*, *Time*, and *Esquire*. She told me she'd heard the rumors about Weinstein "forever." Once, years earlier, she'd even confronted him about them.

"Why are you writing this shit about me?" he'd roared at her at a lunch at the Peninsula in Beverly Hills. "Why do you say that I'm a bully?"

"Well, Harvey," Masters recalled telling him. "I hear you rape women."

"Sometimes you have sex with a woman who's not your wife, and there's a disagreement about what's happened, and you just have to write a check to make it go away," Weinstein replied calmly. Hiltzik, the public relations operative, was also there that day. Masters recalled him looking shocked. He'd later deny that he heard her mention rape.

Masters wasn't convinced so much had changed, all those years later. A few months earlier, she'd worked on a story about an accusation of sexual harassment against Roy Price, the Amazon Studios executive who had canned McGowan's deal, and a figure around whom such claims had long circulated. But the *Hollywood Reporter*, where Masters had written articles for seven years, had passed on the story. That summer, she was still trying to rescue it, shopping it to *BuzzFeed* and then to the *Daily Beast*. Price had hired Charles Harder, the same *Gawker*-slaying attorney Weinstein was using, to approach the outlets. "One of these days," Masters told me wearily, "the dam is gonna have to break."

❖

I came back to Ken Auletta and asked him if he'd give an interview. For us, putting a print reporter who'd worked on a story on camera was routine. For him, it felt like an extraordinary step, relitigating old reporting. But when I told him what we had, including the audio of Weinstein's confession, he said he'd make an exception. We arrived at Auletta's home on Long Island in the midst of a torrential downpour and hauled in our equipment through the rain. He confirmed that he'd seen evidence of the London settlements and concluded, as we had, that Weinstein had routinely purchased women's silence. And Auletta spoke of his quixotic returns to the topic over the decades. Running the story was important, he said, "to maybe stop him from doing it again."

Auletta, unprompted, looked at the camera.

"Tell Andy Lack, who's a friend of mine, he should publish this story. He will."

"Okay," I said.

"If NBC, which has the evidence, doesn't go forward with this story, it's a scandal." Our shooter exchanged a nervous glance with McHugh. I told Auletta that I was sure NBC would run it. "Well, you better hurry," he replied. "If the *Times* is on it—"

"I know," I said. And we both looked out of his living room at the storm.

◆

The same day, Diana Filip followed up with Rose McGowan. "I'm back home, and just wanted to thank you again for the wonderful evening!" she wrote. "It's always a pleasure seeing you and spending time with you :). I sincerely hope I'll be back soon and that this time we'll have more time!"

And then she came to the point: "I was thinking about Ronan Farrow, who you mentioned during our meeting. I still cannot get his photo out of my head. Seems like a really impressive and sweet guy. I read a bit about him and was very impressed by his work, despite the problematic family connection...I was thinking that someone like him could be an interesting and valuable addition to our project (not for the conference, but the annual activity through 2018), due to the fact that he's a pro-female male," Filip continued. "Do you think you could introduce us, in order to look into this opportunity further?"

CHAPTER 20:

# *CULT*

*T*he script we developed, over the course of late July, was spare and economical. It included the tape, naming Gutierrez with her cooperation, as well as McGowan's on-camera, on-the-record interview, and Nestor's interview with her face in shadow, accompanied by images of her messages from Irwin Reiter, documenting how Weinstein's behavior was seen as a serial problem within the company. The evidence we'd uncovered of the two settlements in London was included, based on multiple firsthand accounts of the negotiations and the check from Bob Weinstein's account. And there were sound bites from the four former employees who had gone on camera.

McHugh, in the same period, had stumbled into a subplot. At a hockey game — he played a lot, and periodically limped into the office with arcane injuries sustained on the ice — he'd run into a friend in the film industry who had tipped him off that there was mounting scrutiny of Weinstein's deep ties to amfAR, The Foundation for AIDS Research. Board members there suspected Weinstein had misused funds destined for the charity. Weinstein was trying to get them to sign nondisclosure agreements.

"Feels like 2nd beat," McHugh texted, "but maybe worth being aggressive?"

"I'd pursue quietly," I replied. "Don't want to trigger anything that could adversely impact this first story."

After McHugh sent me his notes on the script, he wrote, "Time to get the real convo going between you, legal, Rich, and me, and see the real tenor of this news org."

"Yup," I replied.

"We make an oddly good combo," he added. "Not b/c we work well, but because it's frustrating i'm sure to someone who is trying to find dirt or disparage us individually." Neither of us knew that McHugh's name — the names, even, of our crew members — were by then all over dossiers quietly making their way around the world.

We both had the sense, as we finished the story, that attacks were coming. We just didn't know what form they'd take. "He has a lot to lose, back up against corner," McHugh pointed out. "It'll be war."

❖

The last week of July, Susan Weiner, the general counsel of NBC News, sat with Rich Greenberg, McHugh, and me in Greenberg's office and paged through the script and elements list. I'd worked with Weiner before on investigations deemed particularly trouble-some or likely to generate litigation. I'd found her to be a good lawyer, with sound instincts. And she'd been supportive of the reporting, even when I'd picked subjects like a litigious Korean doomsday cult. Before her twenty-plus years at NBC, Weiner had been deputy general counsel at the New York Metropolitan Trans-portation Authority. She was thin and pale, with a shock of frizzy hair. In the office that day, she peered over her glasses and pursed her lips. "You've got a lot," Weiner said.

"Can you play her the tape?" said Greenberg, with undisguised excitement. He'd already read, and liked, the script. In a meeting with him earlier that day, McHugh had prevailed in arguing for a longer-than-standard script, with an eye toward airing it on the web. Shorter *Today* show and *Nightly News* versions could easily be slivered off.

As the audio wound down, Weiner's tight expression dissolved into a half smile.

"Wow," she said.

"And the source will meet you, or whomever you want from legal, to show you the contract with Weinstein's signature on it," I said.

I asked her if she saw any outstanding legal issues based on her review of the material so far, and she said she didn't. "I think our next step is to seek comment," she said. McHugh shot me a relieved look. The news division's top lawyer and Greenberg, a veteran of its standards department, both wanted to proceed. Greenberg nodded at Weiner. "I want to let Noah know before we do," he said.

❖

Greenberg was still excited, barely suppressing a smile, as he, Weiner, McHugh, and I sat down with Oppenheim in his office later that day. Oppenheim flipped through his copy of the script, written story, and elements list. A groove deepened in his brow.

"It's just a draft script," I said. "We'll get it tighter."

"Okay," he said flatly.

"We thought you should hear the audio," Greenberg said. He seemed to be caught off guard by Oppenheim's lack of enthusiasm. "It's pretty powerful."

Oppenheim nodded. He was still looking at the pages, not

making eye contact. Greenberg nodded at me. I hit Play and held my phone out.

"No," Ambra Gutierrez said, her voice shot through with fear. "I'm not comfortable."

"I'm used to that," Harvey Weinstein said again.

Oppenheim slouched deeper into the chair, like he was shrinking into himself.

There was a yawning silence after the tape finished playing. Apparently realizing that we were waiting for him to say something, Oppenheim produced a sound somewhere between a weary sigh and an apathetic "eh" and made a shrugging gesture. "I *mean...*," he said, drawing out the word. "I don't know what that proves."

"He admits to groping her," I said.

"He's trying to get rid of her. People say a lot of things when they're trying to get rid of a girl like that."

I stared at him. Greenberg and Weiner stared at him.

"Look," he said, annoyance creeping into his voice. "I'm not saying it's not gross, but I'm still not sure it's news."

"We have a prominent person admitting to serious misconduct on tape," I said. "We have multiple-sourced accounts of five instances of misconduct, with two women willing to put their name out there, we have multiple former employees saying this was a pattern, we have his signature on a million-dollar settlement contract—"

He waved a hand at me. "I don't know if we can show contracts," he said. McHugh and I glanced at each other. We couldn't figure out why a news organization, which reported contractually protected information routinely in national security and business contexts, would suddenly be so concerned about upholding settlements related to sexual harassment.

"We're not relying solely on the contracts, obviously," I said. "But patterns of settlements are newsworthy. Look at the Fox story—"

"This isn't Fox," he said. "I still don't think Harvey Weinstein's a name the *Today* show audience knows." He looked at the pages again. "And anyway, where would we even air it? This looks long."

"We've run seven-minute pieces on *Today* before. I can cut it down to that."

"Maybe Megyn's show, but that's going away now," he said, seeming to ignore this. Megyn Kelly was concluding a brief stint anchoring a Sunday night newsmagazine program.

"We can put it on the web," McHugh suggested.

I nodded. "And the written version can go online, too."

Oppenheim turned to Greenberg. "What are you proposing?"

"We'd like to reach out to Harvey Weinstein for comment," Greenberg said. Oppenheim looked at Weiner. She nodded. "I think there's enough here to proceed with that call," she said.

Oppenheim looked at the pages in front of him.

"No, no, no," he said. A nervous titter of laughter escaped him. "We can't call Harvey. I've got to take this to Andy."

He rose, pages in hand. The meeting was over.

"Thank you. I think it'll make a big impact, whatever platform we put it on," I babbled, as Oppenheim ushered me out.

McHugh shot me a stunned look. Neither of us could make sense of the reaction.

❖

The earlier months of the year had been dominated by the kind of targets Ostrovskiy, the Ukrainian private investigator, was used to: four hours chasing a cheating spouse here, six tailing the wayward teenage son of a nervous mother there. In return, Khaykin, the bald Russian, would send over the agreed-upon thirty-five bucks an hour, plus expenses. But as the summer unfolded, Khaykin was issuing assignments that felt different. These jobs gave Ostrovskiy pause. They drove him back to that troublesome tendency to ask questions.

Before dawn on July 27, Ostrovskiy headed to the next of those jobs. When he arrived at what looked to be a residential address, he found Khaykin's car, a silver Nissan Pathfinder. He and Khaykin agreed that they'd split up, Ostrovskiy keeping an eye on the target's home, Khaykin standing ready to give chase to a work address.

Khaykin hadn't said much about these new assignments. He'd just sent over a series of screenshots, from some kind of dossier from a client. The screenshots featured addresses, phone numbers, birth dates, biographical information. They identified spouses and other family members. Ostrovskiy's first thought was that they were following some kind of custody dispute, but that explanation fit less and less as the summer wore on.

Ostrovskiy flicked through the screenshots as he hunkered down to keep watch on the address. The formatting was identical to that of the documents that had made their way through the offices on Ropemaker Street in London, with blue italic Times New Roman headers and shaky English. As he looked at the details, a strange feeling came over him. He wasn't used to following reporters.

# CHAPTER 21:

# *SCANDAL*

On a muggy morning not long after the meeting with Oppenheim, I made my way through the sweating crowds, past the tilted cube at Astor Place, toward the East Village. I'd texted McGowan and she'd agreed to meet. At the Airbnb where she was staying, she emerged in pajamas, a half-moon silicone pad under each eye. She gestured to the absurd room around her, which was princess-pink, with fuzzy pillows everywhere. "I didn't decorate," she deadpanned. She was drawn, nervous, even more stressed than when we'd last met. I told her we had stronger material than ever, but that her voice was going to be important. I wanted to take her up on her suggestion that we shoot more, and her offer to name Weinstein to the NBC lawyers.

"I don't trust NBC," she said.

"They've been"—I paused—"careful. But I know they're good people and they'll do right by the story."

She took a breath, seeming to steel herself. "Okay," she said. "I'll do it."

She agreed to shoot a follow-up interview a few days later. She had to go replace Val Kilmer at Tampa Bay Comic Con first. "That'll be fun," I said, as I stepped back out into the heat. "No, it won't," she replied.

I was back at work, in the cafeteria, when my phone rang. It was Greenberg.

"Great news," I said. "I spoke with Rose and —"

"Can you talk?" he said.

In his small office, Greenberg let me babble through my update on McGowan.

"So I know you've been asking for an update," he said. In the two days since the meeting with Oppenheim, I had stopped by Greenberg's office three times to ask if he had any word from Lack.

Greenberg took a breath, as if bracing for something. "The story is now *under review by NBCUniversal.*" He wrapped his mouth around these last words strangely, like he was quoting a lyric in a foreign language. *Domo arigato, Mr. Roboto.*

"NBCUniversal," I said. "Not NBC News."

"It's gone upstairs. I don't know whether that involves Steve Burke or Brian Roberts," he said, referring to the top executives at NBC-Universal and its parent company, Comcast, "but it's under legal review." Greenberg was fidgeting, jiggling a knee under the desk. "Maybe once, when we got close to air on a tough story, I saw a high-level corporate review. But this is very atypical."

"What are they basing this review on?" No one had asked us for additional copies of material, or for the audio.

"I don't know," he said absently.

An NBCUniversal legal review meant Kim Harris, the general counsel of NBCUniversal — who had, with Weiner, presided over the "pussy grab" tape imbroglio the year before. Harris had also, years earlier, recruited me as a summer associate at Davis Polk.

"I'd be happy to send the material to Kim," I suggested. "I can play her the tape."

"My gosh, no!" Greenberg said, mortified, like I'd proposed an orgy with his grandparents or something. "No, no, no! Let's—we'll respect the process and remain at arm's length. I'll make sure Susan sends them whatever they need."

I wondered what logic we could have for keeping our own lawyers at "arm's length," but said, instead, "Well, I'd like to know as much as I can, when I can. And I'll keep you updated on the follow-up interview with Rose."

He flinched. "We're supposed to pause all reporting."

"Rich. It's been hell keeping Rose hanging in there at all. Now we have more from her and you want me to go back to her and cancel?"

"Not cancel," he said, "pause."

"There is an actual interview date set. I would be canceling."

I asked him how long we were supposed to "pause."

"I—I would anticipate that it won't move fast," he said. "I mean, I have no idea what their process is. But this could take more than a few days."

"Rich. I don't think anyone in our chain of command wants to be in the position, as a matter of record, of having canceled hard-fought pieces of reporting during a corporate review by our parent company."

"Things get canceled for all sorts of reasons. Nobody outside the company has to know why."

"If you tell them what you told me and Rich, it will matter for what happens to this story," I said, referring to his "fuck it, let him sue" and his decision to go to Weinstein for comment. It was hard to square that guy with this guy.

"This is a Steve Burke decision. It's an Andy decision," he replied. His eyes flicked away from mine. "What I say is not gonna matter." I believed Rich Greenberg when he said he cared about journalism. I believed, absent friction, that he would have supported the reporting and pursued the interview with McGowan. But several colleagues of his said he shied from messy confrontations. "He's really good as long as he's not in front of the pack," one veteran correspondent later told me. "He doesn't have the stomach for somebody's-gonna-be-mad-at-you investigative reporting." Few stories got people madder than this one. That day in Greenberg's office, I remember thinking how small he seemed — not defeated so much as comfortable within the narrow bounds of what he could and could not do inside an organization to which he had devoted seventeen years of his life.

Exasperated, I told him, "Look, Ken Auletta just turned to the camera and said, Andy Lack, this is a scandal if you don't run this."

Greenberg's eyes snapped up. "Do we have that? Is that in the script?"

I looked at him, puzzled. "It's in the transcript."

"Send that to me," he said.

◆

As I pushed out of the back doors of 30 Rock and into the summer heat, McHugh and I texted, debating what to do. There seemed to be no interest, in the loftiest echelons of the corporation, in hearing the tape or learning the full extent of the reporting. The only person who might have access to the corporate review that Greenberg hadn't discouraged us from reaching out to was Weiner, who, as the top lawyer in the news division, reported to Harris. I'd begun calling her the moment I emerged from the meeting with Greenberg. An assistant I reached told me not to stop by. After hours of calls, Weiner emailed to say she was busy, then leaving for a long weekend.

Then there was the dilemma about what to do about the interview with McGowan. "We are shooting with Rose. We are not canceling,"

McHugh texted. We both knew postponing could mean losing the interview entirely. On the other hand, refusing Greenberg's order to cancel the shoot might mean jeopardizing the increasingly tenuous support for the story within the network.

With the legal department not taking our calls, I grappled with whom to turn to. Arriving back at my apartment, I decided to take a risk and call Tom Brokaw. "Tom, I'm going to need to rely on that promise you made," I said. "About not talking to the subject of that story we discussed."

"You have my word," said Brokaw.

I told him about the corporate intercession. I ran him through the list of interviews and evidence.

"This is wrong," he said. He told me he'd reach out to the network's leadership about it. "You need to talk to Andy. You need to go in and play that tape for him."

I sent Greenberg the Auletta transcript, as he requested, with the comment about how it would be a scandal not to air the story highlighted. Then I forwarded it to Oppenheim.

❖

A few hours later, the phone rang.

"I got your email," said Oppenheim. "*Sooo*" — he drew out this word, like an emphatic teenager — "I hope, based on our two-and-a-half-year, or whatever, relationship, that you know you can trust me to do this process right. And this isn't about 'Andy doesn't want to do this,' or 'I don't want to do this.' If we can establish that he's a — a 'predator,' to use your term —"

"To be clear, that's not coming from me. We have documents and sources from within his company making that claim."

"Alright, alright," he said. "I hear you. If we could establish that he's, whatever, of course we'd want to get it out. We just need to, um, stress-test this, and Kim, who I know you've known since you were, like, sixteen, is going to do that and tell us what we can really be bulletproof in saying, what can hold up in court."

I told him that was all well and good as long as reporting wasn't being interrupted. I mentioned the interview we'd scheduled with McGowan.

"You just can't, Ronan," he replied. "If Kim decides that tortious interference or inducement to breach contract are big concerns for us, we can't be rushing ahead with an interview before she makes that call."

"That's not how this works," I told him. "We can get it in the can and then decide to review it later. Airing it is what makes it subject to litigation."

"I don't know," he said, defensively. "I'm not a lawyer. If they're saying tortious interference, I've gotta listen."

"I *am* a lawyer, Noah. That's just not a real rationale. Half our political reporting wouldn't be possible if we refused to talk to sources who were breaching contracts." It was true: there were few solid cases that supported the idea that news organizations, acting in good faith, could be exposed to significant liability in cases like this.

"Well, forgive me if I take Kim Harris's legal advice over yours," he said tartly.

I tried to think how to underline the stakes while conveying that I was a team player. "My sense is this is gonna come out," I said, "and the question is whether it comes out with or without us sitting on the evidence we have."

A long silence. "You'd better be careful," he said at last. "'Cause I know you're not threatening, but people could *think* you're threatening to go public." I knew what he meant, but the choice of words struck me as odd. Weren't we in the business of going public?

"But that's just it," I said. "I think threatening us is exactly what Ken Auletta was doing. And I think that's why Rich asked me to send him that quote. And why I forwarded it to you. A lot of people know we have this."

"Well," he said, "we're not 'sitting on it,' we're reviewing it carefully."

He softened a little, tried something different. "Ronan, you know in my years of supporting you, we've run a series of stories that could get us sued, and we've stood by them."

"I trust you'll do the right thing," I said. "There have just been some odd signals."

"We're just hitting pause while we wrap our arms around this," he said. "That's all I'm asking." On some level, I knew these euphemisms — the "pauses," the wrapping of arms — to be absurd. Canceling an interview was canceling an interview. The word *doubleplusungood* wandered through my mind. But I needed Oppenheim's support to get the story over the finish line.

I looked out of the window. Across the street, the lights were off and the dance studio was in shadow. "I'm glad you called," I said. "I do trust you."

"Just hang tight," he said. "No more reporting for a little bit."

# CHAPTER 22:

# *PATHFINDER*

"**W**e were right to keep our mouths shut," McHugh texted. We decided we'd pushed Oppenheim as far as we could. "I'd just sit back, work the phones and whatnot, but let the NBC team be. You've said your piece." But this still left the tricky proposition of the shoot with McGowan and the order to cancel it.

"Did Noah say don't do it?" McHugh wrote.

"Yes."

"Quandary."

"It's tempting to just push it back and risk losing her," I replied. "Just to avoid the fight with Noah. Think I can freely consult Greenberg on this?"

"Not sure any more," he wrote.

We were starting to concede that we might have to take the risk of rescheduling with McGowan. "I'm not sure another rose intv is critical to our story. But nbc having our back, in some ways, will be," McHugh wrote. "I am thinking, maybe there's a way to push it to LA and buy ourselves a little more time?"

I took a deep breath and dialed McGowan. "We were looking at maybe doing a later date," I said, feeling her out. "We could shoot more with you in Los Angeles, go back to your place."

Her voice was small on the other end of the line. "I'm not sure I can do this," she said. "There's a lot coming at me."

"Just — just hang in there," I said. "Please. For the other sources involved. I promise you it's just a little longer."

"I knew NBC wasn't going to take this seriously."

"They're taking it seriously. I'm taking it seriously."

"I offered to call the lawyers."

"They — we're going to do that, they're just reviewing things," I said. She didn't say anything. "If Tuesday's all you can do, we'll do Tuesday," I said quickly. "Don't worry about it."

She said we could look at options. But I could hear the uncertainty creeping into her voice.

A few minutes later, Jonathan, on the phone from Los Angeles, was working up a lather. He thought I should flout Greenberg's orders and call Kim Harris. He was incredulous at the legal arguments Oppenheim had raised. For any layperson with a dim recollection of the term, "tortious interference" was probably best known as the specious rationale used by CBS News's parent company to shut down that network's tobacco reporting. That day McHugh and Jonathan both made the same comparison: "Hasn't *anyone* in this company seen *The Insider?*" Jonathan asked, exasperated.

❖

The next morning, I called Kim Harris's office several times before she responded by email. Harris wrote that she'd been traveling for several days. We could meet the following week, perhaps. But this would be too late for the McGowan interview. I pleaded. "Canceling it could mean we don't get it back," I replied. I offered to pre-brief with Harris and let her dictate my posture in the interview, as I'd done with Chung before the early interviews. Then I called Weiner and left her a voicemail making the same points again. "Susan, as a matter of record, I don't want us to have to be canceling reporting. I know you're both out, but please respond."

As I hung up, Greenberg motioned me into his office. "So," he said, "I called Harvey back."

"What did you say?" I asked.

"I told him legal is vetting it and nothing's running for now." He said Weinstein had told him he wanted to send a letter to NBC's legal department, and Greenberg had directed him to Susan Weiner. "He may accuse you of maligning him in conversations," he added.

I laughed. Greenberg stayed serious. "Obviously, I've been incredibly careful not to malign him beyond asking neutral questions," I said. "I'll stand by anything I've said or put in writing."

"Just be careful," Greenberg said.

I asked him if he had any word on the McGowan interview, and he said legal was still deciding if it could go ahead. I thought of McGowan's fraying resolve, her reeling at my attempt to cancel.

Not long after, word came back. My begging had worked. Legal would allow the interview to proceed the following week. But the wavering had exacted its toll. As they decided, McGowan texted: "I can't film. Or be in your segment. I'm so sorry. The legal angle is coming at me and I have no recourse."

Over the following hours, my attempts to bring her back into the fold went nowhere. "I'm hamstrung," she said finally. "I can't talk." McGowan seemed increasingly distraught. In the following weeks, her lawyers would follow up with aggressive cease and desist letters.

I walked into Greenberg's office and told him immediately. "I'm going to try to get her back on board," I said. He thought for a moment, then shrugged. "Honestly, it makes me less nervous if she's not in the script," he said. "She always sounded a little — well, you know."

"Emily Nestor was close to going on camera full face. I can go back to her."

"Just wait," he said.

"It'd be calling an existing source."

"Let's just do this by the book from here. No new reporting for now," he said, as Oppenheim had.

I got home from work and my phone chimed: another text asking me to opt into weather alerts. I swiped it away. Another ping: this time, it was an old school friend calling. I pressed my eyes shut. "I can't go out, Erin," I said. Erin Fitzgerald had the kind of high-end consulting job that repeated explanations shed little light on.

"No one's seen you in, like, six months," she said, over a hum of cocktail conversation. "What's going on with you?"

"You know. On a big story."

"Whatever that means."

"Yeah," I said.

"Well, you're coming tonight." And she wouldn't take no for an answer. I sat with her and another friend on a crowded rooftop in Brooklyn and looked at the city, and realized I'd barely left my apartment that summer. "I'm on this assignment where I feel like I'm burning all my bridges one by one," I said. She shrugged. "Here, come!" she said, pulling me over to the parapet. We stood in front of the glittering Manhattan skyline and posed for a picture.

The next day, Ostrovskiy began his routine inspection of my social media accounts and those of my friends and relatives. Coming to an

Instagram post showing me and a pretty girl against the Manhattan sky-line, he lingered and felt, for a moment, relieved. I was in town after all.

By then, he and Khaykin had begun their latest assignment, but without much success. They'd billed a few hours following the woman from the *New York Times*, taking some photographs of her on the subway and then giving up after she disappeared into the *Times* building. The client's attention soon turned to the television reporter with the story that seemed to be in a state of flux.

But this was proving to be a challenge, too. Seeing that I was on the *Today* show one morning, Ostrovskiy and Khaykin disagreed about how best to capitalize on the opportunity.

"Hey, he's on the show," Ostrovskiy had said.

"Is it worth going? To see if we get him coming out?" Khaykin replied.

Ostrovskiy thought about this. Something about it made him uncomfortable. "It's a really busy area, Rockefeller Center," he pointed out. "We can't get there in a car. We don't have enough people to cover all the entrances and exits."

Not long after, as hot July gave way to a still hotter early August, I left home in the morning and walked right by the silver Nissan Pathfinder parked on the street immediately opposite my address. Only later did I register the memory of the two men sitting inside: one thin and bald, the other heavyset, with dark, curly hair.

❖

All that spring and summer, headlines about harassment and abuse had picked up pace: a fresh round of stories about Fox News; more scrutiny about President Trump. I was starting to field inquiries from women's rights activists supportive of my reporting on gender discrimination. As Ostrovskiy and Khaykin debated 30 Rockefeller Plaza's suitability for interception, one of those messages landed in my in-box, describing a women's advocacy program run by a wealth management company. It included a request to meet the following week. I glanced at the email and moved on without responding. "I am very impressed with your work as a male advocate for gender equality, and believe that you would make an invaluable addition to our activities," wrote Diana Filip of Reuben Capital Partners.

CHAPTER 23:

# CANDY

The first week of August, I arrived at Harris's office, in a light-filled corporate suite high in the building. Declining a call from my mother as I arrived, I texted her, "Going into meeting with parent company lawyer. Say a prayer." I'd broken rank to contact Harris and she hadn't added anyone to our emails. But Greenberg arrived a few minutes later, followed by Weiner.

The difference between the two women in the room was elemental, almost atomic. While Weiner was quiet and bureaucratic, Harris possessed outsize charisma. She had graduated from the best Ivy League institutions, in the sequence required to achieve maximum prestige. She'd worked in the Obama White House and as a partner at a top-ranked firm. She was faster on her feet than the company veterans in the room, and less intent on ceremony. She had big, genial features and a quick smile. Harris was the deadliest kind of lawyer, one sophisticated enough that you didn't see her doing the work at all.

She pulled out a copy of the script and ran through a few small language notes. And then: "I also think we're open to a tortious interference argument." I kept my face composed. I wasn't about to parse case law with the company's general counsel, but I knew this was bullshit.

Still, talking to Harris was generally reassuring. Her order, from a legal standpoint — separate from the news division's editorial decision — was not to stand down. She wanted another script, with the edits we'd discussed.

A few hours later, on my way out of the building, I ran into Weiner. Outside, rain was pounding at the lobby's revolving doors. To my surprise, she fixed me with a meaningful stare, and said, "Keep going."

◆

As the Weinstein story had expanded to fill more and more of McHugh's and my days and nights, I'd struggled to keep my canceled foreign policy book alive and find it a new publisher. All of the living secretaries of state had agreed to go on the record for the project, and I'd kept racing from our shoots into interviews with them. Hillary Clinton, who'd known about the book since I described it to her during my time working for her at the State Department, had agreed early and with enthusiasm. "Thank you, my friend, for your message; it is great hearing from you and I am delighted to know that you are close to completing your book project," she wrote that July. The letter was printed on embossed stationery in a curly art deco font, like a *New Yorker* headline or a piece of set-dressing from *BioShock*. It was very lovely, and not the sort of thing that wins Wisconsin. Several rounds of calls and emails had ensued, and an interview date had been promised that month, ahead of the beginning of a promotional tour for Clinton's latest memoir.

The afternoon of the meeting with Harris, as I pushed through the downpour and into my building's front door, a call came in from

Nick Merrill, Clinton's flack. We discussed the book briefly, and then he said, "By the way, we know about the big story you're on."

I sat down on one of the chairs in my building's lobby. "Well, Nick, I'm probably working on a lot of stories at any given time."

"You know what I mean," he said.

"I really can't say anything."

"Well, you know, it's a *concern* for us."

I felt a rivulet of rain run down my neck. "Can I ask who said this to you?" I said.

"Maybe off the record, over drinks," he replied. "Let's just say people are talking."

When I turned the conversation back to the interview with Clinton, he said that she was *"really* busy with the book tour." I pointed out that this was why we'd scheduled the interview for before the book tour. "Like I said," he reiterated, as if he hadn't heard this, *"really busy."* Over the ensuing weeks, every attempt to lock a date for the interview yielded another terse note that she'd become suddenly unavailable. She'd injured her foot. She was too tired. Clinton, meanwhile, was becoming one of the most easily available interviews in all of politics.

Later, Merrill would swear up and down that Clinton's sudden reticence was coincidental. Whatever the motivation, it felt ominous—another screw turning, another sign of my life outside the story shrinking. It was hard not to sense a pattern forming: each time we came back to our bosses with more reporting, word of the story seemed to spread farther. McHugh and I both worried about protecting our sources.

"If someone's leaking to Clinton, what's getting leaked to Harvey?" McHugh wondered.

"Shit," I said. "You don't think they would—"

"I don't know," he said. "That's the problem."

As pressure on the story mounted, fissures between McHugh and me widened. Our exchanges grew terse. After the meeting with Harris, he was miffed he hadn't been included, and seemed to wonder where my loyalties lay. "Just odd that you ended up solo," he said. I explained that I'd been trying to leave the door open to a more candid one-on-one, that I hadn't known Greenberg would join. "Just don't want them isolating us," McHugh said, warily.

As I arrived home from work one day early that August, my superintendent, squat and square-jawed and graying, approached me under the building's awning. He was annoyed.

"You know these guys outside today?" he said, in an Albanian accent.

"What guys?" I asked.

"Eh, two guys. In car. Smoking by car. All the time."

I looked up and down the block. The street was mostly empty. "Why do you think they were here for me?"

He rolled his eyes. "Ronan. Is always you. You move in, address print everywhere, now I have no peace."

I told him I was sure it was just TMZ guys on a slow day. "If they come back, I'll bring them coffee and ask them to leave," I said. He shook his head and looked at me doubtfully.

It was clear that we could bring in more reporting if NBC wanted it. "I know you'd been considering taking that last step and doing an interview showing your face," I told Nestor in a call as the review progressed. "I hate to put this on you, but it could be important if you do."

"I'm applying for jobs. I'm just not sure," she said.

"I wouldn't be asking if I didn't think it might make the difference here."

She thought for a moment. "If it winds up being that important, I'm open to it," she said. "I'd do it."

Despite the strange signals from our bosses, McHugh and I kept working. He helped with research, clicking over to other browser windows as Greenberg walked by. I stayed up late, calling Weinstein's former employees around the world. I needed the kind of big break that could shatter the halt on reporting.

❖

Leaving home one morning, I spotted something outside that made me stop abruptly: a silver Nissan Pathfinder I felt sure I'd seen before in the same spot. Other residents made their way into the sunlight. My neighbor who looked a little like me smiled as he passed. I stood there feeling ridiculous. There were a million reasons for two guys to be parked near Columbus Circle a few times a week, I reminded myself. But I decided I'd have more privacy working from home anyway, and went back upstairs.

It was a minute after noon when the call from Greenberg came in.

"How's the script?" he asked. I'd been revising it according to Harris's specifications.

"It's rock-solid," I said. "And we're continuing to field any relevant incoming calls from sources, of course."

"Legal called and they want you to pause reporting," he said.

*This again*, I thought.

"Why?" I asked. "I assumed, since they gave us a green light to go ahead with Rose—"

"No, we're paused. How's your book? Interviews going well?"

Greenberg had never shown any interest in my book. We talked about Condoleezza Rice for a few minutes before I said, "Rich, about stopping reporting —"

"I gotta go," he interjected. "I'm flying to see my dad. I'll be gone all weekend. We can talk next week."

And then he was gone.

"Greenberg called," I texted McHugh. "Legal wants us to stop any new calls. So be discreet."

"Oh shit," he wrote back. "Why?"

It didn't make sense. Discouragement was one thing, but there was no rationale, journalistic or legal, for ordering us to stop reporting. I called Greenberg again.

"Rich, I'm sorry to bother you again, I just need some clarification here. What, exactly, did 'legal' say? Who in legal? Why?"

"I don't know, I'm not a lawyer. I really have to go now, I have to catch my flight," he said quickly. As if to leaven the tone, he added, "Sorry, man."

I was responding when he hung up. The call had lasted all of thirty-seven seconds.

I paced my apartment. I called Harris's office, said it was urgent, didn't hear back. My phone chimed: another message from Diana Filip of Reuben Capital Partners, entreating me to meet about my reporting on gender issues.

Leaving home that afternoon, I edged up to the front door, where I'd seen the car. Nothing there. *You look like a damn fool*, I thought to myself. But I was starting to take precautions. I was memorializing sensitive information in longhand form. I was moving new documents into the safe-deposit box. Eventually, I'd consult John Tye, a former whistle-blower on government surveillance practices who founded a nonprofit law office called Whistleblower Aid. He set me up with an iPod Touch with only an encrypted messaging app installed, connected to the internet through an anonymous Wi-Fi hot spot purchased with cash. Its number was registered to a pseud-onym. Mine was "Candy."

"Oh, come on," I said, incredulous.

"I don't pick the names," Tye said, all serious.

"I sound like a nice Midwestern girl who should not have moved to LA."

"I don't pick the names."

## CHAPTER 24:

# *PAUSE*

"I've been waiting for this call," a crisp English accent was saying. Ally Canosa, who'd worked for Weinstein since 2010, immediately confirmed she'd been aware of the pattern of honeypot meetings. And there was more: "I was sexually abused by Harvey Weinstein," she said. "Repeatedly." I took a risk, showed my cards, told Canosa exactly what I had.

"Oh my God," she said, beginning to break down. "It's finally going to come out."

When I asked if she'd go on camera, she sounded frightened, but open to the idea. "I want to help," she said. "Let's talk." She agreed to meet me in Los Angeles in person. She was available that weekend. When a source offers you a break like that, you grab it.

I started the process of booking a plane ticket, then stopped. It was a Thursday afternoon. To make it to the meeting with Canosa over the weekend, I'd need to fly out soon. But Greenberg had just issued his latest order to stop reporting, this time invoking the legal department.

McHugh again suggested asking for forgiveness, not permission. "If you don't explain this to anybody, you guarantee this meeting, and you can see her this weekend and have a talk, and maybe convince her to go on camera. If you tell them, you let people far more powerful than we are in this scenario dictate what happens." But going truly rogue, rather than just keeping under the radar, as we had that spring, felt like a bridge too far. I called Weiner and told her the interview was important. Then I sent an email pleading for permission to continue reporting.

No one replied. "They are prob talking," McHugh texted. "Try to put it out of mind."

I waited a day, then booked my ticket to LA.

◆

It was raining again the next morning, an oppressive gray drizzle. McHugh called from the office early as I threw unfolded clothes into a suitcase. "Didn't you say Greenberg was getting on a flight yesterday?" McHugh asked. He was speaking under his breath.

"Yeah," I said. "He had to get off in a hurry."

"Funny," he said. "'Cause he's here."

"Maybe his flight got canceled."

"Maybe."

I was putting the luggage into the trunk of a sedan when Greenberg tried me. Then he texted: "Call me ASAP."

"Hi," I said. "I'm on the way to the airport."

"What?!" he said. He sounded like he was about to leap out of his skin. "I have to get Susan on the phone." Then she joined, speaking slowly and carefully. "We have discussed your email about this weekend's meeting. The company would like to put a pause on all reporting and contact with sources."

"All *contact* with sources?" I asked, incredulous. There was a heaviness to these conversations now, a strange sense that we were not just speaking to each other but also turning out, just a bit, to the crowd that might someday scrutinize our decisions. I felt this, and then felt it might be self-aggrandizing. But it gave me a strange kind of authority to push them to say what they hoped to leave between the lines.

"I don't understand," I continued. "Has anyone at any point raised any issue with the reporting or how I've acted?"

"No, no," Greenberg said.

"Is there any question about the *news value* of this woman offering to discuss a serious allegation of sexual abuse by a prominent person?"

"That's, well — that's above my pay grade," he managed.

"Okay. So where's this coming from? Is this an order from legal?" I asked.

There followed a silence that felt endless.

"It's not —" Weiner began.

"You should know this comes directly from Noah," Greenberg said.

"So legal *hasn't* made a determination that I should stop reporting?"

"*Noah* has made a determination that we should pause reporting and contact with sources."

"No one has expressed a rationale as to why it would place us in any jeopardy to allow reporting to continue, with full caution and in full consultation with legal. Did he articulate any reason why?"

"Well, if I — if I had to guess, from my standpoint," Weiner stammered, "I'd say one might want to review what we, uhh, what we have now before continuing with anything new." She assembled this sentence like she was reading characters off of a newly unearthed cuneiform tablet.

"This isn't new," I said stubbornly, referring to the meeting with Canosa. "It's been scheduled."

The phone vibrated—McHugh calling. I declined the call, tapped in a text. "On w Greenberg and Weiner."

"Should I join?" he responded. It felt like a rescue operation.

"Maybe poke head in," I wrote.

"In light of what Noah said, we think you should not be meeting with any sources," Greenberg was saying.

McHugh texted to say Greenberg had waved away the attempt to enter his office. No rescue.

"I can't prevent sources from reaching out to me," I told Greenberg.

"We understand that," he said.

I said nothing about whether I would obey the order to cancel the meeting, agreeing instead to keep them apprised of what Canosa told me "if" we had any contact. I'd never experienced this before: pretending I wasn't contacting sources, feigning reluctance to hear back from them.

"I think she will very possibly agree to go on camera," I said. "And if she does, I'll feel strongly about proceeding with that."

"We'd—we'd have to go back to Noah on that," Greenberg said.

I got off the call feeling disoriented. I called Jonathan.

"This is insane," he said.

"I don't think I can risk trying to cancel another interview," I said.

"You and Rich McHugh need to start writing each other memos. Detailed descriptions of all of this, sent in real time. They're saying incriminating shit."

I looked out of the car window at a snarl of bumper-to-bumper traffic outside JFK. "This is all fine for you guys," Jonathan was saying. "As long as you keep going, as long as you keep reporting."

"Easy for you to say," I told him. "I'm pissing them off with this stuff. I'm going to be unemployed soon at this rate."

"Who cares?! Look at what's happening! No one on these calls wants to own any of this, because it's so obviously bad! It's like a reverse *Murder on the Orient Express*. Everyone wants it dead, nobody wants to stab it!"

❖

Back at 30 Rockefeller Plaza, McHugh, still lingering outside Greenberg's office, knocked again.

"What's going on?" McHugh said.

"Noah has asked us to pause our reporting while we see what we have and the legal review takes place," Greenberg told him.

"I just don't understand that," McHugh said.

Greenberg hadn't offered any explanations on the phone with me, and he didn't offer any to McHugh. He rattled off a list of Weinstein's lawyers—Charles Harder, David Boies, and, a new name McHugh hadn't heard in connection with Weinstein before, Lanny Davis. "Not that we're afraid of any of them," Greenberg added. "But for the time being you have to stop any calls about this." As I had, McHugh said he couldn't stop incoming calls, and left it at that.

❖

As I arrived at JFK, Canosa called. She sounded nervous. "You're still coming to town?" she asked. I stopped for a moment, anxious travelers dragging heavy luggage coursing around me. I thought how easy it would be to tell her no, to take the order from our bosses, to safeguard the relationships with Greenberg and Oppenheim.

"Ronan?" she asked again.

"Yeah," I told her. "I'm coming."

From the plane, I put the finishing touches on the script, trading notes with McHugh about a word choice in my narration or an edit on a sound bite. Even pared down to the elements the legal department had reviewed and sanctioned, it was explosive. "I'm used to that," said Weinstein near the top, as Gutierrez, panicked, tried to escape. "NBC NEWS HAS EXCLUSIVELY OBTAINED AUDIO COLLECTED DURING THE NYPD STING," I narrated. Gutierrez was named, her story told in detail, followed by a summary paragraph: "NBC NEWS HAS SPOKEN TO FOUR OTHER WOMEN WHO HAVE WORKED FOR WEINSTEIN AND WHO ALLEGE SEXUAL MISCONDUCT . . . ALLEGA-TIONS DATING FROM THE LATE 1990S TO JUST THREE YEARS AGO." Nestor's interview was included, and the messages from Reiter cor-roborating her claim, and sound bites from the executives, describ-ing firsthand recollections of misconduct.

I attached to the script a note that I hoped would put our bosses at NBC on notice about Canosa:

> Rich,
> Attached please find the script, revised according to Kim and Susan's enumerated concerns, and your subsequent suggestions, which have been followed very precisely.
> Please note that one additional former assistant has raised a credible first hand allegation of sexual abuse and claims to have a paper trail relevant to our reporting. She has expressed a willingness to participate in this story and is deciding in what capacity.
>
> Ronan

After the email went out to Greenberg and Weiner, I felt antsy. I depressed the button on my seat and tested the limits of its recline a few times. It felt like we were standing still while the outside world accelerated. While I was on the flight, *HuffPost* ran a story about claims that the Fox News host Eric Bolling had sent lewd texts to

coworkers. The story had used entirely anonymous sourcing—
something that had never been the case in any draft of ours. The
same afternoon, the *Hollywood Reporter* announced that Harvey
Weinstein, for his "contributions to public discourse and the cultural
enlightenment of society," would be receiving the LA Press Club's
inaugural Truthteller Award.

# CHAPTER 25:

# *PUNDIT*

*I* met Ally Canosa at a restaurant way out on the east end of Sunset Boulevard. She sat perfectly upright, every muscle in her body tensed. Like many of the sources in the Weinstein story, she was pretty in a way that would have been striking in most settings, but was just a criterion for employment in Hollywood.

Canosa wasn't sure what to do. She had signed a nondisclosure agreement as a condition of her employment with Weinstein. She was still trying to make it as a producer, and was terrified of retaliation. Weinstein could render her unemployable. And then there were the hesitations of any survivor of sexual violence. She'd allowed her wounds to calcify and learned to carry on. She hadn't told her father, or her boyfriend. "I don't want to suffer more. You know?" she told me. Once, as she'd worked up the nerve to raise the matter with a therapist, "I saw her at a premier for a Weinstein movie," Canosa told me. "I found out she was a producer on one of Harvey's movies."

Canosa had met Weinstein the better part of a decade earlier, when she was working as an event planner at the West Hollywood branch of the members-only club Soho House. She'd organized an event for the Weinstein Company, and he'd spotted her, stared, and then handed her his business card. At first, Weinstein almost stalked Canosa, demanding to meet again and again. When she was "creeped out" and didn't respond, he forced her hand, demanding a formal meeting through Soho House, ostensibly to discuss another event.

At the Montage hotel, their midday meeting was moved to a hotel suite, and Weinstein laid into her with his familiar promises of career advancement followed by sexual overtures. "You should be an actress," she remembered him saying. "You have a face." When he asked, "You're not gonna kiss me?" she said no and left, flustered.

She kept trying to ignore him, but he was persistent, and she was fearful of the impact he might have on her career if she spurned him. She agreed to meet again. During dinner at a hotel restaurant, Eva Cassidy's cover of "Autumn Leaves" drifted over the stereo system. Canosa talked about Cassidy's life story, and Weinstein proposed developing a biopic about her, with Canosa's help. After the meal, he grabbed her by the arm, pressed her against a railing on the steps outside, and kissed her hard. She was horrified.

But afterward, Weinstein "made a big show of being apologetic," she said. "We can just be friends," she remembered him telling her. "I really wanna make this movie with you." He set up a call with a veteran producer of his, and pretty soon they were meeting with rights holders and exchanging script notes.

"I called my parents and was like, 'Oh my God. You would not believe what just happened. Harvey Weinstein wants me to help him produce a movie about an idea I gave him,'" she recalled. "So naïve. Look, it's embarrassing just talking about it. But at the time I was like, 'This is all I ever wanted.'"

❖

Canosa took time to get to these points. After our meeting at the restaurant, she said she'd be more comfortable in private, and came to Jonathan's place in West Hollywood. It was the start of a trend that would soon see more and more distraught sources traipsing through his doors. Pundit, the Goldendoodle my mother had given Jonathan, curled up next to Canosa as she continued the story.

The first year they'd worked together, Canosa had tried repeatedly to brush off Weinstein's advances. During one meeting about the Cassidy film, he casually told her he needed to go up to his hotel room to get something. "It was like midafternoon or something. So, I just didn't think," she said. When they got there, he told her he was going to take a shower. "Would you get in the shower with me?" he asked.

"No," Canosa told him.

"Just get in the shower with me. I don't even need to—I don't want to have sex with you. I just want you to be in the shower with me."

"No," she said again, and went into the living room. Weinstein announced, from the bathroom, that he was going to masturbate anyway, and started doing so through the open door as she averted her gaze. She left Weinstein's hotel room, upset.

Another time, Weinstein left a jacket behind at one of their meetings and asked her to hold onto it. In its pockets, she found a pack of syringes that googling revealed were a treatment for erectile dysfunction. She reeled at the implications of him arming himself for sex ahead of their meetings.

By then she was working on the film for Weinstein; her professional life had come to revolve around him. And they had developed a friendship that was real, if twisted by imbalances of power and by

Weinstein's overtures. At one work dinner with a number of colleagues that summer, he wept over news that Disney would be selling Miramax. He asked her, yet again, to come to his hotel room. When she refused, he roared at her, "Don't fucking refuse me when I'm crying." She relented, and nothing happened. He just sobbed. "I've never been happy," she remembered him saying. "You're one of my best friends. You're so loyal." She hoped the declarations of friendship meant he understood her boundaries. She was wrong.

"What came next," she said, beginning to cry, "was he raped me." The first time had been after another meeting in a hotel. As they discussed the Cassidy project, he said a scene in the script reminded him of a classic film, and asked her to come up to his room to watch a clip. Weinstein had by then apologized for his advances profusely and he was, after all, her boss. "I was like, I can handle myself," she said. The only television in Weinstein's hotel room was in the bedroom. She sat on the bed and watched the clip, feeling uncomfortable. "He made a move, and I told him, 'No.' And he made another move, and I told him, 'No,'" she recalled. Weinstein got angry, aggressive. "Don't be a fucking idiot," she remembered him saying. He departed for the restroom and returned a few minutes later wearing only a robe. Then he pushed her onto the bed. "I said no more than once, and he forced himself on me," she said. "It wasn't like I was screaming. But I was definitely like, 'I don't want to do this.' And his full body weight was on top of me."

Canosa lingered on what she could have done differently. "In my head at the time, it was like I didn't put up enough of a fight." Eventually, she stopped saying no. "I was just numb. I wasn't crying. I was just staring at the ceiling." It was only after she left that she started sobbing and couldn't stop. Weinstein hadn't used protection. He had told her, to her great discomfort, months earlier, how he'd gotten a vasectomy. But she was terrified he might have given her an

STD. She thought of telling her boyfriend but felt too ashamed. "Looking back, I would drag myself kicking and screaming straight to the police if I could."

As she broke down telling the story, Pundit leapt up, concerned, trying to lick Canosa's face. She laughed, relieved to have the tension of the moment punctured. "This is the sweetest dog I think I've ever met," she said.

Canosa kept working for Weinstein. "I was in a vulnerable position and I needed my job," she told me. Later, when she lost her job at a different production company, she signed a formal contract with the Weinstein Company, working on awards campaigns for *The Artist* and *The Iron Lady.*

Weinstein's misconduct continued. Once, he ordered her to accompany him to an appointment with an osteopath and to remain in the room as he stripped naked and received treatment for a worsening case of sciatica. Another time, during an attack of the same condition, he demanded that she massage his thighs. She remembered him screaming at her when she refused. "What the fuck? Why aren't you gonna? Why?"

"Because I don't feel comfortable," she told him. "I'm your employee."

"For fuck's sake, Ally!" he shouted. "For fuck's sake, you can massage my thighs!"

"I'm just not going to."

"Then fucking get out of here! Fuck you! Fuck! Fuck! Fuck!"

When she was working on the production of the Netflix series *Marco Polo*, Weinstein arrived on set in Malaysia and wreaked havoc. At a dinner for the directors and producers, he demanded, in front of her coworkers, that she go to his hotel room. When she tried to go instead to her own room, the barrage of texts from his assistants started up: "Harvey wants to see you, Harvey wants to see you." Sometimes her efforts to evade him failed, and more assaults followed. Later, court documents would itemize "oral sexual conduct or anal sexual conduct with plaintiff by forcible compulsion and/or when plaintiff was incapable of consent by reason of being physically helpless."

All around Canosa, there were signs that she wasn't alone. During that same visit to the set of *Marco Polo*, Weinstein went into the dressing room of one actress for fifteen minutes, "and then she was a ghost of herself for a week afterwards." Canosa felt a moral obligation to do something but was terrified by Weinstein's displays of vindictiveness. "The number of times I've seen people have their lives threatened, or their wives threatened, or their reputation threatened," she said, shaking her head.

I tried to be honest with Canosa about the precariousness of the story, and the importance of her participation to its future. I said, as I had so many times that summer, that the decision was hers; that all I could do was tell her how sincerely I believed talking would make a difference for a lot of people. By the end of our conversations, she was edging tantalizingly close to saying yes to going on camera.

## CHAPTER 26:

# *BOY*

It was early evening and the shadows were lengthening in Harvey Weinstein's offices on Greenwich Street when the call came in. "Can you get Harvey?" said George Pataki, the former New York governor. An assistant made the connection. "Hey, Harvey, it's George. I just want to let you know, Ronan Farrow's still working on the story."

"That's not what I hear," Weinstein said.

Pataki insisted that multiple women were talking to me. "He's ready to go with it. It's supposed to get aired—"

"When?" Weinstein asked. "When is it supposed to get aired?"

"Two to three weeks," Pataki said.

Nowhere was Weinstein more deeply enmeshed in politics than in New York. Between 1999 and that summer in 2017, he and his company had given to at least thirteen New York politicians or their PACs. He'd covered his bases, mostly with Democrats but also occasionally with Republicans like Pataki. He'd been generous with Senator Kirsten Gillibrand, and Attorney General Eric Schneiderman, and Governor Andrew Cuomo.

For Weinstein and Pataki, as had been the case with Hillary Clinton, campaign contributions had helped foster friendship. The former governor was often photographed at the movie mogul's events. Weinstein helped boost the career of Pataki's daughter, Allison, an historical novelist. A year before Pataki's call, Weinstein hosted a book party for her. The year before that, when her husband suffered a stroke, Weinstein helped secure the right specialists. Allison Pataki's book agent, Lacy Lynch, also worked with McGowan. As the summer wore on, Lynch's name began showing up on Weinstein's email and call lists.

Weinstein had kept up his calls to Boies about the NBC problem. After his conversation with Lack, he'd continued to reach out to NBC executives, and had confidently reported back to people around him that the story was dead. But it wasn't long before he called Boies back, sounding less certain. "I think NBC is still working on a story," he said. He sounded angry. "I'm going to get to the bottom of this."

After hearing from Pataki, Weinstein placed a fresh round of calls to Phil Griffin, Andy Lack, and Noah Oppenheim. He'd shouted the names so often—"Get me Phil, get me Andy, get me Noah"—the assistants had taken to calling them "the triumvirate." By that August, Weinstein's attention was increasingly turning to Oppenheim. But Griffin, whom Weinstein told his staff he knew best, had been an object of early and intense focus, and continued to be a mainstay.

◈

Griffin's carefree qualities contributed to his considerable charm. They could also, however, be a source of discomfort for colleagues. He had a temper, and cursed like a sailor. He was notorious for his hard drinking after work. While he was a senior producer at *Nightly News* in the nineties, he'd often retire after work to Hurley's, a Midtown bar. After a few drinks one night, he told three women producers with him that he wanted to go to Times Square.

"I want to go see the lights at Times Square! I love to see the lights!" one recalled Griffin saying.

Griffin moved the drinking to a Times Square hotel. Then the group stumbled over to Eighth Avenue, where Griffin urged the women to come with him to see a peep show. Two of them exchanged uncomfortable glances. He told them to lighten up. In they went, to a circle of darkened booths upstairs, where a window opened and a woman, naked but for her heels, squatted in front of them and asked Griffin for some cash to continue the show.

Griffin looked at the women with what one described as "a flicker of shame." He told the stripper no thanks. The window closed, and the group headed out to exchange awkward goodbyes. For the women, the incident had been gross, but unremarkable: they'd all come up in the business with this kind of behavior from men.

Four colleagues said Griffin was known for making lewd or crass remarks in work emails. In one meeting I'd been in after the television personality Maria Menounos's vagina had been photographed in a bathing suit wardrobe malfunction, Griffin waved around a printed page bearing a zoomed-in image, smirking. "Would you look at that?" he said, and exhaled hard. "Not bad, not bad." On a couch nearby, the female employee in the room with us rolled her eyes.

Griffin seemed to see the news purely as a business, and evinced for journalism little of the fervor he held for sports. When the winds of the industry blew in favor of partisanship, he pushed his anchors toward opinion; when partisanship wore thin, he was the first to turn to straight news. And when you subjected him to any kind of rigorous discussion of reporting, he'd squint at you and look confused.

But Griffin did become passionate when a business interest was on the line. Once, while I was co-hosting a charity concert called the Global Citizen Festival — a big, earnest, low-rent Live Aid — I interviewed the concert's headline act, No Doubt. One of the festival's goals that year was promoting vaccination, even as the anti-vaxxer movement in the United States was producing adherents and measles outbreaks. I asked Gwen Stefani if she vaccinated her kids, and how she felt about the anti-vaxxers. She said she supported vaccines and advised people to talk to their doctors. Mike Wallace at your door this was not. But back at Rockefeller Plaza, assembling the spot in edit, I got a call from an MSNBC producer working on the concert.

"Stefani's people have reviewed the transcript, and they'd like some edits," she said.

"Who sent them a transcript?"

"I — I don't know."

In my in-box was a redlined script, with Stefani's sound bites rearranged and trimmed to make it sound like she was ambivalent to negative on the vaccine front. I told the producer I wouldn't air it.

Pretty soon I was in Griffin's office with him and another member of his team. "What the fuck?" he asked, exasperated.

I looked at the proposed script in front of me.

"Phil, I'm not gonna edit sound bites to change their meaning."

"Why not?!" he said, like this was the craziest thing he'd ever heard.

"It's not ethical?" I offered, less as a statement and more as a kind of reminder, hoping Griffin's question had been rhetorical and he'd finish the thought. Instead, he leaned back in his chair and directed a "Lord give me strength" look at his colleague.

She tried a gentler tone. "We all know you care a lot about the" — she hesitated here, seeming to genuinely struggle to find a nice way to put it —"*journalism with a capital J*, but this is not some sensitive political story."

"It's a puff piece!" Griffin chimed in. "Come on. What the fuck?"

"There are literally kids dying over this issue. She's a famous person. Since when do we send transcripts of interviews outside the building anyway?"

"We don't know how that happened—" his colleague began.

"Who cares?" Griffin interjected, impatient. "You know what happens if we don't make these edits? Stefani's threatening to pull out! That's straight from her manager."

"That's who made these edits?"

Griffin blew past the question. "Point is, she pulls out, *sponsors* start to pull out, the network's pissed..." The channel's partnership with the Global Citizen Festival was, Griffin often remarked, bait to entice corporate sponsors. For weeks, we would run branded segments about Unilever or Caterpillar.

"So let's not air it," I said.

"You have to air it," said Griffin.

"Why?"

"It's part of the deal with the sponsors, with her people—"

"We ran this all the way up," his colleague said, referring to the executive chain of command in the news group. "Your concerns are not shared."

Griffin said he'd tell me what he told another anchor trying to air a tough segment about net neutrality—the principle that internet providers shouldn't charge different rates for different types of data on the internet, which our parent company was lobbying against. "You wanna work for PBS and have complete freedom and make a hundred thousand bucks a year, be my guest," he recalled telling that anchor. "You wanna fight with me on what's good for the bottom line, I'll be happy to put your salary numbers out in the press."

I considered quitting. I called Tom Brokaw, who said I under no circumstances could air sound bites with deceptive edits, and gave me the same warning about fucking my credibility that he'd later lay on me during the Weinstein reporting. Then I called Savannah Guthrie, who had a knack for cutting through bullshit. "What about just not airing that part of the interview?" she suggested.

"I mean, it was most of the interview," I said.

"Just find something else to air."

It was simple and, in hindsight, obvious advice—don't air the deceptive part, but don't self-immolate over a singer's backstage interview. Picking the right fights was a lesson I could be slow to learn. In the end, I sat at the anchor desk and aired a five-minute clip of small talk with No Doubt. I felt neither hella good nor hella bad.

❖

Two years later, as Weinstein continued his calls to the triumvirate of executives, he reached Griffin.

"I thought this was done," Weinstein said.

"Harvey, it is," Griffin responded.

"You need to get your boy in line," he said. He sounded angry.

"Harvey," Griffin said, defensive, "he's not running it with us." Later, Griffin would deny he ever promised the story was killed.

It was, by the estimate of multiple staffers in Weinstein's office, one of at least fifteen calls between Weinstein and the three NBC executives. And by late summer, Weinstein's mood after the calls had again become triumphal. Weinstein told one of his legal advisors that he'd spoken to executives at the network, and that "they tell me they're not doing the story."

# CHAPTER 27:

# *ALTAR*

*T*he news from the executive suites of NBCUniversal at first seemed good. Early that August, Greenberg called to report that legal had signed off on the pared-down version of the script. And from the editorial side, he added, "my view is everything in there is reportable."

"So we seek comment. We go into edit," I said.

"*Reportable* doesn't mean it airs. Now it goes to Noah and Andy."

"But surely if legal approved, and you consider it reportable—"

"What they decide's above my pay grade," he said. "There may be questions that have nothing to do with what's reportable. They may have concerns about whether it's good TV. You know, you have an incredible print piece, an incredible *Vanity Fair* story here."

"I—what?" was all I managed.

"You know, it'd make a perfect *Vanity Fair* story," he repeated.

Later, McHugh and I sat in a conference room and puzzled over the comment. "Maybe he's right," he said heavily. "Maybe you save this by taking it to somewhere else."

"Rich, you know if that happens, you get screwed." He had

produced the hell out of the story, as a television piece. We'd shot, by this point, eight on-camera interviews. All of that would fall by the wayside in the scenario Greenberg had lightly proposed. And even if I wanted to take it elsewhere, would it be possible? The footage was owned by NBCUniversal and, in turn, the Comcast Corporation.

"We're running this here," I said firmly. "Produced by you."

McHugh said, "Okay," and sounded less certain.

◆

It rained ceaselessly that day. In my in-box, inquiries unrelated to the Weinstein story piled up. Diana Filip, the investor with the women's rights project, sent another email, this time through my agents at CAA. The messages related to the story were more anxiety-inducing. One arrived, blunt and short, from Auletta:

Ronanm
Harvey status?
ken

I made my way down through the bowels of 30 Rock, onto a D train. It was sparsely populated, despite the rain. I saw something, or thought I did, and froze. There, in profile, seated on my side at the opposite end of the car, was a bald head that I swore I'd seen in the Nissan. I could make out the same pale face and snub nose. I couldn't be sure. My most rational self thought, *You're seeing things.* But as the train stopped, I felt uncomfortable enough to slip out before my station. I pushed onto the crowded platform, looking over my shoulder.

Outside, New York was a dreamscape, streets and buildings and people suspended in mist and rain. I walked fast, stopping at a CVS, scanning to see if I recognized anyone from the subway car or the platform. When I emerged, the light was failing. I came to the familiar fortress-like church near my apartment, and moved quickly up the steps, and walked through the doors. Where my damp shirt hadn't adhered to my body, rain rolled down the small of my back, my chest, my arms. The nave was smaller than I'd expected from the outside. Under imposing stained-glass windows, an altar loomed. I stood in front of it, feeling out of place. By the altar was a seal, in inlaid marble, showing a book and a sword over a diagram of the earth: the coat of arms of Saint Paul. "PRAEDICATOR VERITATIS IN VNIVERSO MUNDO." I had to google the translation later: "A preacher of truth to the whole world."

"We've been watching you," said a heavily accented voice next to me, and I lurched. It was an older woman with dark hair. Next to her was a younger woman. They looked alarmed at my reaction. "We've been watching," she said again. "From the beginning. Your show. My daughter is a big fan."

"Oh," I said. "Thank you." And then, collecting myself, managed a smile and a stock joke about low ratings: "You and my mom and no one else."

◆

I had arrived home when Berger, my agent at CAA, called. "Ronan!" he boomed. "How's it going?"

"I'm fine," I said.

"You're better than fine, you're fantastic," he said. And then, a little quieter, descending into brisk efficiency, "Look, I don't know the details of this big story —

"Did Noah mention it?" I asked. Berger was agent to both of us, and closer to Oppenheim.

"Ronan, I don't know a thing," he said. He reminded me that my contract was about to be up for renewal. "I'm just saying if this is causing you problems, prioritize the stuff that's working."

◆

I chewed my lip for a second, then dialed my sister.

"So how's the story?" she asked.

"I don't know how it is, honestly."

"Don't you have, like, literally a recording of him admitting to it?"

"Yeah," I said.

"So—"

"I've been pushing. I don't know how much more I can push."

"So you're going to drop it."

"It's not that simple. I might have to prioritize other things while I figure this out."

"I know what it's like to have people stop fighting for you," she said quietly. And there was a long silence before we said our goodbyes.

It was dark by then. I looked at my phone and found Oppenheim had texted: "Let's talk tomorrow. When's good?" I went over to my laptop and opened up a Microsoft Word document. "OTHER STORIES," I typed, and then hit Delete a few times and replaced "OTHER" with "UPCOMING." I pasted in bullet points for two stories we were in the midst of shooting, on health care consolidation and opioid-dependent infants, and a handful of others Oppenheim had liked before, including a "Vicey travelogue" on Facebook's server farm deep in the permafrost of Luleå, Sweden. "It looks like a Bond villain's lair," I had written of the server farm, and other escapist TV pablum followed. Luleå is one of the busiest ports in Sweden and a major hub of its steel industry, but of this I knew nothing. I was picturing a place big and brisk and empty, where a person could breathe, and you could see the northern lights.

At 30 Rock, McHugh stepped into an elevator, turned to find Weiner standing next to him, and smiled. But as she said hello back, she flinched and looked at her feet.

## CHAPTER 28:

# *PAVONINE*

**D**uring my years at 30 Rock, the third-floor waiting area outside of the news executives' offices cycled through several arrangements of furniture. That August, there was a low chair and a little table with a fan of the kind of months-old magazines that tend to ornament waiting rooms. A *Time* cover, jet-black with blood-red lettering, asked, "Is Truth Dead?" It was an homage to a classic '60s *Time* cover that read "Is God Dead?" but not as good. It had been an impossible task: "Truth" just didn't fit like "God" did, despite valiant efforts at kerning. I looked at it, then went over to Oppenheim's assistant, Anna, to make small talk. "Guess you guys are working on something big," she said, and gave me a conspiratorial, *mum's the word* smile.

When I walked into Oppenheim's office, he didn't rise or move to the couch as usual. He looked nervous. "So where's your head at?" I asked. I had, folded in one hand, the print-out of the alternative stories list. Maybe Berger was right. Maybe I could turn from the terrible topic at hand, leaven things, refocus. Oppenheim shifted in his seat. "Well," he said, picking up a copy of the script, "we have some anonymous sourcing in here."

"We're leading with a woman we name, we're showing her face, we're hearing her voice," I said, referring to Gutierrez.

He let out an exasperated breath. "I don't know how credible she is. I mean, his lawyers are gonna say, they're in a public place, nothing actually happens—"

"But he admits to something having happened before, something serious and specific."

"We've gone over this, he's trying to get rid of her. And anyway, you say right here"—he flipped to the relevant section of the script—"she's got credibility problems."

"No," I said. "We've got sources on the force, sources in the DA's office, saying she was credible."

"It says right here in the approved script!" he said.

"Noah, I wrote the script. We're disclosing the stuff that got thrown at her. But the DA, the cops—"

"The DA didn't go with it! And he's gonna say, she's some hooker—"

"Okay, so we disclose all of that. And we let the public listen and decide."

He shook his head, looked at the page again.

"And it's—how serious is this stuff, really?" he asked, as he had in each of our conversations about the story.

◆

As we spoke, a conversation came back to me, from the year before, during the campaign. At the NBC cafeteria, I'd sat with Oppenheim, a green juice in front of me. He'd leaned in, a little more gossipy than usual, and said that women at NBC News had reported harassment by a Trump campaign official on the trail. "That's a huge story!" I said.

"We can't tell it," Oppenheim replied, with a shrug. "They don't want to, anyway."

"Well, surely there's a way to document it without violating confidences —"

"It's just not gonna happen," he told me, as if to say, "that's life," with the nonchalance and confidence I so admired at the time — so much so that I didn't give it, or his wider views on sexual harassment, more thought.

During his years as a writer at the *Harvard Crimson*, Oppenheim had styled himself as a provocateur. He would pose as an earnest attendee at gatherings of feminist groups, then turn out fiery columns in the *Crimson* about how these groups were full of shit. While columnists don't always write their own headlines, Oppenheim's pieces had titles like "Reading 'Clit Notes'" and "Transgender Absurd," which accurately reflected their content. "There is no question that my most impassioned adversaries have been the members of organized feminist groups," he wrote. "The vitriol of their rhetoric has gone unmatched. Of course, so has their hypocrisy. Apparently, it is easy to blame the patriarchy for all of your woes, and to silence your opponents with accusations of misogyny, but it is more difficult to actually deny oneself the pleasures of cavorting with said patriarchy's handsome sons. I will never forget the fateful evening when I encountered the leader of one prominent women's organization emerging from the anteroom of the Porcellian," an all-male social club. "It seems that political dogmatism comes easy, so long as it does not interfere with one's plans for Saturday night."

After attending a meeting related to the merger of Radcliffe, Harvard's former women's college, with the main undergraduate school, young Noah Oppenheim wrote: "Why are women's meetings any more deserving of protected space than anyone else's?" In a column defending the good old days of same-sex clubs at Harvard, he argued,

"To the angry feminists: There is nothing wrong with single-sex institutions. Men, just like women, need to themselves. We need a place to let our baser instincts have free reign, to let go of whatever exterior polish we affect to appease female sensibilities." He added that "women who fell threatened by the clubs' environments should seek tamer pastures. However apparently women enjoy being confined, pumped full of alcohol and preyed upon. They feel desired, not demeaned."

◆

Years had passed and Noah Oppenheim had matured. But, that day in 2017, as I watched him shift and gaze down, I had a sense that part of his vulnerability to criticism of the story was a sincere belief: that this just wasn't a huge deal, some Hollywood bully, famous in SoHo and Cannes, crossing a line.

"Megyn Kelly did that story about women in tech, and we had a couch full of women—" he was telling me.

"If what you're saying is you sincerely just want more, then tell me," I said. "There's more we can get in place quickly."

He seemed not to hear this. "The temp is in shadow," he said.

"She'll go full face. She said she'll do it if we need it."

He swallowed hard, laughed a little. "Well, I don't know," he said. "It depends what she has to say."

"We know what she has to say. She has evidence. She has messages from an executive within the company—"

"Well, I don't know if we want that, I don't know—"

"And there's a third woman, as I've mentioned, with a rape allegation. Noah, she's close to going on camera. If what you're saying is we need more, I will get us more."

"Now, just a second, I don't know if—we'd have to check with legal before we do anything like that." He seemed frustrated, like he'd expected this to be easier. His face was going pale and slick, as it had when he listened to the audio.

"That's the problem, Noah," I said. "Every time we try to get more, you guys push back."

This seemed to make him angry. "Well, none of this matters," he said. "We've got a much bigger problem." He smacked onto the desk a printed page, then leaned back.

I picked it up. It was a *Los Angeles Times* article from the early 1990s about Weinstein's willingness to work with Woody Allen. Weinstein had never produced Allen's movies, but he'd picked up a few for distribution.

"Harvey says you've got a huge conflict of interest," Oppenheim said.

I looked up from the page. "*Harvey* says?"

Oppenheim's gaze shifted off to the side again. "You know," he said. "Harvey told Rich Greenberg. I never talked to Harvey."

"But we knew this," I said, puzzled. "Greenberg and McHugh and I searched and found he'd worked with both my parents — he worked with everyone in Hollywood."

"He worked with Woody Allen when he was a pariah!" He was raising his voice now.

"A lot of distributors worked with him."

"It doesn't matter. It's not just about that, it's — your sister was sexually assaulted. You wrote that *Hollywood Reporter* piece last year about sexual assault in Hollywood, it caused this splash."

"What are you arguing?" I asked. "That no one with a family member who's been sexually assaulted can report on sexual assault issues?"

He shook his head. "No," he said. "This goes directly to the heart of your — your agenda!"

"Do you think I have an agenda, Noah?" I had the same feeling I'd had in the conversation with Greenberg—that I had to ask direct questions, because it was the only way to expose the space between what he was willing to imply and what he was willing to say.

"Of course not!" Oppenheim said. "But I know you. That's not what this is about, this is about public narrative, and the public narrative is gonna be 'I let Ronan Farrow, who just came out as this— this—*sexual assault crusader*, hating his father—'"

"This wasn't a crusade, it was an assignment. An assignment you gave me!"

"I don't remember that," he said. "I don't think I would have done that."

"Well, it's true. I didn't pitch this of my own initiative, and I didn't report it alone, either. This is something your whole news organization worked on." I slid the printout back across the desk to him. "We knew he was gonna try to smear me in some way," I said. "If this is the best he's got, honestly, I'm relieved, and you should be, too."

"I'd be happier," he said, agitated, "if he'd found video of you fucking in a bathroom or something." The friendship we'd had, which might have made this gay joke merit an eye roll and a laugh, was giving way to something else, where he was just a boss and a network head, and I was annoyed by it.

"Insane!" Jonathan would later yell at no one in particular. "It's insane for him to actually present that article seriously. It's not serious. It's not a real objection. It's fully fucking slimy." Later, every journalist I consulted—Auletta, Brokaw even—would say that there was no conflict, that it was a non-issue. What Oppenheim was describing was a journalist caring about a topic, not having a conflict with a specific person. Even so, I told him I'd be more than happy to put a disclosure on the story.

An almost pleading look crossed Oppenheim's face. "I'm not

saying there isn't a lot here. This is an incredible"—he searched for the end of the sentence—"an incredible *New York* magazine piece. And you know, you want to take it to *New York* magazine, go with God. Go with God." He put up his hands in a gesture of surrender.

I looked at him like he was crazy for a moment and then asked, "Noah, is this story dead or not?" He looked at the script again. Over his shoulder, I saw the deco architecture of historic Rockefeller Plaza.

I thought of my sister. Five years earlier, she'd first told the family she wanted to revive her allegation of sexual assault against Woody Allen. We'd stood in the TV room at our home in Connecticut, with stacks of fading VHS tapes.

"I don't see why you can't just move on," I told her.

"You had that choice!" she said. "I didn't!"

"We have all spent *decades* trying to put this thing behind us. I'm just now trying to launch something serious where people focus on the work. And you want to—want to reset the clock completely."

"This isn't about you," she said. "Don't you see that?"

"No, it's about you. You're smart, you're talented, you have so many other things you can do," I said.

"But I can't. Because it's always there," she said, and then she was crying.

"You do not need to do this. And you are ruining your life if you do."

"Fuck you," she said.

"I support you. But you just—you have to stop."

◆

Oppenheim was looking up from the page. "I can go back to the group. But right now, we can't run this."

Alan Berger's creaky voice drifted through my mind. *"Prioritize the stuff that's working."* I wondered if I had it in me to say *"Okay,"* to turn to other things, to focus on the future. In hindsight, it's clear. But in the moment, you don't know how important a story is going to be. You don't know if you're fighting because you're right, or because of your ego, and your desire to win, and to avoid confirming what everyone thought—that you were young, and inexperienced, and in over your head.

I looked at the story list on my lap. I'd been gripping it so hard it was twisted and moist with sweat. The words *"looks like a Bond villain's lair"* peeked up at me. Just beyond my field of vision, the aurora flashed.

Oppenheim was studying me. He said there couldn't be any more work under the aegis of NBC News. He said, "I can't have you going to any more sources."

I thought of McGowan under the TV lights, saying, *"I hope they're brave, too"*; Nestor, falling into shadow, wondering, *"Is this the way the world works?"*; Gutierrez, listening as Weinstein said, *"I'm used to that"*; Annabella Sciorra telling me, *"I'm sorry."*

I looked at Oppenheim hard. "No," I said.

He looked annoyed.

"Excuse me?"

"No," I said again. "I'm not going to—whatever you said. Stop contact with sources." I balled up the page in my hand. "A lot of women have risked a lot to get this out, are still risking a lot—"

"This is the problem," he said, picking up volume. "You're too close to this."

I considered whether this could be true. Auletta had said he had a "fixation" on the story. I guessed I did too. But I had also grilled these sources. And I was skeptical, ready to follow the facts wherever they led. And I was eager to go to Weinstein for comment, which I had not been allowed to do.

"Okay. So I'm close to it," I said. "So I care. We have evidence, Noah. And if there's a chance of exposing this before it happens to anyone again, then I can't stop." I wanted this to sound masculine and assertive, but I could hear my voice cracking. "If you're sending me packing, this is your news organization, and that's your call," I continued. "But you need to tell me."

"I'm not sending you packing," he said, but he was looking away again. There was a long beat, and then he shot me a wan smile. "This was fun. Wish we could go back to California poison water, right?"

"Yeah," I said. "Guess so." I stood up and thanked him.

I walked out of Noah Oppenheim's office, into the elevator bank and past its giant chrome rendering of the NBC crest — a peacock that said, "NBC is in color now. You can watch it in color. Isn't that amazing?" And it was. It truly was. I moved through the cubicles of the *Today* show newsroom and up the stairs to the fourth floor, with battery acid in my mouth and red parentheses in my palms where I had pressed nails into skin.

# PART III: ARMY OF SPIES

## CHAPTER 29:

# *FAKAKTA*

"**G**o with God," Oppenheim had said. To *New York* magazine, of all places. (Only in Manhattan media circles did heaven mean a middlebrow biweekly.) But how to go with God when the interviews were locked up on NBC's servers? I motioned McHugh over to an empty office and told him what had just happened with Oppenheim. "This is why this guy continues to get off," McHugh said. "So they were coming up with this argument with Weinstein's lawyers, not telling us, waiting to deliver it like a . . . like a death nail," he added, mixing metaphors. "They were trying to get us to wrap up our reporting. That's why nobody's particularly interested in this recent victim that we're talking to." I looked at him, nodded. So this was the end. "It's a bunch of bullshit," he said. "What happened here at this company. It's a big story."

"All the reporting," I said wearily. "They own everything."

He looked at me hard.

"Come here."

Back at our cubicles, McHugh glanced around, leaned to open a desk drawer.

"Say," he said, fumbling through a stack of AV paraphernalia and producing a silver rectangle, "you did have the interviews." He slid across the desk a USB hard drive, with "Poison Valley" written in black Sharpie on one corner.

"Rich . . . ," I said.

He shrugged. "Backup."

I laughed. "They're gonna fire you."

"Let's be honest, neither of us is going to have a job after this."

I moved in like maybe I was gonna hug him and he waved me off. "Alright, alright. Just don't let them bury this."

◆

A few minutes later, I was headed for the safe-deposit box at the bank, walking quickly. I didn't want to give Oppenheim the chance to reconsider his suggestion that I take the story somewhere else. But whom to call? Looking at my phone, I saw Auletta's email from the previous day. If there was an outlet that knew the challenges of going up against Weinstein, it was *The New Yorker*. I dialed Auletta.

"They're not running it? With what you have? The recording?" he asked. "That's ridiculous." He told me he'd make some calls and get back to me.

I'd been trying to reach Jonathan since after the meeting with Oppenheim. "Call me," I wrote. Then, pettily: "I'm going through the biggest thing in my life and you have not been there for me. I'm making critical decisions and I'm making them without you, which sucks. I step out of shoots for you, you don't reciprocate."

When he finally called, he was annoyed.

"I can't step out of meetings to these explosions of texts from you, it's ridiculous," he said.

"I'm just dealing with a lot," I said. "And I feel like I'm doing it alone."

"You're not alone."

"So come be with me."

"You know I can't do that. We're starting a company here, which barely registers for you —"

"There are weird things happening around me," I said. "I feel like I'm going crazy." We both got off the call in a huff. By then, I was descending into the subterranean vault. I put the hard drive in the deposit box and watched as it slid back into place with a nails-on-chalkboard squeal.

The next day, Auletta introduced me to David Remnick, the editor of *The New Yorker*. Remnick and I set a time to talk the following week. "It's an issue," he wrote, "about which we have some experience."

At 30 Rock, anxiety pulsed through McHugh's and my interactions in the newsroom. Greenberg seemed on edge. McHugh cornered him and expressed incredulity about the conflict of interest argument. He reminded Greenberg that we'd looked at industry connections between Weinstein and my family and determined there *wasn't* a conflict of interest.

Greenberg said vaguely that they'd find a way forward.

"So this is not dead at NBC?" McHugh asked.

"Look, I'm not going to debate this," Greenberg replied.

"I'm not debating," McHugh said. "But I have to say, for the record, I disagree."

When I saw Greenberg, likewise, I had questions. "This conflict of interest thing," I said. "Noah said Harvey told you about it."

He found time in between looking panicked to appear sincerely puzzled.

"I never talked about that with Harvey," he said.

❖

It was early afternoon when Oppenheim texted, asking to meet. "I spent all day having conversations about this," he snapped, as I arrived in his office. He looked like he hadn't slept. "We all think that there's a potential"—and then, evidently off my look of pirouetting optimism, he repeated—"*potential* solution." Whoever decided that the story couldn't run had now, it seemed, realized the story couldn't *not* run, either—at least not the way Oppenheim had left it the day before. "We're going to have one of the most veteran senior producers in the company, a *Dateline* person who's been here twenty, thirty years—we're going to assign them to retrace everything you've done, scrub everything."

"Who?" I said.

"Corvo, who's unimpeachable, is going to oversee it. He's picking someone."

I thought of Corvo, the *Dateline* veteran—a company man, but, as far as I knew, a principled one.

"If this is genuinely an effort born of wanting to run it, then I welcome it. Vet the hell out of it. The reporting holds up."

"It's not just the checking," Oppenheim said. "My view is that the tape and Harvey Weinstein grabbing a lady's breasts a couple of years ago, that's not national news." I started to talk and he held up a hand. "It's news somewhere. Do it for the *Hollywood Reporter*, great, it's news there. For the *Today* show, a movie producer grabbing a lady is not news."

He said they wanted more, and I said that was great too. I could take Gutierrez up on her offer to come in, and shoot with Canosa, and reshoot with Nestor.

"No, no, no," he said. "We're picking this producer to vet things. Everyone we're considering is on vacation till Monday. Let's just hang tight till then," he said.

"Noah, if you want more, I need to be able to go out and get it."

"I know, I know," he said. "I'm just saying hang tight till Monday."

"This is *fakakt*," McHugh was saying.

"Please, Rich, no more Yiddish, and it's *fakakta*—"

"It calls into question my credibility, which I fucking—"

"No, it doesn't," I said.

"How's that? We *have had* a trusted producer vetting every element of this. I've been there the whole time—"

"Oh, sorry!" a chirpy young *Today* show producer said, opening the door. We were in a mailroom near the *Today* show bullpen. Everything else was full. The producer started sorting through mail and futzing with FedEx forms.

We stood awkwardly for a moment.

"So, life's good?" I managed.

"Yeah," she said. "Great. You know. Sad the summer's over."

"Sure," I said.

When the door swung shut behind her, I turned to McHugh. "Rich, I'm not gonna let them force you out."

"But it *is* forcing me out," McHugh continued under his breath. "What the hell is this?"

"Basically it's a special prosecutor role, and if they wanna shut this thing down, sure, they can, but it was very promising."

Rich looked at me like I was insane. "They said no, then they realized it's a PR scandal. And now they're just gonna rope-a-dope us to death until it's March and we're still talking about this. Basically, 'we need more, we need more'; they're not gonna say no to us — It's okay, come in."

"Sorry!" the producer squeaked, and tiptoed back over to grab some document she'd left behind.

I smiled tightly, then said to McHugh, "Don't you think that's a *little* conspiratorial? Maybe they'll run it."

"Bottom line, it's trouble that the president of NBC News is talking directly with Harvey and lying to us about it." He was sulking. "What are you gonna do about the meeting with Remnick next week?"

I thought about this. "I keep it, and we keep that option waiting in the wings. Potentially propose doing it for both. I don't know."

"You've got to be careful now," McHugh said, "because, say it does come out in another publication, and it does look bad for NBC, they could so easily turn on us —"

"Hello!" said one of three smiling interns who had just opened the door. "Don't mind us."

❖

Despite McHugh's skepticism, I was lifted, as I left Rockefeller Plaza and made my way through the harsh neons of Times Square, by newfound optimism. "NBC's a bird in the hand. As long as they're letting you keep reporting, stick with them," Jonathan said, on the phone from Los Angeles. "Noah's in over his head, he's not malicious."

My feeling that the obstacles of the last month had been a passing fever dream was reinforced when Thomas McFadden, from NBC security, got back in touch to say he had an update. They'd figured out where at least some of the menacing messages came from. It turned out I really did have your run-of-the-mill stalkers with mental health issues. No grand conspiracies, no one lurking outside the apartment, I told myself.

Harvey Weinstein's mood was shifting too. In conversations with those around him, he'd once again gone from jubilant claims that his contacts at NBC had promised the story was killed to concern that it hadn't happened cleanly and I might still be working. Weinstein knew Boies was friendly with Lack, and asked if the attorney might put in a call to the network head.

"I can call Andy and see if he'll tell me," was all Boies would say.

More sources were telling me that they were getting calls from Weinstein or his associates that they found unsettling. Katrina Wolfe, who had gone on camera to say she'd witnessed the London settlement process, nervously told me that she'd gotten a call from a veteran Weinstein producer named Denise Doyle Chambers. Doyle Chambers said that she and another veteran producer, Pam Lubell, were back working for Weinstein, conducting research for a book. A "fun book," Lubell would later say, "on the old times, the heyday, of Miramax." Weinstein had asked them to write down all the employees they knew and get in touch with them. Later, how much the two women believed this cover story would be a subject of public speculation. Lubell, anyway, seemed to have convinced herself: she even put together a book proposal. On its cover, Bob and Harvey Weinstein smiled in black and white. The graphic above them read: "MIRAMAX: THOSE WERE THE DAYS MY FRIEND, I THOUGHT THEY'D NEVER END."

But the cover story, threadbare to begin with, quickly frayed.

In early August, Weinstein called the two women back into the office. "You know what, we're going to put a hold on the book," he said. He asked Doyle Chambers and Lubell to "call some of your friends from the list and see if they got calls from the press."

On the phone with Wolfe, Doyle Chambers didn't make much small talk about the good old days before she came to the point. Weinstein wanted to know if Wolfe had heard from any reporters: if she'd heard, specifically, from me. And he wanted copies of any emails she'd received or sent. Wolfe, rattled, sent my messages to Doyle Chambers and denied she'd ever responded to them.

And there was something else: the names Doyle Chambers and Lubell compiled and called were being added to a larger master list. The list was light on insiders from the glory days, and heavy on women Weinstein had worked with, and troublesome reporters. It was color coded: some names highlighted in red, indicating urgency, especially among the women. As Doyle Chambers and Lubell updated the list based on their calls, they weren't told that their work was being sent to Black Cube's offices in Tel Aviv and London, then onward to operatives around the world, to serve as a basis for their increasingly involved work on Weinstein's behalf.

◆

At the same time, John Ksar, an agent I worked with at the Harry Walker speaking agency, was fielding inquiries from a wealth management firm in London. Its representative, Diana Filip, said that she was planning a gala focused on women's representation in the workplace. She wanted a reporter well-versed in that issue to give a speech, or possibly even several.

Ksar had been in the business a long time and was wise to attempts to fish for information. But Filip had all her answers lined up. She rattled off the particulars, including the investors who would be in the room. She said that her firm was still finalizing its decision. They'd need to meet with me first. "I hope such a meeting could be arranged sometime in the coming weeks, in fact I'm planning to be in NY next week so if Mr Farrow is available that might be a good opportunity," she wrote in an email. It was the first of several messages saying that a meeting had to happen promptly; and eventually, when this failed to gain traction, that she'd settle for a call with me. For more than a month, the emails from Diana Filip kept coming. Ksar figured she was just really, really into investigative reporting.

## CHAPTER 30:

# *BOTTLE*

*T*he dawn after my latest meeting with Oppenheim, the private investigators settled in outside of my front door. Khaykin was already there when Ostrovskiy ambled over from the bagel place around the corner. "Wang anything?" Ostrovskiy had texted. "No man, Ty," Khaykin replied. A few minutes later, they assumed their positions on the street outside, watching.

Immediately after emerging from the meeting with Oppenheim, I'd sent an email to David Corvo, and we'd agreed to meet. Inside my apartment, I put on a white button-down shirt, stuffed my notes into a bag, and headed out into the light.

At just after eight thirty, the private investigators spotted a young man with fair hair, wearing a white shirt and carrying a knapsack. They scrutinized the figure. They'd been given reference photos of me and, the day before, had undertaken additional database searches. A lot of the surveillance business was guesswork, but this looked like their mark. Ostrovskiy drove, rounding the corner just after the target, recording on a Panasonic camcorder. "I'm heading to 30 rock for now," he texted. Khaykin gave chase on foot, descending into the Columbus Circle subway stop, then getting on a downtown train.

For the private investigators, long days of surveillance often meant few opportunities for bathroom breaks. "How far are you?" Ostrovskiy texted his boss later that day, while sitting in his car awaiting the next emergence of their target. "I need to use a bottle. If you nearby I can wait." Khaykin was not, it came to pass, nearby. Ostrovskiy eyed the beverage he'd finished off earlier, resigned himself, picked it up, and went.

"Ok all good now," he texted his boss.

By the time I made it to Rockefeller Plaza, I'd sweated through the white shirt. Corvo, in his office near the rest of the *Dateline* team, smiled and asked, "How's it going?"

"I gather we're going to be working together," I said.

"Oh, that," he said. "I've only gotten the broad strokes."

I ran Corvo through the basics: the audio, the numerous allegations against Harvey Weinstein that had remained in the script after the legal review, Gutierrez's unwavering willingness to be named and to lead the story, Nestor's openness to showing her face to replace McGowan. His head bobbed genially as he listened. "Sounds compelling," he said, and smiled.

Corvo had dealt with tough stories about sexual assault allegations before. In 1999, during Andy Lack's previous tenure at NBC News, Corvo had overseen the network's interview with Juanita Broaddrick, who had accused Bill Clinton of rape twenty-one years earlier. The network had reviewed the interview for a little more than a month after it was recorded, airing it only after Broaddrick, frustrated, had taken the story to the *Wall Street Journal*, the *Washington Post*, and the *New York Times*. "If Dorothy Rabinowitz hadn't come to interview me, I don't think NBC would ever have played it,"

Broaddrick later said, referring to the *Wall Street Journal* reporter who ultimately broke the story. "I had absolutely given up."

I was unaware that Corvo also had a personal history with sexual harassment issues. In 2007, he'd appeared to fixate on one employee, sending her leering messages. "In our renewed effort to avoid misunderstandings," he wrote, "we have to get one 'ground rule' very clear: whenever you go to the pool, you must let me know. A long distance glimpse, even, will make my day." On a hot day, he'd added, "I love warm weather, but are you going to a school event dressed like that?" Repeatedly, he'd find or create openings to be alone with the woman. Eventually she complained to management. She was promoted into a new role and stayed at the company for years after. Corvo's ascent within the network continued uninterrupted.

I left the meeting with Corvo feeling reassured. The next day, unbeknownst to me, NBC finalized a nearly $1,000,000 separation agreement with Corvo's accuser. When the *Daily Beast* later reported on the allegations, the network would say that the payout had been a mere coincidence, unrelated to her complaint. The agreement forbade her from ever speaking negatively about her time at NBC.

❖

A few mornings later, the private investigators were in position on the Upper West Side again. This time, Ostrovskiy was on duty. "So far haven't seen him," he texted his boss. Then he spotted the young man with fair hair again. Ostrovskiy hopped out of his car and followed on foot. He drew close, within touching distance. Then he frowned, punched a number into his phone.

Upstairs in my apartment, I picked up. "Hello?" I said, and heard a brief exclamation in Russian, before the line went dead. In front of Ostrovskiy, the neighbor to whom I bore a passing resemblance walked on, blithely unaware, definitely not taking a call.

"Seems like no march," Ostrovskiy texted Khaykin. "Back at residence now." In his car, he googled for better photos of me. "Found a good ID pic," he wrote, and sent his boss a picture of me and my sister Dylan, aged four and six, perhaps, in our parents' arms. "Going off this one we should be good."

"Lol," replied Khaykin. Later, as if to make sure Ostrovskiy was kidding, Khaykin sent a screenshot from one of the dossiers with the blue Times New Roman headers, showing my birthday.

❖

The offices of *The New Yorker* encircled the thirty-eighth floor of One World Trade Center, an ouroboros of news and highbrow commentary and tote bags. It was bright and airy and modern. My meeting with David Remnick was set for midday. As I walked in, my phone played a scherzo of alerts. A series of new spam texts, this time asking me to opt into or out of some kind of political survey. I swiped them away as a gangly assistant ushered me into the small conference room adjoining Remnick's office.

David Remnick would someday be a hundred years old and they'd still call him a wunderkind. He'd started as a reporter covering both sports and crime for the *Washington Post* before becoming the paper's Moscow correspondent, which had led to a celebrated book about Russia, and a Pulitzer Prize in his thirties. By that summer, he was in his late fifties, gray creeping into his black curls, and still, there was a boyishness to him. When his wife later mentioned that he was tall, this was somehow news to me. He was the rare man of his stature, physical and professional, who did not make you feel small. He sat, in jeans and a jacket, in one of the office chairs around the conference room table, body language relaxed but curious.

He'd brought with him a young editor, Deirdre Foley-Mendelssohn, who'd joined the magazine earlier that year after stints at *Harper's* and the *Paris Review*. Foley-Mendelssohn was thin and quiet and intense. The evening before, Remnick had sat in her office and suggested she review Auletta's old profile of Weinstein. She'd done more than that, reading widely.

As we sat together and I outlined the reporting, I could see Remnick thinking hard. "And you think you can get more?" he said.

"I know I can," I replied, and told him about the leads NBC was stalling on.

He asked if he could hear the tape, and, for the second time that summer, I sat in front of leadership at a media outlet and put my phone on a table and hit Play.

Remnick and Foley-Mendelssohn listened. Their reaction was the polar opposite of Oppenheim's. There was a stunned quiet afterward. "It's not just the admission," Foley-Mendelssohn said finally. "It's the tone, the not taking no for an answer."

"And NBC is letting you walk away with all this?" Remnick asked. "Who is this person at NBC? Oppenheim?"

"Oppenheim," I confirmed.

"And he's a screenwriter, you say?"

"He wrote *Jackie*," I replied.

"That," Remnick said gravely, "was a bad movie."

Ostrovskiy and a colleague had made a last, fruitless stop outside the New York Times Building that morning. Then Khaykin called to relay fresh orders about me: *"Track his cell phone."* Ostrovskiy thought back to Khaykin's boast, the previous fall, that he was capable of doing that.

Shortly after noon, Khaykin started sending screenshots of maps, marked with pin-drops indicating the latitude, longitude, and elevation of a moving target. Maybe Khaykin hadn't been full of shit after all: the pinpointed locations synced up exactly with my trip to the meeting with Remnick.

❖

I was frank with the *New Yorker* editors about every aspect of the reporting, including my hopes about its future at NBC. "I honestly don't know what's happening over there," I said. "But I work there, and if there's a chance this last review is sincere, I have to give it a shot. I owe it to my producer there."

Remnick made it clear that if NBC either killed the story again or didn't intend to run its version first, he was interested. There would be more work to do, of course. The more evidence I accumulated, the better. Weinstein and his legal team, Remnick knew from experience, would be ready for a fight. But for the first time that summer, a news outlet was actively encouraging me. Remnick told me to keep Foley-Mendelssohn apprised as the outstanding pieces of reporting, including the on-camera interview Canosa was contemplating, fell into place.

"I'm not expecting you to promise anything yet, but I think there's enough here to publish something substantial," I said.

He nodded. "I think there may be."

After the meeting, Remnick went back into his office, and I said my goodbyes to Foley-Mendelssohn. "If they don't let you continue for some reason," she said, "call."

As I stepped out into the lobby, perhaps two hundred text messages flooded my phone. "(Survey) Should Trump be impeached?" they read, identically, one after another. "Reply to cast your vote. To unsubscribe from our list..." Each came from a different number. I stood, swiping away the texts, finally giving up and responding to opt out, which seemed not to help.

◆

"It's the area near World Trade Center," Ostrovskiy wrote to Khaykin after receiving the maps. "Heading there now." And then: "Any additional info where to expect him to come out from?" and "Building at that address? Or he's outside possibly?"

"No data," Khaykin replied.

"Ok will look around."

Amid the flurry of survey texts, a message from McHugh came in, asking for an ETA. I was due back at NBC. I moved toward the subway, then reconsidered. I'd felt an odd anxiety since the day I'd wondered whether I was being followed. I moved out onto the street instead and hailed a cab. As I made my way uptown, I went right by the private investigators.

◆

Soon after, McHugh and I sat with the two producers Corvo had assigned to work on his review of the reporting. Both seemed earnestly interested, but it was also clear that the decisions about the fate of the story would be made above their pay grade. The meeting was rushed: both producers were in and out of screenings of *Dateline* stories. McHugh and I gave them what reporting materials we could print quickly, making it clear that there was more, including the sensitive material in the bank vault. Corvo didn't listen to the tape. Neither did the lead producer. As it turned out, they never would.

When we stepped out of the meeting, McHugh had a missed call from a number he didn't recognize. It was Lanny Davis, the lawyer and public relations operative.

"I understand you're working with Ronan Farrow on a story about Harvey," Davis said. "Is that correct? Is that story still running? When do you plan to run it?"

McHugh told him he couldn't say anything about ongoing reporting. Davis said he was on vacation and gave McHugh his cell phone number. "I've worked with the Clintons for many years and now I'm working with Harvey," Davis said. "And I'm here to help." McHugh hurried off the phone and for the rest of the afternoon seemed a little off balance.

❖

I'd booked a flight to Los Angeles that evening. I hoped I might finally persuade Canosa to go on camera. Nestor, too, had agreed to meet, to map out a potential full-face interview.

As I stepped into the departures terminal at JFK, Canosa called. She sounded nervous. "He's been calling me," she said. Weinstein seemed to be keeping her close, telling her how much he valued her loyalty.

"If you feel like you can't do this—"

"No," she said, firmly. Her face would be in shadow, but she would do it. "I'll give the interview." We set a time.

The most recent rationale Oppenheim had offered for stopping the reporting—waiting for Corvo to assign a producer—had come and gone. McHugh and I let NBC know that we'd be proceeding with the interview.

❖

After our near-miss at the World Trade Center, the private investigators idled in the neighborhood. Khaykin chain-smoked, glancing at his phone, awaiting further GPS data that never came. That evening, Ostrovskiy staked out my apartment again, fruitlessly. "Don't worry about the Ronan time at all," he texted his boss. "Seriously I understand the situation and did not expect to get paid unless we actually found him."

But Weinstein did seem worried by the lack of updates. By then, he was trying to enlist additional investigators. He met with Glenn Simpson, whose firm Fusion GPS was best known for hiring former MI-6 agent Christopher Steele to compile a dossier about Donald Trump. Simpson declined to take the job. Weinstein also called Sam Anson, an investigator at Guidepost Solutions. They spoke for about twenty minutes. Anson would later recall that Weinstein sounded "agitated, distressed, not happy." He made clear that the work would focus on women accusing him of sexual misconduct and reporters on the story. Anson had a follow-up conversation with Weinstein's lawyers, but didn't take the job either. The day after Khaykin and Ostrovskiy lost me, Weinstein sent Anson an email with the latest version of his target list. Familiar names were highlighted in red: McGowan; Sciorra; Gigliotti; Irwin Reiter, the executive who had sent Emily Nestor the sympathetic messages. "The red flags," Weinstein wrote, "are the first to call."

# CHAPTER 31:

# *SYZYGY*

*P*rivate investigators weren't the only way Weinstein was seeking answers. David Boies placed the call to Andy Lack as he'd promised Weinstein he would. Boies asked Lack whether work on the story was ongoing.

Lack was reasonable and warm. He stayed quiet for most of the call, as he had during the earlier conversation with Weinstein, when the studio head had suggested that sleeping with employees was common practice. During his tenure as executive producer of *West 57th* in the late eighties, Lack, who was married at the time, had pursued sexual relationships with underlings and talent. Jane Wallace, one of the show's correspondents, said that Lack was "almost unrelenting." When she started work at the show, she said, Lack asked her to go to dinner with him "every day for almost a month," saying he wanted to celebrate her contract. "If your boss does that, what are you gonna say?" she later told me. "You know if you say 'I don't want to celebrate with you,' you're asking for trouble." Wallace said that it was "ultimately consensual, but I didn't just get flirted with. I got worked over." The relationship eventually soured. Lack, she said, became volatile. As she left the show, she recalled him yelling, "You will never get credit." Then the network deployed a tactic that the public was barely conscious of at the time: it offered her a substantial payout to sign a binding nondisclosure agreement. Wallace accepted. "It wasn't till I really got out of there that I felt the full force of it. Of how disgusted I was," she told me. "The truth is, if he hadn't been like that, I would have kept that job. I loved that job."

Several other former employees of Lack's recalled another relationship with a young associate producer who worked for him named Jennifer Laird. When the relationship ended, colleagues recalled Lack turning hostile, taking what they saw as punitive actions. When Laird asked to be reassigned, Lack wouldn't allow it. He compelled her to work longer hours, and on weekends, and proposed she cancel vacations. Through a spokesperson, Lack denied taking any retaliatory actions against Laird. Laird confirmed that the relationship had happened, and said the aftermath was "extremely uncomfortable." She told me, "There's clearly a reason you don't get involved with your boss."

Lack's reputation had preceded him in his latest role at NBC. "Why would you do that?" one executive recalled asking Steve Burke upon learning of his decision to reinstate Lack. "The reason you have those cultural problems down there—he created that!"

That day on the phone with Boies, Lack was less quiet when the conversation turned to the story's fate at NBC. "We've told Harvey we're not doing a story," Lack said. "If we decide to do a story, we'll tell him."

◆

As I flew to Los Angeles the evening after the meeting at *The New Yorker*, Greenberg called McHugh, sounding frantic. He said Oppenheim had told him to "hit the pause button on this."

"Meaning I can't report anything else?" McHugh said.

"That's coming from our boss," Greenberg replied. "That's an order."

Then, the following morning, Greenberg called me and said the same thing.

"Noah's directive is very clear-cut," he told me. "We can't shoot this interview. We are pausing."

I was at Jonathan's place in West Hollywood. He walked over, agape. "To be clear, you're ordering me to cancel this interview," I told Greenberg.

There was a long silence. "It's a pause," he said.

"The interview is scheduled. You're asking me to un-schedule it. How is that a pause?"

"Ronan," he said, in a huff now. "You have to stop."

"Do we know how long this pause is?" I asked. "Why exactly is NBC News ordering us to stop reporting?"

He sounded at sea.

"I—he—Harvey's lawyers have made the argument that every employee is subject to a nondisclosure agreement," he said. "And we can't just go encouraging them to breach those."

"Rich, that's just not how legal exposure works. *Conducting* the interview doesn't—"

"This is Noah's decision," he said. "I understand if you don't like it, but I don't think any of us is in a position to disagree with it."

❖

I paced the length of the apartment, debating the situation with Jonathan. Oppenheim's suggestion that I bring the story to another outlet felt precarious. "He knows this is a scandal when it runs somewhere else, doesn't he?" Jonathan pointed out. I wanted to keep fighting the ban on reporting. But if I did so, the dynamic might turn openly acrimonious, and the network might try to block me from taking the material out the door.

Jonathan proposed what I did next. I called Oppenheim and said I'd like to take him up on the offer to "go with God" to a print outlet, but presented it as something nonthreatening and friendly. I told him, truthfully, that I had preliminary interest from a print editor. I didn't say which one. I suggested that NBC could continue to shoot my interviews and run a television version after I broke the story in print.

"I don't want to sort of stand in the way of you proceeding with something. My instinct is it sounds like a reasonable proposal," Oppenheim said. He sounded overcome with relief. "Let me take ten minutes and take a breath, and I'll come back to you."

As promised, ten minutes later, he texted saying that sounded fine. I asked if I could still have an NBC crew in the next interview, with Canosa. I pointed out that it wouldn't obligate him to air it, it would just preserve the option. "Unfortunately," he replied, "We can't move forward with anything for NBC until the review is complete."

Within twenty-four hours, Oppenheim would meet with Corvo and the producers working under him and halt the review. One of the producers told the group that Nestor was "not ready to be outed." Nestor, who had already told me she'd go on the record if I needed it, denied saying anything of the kind. Corvo, at one point, argued that the reporting was insufficiently visual and wouldn't make for good television.

Greenberg then gave McHugh a final order to stop taking calls about the story. "You are to stand down," he said. McHugh thought of all the times Weinstein had successfully quashed the story in the past, and replied, "We are letting him win."

With no news organization behind the story, I had no one to consult about security, and no protection if Weinstein decided to sue me personally. I called Foley-Mendelssohn. "He's obviously already threatened NBC," I said, "I know the story's the important thing, but I'm trying to figure out how exposed I am here."

"Send me everything you have," she said. "We can start a conversation about this."

"But your gut is I keep these interviews going, without a news outlet behind me?"

She considered this.

"I don't know the specific legal risks here. But I don't think you should cancel things. You never stop reporting."

Foley-Mendelssohn offered to introduce me to *The New Yorker*'s lawyer, Fabio Bertoni. Rendering legal advice, even informal legal advice, to someone the magazine hadn't taken on as a writer was outside of standard operating procedure. But Foley-Mendelssohn sensed how far out on a limb I was.

As I waited for word from Remnick, I sent Foley-Mendelssohn too many nervous texts, letting her know I was proceeding with reporting calls, reading the tea leaves of her responses for any trace of further commitment.

I did, as promised, hear from Fabio Bertoni. He had previously worked at *American Lawyer* magazine and HarperCollins, fending off precisely the kind of threats to publication that I was confronting. When I explained NBC's insistence on halting reporting, supposedly due to concerns about legal exposure, he seemed genuinely at a loss. "The exposure happens when you run the story," he said. "It would be extremely unusual to see any legal action over unpublished reporting." When I told him the argument had been tortious interference, he was even more confused. He made the same point I'd tried to make in my own conversations with the network: a significant portion of all political and business reporting would be impossible if news organizations looked askance at talking to employees with nondisclosure agreements. My early experiences at *The New Yorker* felt like those videos where lab animals walk on grass for the first time.

"So do I keep going, even knowing he's actively threatening?" I asked.

"Here's the thing," Bertoni said. "It's easy for people to make scary legal threats. It's another thing entirely to act on them."

❖

I'd promised Canosa I'd put her on camera, and I didn't want to spook her by changing that plan. And so I set about trying to hire a crew myself. McHugh—ordered not to help with the shoot but still bent on doing so, because he was just that kind of guy—sent me name after name. The Monday in late August chosen for the interview coincided with a rare total eclipse of the sun. Most of the freelance crews we contacted were busy shooting the eclipse from ideal vantage points in places like Wyoming. For the few still in town, there was a further wrinkle: almost everyone had worked on Weinstein productions or stood to in the future. I finally found a shooter named Ulli Bonnekamp. Either because he knew I was doing it alone or because he could sense it was a subject matter worth caring about, he gave me a reasonable rate.

I asked Canosa if she'd be more comfortable shooting in a hotel room, and she said being back at Jonathan's place, where she'd bonded with the dog, suited her fine. As the syzygy commenced, the crew and I got to work retrofitting the house in West Hollywood. We carted around sandbags and tripods, and taped blackout cloth over the windows, and generally did not treat Jonathan's furniture with great compassion.

Midafternoon, a text came in from Oppenheim. "Just to reiterate in writing, any further reporting you're doing, including today's interview, is not on behalf of or with the blessing of NBC. That needs to be clear not only to you, but anyone you make speak with."

"You know my view," I wrote back. "But I understand and am honoring this."

When Canosa arrived, I was honest with her about the uncertainty of the story's future. I told her the interview still had value. That I'd go to the mat to make it public somewhere. She didn't balk, and that evening, we started rolling. The interview was devastating. "He creates the situation in which your silence will benefit you more than speaking out will," Canosa said of Weinstein.

"And for any news outlet grappling with the decision of whether this is an important story, whether your allegation is serious enough, credible enough," I asked, "what would you say to them?"

"If you don't run with this, if you don't move forward with this and expose him, you're on the wrong side of history," she said. "He's going to be exposed. It benefits you to do it and not wait till he is and everyone knows you were sitting on information that could have prevented other women going through it, for potentially years to come."

# CHAPTER 32:

# *HURRICANE*

All through those last weeks of August, what would eventually become a Category 4 hurricane bore down on the Gulf of Mexico. As Emily Nestor and I sat down at a coffee shop in Brentwood, scenes of devastation flickered on a television in the corner. Since Nestor had told me she was open to showing her face if NBC wanted it, she hadn't evinced any signs of backing down. But I also hadn't told her that the story's institutional support had dissipated, and that going on the record now meant a print fact-checking process.

"I'm asking you if you'll still put your name on this," I said. I told her that I was going to send my draft to *The New Yorker*, and that the magazine would decide whether to take on the story based on it. I told her every name still counted.

"I've had a lot of time to think about this," she said. I studied the worried face of this stranger I'd asked to upend her life, then jerked around for months. She was quiet for a moment, then said, "I'm going to do it."

I raced out of the coffee shop to put the finishing touches on the draft. Here is how it described the reporting *The New Yorker* would be considering, that NBC News had sent away:

In the course of a nine month investigation, five women alleged to me directly that Harvey Weinstein committed multiple acts of sexual harassment and abuse. The allegations range from inappropriate sexual propositions directed at employees, to groping and touching of the kind confessed to in the NYPD tape, to two claims of rape. The allegations span nearly twenty years. Many of the women worked for Weinstein, and all of their claims involved ostensibly professional meetings, which they claim Weinstein used to lure them to hotels where they experienced unwanted sexual advances. In at least three cases, Weinstein used large financial settlements with strict nondisclosure agreements to prevent criminal proceedings and public revelation.

Sixteen former and current executives and assistants at Weinstein's companies corroborated those allegations, saying they witnessed unwanted sexual advances, inappropriate touching, and a pattern that included Weinstein using company resources to set up sexual liaisons of the type described in the allegations.

I sent the draft to Foley-Mendelssohn. On a muted TV in Jonathan's living room, Hurricane Harvey wreaked havoc.

◆

Back at 30 Rockefeller Plaza, the calls kept coming in from Weinstein and his intermediaries. One afternoon, Lanny Davis received a request from Weinstein much like the ones Boies was fielding. Davis was in a meeting between Weinstein's team and the *New York Times* focused on the allegations that Weinstein had misused funds raised for amfAR, The Foundation for AIDS Research.

Afterward, Weinstein told Davis, "I just talked to someone at NBC. Would you go over there and find out the status of the story?"

"Harvey," Davis replied, "I told you I'm not involved in this women's issue."

"All I'm asking is for you to go over and meet someone in the lobby and ask what's the status on the story," Weinstein said.

"If I'm gonna do this, I want someone else with me," Davis replied.

At this, Weinstein sounded nervous. "Why do you want that?" he asked.

"Because I'm not supposed to be doing this issue, and I want someone to be available to confirm exactly the words I used."

Weinstein, a little huffy, said that was fine, and Davis, joined by a Weinstein Company employee, headed to 30 Rock. At the marble visitors' desk, Davis said he was there for Noah Oppenheim.

"Mr. Oppenheim knows I'm coming," he told the assistant working the desk. Later, NBC would say that Davis ambushed Oppenheim. Of that claim, Davis told me, "This is a rare exception to my usual reluctance to use the word 'lie.' I'm absolutely certain someone knew that was a deliberate misrepresentation."

What is not in dispute is that, a few minutes later, Oppenheim came down. The Weinstein Company employee Davis had brought with him watched from a short distance away.

"What is the status of the Ronan Farrow story on Harvey?" Davis asked.

Oppenheim answered quickly. "Oh, he's no longer working on the story," he said. "He's not working for us." The way he said it made Davis wonder if I'd been fired altogether.

❖

It was September 5 and still hot when I headed back to *The New Yorker*. In the elevator up, I did a little sign of the cross, almost involuntarily. Remnick and Foley-Mendelssohn, along with Bertoni, the lawyer, Dorothy Wickenden, an executive editor, and Natalie Raabe, the magazine's head of communications, sat opposite me at the table in Remnick's conference room. I had no idea what Remnick would say.

"I think everyone's aware of the story," he said. "But why don't you update us."

I ran through much the same summary from the top of the draft, culminating in how the interview with Canosa had fallen into place. I mentioned the ongoing pressure on sources, the calls they were getting.

"Are these sources willing to stand by what they've told you in court?" Bertoni asked. "Can you see if they'll do that?"

I told Bertoni that I'd already put the question to several major sources, and that they'd said yes.

The rhythm of the conversation picked up: Remnick and Bertoni took turns asking questions about specific pieces of reporting and the evidence that backed them up. Did I have the messages from Reiter, the executive who acknowledged to Nestor the pattern of misconduct? I did. Was Gutierrez willing to show us her contract? She was. Foley-Mendelssohn, by then intimately familiar with the story, chimed in periodically, reminding them of the existence of a secondary source here, a document there.

Later, several people in that room would reach for the same adjectives to describe me: sad, desperate, trying to preempt pushback at every turn. It was, one said, like I was defending a dissertation.

I thought of the meeting weeks before, when Oppenheim had first killed the story. I studied the faces across from me, trying to decide how to convey the stakes. Wickenden, a veteran of decades in the magazine business, said gently, "You've been working on this a long time, haven't you?"

I thought, again, of Sciorra's voice; of Gutierrez, flinching as the recording of Weinstein played; of Nestor, making her decision. "I know there's a chance of litigation here," I said. "I know bringing the story here would mean more reviewing, more fact-checking. I just think there's enough here that it deserves that chance."

A silence across the room, a few glances exchanged.

"Alright," said Remnick, without drama, in a scene from a different movie. "You'll work with Deirdre. No guarantees until this is fact-checked."

Remnick was thoughtful, restrained. He had published Seymour Hersh's contentious national security reporting on Afghanistan and Pakistan, and Lawrence Wright's investigation into the Church of Scientology. But this would be a new and specific kind of challenge. "We do this straight down the middle," he said. "Just the facts."

❖

Not long after, at the Loews Regency hotel on Park Avenue, Harvey Weinstein met with an actress, then retired to a corner with a familiar companion: Dylan Howard, of the *National Enquirer.* By then, Howard and Weinstein were spending more time together. Often, Howard told colleagues trying to reach him, "I'm with Harvey." Howard produced several thick manila folders. He and Weinstein spent the following hours scrutinizing their contents, heads bowed in hushed conversation. At one point, one of Weinstein's assistants walked over to the two men's table to inform Weinstein that he had an incoming call. Weinstein scrambled to cover up the documents. "What the *fuck* are you doing back here?!" he shouted. Howard offered a sympathetic glance. Later he whispered to the assistant, "Not jealous of your job!"

Howard's focus on Weinstein's opponents had continued. So had his interest in Matt Lauer, a figure the *Enquirer* had long circled.

Discussing his targets that summer with a reporter, Howard joked about his focus on the anchor. "I'm sure I'm not on Matt Lauer's Christmas card," he deadpanned. Since Howard had examined the "kill file" of unpublished reporting about Lauer, the *Enquirer* had run three negative stories about the *Today* show anchor. A fourth would arrive shortly after the meeting with Weinstein at the Loews Regency. The stories were preoccupied with Lauer's infidelity, particularly at work. "NBC Gives Sleazy Lauer One More Chance," read one headline. "Hey Matt, That's Not Your Wife!" read another.

CHAPTER 33:

# *GOOSE*

*B*y then, Weinstein was acting frantically, deploying his usual mix of intimidation and influence in the media. Howard's boss, David Pecker of American Media Inc., had long been a close ally, but started appearing more frequently in Weinstein's emails. "Dear David, I just tried you," Weinstein wrote late that September. "Are you available for a call now?" Pecker responded, "I am in Saudi Arabia on business." Later, Weinstein proposed an alliance to purchase *Rolling Stone* magazine for Pecker to add to his media empire and run behind the scenes. Pecker at first demurred, then acceded. "I can reduce costs and bring the profits to $10mm.... If you want it you can own 52% for $45mm. I would be happy to do all the back office for you and be responsible for the magazine print and digital operations."

Weinstein amplified his outreach to NBC, too. There were emails and calls to Deborah Turness, Oppenheim's predecessor, who was now in charge of international content. Weinstein proposed cutting a deal with Turness around a documentary he was making about Clinton. "Your Hillary doc series sounds absolutely stunning," Turness wrote. "I am here and would commit to turning our platforms into dedicated 'Hillary channels' for several nights!"

Late that month, Weinstein sent an email to Ron Meyer, the veteran head of Universal Studios and still, at the time, vice chairman of NBCUniversal. "Dear Ron," he wrote. "I wanted to talk to you about Universal doing our home video and VOD—we're talking to your guys and I think it's always good to have a word from the top." Meyer replied, "I would love to make this work." Emails from the Weinstein Company's COO, David Glasser, show the proposed deal coalescing. A term sheet was drafted, then submitted to the company's senior management for approval. Glasser's team began discussing the finer points with two home entertainment executives at NBCUniversal. "I look forward to us being in business together," Meyer wrote soon after. "As I told you, if there is anything but a yes please let me know." The deal never went ahead.

Weinstein had seemed relieved after Lanny Davis's report back on the meeting with Oppenheim and Boies's update after the call with Lack. Weinstein had taken both as unambiguous confirmation that the story was dropped, and possibly me with it. But he wanted more. He ordered another round of calls from his legal team to NBC's. It wasn't long before Susan Weiner was on the phone with one of Davis's attorneys, using similar language: I was, she said, no longer working for NBC News.

I knew nothing of this. I still had time left in my contract with NBC News and, as far as I knew, was still planning to renew it. The killing of the story had shaken me, but I still felt loyal to the network, and to my bosses there. Greenberg sounded enthused about expanding my investigative work over the upcoming years. Don Nash, the *Today* executive producer, proposed an expanded role for me as the show's main investigative correspondent.

On September 11, after McHugh and I returned from one of our ongoing shoots, for a story about health care, I sat down with Oppenheim again. There was a beat of small talk about his Hollywood projects, including a long-gestating script about Harry Houdini. He was mulling possible lead actors. I suggested Michael Fassbender. Oppenheim said, like a screenwriter's caricature of a Hollywood agent, that the actor couldn't open a movie. I murmured something about *Assassin's Creed*, and finally, it seemed, we'd agreed on something we found objectionable in Hollywood.

I told Oppenheim about my hopes for the future. He looked at me sympathetically, told me he'd looked into it. "There's just no room in the budget for you anymore."

"Oh," I said.

He told me that maybe the network could have me back for one-off stories here and there. "We can't commit to anything regular," he said. "Sorry. I tried."

After the meeting, I called Jonathan and told him, "So I'm about to be unemployed. Guess it's not going to happen. You a media mogul, me on the show . . ."

"You're not a morning person anyway," he said.

❖

Back in Los Angeles, at Jonathan's place, I got a call from a UK number I didn't recognize. The caller identified himself as Seth Freedman, a frequent writer for the *Guardian*. He said he was working "on a kind of collaborative piece with journalists from other papers on a very kind of soft piece about life in the film industry."

The description was off, strangely vague. "We've come across some stuff doing our research that we really can't use," Freedman continued. "I just wondered if what we have could be useful to you, basically."

He asked about McGowan, saying she'd "been very helpful for the piece we're doing." Then he offered to connect me with another high-profile source if I could tell him more about my work.

"Someone I spoke to said, 'Mr. Farrow might be working on something related.'"

"And who was it that suggested that this might be a topic of interest for me?"

"If you don't mind, I'd rather not say, not in a kind of hostile way, just that the person who'd said 'Mr. Farrow might be working on it' doesn't want to be involved himself."

I told Freedman I was open to leads, but couldn't tell him anything. He was silent for a beat, unsatisfied. "If someone makes an allegation against someone, libel law in the UK is very strict and no one will publish if you say, 'Ms. X said this about Mr. Y.' Unless you've got some kind of proof to back it up. Is it different in the States, can you publish 'This person said that about someone else,' or would you also have to stand it up in some way?" It sounded like a warning. "Without knowing more about the details of your story, I really couldn't advise," I told him, and politely ended the call. It was one of several similar calls Freedman made that month, based on instructions he received via email and WhatsApp, from a project manager at Black Cube.

❖

About two weeks after my meeting with Oppenheim, Susan Weiner called. "The reason I'm calling is we have continued to have concerns raised to us about the reporting regarding Mr. Weinstein," she said. "We thought we had made it clear to you that NBC is not involved in this story in any way."

I told Weiner that, while Oppenheim had made it clear that he couldn't go first, we were still looking at the possibility of resurrecting the TV version after the story broke in print. Greenberg had told McHugh several times that this prospect wasn't completely dead.

"I can't speak for Rich and Noah, but my understanding is that NBC has no interest in ever being a part of this story," she said. "NBC does not want to be mentioned in connection with this at all. And we are being advised that you have been identifying yourself as an NBC reporter."

Harvey Weinstein had by then acquired an expansive collection of my introductory emails to sources. Weiner began reading one of these aloud. "I see here you say you've reported for NBC News," she said.

"Well, that's accurate, of course," I replied. I'd been transparent with sources. Since the story had been picked up by a print publication, I'd said nothing to suggest NBC had any ongoing involvement. But I'd mentioned my wider work with the network as a credential. And even after the conversation with Oppenheim about the budget, I hoped to continue that work, in the context of whatever small, piece-by-piece deal he could offer.

"My understanding is your contract is now terminated," Weiner said. "If you in any way imply that NBC had any involvement in this story, we will be forced to publicly disclose that."

"Susan, we've worked together for years," I said. "You can reassure Noah that I won't say NBC's working on this, but there's no need to —"

"Obviously we don't want to publicly discuss your contract status, but we will be forced to do so if we receive any more complaints about this. Noah wants to make sure the word 'NBC' does not appear in any communications about this story."

❖

In conversations with people around him, Weinstein was ecstatic. "He kept saying, 'If I can get a network to kill a story, how hard can a newspaper be?'" recalled one of them. Weinstein seemed to be referring to his trouble at the *Times*. "He was triumphant," added a senior Weinstein Company executive. "It was the kind of thing he'd be yelling at us. He'd say, 'I got them to kill this fucking story, I'm the only one getting anything done here.'"

At around close of business the day before Weiner's call to me, Weinstein had sent Oppenheim a warm note, burying the hatchet:

From: ""Office, HW"" <HW█████████████████████

Date: Monday, September 25, 2017 at 4:53 PM

To: NBCUniversal <noah█████████████████

Subject: From Harvey Weinstein

Dear Noah,

I know we've been on opposite sides of the fence, but my team and I watched Megyn Kelly today and thought she was terrific—congratulations, I'm going to send you a little gift to celebrate. The format is outstanding as well. If there's anything we can do to help, we have a pretty significant film and television lineup coming up. The WILL & GRACE part was warm and hilarious—really, the whole format was just smart, smart, smart.

All my best,
Harvey

To this, Oppenheim replied: "Thanks Harvey, appreciate the well-wishes!"

Shortly thereafter, Weinstein's staff received a message in the usual format keeping them apprised of mailed gifts: "UPDATE," it read. "Noah Oppenheim received a bottle of Grey Goose."

# CHAPTER 34:

# *LETTER*

*A*ll that September, my representatives at CAA had been calling. First Alan Berger, my agent, and Bryan Lourd, his boss and
one of the heads of the agency, called to say Weinstein had been
hounding them. I told them both that if there was a story about
Weinstein moving ahead, I would meet with him, as early as
was appropriate. When Lourd passed on the message, Weinstein
wouldn't take no for an answer. As Lourd told the story, Weinstein
showed up at the agent's office in Los Angeles and ranted for more
than an hour.

"He said he's far from perfect and has been working on himself for
a very long time now, and felt like he was being painted with an old
brush, so to speak," Lourd said. "Honestly, I kept thinking, *I did not
volunteer for this. Why is this happening right now.*" Weinstein said he'd
hired a lot of lawyers. That he didn't want to create problems for me.
That a meeting had to happen straightaway.

The next Tuesday, the same day I spoke with Weiner, there was
another email from Weinstein to Lourd demanding to talk immediately, and an update from Lourd in response.

This guy won't meet right now
He did say he will call you soon
I think he is absolutely pursuing the story
B

That Friday, Weinstein kept calling Berger and Lourd. Weinstein told Berger his legal team was at the ready. He specifically mentioned Harder, and Boies, and—I felt a jolt when Berger repeated the name to me—Lisa Bloom.

A few hours later, copies of a letter started arriving at various offices at CAA. I thought of the scene from *Harry Potter* where invitations to attend Hogwarts start flying in through the fireplace and the letterbox and the windows. Berger called to read me the letter. It was not an invitation to attend Hogwarts. It was Charles Harder conveying Harvey Weinstein's threat to sue me, based on an arrangement he suggested had been reached with NBC News:

> Dear Mr. Farrow:
>
> This law firm is litigation counsel for The Weinstein Company.
>
> We understand that you have interviewed certain people affiliated with The Weinstein Company and/or its employees and executives (collectively, "TWC"), and have been reaching out to other persons affiliated with TWC, seeking additional interviews, based on the representation to each such person that you are working on a story for NBCUniversal News Group ("NBC"). NBC has informed us, in writing, that it is no longer working on any story about or relating to TWC (including its employees and executives), and all such activities have been terminated. Accordingly:
>
> 1. All interviews that you have conducted or been involved in relating to TWC (including its employees and executives) are

the property of NBC and do not belong to you, nor are you licensed by NBC to use any such interviews.

2. Demand is hereby made that you turn over all of your work product relating to TWC (including its employees and executives) to Susan Weiner, Esq., Executive Vice President, Deputy General Counsel, NBC Universal, 30 Rockefeller Plaza, New York, NY 10112.

3. Should NBC license any content to you for any purpose, TWC will hold NBC jointly and severally liable for your unlawful acts, including defamation.

4. All interviews that you have conducted or been involved in relating to TWC (including its employees and executives) are now invalid, because they were based on the representation that the interview was for story by NBC. NBC has terminated its involvement. Therefore, you have no right to use any such interview for any purpose, and should you do so, you would be engaged in misrepresentation, deception and/or fraud.

5. If you are now working with any other news outlet regarding your investigation and story about TWC (including its employees and executives), please provide me with the name and contact information of that news outlet and the person(s) at that company to whom you report, so that we can place that company on notice of my client's legal claims against them.

6. If you have any intention of publishing or disseminating any story or statements about TWC (including its employees and executives), now or in the future, we demand that you provide my client, in care of this office, a list of every single statement that you intend to publish or disseminate about TWC (including its employees and executives), including all statements by

you and by any third parties, so that my client can place you on specific notice of any false and defamatory statements, and demand that you cease and desist from publishing or disseminating any such statements or face a lawsuit for millions of dollars in damages, and that you give my client at least fifteen (15) days to provide you with a response before any story or statements are published or disseminated.

7. Cease and desist from any and all further communications with TWC's current and former employees and contractors. All such persons have signed confidentiality agreements, and your past communications, and any future communications, with them constitutes an intentional interference with contractual relations.

Pages of demands that I preserve documents in anticipation of potential litigation followed. NBC later denied ever reaching an agreement with Weinstein and said Harder was misrepresenting their communications.

I forwarded the letter to Bertoni. "I don't want to disregard it, but it strikes me as silly right now," he said. He thought a copyright claim from NBC on the underlying contents of the interviews was dubious, and that, in any case, he couldn't imagine the network actually following through on the threat. Still, the line about written assurances that reporting had been terminated "was just shocking to me," he recalled later.

❖

The last time I answered a call from Lisa Bloom that summer, I expressed astonishment.

"Lisa, you swore, as an attorney and a friend, that you wouldn't tell his people," I said.

"Ronan," she replied. "I *am* his people."

Bloom told me Weinstein had optioned her book, that she'd been in an awkward position. "Ronan, you need to come in. I can help. I can talk to David and Harvey. I can make this easier for you."

"Lisa, this is not appropriate," I said.

"I don't know what women you're talking to," she said. "But I can give you information about them. If it's Rose McGowan, we have files on her. I looked into her myself when this first came up. She's *crazy*."

I thought of Bloom's calls and texts and voicemails pressing me for information, dangling clients, enticing me to meet about Blac Chyna. Bloom reminded me that she'd mentioned she knew Weinstein and Boies. But that was after she made the promise not to disclose anything I told her. And she hadn't let on that she'd actually been *representing* Weinstein in the matter she kept asking about.

But she had been, since he retained her in December 2016. From the beginning, she'd explicitly offered to discredit women with sexual abuse claims. "I feel equipped to help you against the Roses of the world, because I have represented so many of them," she wrote in her first memo to Weinstein. "They start out as impressive, bold women, but the more one presses for evidence, the weaknesses and lies are revealed." Referring to McGowan, she offered to "place an article re her becoming increasingly unglued, so that when someone Googles her this is what pops up and she's discredited." Bloom ended the note with a cheery reminder to pay her fee. Weinstein paid $50,000 initially. She'd been billing him $895 an hour since.

On the phone that day, I collected myself, then told her, "I welcome any information you think might be relevant for any story I might be working on." Then I got off the phone. Bloom never got around to sending the supposed dirt on McGowan.

# CHAPTER 35:

# *MIMIC*

I didn't accede to Harder's threat—didn't even, on Bertoni's advice, respond to it. I just kept reporting. That month, I finally got Mira Sorvino on the phone. Sorvino, the daughter of actor Paul Sorvino, had come to prominence in the nineties. She'd won an Oscar, in 1995, for *Mighty Aphrodite*—one of Woody Allen's films Weinstein had distributed and had emphasized in his threats to NBC. And she'd been a bona fide movie star for the following year or two, culminating in a leading role in another Weinstein film, *Mimic*. After that she more or less disappeared.

In our first call, Sorvino sounded petrified. "I already lost so much of my career to this," she told me. "This" was a pattern of sexual harassment from Weinstein while they were working together. At the Toronto International Film Festival in September 1995 to promote *Mighty Aphrodite,* she found herself in a hotel room with Weinstein. "He started massaging my shoulders, which made me very uncomfortable, and then tried to get more physical, sort of chasing me around," she said. He was trying to kiss her when she scrambled away, improvising ways to ward him off, telling him that it was against her religion to date married men. Then she left the room.

A few weeks later, in New York City, her phone rang after midnight. It was Weinstein, saying that he had new marketing ideas for *Mighty Aphrodite* and asking to get together. Sorvino offered to meet him at an all-night diner, but he said he was coming over to her apartment and hung up. "I freaked out," she told me. She called a friend and asked him to come over and pose as her boyfriend. The friend hadn't arrived by the time Weinstein rang her doorbell. "Harvey had managed to bypass my doorman," she said. "I opened the door terrified, brandishing my twenty-pound Chihuahua mix in front of me, as though that would do any good." When she told Weinstein that her new boyfriend was on his way, he seemed dejected and left.

Sorvino said that she felt afraid and intimidated; when she told a female employee at Miramax about the harassment, the woman's reaction "was shock and horror that I had mentioned it." Sorvino recalled "the look on her face, like I was suddenly radioactive."

Sorvino was convinced that, after she rejected Weinstein, he'd retaliated against her, blacklisted her, hurt her career. But she acknowledged the difficulty of ever proving this point. Sorvino appeared in a few more of Weinstein's films after *Mighty Aphrodite*. On *Mimic*, when Weinstein and his brother, Bob, had fired the film's director, Guillermo del Toro, and recut the film against his wishes, she'd objected and fought on del Toro's behalf. "I can't say definitively whether it was the *Mimic* fight or it was his advances," she told me, "but it is my strong feeling I was retaliated against for refusing and then reporting this harassment." Later, her suspicions would be borne out: the director Peter Jackson said that, when he was considering casting Sorvino and Ashley Judd in *The Lord of the Rings*, Weinstein had interceded. "I recall Miramax telling us they were a nightmare to work with and we should avoid them at all costs," Jackson later told a reporter. "At the time, we had no reason to question what these guys were telling us. But in hindsight, I realize that this was very likely the Miramax smear campaign in full swing."

Sorvino told me that she'd struggled for years with whether to come forward with her story and argued—to me but also, it seemed, to herself—that her experience was mild enough that maybe she didn't have to. But Sorvino's claim, like the others that involved unwanted advances but not assault, were pivotal in establishing Weinstein's M.O.

Sorvino was formidable. She'd graduated magna cum laude from Harvard. And she'd advocated for charitable causes related to the abuse of women, including as a UN Goodwill Ambassador to Combat Human Trafficking. It was evident, from our first conversations, that she was undertaking a careful analysis, and that her sense of wider ethical obligations weighed heavily in it.

"When you first wrote," she said, "I had a nightmare, that you showed up with a video camera and asked about working with Woody." She was sorry for my sister, she said. I told her—awkwardly, talking too fast, changing the subject—that half my friends in the industry had worked with Allen, that it didn't take away from her performance, that it was my sister's issue, not mine, that she shouldn't worry about it. But I could sense her worrying, and reflecting, just the same.

Sorvino decided she'd help and, over the course of several calls, went fully on the record. But the fear in her voice never left. "When people go up against power brokers there is punishment," she said. I realized her anxieties went beyond career considerations. She asked if I had security, if I'd thought about the risk of disappearing, of an "accident" befalling me. I said I was fine, that I was taking precautions, then wondered what precautions I was actually taking, other than glancing over my shoulder a lot. "You should be careful," she said. "I'm afraid he has connections beyond just professional ones. Nefarious connections that could hurt people."

The voices kept tumbling in. After Rosanna Arquette's representatives went dark, I found her sister, who promised to pass on the request. A few days later, Arquette and I were on the phone. "I knew this day would come," she said. "The anxiety that's in my chest right now—it's off the charts." She sat down, tried to collect herself. "I just have this '*danger, danger*' alarm going on," she told me.

Arquette told me that, in the early nineties, she'd agreed to meet Weinstein for dinner at the Beverly Hills Hotel to pick up the script for a new film. At the hotel, she was instructed to meet him upstairs, in his room. Arquette recalled that, when she arrived at the room, Weinstein opened the door wearing a white bathrobe. He said that his neck was sore and that he needed a massage. She told him that she could recommend a good masseuse. "Then he grabbed my hand," she said. "He put it on his neck." When she yanked her hand away, Weinstein grabbed it again and pulled it toward his penis, which was visible and erect. "My heart was really racing. I was in a fight-or-flight moment," she said. She told Weinstein, "I will never do that."

Weinstein told her that she was making a huge mistake by rejecting him, and named an actress and a model who he claimed had given in to his sexual overtures and whose careers he said he had advanced as a result. Arquette said she responded, "I'll never be that girl," and left. Arquette's story was important because of how closely it hewed to others I'd heard: professional pretext, meeting moved upstairs, hotel room, request for massage, bathrobe.

Arquette shared Sorvino's conviction that her career had suffered because she rejected Weinstein. "He made things very difficult for me for years," she said. Her small role in *Pulp Fiction* did come afterward. But Arquette felt she only got the part because of its size and Weinstein's deference to the director, Quentin Tarantino. This, too, was a leitmotif: Sorvino had suspected that her romantic relationship with Tarantino at the time had shielded her from retaliation, and that this protection had dissipated when the two split up. Later, Tarantino would say publicly that he could have, should have, done more.

Arquette, like Sorvino, had a history of advocating for vulnerable and exploited people. The bigger picture was inescapable for her. She spoke of a cabal that was wider and deeper than Weinstein. "This is the big boys' club, the Hollywood mafia," she said. "They protect each other." Over the course of several conversations, she agreed to be a part of the story.

When I told her Weinstein was already aware of my reporting, Arquette said, "He's gonna be working very hard to track people down and silence people. To hurt people. That's what he does." She didn't think the story would ever break. "They're gonna discredit every woman who comes forward," she said. "They'll go after the girls. And suddenly the victims will be perpetrators."

By then, Black Cube had already circulated another profile. It assessed Arquette's likelihood to talk, mentioning her friendship with McGowan, her social media posts about sexual misconduct, and even a family member who had experienced abuse.

The day of my first conversation with Arquette, Lacy Lynch, the literary agent working with McGowan, sent an email to Harvey

Weinstein, suggesting they meet up. A week later, Weinstein, Lynch, and Jan Miller, the founder of the agency where Lynch worked, sat together at the Lambs Club, a restaurant in midtown Manhattan decorated with pictures of old Broadway and Hollywood. Lynch and Miller pitched Weinstein on various literary properties they'd acquired. "I just had dinner with Lacy Lynch and Jan," Weinstein wrote afterward to Glasser, his company's COO. Weinstein described his favorite pitch, a story drawn from a book Lynch had sold about police brutality. "I think this could be great for Jay Z," Weinstein wrote.

That summer, Lynch had been drawing closer to Weinstein. She feared his ability to retaliate against her clients with ties to him. Later, she would say publicly that she knew he was interested in her because of her connection to McGowan, and that she was just playing along. If that was the case, he never caught on. At the Lambs Club, Weinstein, Lynch, and Miller talked shop. Then Weinstein offered the women tickets to see a performance of *Dear Evan Hansen* on Broadway.

◆

In the months since Lynch had introduced them, McGowan and Diana Filip had continued to spend time together. Sometimes they met at hotel bars in LA and New York. Other times they took long walks. Once, McGowan brought Filip to the Venice boardwalk. They ate ice cream as they strolled. The potential speaking engagement had been just the beginning. By that fall, Filip was talking seriously about investing in McGowan's production company.

That September, in Los Angeles, the two met with one of Filip's colleagues from Reuben Capital Partners. He, like Filip, was attractive, with a refined, indeterminate accent. He introduced himself as

Paul Laurent. He was just as curious about and attentive to McGowan as Filip had been. The three talked about the potential for collaboration and about their shared belief in telling stories that would defend and empower women.

McGowan was still figuring out how to tell her own story, and Filip was there to help. The two discussed how explicitly McGowan was going to identify Weinstein, and under what circumstances. They talked through what McGowan had said to the press, what she was writing in the book. During one of their emotional heart-to-hearts, McGowan told Filip that there was no one else in the world she could trust.

# CHAPTER 36:

# *HUNTER*

For months, sources had been telling me that Asia Argento, the Italian actress, had a story to tell about Weinstein. Argento's father, Dario, was a director famous for his horror films. Argento played a glamorous thief in a crime drama Weinstein had distributed, *B. Monkey*, and Hollywood had briefly sized up her potential as a stock exotic femme fatale type, a role she gamely played in the Vin Diesel vehicle *XXX*. But this proved an imperfect fit. There was an edge to Argento, a hint of something dark and maybe damaged.

As with so many others, conversations with her agents and managers had dead-ended. But I had followed Argento on social media and we'd begun "liking" each other's photos. The day I first spoke to Arquette, Argento and I exchanged messages too. Soon after, we were on the phone.

Argento was terrified, her voice shaking. In a series of long and often emotional interviews, she told me that Weinstein assaulted her while they were working together. In 1997, she was invited to what she understood to be a party thrown by Miramax at the Hotel du Cap-Eden-Roc, on the French Riviera. The invitation came from Fabrizio Lombardo, the head of Miramax Italy—though several executives and assistants told me that his title was a thin cover for his actual role, as Weinstein's "pimp" in Europe. Lombardo denied it then and has since.

He also denied what Argento told me next: that Lombardo led her not to a party but to Weinstein's hotel room. She recalled Lombardo telling her, "Oh, we got here too early," before he left her alone with Weinstein. At first, Weinstein was solicitous, praising her work. Then he left the room. When he returned, he was wearing a bathrobe and holding a bottle of lotion. "He asks me to give a massage. I was like, 'Look, man, I am no fucking fool,'" Argento told me. "But, looking back, I am a fucking fool."

Argento said that, after she reluctantly agreed to give Weinstein a massage, he pulled her skirt up, forced her legs apart, and performed oral sex on her as she repeatedly told him to stop. "It wouldn't stop," she told me. "It was a nightmare." At some point, she stopped saying no and feigned enjoyment, because she thought it was the only way the assault would end. "I was not willing," she told me. "I said, 'No, no, no.'... It's twisted. A big, fat man wanting to eat you. It's a scary fairy tale." Argento, who insisted that she wanted to tell her story in all its complexity, said that she didn't physically fight him off, something that prompted years of guilt.

"The thing with being a victim is I felt responsible," she said. "Because if I were a strong woman, I would have kicked him in the balls and run away. But I didn't. And so I felt responsible." She described the incident as a "horrible trauma." Afterward, Argento said, "He kept contacting me." She described it as "almost stalking." For a few months, Weinstein seemed obsessed, offering her expensive gifts. What complicated the story, Argento readily allowed, was that she eventually yielded to his further advances. "He made it sound like he was my friend and he really appreciated me." She had occasional sexual encounters with him over the course of the ensuing years. The first time, several months after the alleged assault, came before the release of *B. Monkey*. "I felt I had to," she said. "Because I had the movie coming out and I didn't want to anger him." She believed that Weinstein would ruin her career if she didn't comply. Years later, when she was a single mother dealing with childcare, Weinstein offered to pay for a nanny. She said that she felt "obliged" to submit to his sexual advances. She described the encounters as one-sided and "onanistic."

This was the complex reality of sexual assault for so many survivors: these were often crimes perpetrated by bosses, family members, people you can't avoid afterward. Argento told me that she knew the later contact would be used to attack the credibility of her allegation. She offered a variety of explanations for why she returned to Weinstein. She was intimidated, worn down by his stalking. The initial assault made her feel overpowered each time she encountered Weinstein, even years later. "When I see him, it makes me feel little and stupid and weak." She broke down as she struggled to explain. "After the rape," she said, "he won."

Argento embodied, more than any other source, a collision of complications. After her involvement in my reporting, she reached a financial settlement with an actor, Jimmy Bennett, who alleged she had sex with him when he was seventeen. She stood accused of child abuse. In California, where Bennett said the incident took place, it would be illegal, statutory rape. Argento's attorney later disputed Bennett's account, accusing him of "sexually attacking" Argento and stating that, while the payment was an appeasement gesture, the arrangement didn't bar Bennett from disclosing his claim. But the press observed the hypocrisy of Argento's use of a settlement, given her own claims of victimization by someone who so routinely employed them.

The later settlement had no bearing on an undeniable truth: Argento's story about Harvey Weinstein checked out, with corroboration from people who had seen things or been told at the time. Perpetrators of sexual abuse can also be survivors of it. Any psychologist familiar with sex offenders will tell you, indeed, that they often are. But this idea found little purchase in an environment where victims were expected to be saints and otherwise were disregarded as sinners. The women who spoke that summer were just people. Acknowledging that all did a courageous thing — Argento included — does not excuse any choices made in the years that followed.

Even before that later scandal, Argento was a lightning rod. As agonizing as the social stigma was for every source in the story, in Italy, as Gutierrez's case had illustrated, the cultural context was still more viciously sexist. After her allegation against Weinstein, the Italian press branded Argento a "whore."

In our calls that fall, Argento seemed aware that her reputation was too checkered, the environment in Italy too savage, for her to survive the process. "I don't give a fuck about my reputation, I've already destroyed that myself over the years, as a result of many traumatic experiences, including this," she told me. "It will definitely destroy my life, my career, everything." I told her the choice was hers alone, but that I believed it would help the other women. As Argento grappled with the decision, her partner, the television personality and chef Anthony Bourdain, interceded repeatedly. He told her to keep going, that it was worth it, that it would make a difference. Argento decided to go on the record.

❖

The stories multiplied. Sorvino pointed me to Sophie Dix, an English actress who, years earlier, told her a horror story. Dix had appeared in the Weinstein-distributed Colin Firth film *The Advocate* in the early nineties and then slipped from the spotlight. When I reached her, she was at first apprehensive. "I'm really scared he'll come after me," she wrote at one point. "Maybe I shouldn't stand up and be counted." But over the course of half a dozen calls, she told me that Weinstein had invited her to his hotel room to view footage from their film, then pushed her onto a bed, tugging her clothes off. She'd fled to a bathroom, hidden for a time, then opened the door to find Weinstein masturbating on the other side of it. She'd been able to escape when room service knocked on the door. It was "a classic case" of "someone not understanding the word 'no,' " she told me. "I must have said no a thousand times."

Like all of the allegations that made it into the story, Dix's account was backed up by, among other things, people she had told, in detail, at the time. Dix's friends and colleagues were sympathetic but did nothing. Colin Firth, like Tarantino, would later join the ranks of men in the industry who publicly apologized for hearing without really listening. Dix told enough people that Weinstein called her later that year, telling her, "I'm sorry, and is there anything I can do for you?" She sensed, despite the apology, a note of menace. She got off the phone quickly. Afterward, Dix felt disillusioned about the industry, began to drift from acting. She was, by the time we spoke, working as a writer and producer. She feared fallout among the industry colleagues she now depended upon to get films made. The actress Rachel Weisz was part of a contingent of friends who convinced her it was worth the risk. Dix put her name in the story, too.

❖

Argento, in turn, helped me reach French actress Emma de Caunes. De Caunes told me how she'd met Weinstein in 2010, at a party at the Cannes Film Festival, and, a few months later, received an invitation to a lunch meeting with him at the Ritz, in Paris. In the meeting, Weinstein told de Caunes that he was going to be producing a movie with a prominent director, that he planned to shoot it in France, that it had a strong female role. As in Dix's story and Canosa's, there was an excuse to adjourn to his room: the project, he said, was an adaptation of a book whose title he could tell her, if only they could go upstairs to retrieve his copy.

De Caunes, wise to this, replied that she had to leave, since she was already running late for a TV show she was hosting. But Weinstein had pleaded until she agreed. In the room, he disappeared into a bathroom, leaving the door open. She assumed that he was washing his hands, until the shower went on. "I was like, What the fuck, is he taking a shower?"

Weinstein came out, naked and with an erection. He demanded that she lie on the bed and told her that many other women had done so before her. "I was very petrified," de Caunes said. "But I didn't want to show him that I was petrified, because I could feel that the more I was freaking out, the more he was excited." She added, "It was like a hunter with a wild animal. The fear turns him on." De Caunes told Weinstein that she was leaving. He panicked. "We haven't done anything!" she remembered him saying. "It's like being in a Walt Disney movie!"

De Caunes told me, "I looked at him and I said—it took all my courage, but I said, 'I've always hated Walt Disney movies.' And then I left. I slammed the door." Weinstein called relentlessly over the next few hours, offering de Caunes gifts and repeating his assertion that nothing had happened. A director she was working with on the TV show confirmed that she arrived at the studio distraught and that she recounted what had happened.

De Caunes, who was in her early thirties at the time, was already an established actress. But she wondered what would happen to younger and more vulnerable women in the same situation. She, too eventually went on the record—for their sake. "I know that everybody—I mean everybody—in Hollywood knows that it's happening," de Caunes told me. "He's not even really hiding. I mean, the way he does it, so many people are involved and see what's happening. But everyone's too scared to say anything."

## CHAPTER 37:

# *HEIST*

**V**irtually every day, I encountered dead ends. Some accusers declined to talk at all. All summer, I'd pursued Lauren O'Connor, a former literary scout at the Weinstein Company. In 2015, she'd written an internal memo complaining about Weinstein's behavior with employees. He'd been verbally abusive to her, and she'd learned of his predation. At one point, a young woman had pounded on her hotel-room door, crying, shaking, and eventually recounting a familiar story about Weinstein propositioning her for a massage. "I am a 28 year old woman trying to make a living and a career," O'Connor wrote in the memo. "Harvey Weinstein is a 64 year old, world famous man and this is his company. The balance of power is me: 0, Harvey Weinstein: 10." But O'Connor had signed a nondisclosure agreement and was still too afraid to talk. Late that September, an intermediary called to say that O'Connor had consulted a lawyer and made her final decision. "She is terrified and will not engage. With anyone," the intermediary told me. O'Connor didn't want me to use her name.

It was a blow. I had her name from documents. But the intermediary had described O'Connor's raw panic. I was painfully aware that

I was a man writing a story about women's consent, confronting a woman saying she didn't want her life upended in this way. Eventually, she would begin to tell her story publicly. But at the time, I promised I wouldn't include her.

Then there were those who hesitated. The actress Claire Forlani would later post an open letter on social media about her struggle over whether to describe to me her claim that Weinstein had harassed her. "I told some close men around me and they all advised me not to speak," she wrote. "I had already told Ronan I would speak with him but from the advice around me, interestingly the male advice around me, I didn't make the call."

❖

I canvassed Hollywood for more leads. Some of Weinstein's contacts seemed sincerely to know little about the claims surrounding him. Late that September, I reached Meryl Streep, who had made films with Weinstein for years, including *The Iron Lady,* the Margaret Thatcher biopic that had won Streep her most recent Oscar. When we connected, Streep was hosting a fiftieth reunion with school friends. "I am hosting and cooking tearing my hair," Streep wrote.

"Sounds like you've been in a maelstrom there," I said, on the phone. She replied, not missing a beat, "a *female*strom."

She hummed along, luminous and buoyant, asking who it was I was reporting on.

I told her Harvey Weinstein. Streep gasped. "But he supports *such good causes*," she said. Weinstein had always behaved around her. She'd watched and sometimes joined in his Democratic fund-raising and philanthropy. She knew him to be a bully in the edit room. But that was it.

"I believe her," I told Jonathan later.

"But you would either way, right?" he replied, considering it a thought exercise.

"Yeah, I get it."

"Because she's Meryl—"

"Because she's Meryl Streep. I get it."

❖

Other industry veterans I spoke with sounded a different note. Weinstein's predation was an open secret, they said, and if they hadn't seen it, they'd heard about at least some of it. Susan Sarandon, the kind of ethical futurist who had stubbornly refused to work with accused predators for years, gamely brainstormed leads. She let out a cackle when I told her what I was up to. "Oh, Ronan," she said, going into a teasing, singsong delivery. Not mocking, just delighting at the impending drama about to befall me. "You're gonna be in *trouble*."

Still others appeared to report back to Weinstein. When I reached the director Brett Ratner, I implored him to keep the conversation in strict confidence. I told him there were vulnerable women who might get blowback if Weinstein became agitated. "Do you feel comfortable not repeating anything I mention, for their sake?" I asked. Ratner promised he wouldn't. He said he knew of a woman who might have a story about Weinstein. But he sounded jittery. Months later, six women would accuse Ratner of sexual harassment in a *Los Angeles Times* report—though he denied several of their claims. He informed Weinstein of my inquiry almost immediately.

"Harvey says Brett Ratner called him and now he's all spun up," Berger told me, in the *this-is-gonna-be-the-death-of-me* inflection that by then dominated our exchanges. Berger had been supportive of the story, if occasionally fretful about its effect on my professional prospects. "It's causing too many speed bumps," he said. "Either run it or move on."

❖

Weinstein was doing canvassing of his own. As September turned to October, he sought out the figure at the heart of his claims that I had a conflict of interest. Weinstein had his assistants place the call. On a movie set in Central Park, another assistant brought a phone to Woody Allen.

Weinstein seemed to want a strategic playbook — for quashing sexual assault allegations, and for dealing with me. "How did you deal with this?" Weinstein asked at one point. He wanted to know if Allen would intercede on his behalf. Allen shut down the idea. But he did have knowledge that Weinstein would later put to use. That week, Weinstein's credit card receipts show his purchase of a book of interviews with Allen, written by a die-hard fan of his, documenting all of the arguments Allen and his army of private investigators and publicists had come up with to smear the credibility of my sister, the district attorney, and a judge who had suggested she was telling the truth.

"Jeez, I'm so sorry," Allen told Weinstein on the call. "Good luck."

Weinstein was also placing calls to my sources, sometimes frightening them. The day after I received the legal demand letter from Harder and company, Weinstein called Canosa again. It was Yom Kippur, the Jewish day of atonement, but this seemed not to inform the sentiment of the call. He told her that he knew people were talking. "You'd never do something like that to me," he said. Unsure if this was a question or a threat, Canosa got off the phone shaken. I told Remnick sources were getting jittery, that Weinstein appeared to be redoubling his efforts to shut people up. "I fast and he threatens," Remnick replied. "Judaism comes in many forms."

◆

Late that month, Weinstein met again with his team in the back room of the Tribeca Grill. He had been there for some time, huddled with his lawyers, discussing the latest developments in the amfAR story. Then there was a changing of the guard, some of the team members focused on that scandal shifting out as several operatives from Black Cube arrived. Their update was triumphant. "We got something good for you," one of them said, smiling. They'd been mindful of the ways they'd fallen short earlier, but this time they'd gone big. They'd obtained a crucial, elusive piece of property that Weinstein had sought all summer long, and described the elaborate heist that had achieved this.

There were three Black Cube operatives present that day: Yanus, the director, was there, and the project manager who worked under him; the third member of the team was a working-level employee who had been deeply involved in the operation. In a white shirt and blazer, she evinced crisp professionalism. She was blond, with high cheekbones, a strong nose, and an elegant, hard-to-place accent. She was introduced, in her meetings with Weinstein, as Anna.

Anna was deferential to Yanus and their colleague, letting them direct the conversation. When they turned to her, she explained, with enthusiasm, the many months she'd spent gaining an important target's trust and secretly recording hours of conversation. Then, as Weinstein's eyes widened, and he muttered, "Oh my God, oh my God," the Black Cube operatives read aloud what they said were the passages about Weinstein from Rose McGowan's forthcoming book.

# CHAPTER 38:

# *CELEBRITY*

Throughout September, *The New Yorker*'s work on the story picked up pace and intensity. Foley-Mendelssohn and Remnick and the rest of the team scrutinized the accumulating reporting and pored over drafts. I stayed at the World Trade Center late, making reporting calls. Arriving home near dawn one day, I saw a silver Nissan Pathfinder parked outside and felt a cold jolt of recognition. I still had no proof that I was being followed, but a jittery suspicion persisted.

A few friends had offered to put me up that summer, and mostly these conversations had ended with a laugh from me and a promise that I was okay. Only one of those friends, Sophie, the daughter of a wealthy executive, said she was accustomed to security threats and told me to take my suspicions seriously. She said to call her if I needed somewhere safe to stay. Finally, I did.

At the end of that month, I packed up my things and moved into what would become my safe house: a section of a building in Chelsea where Sophie's family owned several floors. It was a space to comfortably house everyone you've ever met. The rooms were proportioned like airplane hangars—imposing and beautiful and full of ornate couches you'd be afraid to sit on and objets d'art you'd be afraid to touch.

The place had several layers of security: card, physical key, code. I felt safer. But I still couldn't shake the paranoia that I was being watched. *"I'm saying get a gun,"* Polone had said. And I'd laughed. But later, as others said the same thing, I started to consider it. At a range in New Jersey, I brushed up on pistols and revolvers. I told myself this was just recreational. But, aiming a Glock 19 downrange, feeling its weight, squeezing the trigger, I felt nervy and flushed, and not much like a guy with a hobby.

◆

The signs that the *New York Times* was closing in on the story were picking up, too. I'd learned that two respected investigative reporters—Kantor, who'd been mentioned in the dossiers sent by the private investigators, and Megan Twohey—were leading the paper's effort. They were formidable, chasing sources just as aggressively as I had. After Arquette and Nestor received calls, I told them they should work with whomever they were comfortable with. "In the end it's good for us all that multiple people are working on this," I texted Nestor. I was sincerely glad the *Times* was there to draw some of the heat and ensure the story saw the light of day, whatever happened to my effort. But privately, I was also feeling competitive, with some self-pity mixed in. For six months, the only support I'd had was Noah Oppenheim scrunching his nose and holding journalism at arm's length, afraid it might get on him. Now, finally, I had *The New Yorker*, but it might be too late. I had no idea what the *Times* had. For all I knew, if it published first, our work at the magazine would be rendered moot. The arms race was another source of pressure, another way in which it felt like I was working in an air-lock, waiting to be blown out into the vacuum.

McHugh texted in late September that he was hearing from his sources that the *Times* was on the verge of running something. NBC had banned him from taking calls about the sexual assault allegations, but he had kept at the story about amfAR, the AIDS charity. A source had pointed him to a line item buried in the charity's tax returns suggesting that $600,000 had been diverted to the American Repertory Theater, which had incubated *Finding Neverland*, the musical Weinstein had later produced on Broadway and had entreated Gutierrez to see after their first encounter. McHugh had sought permission to work on the story. Greenberg, after conversations with Oppenheim, had appeared to allow it. But the permission had been hard-fought, and McHugh felt that the network dragged its feet afterward. "They were slow playing it," he lamented later. He wasn't sure whether they wanted him to be reporting, or just wanted the appearance of not having killed two stories about Weinstein in rapid succession.

"Twohey filed her story today," McHugh wrote to me. We debated about what might be in the *Times* story — whether it was their main story about sexual misconduct at all. "Either way," McHugh wrote, "it's showtime soon for Harvey."

Weinstein and Dylan Howard were having a similar conversation that day. The bond between the two men continued to grow stronger. "Dear Dylan," Weinstein wrote after Twohey filed, "I just wanted to let you know that the New York Times are going to be posting their article today."

The next day, there was a *Times* breaking news alert about Weinstein. I clicked through. "It's all amfAR," McHugh texted. It was a false alarm.

"How quickly can you get it out?" asked McHugh. "Get Remnick aware of the Weinstein news swirl. You've got the story. Time to get it out." Auletta, calling in anxiously, applied similar pressure: "Hurry! Meet with him stat, then get this online."

I badgered Foley-Mendelssohn and then Remnick. He was fiercely competitive, but the magazine's priorities were accuracy and caution. "We're not going to race to beat anyone," Remnick told me. The story would be ready when it was ready, after an intensive fact-checking process. "We're an ocean liner, not a speedboat. We always knew that the *Times* might scoop us."

Nevertheless, Remnick dug into editing, peppering me with questions as he went ("Where is the Weinstein Co? Why does he stay in hotels all the time?"). When I wasn't meeting with or calling sources, I was holed up with Foley-Mendelssohn or with Remnick, chiseling away at the language of the piece. We debated when to seek comment from Weinstein. "The sooner we speak to him the better," I wrote to the editors.

Remnick decided, in the interest of fairness and to limit Weinstein's ability to badger the women whose names we would be revealing when we sought comment, to complete as much of the fact-checking as possible before we called Weinstein. Peter Canby, the magazine's veteran head of fact-checking, assigned two checkers, for speed and added scrutiny. For one of the checking roles, Foley-Mendelssohn suggested E. Tammy Kim, a former attorney with a cool and serious disposition. When she was approached about the job, Kim folded her arms and said, unsmiling, "Is this gonna be a celebrity thing or something?" The other assignment went to Fergus McIntosh, a young Scot who had joined the magazine two years earlier after finishing his studies at Oxford. McIntosh was polite to a proper British standard and a little shy. On September 27, Kim and McIntosh began their work on the story, moving fast, putting in grueling hours, calling source after source after source.

# CHAPTER 39:

# *FALLOUT*

*I*n New York City, the rippling heat wavered but did not break. Both my sources and Weinstein's intermediaries who periodically called to sound notes of menace were spread across time zones — Europe, Australia, China. At all hours, my phone felt like a ticking bomb. Sleep was becoming an involuntary reflex, a brief moment when, with a harsh *crack* like a light switch, I blinked and the shadows had changed, and I'd been out for an hour, my face embossed with the grain of whatever desk at *The New Yorker* I'd borrowed that night. I hoped Jeffrey Toobin or Dexter Filkins or whichever other reporter wouldn't have occasion to discover all this drooling on their mouse pads. When I made it back to Chelsea to lie down, I managed only twilight half-sleep. In the mirrors around the place, I looked drawn and pale and thinner than I had at the beginning of the summer, like a consumptive child in an ad for some Victorian-era tonic.

As the fact-checkers began calling sources widely, Weinstein picked up his threats. On the first Monday of October, he sent his first legal letter to *The New Yorker*. "This law firm, along with my co-counsel, David Boise, Esq. of Boise Schiller Flexner LLP and Lisa Bloom, Esq. of The Bloom Firm, are litigation counsel for The Weinstein

Company," Charles Harder wrote this time. The reporting was "defamatory," he argued. "We demand that you refrain from publishing this story; provide TWC with a list of all statements about TWC (including its employees and/or executives) that you intend to publish." There was the expected invocation of NBC: "Importantly, NBC News was previously working with Ronan Farrow regarding a potential story about TWC. However, after reviewing Mr. Farrow's work, NBC News rejected the story, and terminated the project. It would be troubling if The New Yorker were to take Mr. Farrow's work product, rejected by NBC News, and publish it—thereby exposing The New Yorker to liability and tremendous damages in connection therewith."

Weinstein's recent conversation with Woody Allen appeared to inform the letter. Harder devoted several pages to the argument that my sister's sexual assault disqualified me from reporting on Weinstein. "Mr. Farrow is entitled to his private anger," Harder wrote. "But no publisher should allow those personal feelings to create and pursue a baseless and defamatory story from his personal animus." He went on to quote the book Weinstein had purchased by the Woody Allen biographer, and to echo Allen's argument that I'd been brainwashed into finding my sister's claim credible.

There were other colorful personal arguments. "As a second example, Ronan Farrow's uncle, John Charles Villers-Farrow, was prosecuted, pled guilty and sentenced to ten (10) years in prison for sexually abusing two boys. We have yet to find any evidence that Ronan Farrow has publicly denounced his uncle, and he might have publicly supported him. Either way, and in light of Mr. Farrow's outspoken criticism of his estranged father, Mr. Farrow's actions call into question his credibility and perspective as a journalist."

As far as I could recall, I'd never met that uncle. My understanding was that the case against him was credible. My mother and his daughter had both cut him out of their lives. I'd never been asked about my extended family members who weren't public figures. Had I been, I wouldn't have avoided the subject. What any of this had to do with the allegations against Weinstein was unclear.

I was struck by how closely the arguments in the letter mirrored the talking points Oppenheim had recited to me. And I was reminded of the op-eds and television appearances Bloom had devoted to defending my sister's credibility and burnishing her own brand as an advocate for women. I was becoming inured to people contorting their bodies into the shapes of gears for Harvey Weinstein's machine. But I still wondered at Bloom's name at the end of the letter, alongside Harder's.

◆

The first week of October, Weinstein's assistants emailed Dylan Howard: "We just tried you, but Harvey wanted to see if you could instead meet him in front of the NY Times Building on 8th Ave near 43rd Street. He's on his way up there no so should be there in about 30 minutes." Originally, Weinstein had asked his staff to make sure Howard joined him and Lisa Bloom for the drive uptown from the Weinstein Company offices to the *Times*. But Bloom and Weinstein had left without Howard, so the *Enquirer* editor would have to scramble uptown himself, manila folders in hand, containing "basically dirt" on Weinstein's accusers, by the recollection of one person involved. Howard later disputed that he ever went to the *Times* building. What's not in dispute is that Weinstein was soon in the meeting, hearing that the *Times* was preparing to publish its story about sexual misconduct.

When sources reached me with the same message, I was in a cab. I tried Jonathan, then tried him again. He was increasingly busy with work, and I was increasingly needy and annoying.

"What?!" he snapped, when he finally called back. He was stepping out of another meeting.

"The *Times* is running," I said.

"Okay," he said, a little impatiently. "You knew they might."

"It's good it's breaking," I said. "It's just—all these months. This whole year. And now I have no job." I was losing it, actually starting to cry. "I swung too wide. I gambled too much. And maybe I won't even have a story at the end of it. And I'm letting down all these women—"

"Calm down!" Jonathan shouted, snapping me out of it. "All that's happening right now is you haven't slept or eaten in two weeks."

A horn sounded outside.

"Are you in a *cab*?" he asked.

"Uh-huh," I sniffled.

"Oh my God. We are going to talk about this, but first you are going to tip that driver really well."

After the letter from Weinstein and Harder came in, Remnick called me into his office, along with Bertoni and Foley-Mendelssohn. Weinstein's legal argument, in order of ascending absurdity and descending seriousness, was that anything negative about him was defamatory; that reporting on any company that used NDAs was impermissible; that he had cut a deal with NBC; that my sister was sexually assaulted; and that there was a child molester in my extended family. (Jonathan howled with laughter at it. "This letter is *adorable*," he said. "I love this letter.") But I'd watched a news organization internalize thin arguments before. As I filed into Remnick's office, part of me was still braced for capitulation or skittishness. He said plainly, "This is the most disgusting letter I've ever gotten about a story."

Still a little apprehensive, I reminded Remnick that Weinstein was also threatening to sue me personally and that I didn't have a lawyer. "I want to be clear," he said. "We will defend you legally, no matter how far Harvey Weinstein goes." Bertoni responded briefly to Harder: "With regard to your statements about the independence and ethics of Mr. Farrow, we find the issues you raise to be without any merit whatsoever."

As I left work that evening, Remnick called to say that Asia Argento's partner, Anthony Bourdain, had contacted him. Bourdain had been supportive of Argento speaking before, but even so, my heart sank: over and over, women who had withdrawn from the story had done so after an intervention from a husband, a boyfriend, a father. Outreach from significant others was seldom good news. But there are exceptions to every rule: Bourdain said Weinstein's predation was sickening, that "everyone" had known about it for too long. "I am not a religious man," he wrote. "But I pray you have the strength to run this story."

The *New Yorker* team rallied around the reporting, which was proving out, one allegation after another, under pressure from the fact-checkers. We were still waiting until all the claims were fully checked before seeking comment from Weinstein. But several Weinstein intermediaries had already made contact, their tone not combative but resigned. One member of his legal team took the extraordinary step of calling the magazine shortly after Harder's letter arrived, saying that the threats in it had been wrong, inadvisable. "This is not a situation where I'm telling you you're getting it wrong," that attorney said. "The allegations of gross improper conduct—a great many of the instances are true."

The temperature rose, turning Foley-Mendelssohn's office into a sweatbox. She and I sat bowed over print-outs of the draft, with perspiration beading on our foreheads. There was impassioned debate over choices of language, Remnick pressing for caution wherever possible. Initially, we'd excluded the term "rape," fearing it might be distracting or prejudicial. Foley-Mendelssohn and Kim, the fact-checker, pushed back. To exclude the word, they argued, would be a whitewash. In the end, Remnick and Bertoni agreed, and the word stayed in.

One of those days, I stepped out of the heat and into Remnick's apartment on the Upper West Side. Outside, at the margin of the building's limestone facade, there was a tin Fallout Shelter sign. Inside, a double-height living room was lined with books. Remnick's wife, the former *Times* reporter Esther Fein, shooed me into the kitchen, insisting I eat. The couple met in the late eighties and went to Moscow on assignment for rival papers, Remnick for the *Washington Post*. The family had preserved a section of wall bearing the recorded heights of its two sons and one daughter through their years of growth, just like in the movies. In his small home office, Remnick and I fine-tuned the draft. I was frazzled and sleep-deprived, and he was generous, even when I was dead wrong about edits.

If this passed for calm, there was a sense that it was before a large storm. Early that first week of October, Kim Masters ran a story for the *Hollywood Reporter*, headlined "Harvey Weinstein Lawyers Battling *N.Y. Times*, *New Yorker* Over Potentially Explosive Stories." *Variety* ran its version a few minutes later. The cable news cycle began to chatter. This development had the upside of emboldening sources. That day, the actress Jessica Barth, who had appeared in the *Ted* films with Seth MacFarlane, reached out to tell me that Weinstein had sexually harassed her during a hotel-room meeting—a story that ultimately checked out. But the headlines also made me feel exposed. Whatever happened next would take place under stadium lights.

# CHAPTER 40:

# *DINOSAUR*

*T*he world was changing around Harvey Weinstein that October. He looked haggard. Fits of rage were his baseline, but the outbursts that month were more erratic than usual. Inside the Weinstein Company he grew suspicious. It would later be reported that he'd been monitoring the work communications of Irwin Reiter, who sent Nestor the sympathetic messages and whom Weinstein had branded "the Sex Police." On October 3, Weinstein had an IT specialist pull up and delete a file entitled "HW friends" that mapped out the locations and contact information of dozens of women in cities around the world.

On the morning of October 5, Weinstein summoned much of his defense team to his offices on Greenwich Street, where a makeshift war room took shape in a greenroom. Bloom was there, and Howard. Pam Lubell and Denise Doyle Chambers, the veteran employees who had been brought back to help assemble the target list, were also there, not very confused about the status of their book proposal. Davis and Harder called in, the assistants placing them on speakerphone. Weinstein was crazed, shouting at the top of his lungs. The *Times* story hadn't broken yet, but he had been told it was imminent.

He roared name after name at Lubell and Doyle Chambers and the assistants, of board members and allies in the entertainment industry who he hoped would defend him after the stories started breaking. Bloom and others pored over printed and digital pictures that showed ongoing contact between Weinstein and women on the target list: McGowan and Judd, on his arm, smiling politely. "He was screaming at us, 'Send these to the board members,'" Lubell later recalled. And she dutifully sent them on.

Farther downtown, I took a seat at a vacant desk at *The New Yorker* and called the Weinstein Company for comment. Sounding nervous, the front desk assistant I reached said he'd check if Weinstein was available. And then there was Weinstein's husky baritone. "*Wow!*" he said with mock excitement. "What do I owe this occasion to?" The writing about the man before and after seldom lingered on this quality: he was pretty funny. But this was easy to forget as he veered swiftly toward fury. Weinstein hung up on me several times that fall, including on that first day. I told him I wanted to be fair, to include anything he had to say, then asked if he was comfortable with my recording. He seemed to panic, and was gone with a *click*. The pattern repeated that afternoon. But when I got him to talk for a sustained time, he abandoned his initial caution, didn't put the conversation off the record, just got sharply combative.

"How did you identify yourself to all these women?" he demanded.

I was caught off balance a little.

"Depending on the timing, I accurately described the outlet." I started to say that this wouldn't help us hear him out on the allegations, but he jumped in again.

"Oh, really? Like you're a *reporter* at NBC. And what do your *friends* at NBC have to say about that now?" I felt a flush rising in my cheeks.

"I'm calling because I want to hear you out," I said.

"No. I know what you want. I know you're scared, and alone, and your bosses abandoned you, and your father—"

Remnick was outside at this point, tapping on the glass quietly. He shook his head, made a "wrap it up" gesture.

"I'm happy to talk to you, or whomever you want on your team," I said.

Weinstein laughed. "You couldn't save someone you love, and now you think you can save everyone." He really said this. You'd think he was pointing a detonator at Aquaman.

Weinstein told me to send all my questions to Lisa Bloom. By the end of the calls, he was charming again, politely thanking me.

◆

At just after 2:00 p.m., phones chimed and an assistant walked into the Weinstein Company greenroom with the news about the *Times*. "The article's up," the assistant said. "Oh shit," said Dylan Howard, and asked staffers to print copies for everyone. As the team read the article, the tension broke. For a brief moment, Weinstein was relieved. It was good news, he told the assembled staffers, that the story had come out on a Thursday rather than a Sunday, which he deemed to be the *Times*'s preferred real estate for major stories. Then he departed to see his wife, Georgina Chapman, who was attending a fashion show for her clothing label, Marchesa. "She said, 'I'll stick with you,' " Weinstein told several of the team members when he got back. But he was already turning to the reporting still to come. After the *New Yorker* story, he said under his breath, "She's gonna leave me."

Foley-Mendelssohn and I sat opposite Remnick in his office and read the *Times* article, him on a monitor, the two of us scrolling on our phones. The story was powerful, with Ashley Judd finally attaching Weinstein's name to the account she'd given *Variety* two years earlier about unwanted advances from a producer, which finally made sense of the odd call I'd had with Nick Kristof months earlier. It also discussed O'Connor's story about verbal abuse, and Nestor's about workplace propositions, though without their involvement.

There were no allegations of assault or rape. Lisa Bloom quickly put out a statement, referring to the allegations as, mostly, a matter of misunderstanding. "I have explained to him that due to the power difference between a major studio head like him and most others in the industry, whatever his motives, some of his words and behaviors can be perceived as inappropriate, even intimidating." Weinstein was just an "old dinosaur learning new ways," she argued. By the next day's morning programs, Bloom was working to frame the allegations in the *Times* piece as mild indiscretions. "You're using the term *sexual harassment*, which is a legal term," she said to George Stephanopoulos. "I'm using the term *workplace misconduct*. I don't know if there's a real significant difference, to most people, but sexual harassment is severe and pervasive." She said that she'd counseled Weinstein sternly against talking in the office "the way you talk to your guy friends, you know, when you're going out for a beer." Weinstein, in his own statements, said that he "came of age in the '60s and '70s, when all the rules about behavior and workplaces were different," and professed to be on a "journey" to "learn about myself," with "Lisa Bloom to tutor me." Weinstein pledged to devote himself to fighting the National Rifle Association. As far as Bloom and Weinstein were concerned, he would get therapy, start a foundation for female directors at USC, and that would be that.

In Remnick's office, I looked up from the *Times* story. My phone vibrated on the desk, a text from Jonathan. "Times ran. They have harassment, not assault," he wrote. "Race race race." And then, rapidly, another text from McHugh, making the same point. The *Times*, he added, had "less than what we were stopped for."

"It's very strong work," Remnick said, looking up from the story.

"But they don't have anywhere near what we have," Foley-Mendelssohn said, with undisguised relief.

"So we keep going," I ventured.

"We do," Remnick said.

# CHAPTER 41:

# *MEAN*

*A*fter declaring his relief at the *Times* story and its timing, Weinstein issued what was supposed to be a galvanizing message to the staff. "Roll up your sleeves," he announced. "We're going to war." One assistant responded, "I'm done, Harvey," and left. Weinstein said to stop, offered to write a glowing recommendation. "I looked at him like *are you fucking kidding me?*" the assistant recalled.

That evening, the Weinstein Company board of directors convened an emergency conference call. The nine members of the all-male board would be on the line, including Weinstein. For several years, rancor had deepened between a small group of directors seeking to oust Weinstein and a majority of loyalists who considered him indispensable to the company's success. With painful frequency, stories of abuse by powerful people are also stories of a failure of board culture. Weinstein and his brother, Bob, held two seats on the board, and the company's charter allowed them to name a third. Over time, Weinstein was able to install loyalists in many of the remaining seats, too. By 2015, when Weinstein's contract was due to be renewed, he essentially controlled six out of nine board seats, and used that influence to evade accountability. When an adversarial board member, Lance Maerov, demanded to see Weinstein's personnel file, Boies and Weinstein were able to prevail in preventing this, instead enlisting an outside attorney to render a hazy summary of its contents. Maerov later told a *Fortune* writer that there had been a cover-up.

That evening in early October, Weinstein got on the phone with the board. He denied everything, then argued that the *Times* story would blow over. The call devolved into bitter recrimination between the factions within the board and between the Weinstein brothers. "I've never heard such mean people all around," Lubell recalled. "You know, Bob: *'I'm gonna finish you, Harvey, you're done!'* Harvey: *'We're gonna open up the books on you!'* "

In the small hours after the emergency board meeting and on into the following morning, Weinstein bombarded his allies with emotional calls and emails. Among them were executives at NBC and Comcast. Meyer, the NBCUniversal vice chairman, reached out. ("Dear Ron," Weinstein responded that morning. "I just got your message, and thank you—I will. I'm on my way to LA. All my best, Harvey." The two men agreed to talk.)

At 1:44 a.m. on October 6, Weinstein sent an email to Brian Roberts, the head of Comcast, Noah Oppenheim's boss's boss's boss, calling in a favor. "Dear Brian," he wrote. "There comes a moment in everyone's life when someone needs something, and right now, I could use some support."

In Auletta's files, I'd found a taped interview with Roberts, in which he'd served as a rare defender of Weinstein against those who characterized him as a bully. "It's been sort of a joy," Roberts said of Weinstein's and his friendship, and their time spent hobnobbing in New York and on Martha's Vineyard. "I don't personally get put off by all these Hollywoodisms," Roberts said of Weinstein's personality.

"I look and see a guy who is doing great things and built a company." Roberts called Weinstein a good father, a good person. "I think," Roberts added, "he's like a teddy bear."

◆

Comcast, NBC's parent company, was a family business, founded by Roberts's father. The company's articles of incorporation gave Roberts unshakable power: "The Chairman shall be Mr. Brian L. Roberts if he is willing and available to serve.... The CEO shall be Mr. Brian L. Roberts if he is willing and available to serve." Several current and former senior NBCUniversal executives called him mild-mannered or gentle. He was the only person in the corporate chain of command who later approached me to apologize, saying that he had daughters and believed in the reporting. But the executives also said that Roberts avoided conflict. On contentious issues, he "doesn't stand up," one said. "He won't get in the way of Steve doing dirty work"—that is, Steve Burke, who served under Roberts as CEO of NBCUniversal.

Prior to his time at NBCUniversal, Burke worked at Disney, with considerable accomplishments in the company's retail and theme park businesses. But the senior executives said that he was less attuned to news. One recalled a case in which another Hollywood power broker began to call NBC News, demanding that the network not air an interview. The executive recalled informing Burke that the network was proceeding with the story, and Burke replying, "Pull it," adding that the Hollywood power broker "will owe you his life."

"Steve, oh my God, we will have destroyed the reputation of NBC News," the executive remembered saying. "I don't think it's even about protecting his friends, it's just, 'This guy is powerful, I'm getting these calls, I don't need this problem,'" the executive continued. "He doesn't know it's not ethical."

Burke had a rapport with Weinstein as well. A former member of Weinstein's staff—who facilitated Burke's provision of *Minions* costumes for the Weinstein-produced show at Radio City Music Hall where the studio head met Ambra Gutierrez—described Burke as being "in Weinstein's pocket." Several of the senior executives said that Burke was open that summer and fall about his conversations with Weinstein about my reporting. Still another of them recalled how, around the same time the legal department warned me not to disclose the company's involvement, Burke had groaned and said Weinstein was calling incessantly. "I keep having to have these conversations with him promising we're not doing the story," Burke said. When asked if the story might be true, Burke looked baffled by the question. "We can't *run* it," he said. "I'll be getting these calls from Harvey for the next year. I'll never hear the end of it."

❖

At NBC News, there were more signs of anxiety about Weinstein. Soon after Twohey published her story about the amfAR scandal, McHugh was set to publish what he considered a significant follow-up based on his own reporting. At the last minute, management spiked it. Greenberg, who had for days expressed enthusiasm about McHugh's reporting, changed his posture, saying it didn't sufficiently advance the story. It was only after Janice Min, the former *Hollywood Reporter* editor, tweeted that more Weinstein-related news was languishing at NBC that Greenberg came back to McHugh and asked if he could revive his work quickly.

Oppenheim had said I could finish out the other stories I was still working on for NBC. But when the next one's air date arrived, I was told there was no time in the schedule for me to appear on set. Then, when the story was rescheduled, I was given the same excuse again. "Noah says Ronan's not allowed on set," a senior producer told McHugh. "Did something happen?" Lauer read my introduction instead.

❖

The night after the *Times* story ran, CBS News and ABC News prominently covered the deepening scandal on their evening programs. Both networks did so again the following morning, airing detailed segments with original interviews. Only NBC didn't mention the news that first evening, and only NBC offered no original reporting the next morning. Instead, Craig Melvin, filling in for Lauer, read a script that ran less than a minute and was dominated by Weinstein's rebuttals to the allegations. That weekend, the pattern repeated: *Saturday Night Live*, which had eagerly riffed on similar stories about Bill O'Reilly, Roger Ailes, and Donald Trump, didn't mention Weinstein once.

Nevertheless, NBC News was quietly shaping the public narrative around the story. Oppenheim and Kornblau, the head of communications, began talking to media reporters. The two executives suggested NBC had only passing involvement in the story. "Oppenheim says Ronan came to him several months ago and said he wanted to pursue sexual harassment, and after about two or three months, never secured any documentation and never persuaded any women to go on camera," read a memorandum filed internally within an outlet Oppenheim and Kornblau spoke with. "This was a guy who really didn't have anything," Oppenheim said in one of the calls, "I understand this is very personal for him and he may be emotional about it." Asked if he'd had any contact with Weinstein, Oppenheim laughed and said, "I don't travel in those circles."

Several people involved later told me that, in those first days after the *Times* published, NBC avoided covering Weinstein at Oppenheim's direction. "Noah literally went to them and said, 'Do not run this story,'" one person recalled of Oppenheim's conversations with producers at the time. As the story accelerated late that week, Oppenheim and a group of senior staff assembled for a routine coverage meeting. "Should we be doing something on this?" one of the producers present asked. Oppenheim shook his head. "He'll be fine," he said of Weinstein. "He'll be back in eighteen months. It's Hollywood."

# PART IV:
# SLEEPER

# CHAPTER 42:

# *EDIFY*

One additional source joined our story after the *Times* published. A mutual friend alerted me to an allegation by Lucia Evans, a marketing consultant. In the summer of 2004, Weinstein had approached Evans at Cipriani Upstairs, a club in Manhattan. She was about to start her senior year at Middlebury College and was, at the time, trying to break into acting. Weinstein got her number and was soon calling late at night, or having an assistant call her, asking to meet. She declined the late-night advances but said that she would meet with a casting executive during the day.

When she arrived for the meeting, the building was full of people. She was led to an office with exercise equipment in it and takeout boxes on the floor. Weinstein was there alone. Evans said that she found him frightening. "Even just his presence was intimidating," she told me. In the meeting, Evans recalled, "he immediately was simultaneously flattering me and demeaning me and making me feel bad about myself." Weinstein told her that she'd "be great in *Project Runway*" — the show, which Weinstein helped produce, premiered later that year — but only if she lost weight. He also told her about two scripts, a horror movie and a teen love story, and said one of his associates would discuss them with her.

"After that is when he assaulted me," Evans said. "He forced me to perform oral sex on him." As she objected, Weinstein took his penis out of his pants and pulled her head down onto it. "I said, over and over, 'I don't want to do this, stop, don't,'" she recalled. "I tried to get away, but maybe I didn't try hard enough. I didn't want to kick him or fight him." In the end, she said, "he's a big guy. He overpowered me." She added, "I just sort of gave up. That's the most horrible part of it, and that's why he's been able to do this for so long to so many women: people give up, and then they feel like it's their fault."

She told me that the entire sequence of events had a routine quality. "It feels like a very streamlined process," she said. "Female casting director, Harvey wants to meet. Everything was designed to make me feel comfortable before it happened. And then the shame in what happened was also designed to keep me quiet."

♦

We'd sent a detailed fact-checking memo to Bloom that Friday, and she'd promised to respond. When we still hadn't heard back on Saturday, I called. She let it go to voicemail, then texted, "I'm not available today." When she finally picked up, I was at Remnick's place, the two of us huddled over the draft and our respective phones. Bloom sounded disconsolate. "*What?*" she snapped. And then, when I reminded her that Weinstein had asked me to work with her: "I can't talk! I can't comment on any of this!" She told me to call Harder, Boies, anyone else.

Bloom's voice gathered into something accusing and injured. She reminded me how persistently she'd tried to reach me. "For months!" she spat—as if my sharing more information might have led her to step away from Weinstein. Only Bloom and I *had* talked and, as far as I could tell, she'd used the occasion to offer opposition research on women, not to solicit information about her client. It had been a busy summer for Bloom. She'd also begun representing Roy Price, the Amazon Studios executive, after a harassment allegation against him was reported—representation she'd end that fall, amid criticism. Forty minutes after we got off the phone, Bloom tweeted that she'd resigned. She'd been sending emails to the Weinstein Company board describing her plans to discredit accusers virtually until the end.

◆

With Weinstein's team in chaos, we decided to go back to the man himself. Over that weekend and into the following week, I reached him first for less formal calls, and then for long sessions during which I was joined by Remnick, Foley-Mendelssohn, and Bertoni, and Weinstein by lawyers and crisis advisors. Weinstein had added to his team the public relations firm Sitrick and Company, which handed the assignment to an even-tempered former *Los Angeles Times* reporter named Sallie Hofmeister.

Large portions of the conversations with Weinstein were placed off the record. But there were also, among the calls, exchanges for which no ground rules were set, or which Weinstein explicitly placed on the record. At times he sounded defeated. There could be an almost boyish charm in the small "Hi, Ronan," at the top of each call. But more often, there were flashes of the old Harvey Weinstein, arrogant and raging. "Allow me to *edify* you," he'd say. "I'm giving you *insights*."

Weinstein suggested repeatedly that an interaction wasn't rape if the woman in question came back to him later. That this was at odds with the reality of sexual assault as it so often transpires within inescapable workplace or family relationships—that it was at odds with the law—seemed to escape him. He was skeptical, too, of the theme of retaliation that ran through the women's claims. "There's no retaliating in Hollywood," he said, calling the concept of powerful men intimidating women in the industry a "myth." And when I wondered how he figured this was the case, he said that people could simply call up a Ronan Farrow or a Jodi Kantor or a Kim Masters and the retaliation would go away. I marveled at this logic: helping to create a problem, then pointing to the response it had generated to claim the problem didn't exist.

In the earlier, less formal calls, there was a sense that Weinstein was still living in a parallel reality. He would acknowledge wrongdoing, then characterize his actions by discussing a time he wrote an offensive comment in a girl's yearbook, or looked at a colleague the wrong way. Each time I reminded him that we were reporting multiple allegations of rape, he sounded startled. He'd been overwhelmed, he'd say, and hadn't focused on the fact-checking messages in detail. And this seemed likely enough.

Later, as the advisors joined the fray, the response that we ultimately included in the story came to the fore: a blanket denial of all "nonconsensual sex," with little engagement on the specific allegations. This seemed to reflect Weinstein's sincere view: he seldom suggested events hadn't transpired, instead insisting that the interactions had been consensual and were being recast years later in a spirit of opportunism.

He spent an inordinate amount of time attacking the character of women in the story. "Harvey, I have a question," Remnick interjected at one point, in all earnestness. "How does this relate to your behavior?" Weinstein seemed comparatively unconcerned with disputing specific facts. Sometimes, he simply couldn't recall them. Once, he launched into a detailed discussion of an allegation not included in the story. He'd mixed up a name we'd given him and a similar-sounding one from his own memories.

Each time I brought up the audio from the police sting, Weinstein would bristle, outraged that a copy had survived. "You have a copy of a tape that was *destroyed* by the district attorney?" he asked, in disbelief. "The tape that was *destroyed?*" Later, spokespeople in Vance's office would say they never agreed to destroy evidence. But Weinstein was convinced of it. Hofmeister later called and put the point on the record. Weinstein, she told me, was very concerned that a deal he'd reached was being breached. "There was an agreement between the police and our — or the DA, I'm not sure who the agreement was with," she said. "But it was with our law firm that the tape that the police had would be destroyed."

Weinstein continued to emphasize what he took to be an arrangement with NBC News. "NBC is pissed," Weinstein said on several occasions. He wanted to know what I was going to do with the footage I'd shot there. He said that the network had promised him it would explore legal remedies against me if I ever used those recordings. When these points came up on the group calls, Remnick listened patiently, then dismissed the arguments. "NBC is not a consideration here," he said. "This business of NBC is just — you're gonna find that's a nonstarter."

◆

As the calls progressed, Weinstein's temper flashed and flared. "Emily has an NDA," he said of Nestor. "Be careful for her. We like her." Dismayed handlers stepped in and began rapidly talking over him, with limited success. "She's a sweetie and a sweetheart," he continued. "Doesn't deserve it." There were threats to *The New Yorker*, as well: to sue, or to leak our fact-checking memo to preempt our story. "Careful," Weinstein would say. "Guys, careful."

Once, when Hofmeister and the other handlers found themselves unable to stop Weinstein, they appeared to hang up. "We lost you," Remnick said after the abrupt disconnection.

"They didn't want him to say that," said Foley-Mendelssohn.

"Yeah, that's good lawyering right there," Bertoni added, shaking his head in disbelief. "That's what he's paying them the big bucks for, to fucking hang up the phone."

When we got them back on the line a few minutes later, Remnick said, "Sallie? Did a lawyer press the button?"

"Are you on the phone?" Hofmeister replied.

"*I* certainly am," Remnick said.

Where Weinstein offered specifics, the draft did evolve to reflect them. And by the end, even as his anger arced, Weinstein sounded resigned. Several times, he conceded that we'd been fair—and that he "deserved" a lot of it.

❖

On October 10, Foley-Mendelssohn circulated the final edit of the story at 1:00 a.m., and a final copyedit began at 5:00 a.m. By opening of business, the rest of the team had signed off, Kim and McIntosh scrutinizing the last small details. Michael Luo, the respected *Times* alumnus heading *The New Yorker*'s website, oversaw the final details of the web presentation. When I arrived, the magazine's offices were quiet and flooded with sunlight, like a prism. As Monica Racic, the magazine's multimedia editor, stood at her desk, preparing to go live, Foley-Mendelssohn and a few others began to gather, and I moved to take a picture. The idea had been unsmiling documentation, not triumphalism, but Remnick broke it up all the same. "Not our style," he said, and shooed people away, and departed to get back to the grind.

When it was done, I wandered over to one of the office's windows and looked out at the Hudson. There was a numb feeling; Peggy Lee droning, *"Is that all there is to a fire?"* I hoped the women would feel it was worth it; that they'd been able to protect others. I wondered what would become of me. I had no arrangement with *The New Yorker* beyond that first story, and no path forward in television. In the glass, I could make out the dark circles under my own eyes and, beyond that, the world clear to the glittering horizon. A news chopper hovered over the Hudson, watching.

My phone chimed, chimed again. I hurried to the nearest computer, pulled up a browser. From my email in-box and on Twitter and Facebook, the *ping, ping, ping* of alerts sounded. Message after message arrived, quickening to a constant scroll.

Eventually, I'd hear from fellow journalists, including Kantor and Twohey, who'd labored long and hard over their story. Several reporters said they'd fielded efforts to intimidate them. One magazine writer who broke a significant story about Weinstein showed me the messages and played me the voicemails that eventually graduated to explicit threats of harm to him and his family. The FBI had gotten involved. He'd run his report anyway.

But mostly the messages came from stranger after stranger, saying they, too, had stories. Some were from women and others from men. Some were searing accounts of sexual violence and some focused on other species of crime or corruption. All whispered of abuses of power and of the systems — in government, media, law — deployed to cover them up.

That first day, Melissa Lonner, the former *Today* show producer who'd met with me while she was working at Sirius XM, sent a message I barely noticed: "There are more Harveys in your midst."

# CHAPTER 43:

# *CABAL*

"**C**onfident we can get new deal done," Noah Oppenheim texted that day. I'd been a liability inside the building; now I'd be a liability if I left. He called less than an hour after the story ran. "I'm glad it worked out," he said. "Good, good, good!" He continued: "As I'm sure you can imagine, *Nightly*, MS"—as in, MSNBC—"everyone is sort of calling and saying 'Hey, how do we reach Ronan? Can we book him to come on and talk about the article?' So, I just wanted to see where your head was on that." Oppenheim said they'd give me an NBC title again for the appearances.

"The only reason I would be hesitant about going on NBC is I don't want to put anyone there or put you in an awkward position. Obviously Harvey made the story behind the story and the history of it at NBC a big part of his thrust against me," I told Oppenheim. "If I'm asked about the history of it at NBC, I don't want to be in a position where I have to be hiding anything."

Oppenheim and Kornblau were making the issue harder to avoid. By then, several media reporters had called me, claiming that the two executives had been dissembling about the history of the story in background conversations. Stressed, I'd punted the calls to

Raabe, *The New Yorker*'s head of communications, and to Jonathan. While Oppenheim and I spoke, Jake Tapper, of CNN, had tweeted, "Speaking of media complicity ask yourself why NBC reporter Ronan Farrow wrote this for The New Yorker." Soon, Tapper was on air reading a quote. "An NBC source told the *Daily Beast*, quote, 'He brought NBC News early reporting on Weinstein that didn't meet the standard to go forward with the story. It was nowhere close to what ultimately ran. At that time, he didn't have one accuser willing to go on the record or identify themselves. The story he published is radically different than what he brought to NBC News.'" Then he furrowed his brow and said, "That seems like a real lie to me."

When I mentioned not being able to lie if the matter arose on air, Oppenheim laughed nervously. "I mean, look, unless — unless you're gonna, like — I mean, it doesn't sound like you're inclined to do it — unless you're gonna bring up —"

"No. No," I replied. "My honest goal here, Noah, as it has been throughout this process, is to not have anything overshadow the stories of these women."

Oppenheim asked if I'd get over to 30 Rock quickly to shoot a spot for *Nightly News*. I sensed I was being sent to deodorize a public relations problem. But the women's claims really did deserve exposure on NBC's platforms. And the truth was, I wanted my job back. I told myself that avoiding the story behind the story wouldn't be the same as lying about it.

A few hours later, my phone pinged: "Ronan, it's Matt Lauer. Let me be the 567th person to say congratulations on an amazing piece!"

The arrangement with Oppenheim was a tightrope walk. On other networks, I dodged questions, redirecting the conversation toward the women. On NBC programs, I appeared under shifting titles: contributor or correspondent, investigative or not, the detritus of hasty resurrection. When I arrived that afternoon to record the *Nightly News* segment, colleagues approached, ashen-faced. A producer who often worked the police beat, trembling with something like grief, said that he would have loved the chance to help and that he couldn't understand what had happened. A correspondent texted, "As a survivor of sexual abuse, I feel like we are working for a media cabal akin to the Vatican, willing to cover up sex crimes." These were some of the best journalists I knew, the people who had made me proud to be associated with NBC News. They were fiercely committed to the network's ideals of truth and transparency. "People who cared about journalism in the building were very discomforted by all this," a different member of the investigative unit later told me. "It's taken a long time for things to heal here."

It felt strange, not fronting the package McHugh and I had labored over but being interviewed by another correspondent, assigned to cover it as news of the day. The spot included material Harris and Weiner had struck from my script, including the legion of employees saying they witnessed misconduct. "New accusations are rippling through Hollywood as a recording emerges of an encounter between Weinstein and one of his accusers during a police sting," Lester Holt intoned on air that evening. "Here's NBC's Anne Thompson." And this, too, was strange: "a recording emerges." Who could say where it had been before? Not in Noah Oppenheim's office for five months, surely.

❖

Several hours later, in a greenroom where I'd once greeted guests on my show, I watched Rachel Maddow begin her program on a small screen in the corner. For twenty minutes, she recounted the recent history of high-profile sexual assault and harassment stories, lingering on the media's failures of responsibility. She traced the line from Cosby to the Fox News allegations and the conflagration around the *Access Hollywood* tape. "That tape came out a year ago this week," she said pointedly.

Coming to Weinstein, Maddow, like everyone else, made much of the recording. She sat in front of a backdrop that read "I'm used to that" and questioned how it all stayed secret for so long. "These allegations were so widely known and apparently accepted," she said. The public was "coming to terms with the fact that a large corporate conspiracy was involved in covering this all up."

I felt exhausted and conflicted. Oppenheim's dangled promise to un-fire me had actually worked. Despite it all, I still aspired to be an anchor and reporter at NBC News. And I was looking past this moment of attention, of TV hits and tweets, and wondering what I'd actually do next. But there was Maddow, in her meticulous way, setting up our conversation, and pressing on the doubt I felt about even being in this building.

On set, Maddow sat mascaraed and black-jacketed. She leaned in, both empathetic and wolfish. "Obviously this was a long chase for you," she said. "You were working at NBC News when you started working on this. You ended up publishing it with *The New Yorker*—if you can speak to that, I'd love to hear about that." And when I diverted to other topics, she looked at me hard and said, "Ronan, I have a couple more questions for you about this. I was not supposed to keep you for a second segment, but I'm overruling everybody." After a commercial break, she returned to the themes of complicity and cover-up, and the question: "Why did you end up reporting this story for *The New Yorker* and not for NBC News?"

I felt Maddow's gaze, and the harsh lights overhead. For all the warning shots she'd given, I hadn't planned an answer. "Look, you would have to ask NBC and NBC executives about the details of that story," I said. "I will say that over many years, many news organizations have circled this story and faced a great deal of pressure in doing so. And there are now reports emerging publicly about the kinds of pressure that news organizations face in this." I explained that I'd been threatened with a lawsuit personally. That the *Times* had been threatened. That I couldn't describe any threats others might have faced, but you could rest assured there was pressure.

"NBC says that, you know, you didn't—that the story wasn't publishable, that it wasn't ready to go by the time you brought it to them," she said, referring to Oppenheim's and Kornblau's suggestions that I'd pitched the story, come up empty, then gone off to report it elsewhere of my own volition. Maddow pressed an index finger on her Lucite desk. Her real eyebrows arched up and, in the desk, her reflected ones plunged down: a Cirque du Soleil of skepticism. "But obviously it was ready to go by the time you got it into *The New Yorker*."

I'd been clear with Oppenheim that I'd avoid, but wouldn't lie. "I walked into the door at *The New Yorker* with an explosively reportable piece that should have been public earlier, and immediately, obviously, *The New Yorker* recognized that," I said. "It is not accurate to say that it was not reportable. In fact, there were multiple determinations that it was reportable at NBC."

I could feel my promise of keeping the peace slipping away, and my future at the network with it. Maddow gave me a sympathetic look. "I know parts of this story, in terms of the reporting side of it, is not the easiest stuff to talk about and I know you don't want to make yourself the center of this story," she said.

"That is important," I said. "These women came forward with incredibly brave allegations. They tore their guts out talking about this and re-traumatized themselves because they believed they could protect other women going forward. So, this should not be about me, or the wonderful, important work that Jodi Kantor did...ultimately, we are there in service of women doing something really tough, and I hope people hear their voices and focus on that."

I walked off set and burst into tears.

# CHAPTER 44:

# *CHARGER*

The moment she was off air, Maddow got her call. She paced up and down the set, phone pressed to her ear, Griffin's raised voice audible even at a distance. Then Oppenheim was calling. "So, am I an ex-NBC-contributing—whatever you came up with?" I joked.

"I cannot account for Rachel Maddow's behavior. *And believe me*—" Oppenheim began. "Look, it is what it is. Here's what I would say. Unfortunately, it has obviously set off a firestorm."

Oppenheim sounded nervous. He said that he was being told we had to release a statement saying more forcefully, on the record, that NBC never had the story. He wanted me to sign on to it.

Quickly, we were back in the circular arguments from his office, though Oppenheim had now gone from making the case for why the story shouldn't run to arguing, in effect, that he hadn't made that case in the first place.

When I asked him if he talked to Weinstein, he said: "I never did!"

"Noah, when you presented me with that article about Harvey working with Woody Allen, you said, 'Harvey says,'" I reminded him. And at this he groaned, revised, wailed instead: "Harvey Weinstein called me *once*!"

The call stretched on for hours. Mark Kornblau conferenced in and pressed me to sign a Kafkaesque compromise statement that conceded the story had passed a legal and standards review but said it also failed to meet "our standards." My head hurt. Kornblau, it turned out, had a track record of dissembling statements about scandals. In 2007, as then–presidential candidate John Edwards's spokesperson, he spent months stamping out stories that Edwards had fathered a child with Rielle Hunter, a campaign videographer. Kornblau asked Edwards to sign an affidavit denying paternity. When Edwards declined, Hunter later wrote that "it was the moment when Mark knew the truth." But Mark Kornblau, who remained on the campaign until its end a month later, continued to preside over public denials, evidently believing Edwards's thin cover story. Later, when Edwards was tried for violations of campaign finance law in the course of covering up the affair, prosecutors accused Kornblau of concealing the incident in pretrial interviews. Kornblau said prosecutors just hadn't asked the right questions. Edwards was later acquitted of one criminal count, and a mistrial was declared on the others.

At the time, I knew none of this. I still wanted to salvage my future with the executives. I told them I couldn't join a false statement. But I promised them I'd avoid answering further questions like Maddow's.

At one point, my phone died, Oppenheim cut off mid-shout. I was still in the greenroom at MSNBC. I borrowed a charger and plugged in. As I waited, a prominent on-air personality who hadn't yet left the office sat with me and remarked casually:

"Noah's a sick fuck, and Andy's a sick fuck, and they both need to go."

"You mean beyond this?" I asked.

"There have been three things that I know of personally."

"The *Access* tape," I said. "This . . ."

"And something else. Involving talent here."

My eyes widened. But the phone was alive again, and Oppenheim was calling back.

◆

Under the lights of studio 1A, Matt Lauer eyed me like a lit stick of TNT and offered the latest reframing of the matter: "You've been working this story for a long time, both for NBC News and *The New Yorker*. I know it has been a long and difficult process to get these actresses to be identified and go on the record with their allegations." There had been no utopian collaborative effort "both for NBC News and *The New Yorker*." Within the first days of shooting, we'd had a woman on the record. You can see, on the tape of the segment, my eyebrows dart up. Lauer seemed strange on set that day, restless. When I spoke about the complexity of workplace sexual misconduct and retaliation, he shifted in his seat, then jumped in to read Hofmeister's statement about Weinstein. As he moved, a sheen of light slid across his navy blue, impeccably tailored suit.

A few hours later, Oppenheim gathered the producers and reporters of the investigative unit to "clear the air" and allay "misconceptions." When he reiterated the claim that the network simply never had the story, McHugh spoke up. "Forgive me, Noah," he said. "But I have to disagree." Oppenheim looked startled. The meeting turned contentious, the journalists asking one question after another. Why hadn't the network just run the audio? If Oppenheim had wanted more, why weren't McHugh and I allowed to seek it? None of the answers seemed to satisfy. "I don't understand what circumstance would exist as a journalistic organization where—even if they didn't believe you had it at that moment—they didn't say, 'We're gonna give you more resources, we're gonna double down,'" said one veteran journalist there that day. "It didn't ever pass the laugh test for me. And I don't think it did to the rest of the group."

The next morning, McHugh got a call on his cell from Oppenheim's assistant. "Noah would like to see you." Oppenheim said he wanted to address the concerns McHugh had referenced in front of—he said, with a note of distaste—*the whole group.* "Harvey Weinstein's lawyers were calling us all through the seven months and never once did I say to anyone, 'Don't do it,'" Oppenheim said.

"I was ordered to stop on the story," McHugh said. "Ronan and I sensed that NBC was going down a direction where they were not gonna publish this story."

"I'm the one who *launched the fucking story!*" Oppenheim said, losing his cool, getting angry. "I'm now being accused widely," he said, "of being somehow complicit in covering up for a rapist. *Okay!* As the only person here who gave Ronan a job after MSNBC canceled his show, as the person whose idea it was for the story—"

"I'm not accusing you," McHugh said calmly.

But Oppenheim was injured now. That David Remnick had answered plainly the questions he was fielding seemed particularly galling. ("From the moment he walked in the doors here, you were determined to get this in print?" a CBS reporter had asked Remnick. "You're damn right," he'd replied.) "David Remnick spiked the Ken Auletta story!" Oppenheim shouted at McHugh. "He just did nothing for the last sixteen years until Ronan walked in his door. It's a little hard to stomach the self-righteousness from somebody like that who killed their story, didn't do anything for years and years and years, and is now claiming, *I'm just a big hero here because I let Ronan continue reporting.'"* But Remnick *had* let me continue reporting. And

Oppenheim hadn't. The meeting was "crazy," McHugh would reflect later. It seemed clear to him that Oppenheim wanted someone on the inside who'd sign on to the dissembling. He weighed up the stakes. This was his boss's boss cursing at him. McHugh didn't have the platform or profile I did. The network's power to quietly end his ability to make a living was greater, the likelihood of anyone caring smaller. McHugh had his four girls to worry about, and his contract was up soon.

He left the meeting feeling acutely aware that his future was on the line, and wondering how long he could resist these entreaties from the top.

❖

The story left a blast radius, and the NBC executives weren't the only ones caught in it. Hillary Clinton had said nothing over the weekend between the stories from the *Times* and *The New Yorker*, declining inquiries from reporters while other politicians issued moralizing statements. Tina Brown, who had edited *Talk* magazine for Weinstein, began telling the press that she'd warned Clinton team members about Weinstein's reputation during the 2008 campaign. The writer and actor Lena Dunham disclosed how, during the 2016 campaign, she'd told Clinton's staff that the campaign's reliance on Weinstein as a fund-raiser and event organizer was a liability. "I just want to let you know that Harvey's a rapist and this is going to come out at some point," she recalled telling a communications staffer, one of several she said she warned.

After five days, Clinton issued a statement saying she was "shocked and appalled." I went back to Nick Merrill, her representative who had expressed anxieties about my reporting, and told him that my foreign policy book was about to feature interviews with every other living secretary of state and my best efforts to explain why Clinton had withdrawn. A call with her was hastily scheduled after all.

Woody Allen, who had expressed his sympathies to Weinstein on the phone the preceding month, expressed sympathies again in public. "No-one ever came to me or told me horror stories with any real seriousness," he said. "And they wouldn't, because you are not interested in it. You are interested in making your movie." And then: "The whole Harvey Weinstein thing is very sad for everybody involved. Tragic for the poor women that were involved, sad for Harvey that [his] life is so messed up." Later, in response to criticism about the comments, he said he'd meant Weinstein was "a sad, sick man." In any case, he emphasized, the important thing was "to avoid 'a witch hunt atmosphere' where 'every guy in an office who winks at a woman is suddenly having to call a lawyer to defend himself.'"

Streep, who had been so surprised to learn of the allegations when I spoke with her, said as much again. She was fielding criticism, much of it unfair. A right-wing guerrilla artist posted around Los Angeles an image of Streep and Weinstein huddled together, with a slash of red paint over Streep's eyes bearing the words "She knew." Streep released a statement through her publicist. (Because Hollywood values economy of characters, this was also Woody Allen's publicist, Leslee Dart, who had overseen his periodic efforts to discredit my sister.) "One thing can be clarified. Not everybody knew," Streep's statement said. "And if everybody knew, I don't believe that all the investigative reporters in the entertainment and the hard news media would have neglected for decades to write about it." I believed that Streep didn't know. But her optimism was misplaced: the media had tried, but it had also known, and neglected, so much.

CHAPTER 45:

# *NIGHTGOWN*

The women in the story were reacting too. Some were pained, others ecstatic. All described feeling a weight lifted. McGowan, after her months of ups and downs, thanked me. "You came in with a glorious flaming sword. So fucking well done," she wrote. "You did a huge service to us all. And you were BRAVE." McGowan said that she'd been staring down Weinstein's mounting offensive and her own spiraling legal fees. "I know you're mad at me and I had to go hard," she explained. "Behind the scenes Harder and Bloom were terrorizing me."

It had been a lonely time for McGowan. She'd let few people in, except for her new friend "Diana Filip" —"Anna" in the recent meeting with Weinstein. The day my story broke, she checked in with McGowan:

Hi Love,
I've been thinking about you a lot these past few days. So crazy, everything that's going on!

How are you feeling? It must be a relief and a lot of stress at the same time. you must be getting a lot of messages, I hope that all of them are supportive.

Anyway, just wanted to tell you how brave I think you are. I'm so proud of you.

I will send an email soon linking you with Paul, so that the two of you can arrange a follow up meeting to discuss the business.

Xx

By then, multiple sources had described contact from individuals they found suspicious. Zelda Perkins, the assistant involved in the London settlements, finally began responding to me, first to insist that she was legally barred from speaking about her time with Weinstein, then, over time, to share the full story of the London settlements. She said she'd also received what felt like not quite a normal reporting inquiry from a writer for the *Guardian* named Seth Freedman.

Annabella Sciorra sent word the day the story broke, too: "You did an incredible job of not only outing him but also conveying the pain that all of those women went through and continue to go through," she wrote. When I called her back, she began to explain that she was one of the women who continued to experience pain. During our first call, she'd stared out of her living room window at the East River, and struggled to tell her story. "I was like, 'This is the moment you've been waiting for your whole life...'" Then, panic had set in. "I was shaking," she recalled. "And I just wanted to get off the phone."

The truth, she said, was that she had been struggling to speak about Weinstein for more than twenty years. She lived in terror of him; she still slept with a baseball bat by her bed. Weinstein, she said, had violently raped her and, over the next several years, sexually harassed her repeatedly.

In the early nineties, after Sciorra starred in *The Night We Never Met*, which Weinstein produced, she said that she became ensconced in "this circle of Miramax." There were so many screenings and events and dinners that it was hard to imagine life outside of the Weinstein ecosystem. At one dinner, in New York, she recalled, "Harvey was there, and I got up to leave. And Harvey said, 'Oh, I'll drop you off.' Harvey had dropped me off before, so I didn't really expect anything out of the ordinary — I expected just to be dropped off." In the car, Weinstein said goodbye to Sciorra, and she went upstairs to her apartment. She was alone and getting ready for bed a few minutes later when she heard a knock on the door. "It wasn't that late," she said. "Like, it wasn't the middle of the night, so I opened the door a crack to see who it was. And he pushed the door open." Sciorra paused. The story seemed almost physically impossible for her to tell. Weinstein "walked in like it was his apartment, like he owned the place, and started unbuttoning his shirt. So it was very clear where he thought this was going to go. And I was in a nightgown. I didn't have much on." He circled the apartment; to Sciorra, it appeared that he was checking whether anyone else was there.

Sciorra told me that listening to Gutierrez's recording from the sting operation "really triggered me." She remembered Weinstein employing the same tactics as he cornered her, backing her into her bedroom. "Come here, come on, cut it out, what are you doing, come here," she remembered him saying. She tried to be assertive. "This is not happening," she told him. "You've got to go. You have to leave. Get out of my apartment."

"He shoved me onto the bed, and he got on top of me." Sciorra struggled. "I kicked and I yelled," she said, but Weinstein locked her arms over her head with one hand and forced sexual intercourse on her. "When he was done, he ejaculated on my leg, and on my nightgown." It was a family heirloom, handed down from relatives in Italy and embroidered in white cotton. "He said, 'I have impeccable timing,' and then he said, 'This is for you.'" Sciorra stopped, overcome, hyperventilating. "And then he attempted to perform oral sex on me. And I struggled, but I had very little strength left in me." Sciorra said that her body started to shake violently. "I think, in a way, that's what made him leave, because it looked like I was having a seizure or something."

The renderings of these stories that were ultimately published in *The New Yorker* were precise and legalistic. They made no attempt at communicating the true, bleak ugliness of listening to a recollection of violent rape like Sciorra's. Her voice caught. The memory erupted in ragged sobs. You heard Annabella Sciorra struggle to tell her story once, and it stayed inside you forever.

◆

In the weeks and months that followed the alleged attack, Sciorra didn't tell anyone about it. She never spoke to the police. "Like most of these women, I was so ashamed of what happened," she said. "And I fought. I fought. But still I was like, Why did I open that door? Who opens the door at that time of night? I was definitely embarrassed by it. I felt disgusting. I felt like I had fucked up." She grew depressed and lost weight. Her father, unaware of the attack but concerned for her well-being, urged her to seek help, and she did see a therapist, but, she said, "I don't even think I told the therapist. It's pathetic."

Sciorra, like so many others, suspected that Weinstein had retaliated. She said that she felt the impact on her livelihood almost immediately. "From 1992, I didn't work again until 1995," she said. "I just kept getting this pushback of 'we heard you were difficult; we

304 • CATCH AND KILL

heard this or that.' I think that that was the Harvey machine." The actress Rosie Perez, a friend who was among the first to discuss Sciorra's allegations with her, told me, "She was riding high, and then she started acting weird and getting reclusive. It made no sense. Why did this woman, who was so talented, and riding so high, doing hit after hit, then all of a sudden fall off the map? It hurts me as a fellow actress to see her career not flourish the way it should have."

Several years later, Sciorra did begin working again, and Weinstein again pursued her with unwanted sexual advances. In 1995, she was in London shooting *The Innocent Sleep*, which Weinstein did not produce. According to Sciorra, Weinstein began leaving her messages, demanding that she call him or that they meet at his hotel. She didn't know how he'd found her. One night, he showed up at her room and began pounding on the door, she said. "For nights after, I couldn't sleep. I piled furniture in front of the door, like in the movies."

Two years later, Sciorra appeared in the crime drama *Cop Land* as Liz Randone, the wife of a corrupt police officer. She said that she auditioned for the part without realizing at first that it was a Miramax film, and she learned that Weinstein's company was involved only when she began contract negotiations. In May 1997, shortly before the film's release, Sciorra went to the Cannes Film Festival. When she checked into the Hotel du Cap-Eden-Roc, in Antibes, a Miramax associate told her that Weinstein's room would be next to hers. "My heart just sank," Sciorra recalled. Early one morning, while she was still asleep, there was a knock on the door. Groggy, and thinking she must have forgotten about an early hair-and-makeup call, she opened the door. "There's Harvey in his underwear, holding a bottle of baby oil in one hand and a tape, a movie, in the other," she recalled. "And it was horrific, because I'd been there before." Sciorra said that she ran from Weinstein. "He was closing in really quickly, and I pressed all the call buttons for valet service and room service. I kept pressing all of them until someone showed up." Weinstein retreated, she said, when hotel staff arrived.

Over time, Sciorra opened up to a small number of people. Perez said that she heard from an acquaintance about Weinstein's behavior at the hotel in London and questioned Sciorra about what happened. Sciorra told Perez about the attack in her apartment, and Perez, who was sexually assaulted by a relative during her childhood, began crying. "I said, 'Oh, Annabella, you've gotta go to the police.' She said, 'I can't go to the police. He's destroying my career.'"

Perez said that she urged Sciorra to speak by describing her own experience of going public about her assault. "I told her, 'I used to tread water for years. It's fucking exhausting, and maybe speaking out, that's your lifeboat. Grab on and get out,'" Perez recalled. "I said, 'Honey, the water never goes away. But, after I went public, it became a puddle and I built a bridge over it, and one day you're gonna get there, too.'"

When Sciorra decided to go on the record, I told Remnick that I had more. He assigned David Rohde, a veteran war reporter for Reuters and the *Times*, as an additional editor. Rohde, who had once been kidnapped by the Taliban, had an angelic face that seemed incapable of arranging itself into expressions of malice or deception.

That October, he and Foley-Mendelssohn oversaw what became a story about the complex struggle each of the women had faced over whether to speak. We included Sciorra's account, and that of the actress Daryl Hannah, who told me Weinstein had sexually harassed her, too. Hannah said that, during the Cannes Film Festival in the early 2000s, Weinstein had relentlessly pounded on her hotel-room door until she slipped out via an exterior door and spent the night in her makeup artist's room. The night after, he'd tried again, and she'd had to barricade her hotel door with furniture to keep Weinstein out. Several years later, while she was in Rome for the premiere of *Kill Bill: Volume 2*, which Miramax distributed, he simply showed up in her room. "He had a key," Hannah told me. "He came through the living room and into the bedroom. He just burst in like a raging bull. And I know with every fiber of my being that if my male makeup artist was not in that room, things would not have gone well. It was scary." Weinstein, appearing to cover for the bizarre intrusion, demanded that she go downstairs for a party. But when she got there, the room was empty; it was just Weinstein, asking, "Are your tits real?" and then asking to feel them. "I said, 'No, you can't!' And then he said, 'At least flash me, then.' And I said, 'Fuck off, Harvey.'" The next morning, the Miramax private plane left without Hannah on it.

Sciorra and Hannah both talked about the forces that keep women quiet. Hannah said she'd told anyone who would listen from the get-go. "And it didn't matter," she told me. "I think that it doesn't matter if you're a well-known actress, it doesn't matter if you're twenty or if you're forty, it doesn't matter if you report or if you don't, because we are not believed. We are more than not believed — we are berated and criticized and blamed."

Sciorra, on the other hand, had been afraid to talk for all the reasons survivors of rape so often are: the bludgeoning psychic force of trauma; the fear of retaliation and stigma. "Now when I go to a restaurant or to an event, people are going to know that this happened to me," Sciorra said. "They're gonna look at me and they're gonna know. I'm an intensely private person, and this is the most unprivate thing you can do."

But there had been something separate and more specific behind her silence. Weinstein's vice grip on the media had made it hard to know whom to trust. "I've known now for a long time how powerful Harvey became, and how he owned a lot of journalists and gossip columnists," she said.

And she couldn't prove it, but she was convinced Weinstein was spying on her, keeping tabs, sending intermediaries with concealed motives. She conceded it sounded crazy. "I was afraid of you, because I thought it was Harvey checking up on me," she said. "As I was talking to you, I got scared that it wasn't really you." When I asked her if anyone suspicious *had* contacted her, she strained to remember. There had been a call, she said, from a British reporter that had unsettled her. "It struck me as BS," she told me. "And it scared me that Harvey was testing to see if I would talk." She fished through her texts. There he was, in August, not long after I'd heard from him: "Hi Ms. Sciorra it's Seth, the journalist in London....Might you have time for a very quick call to help with our piece? No more than ten minutes, and it'd be really useful for our research..."

## CHAPTER 46:

# *PRETEXTING*

**S**eth Freedman cut a colorful profile. He was a small man with wild eyes, a thick beard, and hair that seemed perpetually askew. He'd been a London stockbroker, then moved to Israel and served in a combat unit in the Israel Defense Forces—IDF—for fifteen months in the 2000s. Later, he turned whistle-blower, taking to the pages of the *Guardian* to expose his financial firm's manipulation of wholesale gas prices, eventually getting fired for it. His articles had a rambling, jocular quality and were laced with frank references to a drug habit. In 2013, he'd written a novel called *Dead Cat Bounce*, about a coked-out London-based Jewish finance guy who runs away to join the IDF and gets swept up in a world of espionage and crime, all under the guise of being a writer for the *Guardian*. Freedman wrote like a gangster in a Guy Ritchie movie talks: "The perfect mojito is a line of coke. See what I'm saying? Rum, lime, sugar, mint—yeah, yeah, yeah, but trust me, it's the poor man's Charlie. The scared man's snow. The straight man's chang."

In late October 2017, after the conversation with Sciorra, I followed up on Freedman's call, saying I wanted to talk. I told him it was time-sensitive. A tumble of WhatsApp messages came back.

"Massive congratulations on your reporting," he said. "Have been following closely." He said he'd been working with an English paper to get some of the stories out. Later, he'd explain how he passed recordings he'd made of his conversations with McGowan and another Weinstein accuser to the *Guardian*'s Sunday publication, the *Observer*, and how it published articles based on the interviews. The articles made no mention of Freedman, and talked around who conducted the interviews, and why.

Freedman professed to have shared the recordings out of a sincere desire to help expose the truth. And he offered to help with my reporting too. Quickly, he sent a screenshot of a document entitled "List of targets." It was a portion of a list of nearly a hundred names: former Weinstein employees, unfriendly journalists, and, most of all, women with allegations. Rose McGowan. Zelda Perkins. Annabella Sciorra. Many of the sources in my reporting were on it, including several who had expressed uneasy suspicions that they were being watched or followed. Priority targets were in red. It was the same list Lubell and Doyle Chambers had helped assemble. In some cases, it was annotated with their updates on conversations with targeted individuals.

A few hours after we began exchanging messages, I was on the phone with Freedman. At first, he repeated his story about having only journalistic interest in the matter. "I got tipped off in about November last year that something was gonna happen, and people were looking into a story about Harvey Weinstein," he said. "At the time, I wanted to just write a piece about Hollywood, about what life was like there."

But over the course of the conversation, more fine details emerged about the "people" who were "looking into" Weinstein's accusers. First he referred to this shadowy group as "them." "I kind of knew them already, but in an extremely different context," he said. Then it was "we." "Initially, we thought this was . . . the normal kind of business dispute you have with Oligarch 1 against Oligarch 2, the equivalent in Hollywood," he said. The earliest dossiers he received scrutinized Weinstein's business rivals, including board members at amfAR. But as the focus turned to McGowan, and Perkins, and Dix, he said, he began to grow uncomfortable with his involvement. "It turned out that it was actually about sexual assault. We pulled back and we said there's no way we're getting involved with this. How do we extricate ourselves? Because he's hired us."

I struggled to make sense of who Seth Freedman was working with on Weinstein's behalf. "Are we talking about private investigators working for him or other journalists?" I asked.

"Yeah, the first, yeah," he said cautiously. "I was in the Israeli army," he continued. "I know a lot of people involved in Israeli intelligence. That should be enough to give you a guide to who they are without me telling you who they are."

I tried one more time. "Can you name any of the individuals in this group or the name of the group?"

Finally, he said, "They're called Black Cube."

For you or me, the term "private detective" might conjure images of hard-drinking ex-cops working out of rundown offices. But for moneyed corporations and individuals, the profession has long offered services that look very different. Back in the '70s, a former prosecutor named Jules Kroll founded his eponymous firm, catering to law firms and banks, and staffed by former cops, FBI agents, and forensic accountants. The formula, and a generation of copycats, flourished. In the 2000s, Israel became a hotbed for such firms. The country's mandatory military service, and the legendary secrecy and accomplishment of its intelligence agency, Mossad, created a ready pipeline of trained operatives. The Israeli firms began emphasizing less conventional forms of corporate espionage, including "pretexting": using operatives with false identities.

Black Cube perfected the formula. It was founded in 2010 by Dan Zorella and Dr. Avi Yanus, who had been on the emails with Weinstein's lawyers. Zorella and Yanus were both veterans of a secret Israeli intelligence unit. From the beginning, Black Cube had close connections to Israel's military and intelligence leadership. Meir Dagan, the legendary former director of Mossad, sat on the company's advisory board until his death, in 2016. Dagan once pitched Black Cube's services to a tycoon by saying: I can find a personal Mossad for you.

Black Cube's workforce grew to more than a hundred operatives, speaking thirty languages. It opened offices in London and Paris and eventually moved its headquarters to a massive space in a gleaming tower in central Tel Aviv, behind a jet-black unmarked door. Inside, there were more unmarked doors, fingerprint readers sealing many of them. In the company's reception area, just about everything fit a black cube motif, from the plush furnishings to the art on the walls. In other rooms, agents took pretexting to new extremes. A single desk might have cubby holes containing twenty different cell phones, each tied to a different number and fictional persona. Everyone submitted to routine polygraphs to ensure they weren't leaking to the press. Even the janitors got tested.

The line between Black Cube and Israel's actual intelligence apparatus could be fine. The private agency was "the exclusive supplier to major organizations and government ministries," one court document revealed. So it was unsurprising that Ehud Barak, the former prime minister, had recommended Black Cube to Weinstein.

I blanketed Tel Aviv with calls and emails, and soon, a firm that prided itself on silence was beginning to whisper, up to its very highest levels. There was a formal, bland denial, orchestrated by a freelance Tel Aviv flack named Eido Minkovsky, who flirted and flattered his way through calls. "My wife's seen your pictures," he said. "There's no way she's gonna come to New York. She's not allowed to. I confiscated her visa."

"You're a sweet talker. I respect that," I said.

"Yeah, that's my game."

And then there was a series of more revealing calls that I took alongside Rohde, the editor, huddled in his office early each morning to account for the time difference. These were with two men close to the Black Cube operation, who spoke on condition of anonymity. At first, their party line was denial. They said the agency had only done internet research for Weinstein, and that its operatives had never contacted women with allegations or reporters. "We never approached any of these," said the deeper of the two Israeli-accented voices, belonging to the more senior of the sources. "I also made sure with my team here, any of these you wrote here: Annabella Sciorra, Sophie Dix, Rose McGowan…." And, when I raised Ben Wallace's and my suspicions that we'd been targeted: "We don't generally work on journalists as a target." They "swore" it, said the more junior man close to the operation, who had a higher, lighter voice. "We're Talmud Jews!" he continued. "We don't swear for nothing!" The calls were both ominous and entertaining.

They promised to send documents from within the operation that would dispel any claims that Black Cube had followed accusers or reporters. "I will send you the documents today," the lower voice said. "We'll use a onetime email or one of our servers, we'll see."

Thirty minutes after we hung up, a message arrived from the encrypted email service ProtonMail, with documents attached. Another message followed a few hours later, from a different email service, Zmail, with more documents. Smart to disperse them across multiple accounts, I thought. "Hello mutual friend," read the first email. "Attached you'll find new information concerning the HW&BC affair. Best, cryptoadmin."

The ProtonMail account it came from bore the name "Sleeper1973."

# CHAPTER 47:

# *RUNNING*

*A*ttached to that email was a complete record of Black Cube's work for Weinstein. There was the first contract, signed October 28, 2016, and several others that followed, including a July 11, 2017, revision after the squabble over invoices. That last arrangement promised services through November:

> The primary objectives of the project are:
> a) Provide intelligence which will help the Client's efforts to completely stop the publication of a new negative article in a leading NY newspaper (hereinafter "the Article");
> b) Obtain additional content of a book which currently being written and includes harmful negative information on and about the Client (hereinafter "the Book").

Black Cube promised "a dedicated team of expert intelligence officers that will operate in the USA and any other necessary country," including a project manager, intelligence analysts, linguists, and "Avatar Operators" specifically hired to create fake identities on social media, as well as "operations experts with extensive experience in social engineering." The agency agreed to hire "an investigative journalist, as per the Client request," who would be required to conduct ten interviews a month for four months and be paid $40,000. The agency would "promptly report to the Client the results of such interviews by the Journalist."

Black Cube also promised to provide "a full time agent by the name of 'Anna' (hereinafter 'the Agent'), who will be based in New York and Los Angeles as per the Client's instructions and who will be available full time to assist the Client and his attorneys for the next four months."

The invoices attached were eye-popping: fees that might have totaled up to $1.3 million. The contracts were signed by Dr. Avi Yanus, the Black Cube director, and by Boies Schiller. This was an astonishment. Boies's law firm *represented* the *New York Times*. But here was the esteemed lawyer's signature, in genteel blue-inked cursive, on a contract to kill the paper's reporting and obtain McGowan's book.

◆

Black Cube stressed that its tactics were vetted by attorneys around the world and that it kept to the letter of the law. But I was soon hearing from sources in the private intelligence world that the agency had a reputation for flouting rules. In 2016, two Black Cube operatives were jailed in Romania for intimidating a prosecutor and hacking her emails. They were later convicted, receiving suspended sentences. "Privacy laws, data laws," one person directly involved with Black Cube's operations told me. "It's impossible to do what they do without breaking the law." The head of a competing Israeli private intelligence firm who'd had dealings with Black Cube told me, "More than fifty percent of what they do is illegal." I asked him what to do if I suspected I was being followed, and he said, "Just start running."

As our conversations with the Israelis grew tense, I spent a few nights at my borrowed desks at *The New Yorker* rather than move around on the streets after dark.

❖

Within hours of the contracts coming in, I was on the phone with David Boies, the beginning of what would sprawl into days of conversation. At first, he wasn't sure he wanted to go on the record. He said he was busy with his pro bono work, including negotiating to get a young American out of jail in Venezuela. And he was concerned that he might be misinterpreted. "As the bad guy says in one of the Mission Impossible films, it's complicated," he wrote in one email. I puzzled over the choice of quotes. It was from a scene in the third film in that series. Billy Crudup, thus far made out to be a good guy, sits down in front of a bloodied Tom Cruise, tied to a chair in the way heroes have to be at this point in the third act, and gives a similarly obligatory speech about how he was working for the bad guy. "It's complicated," says Crudup. He's concerned about being found out. "Did anyone else see it?" he asks of evidence tying him to the villain, chewing scenery like he's read the script and knows it's his last scene.

Boies eventually went on the record. "We should not have been contracting with and paying investigators that we did not select and direct," he told me. "At the time, it seemed a reasonable accommodation for a client, but it was not thought through, and that was my mistake. It was a mistake at the time." Boies conceded that efforts to profile and undermine reporters were problematic. "In general, I don't think it's appropriate to try to pressure reporters," he said. "If that did happen here, it would not have been appropriate." And he edged toward something like personal regret. "In retrospect, I knew enough in 2015 that I believe I should have been on notice of a problem, and done something about it," he added, referring to the time frame when Nestor's and Gutierrez's allegations surfaced. "I don't know what, if anything, happened after 2015, but to the extent it did, I think I have some responsibility. I also think that if people had taken action earlier it would have been better for Mr. Weinstein."

It is to Boies's credit that he unhesitatingly copped to everything, including the agent the contract called Anna and the reporter-for-hire, whom he identified as Freedman, the former *Guardian* writer. When I sent him the signed contracts with Black Cube, he wrote back simply, "Both are my signatures." The best characters know when it's time for a confessional speech.

◆

In Rohde's office the next morning, we were back on the phone with the two men close to the Black Cube operation. I thanked them for sending the documents. They sounded cheerful, confident that what they'd sent would exonerate them of any claims that they'd relied on intrusive human surveillance on Weinstein's behalf. "We did not approach any of these women undercover," the deeper of the two voices said again. "We did not approach any of these journalists undercover."

When I began asking questions about the contract that alluded to those very tactics, they sounded confused. "We never drafted. I can one hundred percent tell you that we never drafted," the higher voice chimed in.

Rohde and I exchanged a puzzled glance. "I'm looking at it. It's on

Black Cube's stationery, it's signed by Avi," I said. " I'm referring to a document you guys sent me."

"When you say 'we guys,' what do you mean by 'we guys?' " said the deeper voice, cautious, worried.

"This was in the binder of documents that you sent to me yesterday. Not the second dump from Zmail, but the very first one, from the Sleeper email," I said.

A pin-drop silence.

"We did not send you any burner email yesterday," the deeper voice replied. "The only thing we sent you yesterday was from Zmail."

Realization prickled my skin. The men had promised a Black Cube document dump from a discreet account. What was the likelihood that another source would intercede with a conflicting and more devastating leak at the exact same time? But two distinct leaks seemed the only possibility. I'd stumbled into a civil war among spies.

I got off the subject of the source of the documents in a hurry, told them that we'd already authenticated them with Boies and others. "They are genuine," I said. There was a flash of panic in the deeper voice. "I . . . I don't know who sent that, but we will definitely investigate." Then, collecting himself, he added: "We should do this friendly, I would say." I wondered what the alternative looked like.

I fired off an email to the mystery address quickly. "Can you give any information that would help authenticate these documents? Some parties involved are denying several pieces of this." A response, immediately: "I'm not surprised they denied it, but it is all true. they were trying to get Rose's book, via a girl named 'Ana' . . . a HUMINT agent."

Another set of files was attached: a wide-ranging history of correspondence and ancillary documents underpinning and surrounding the contracts. Over time, these would check out, too.

I leaned back, rubbed a palm over my mouth, thinking.

*Who are you, Sleeper?*

# CHAPTER 48:

# *GASLIGHT*

"**W**e need to find out who he is," Rohde, and just about everyone else at *The New Yorker*, pressed. We turned over the question. "Sleeper1973 is possibly a Woody Allen reference," I wrote, referring to the film of the same name released that year. "Which is certainly cheeky." Someone with a sense of humor, then.

But Sleeper rebuffed my every plea for identifying information, to get on an encrypted call, to meet in person. "I can understand your editors' concern although I'm afraid to reveal my identity. Every online method can be monitored these days...its hard for me to trust it wont come back at me," Sleeper wrote. "I'm sure you know NSO so I'm not interested in taking unnecessary risks." NSO Group was an Israeli cyber intelligence firm, famed for its Pegasus software, which could take control of a cell phone and strip-mine it for data. It had been used to target dissidents and journalists around the world.

But Sleeper kept sending information from the encrypted email address, and it always checked out. After McGowan told me she'd spent time with only a few trusted contacts in recent months and couldn't recall anyone who might have been Anna, the undercover operative, I asked Sleeper for leads. Another lightning-quick response:

"Regarding Anna, her genuine name is Stella Pen. I've attached pictures as well. She allegedly got 125 pages of Rose's book (as appears on BC's agreement with Boies), and discussed the findings with HW himself."

Attached were three photos of a statuesque blonde with a prominent nose and high cheekbones.

I was in a taxi, the West Side Highway slipping by outside. I texted the photos to McGowan and Ben Wallace.

"Oh my God," McGowan wrote back. "Reuben Capital. Diana Filip. No fucking way."

Wallace remembered her immediately too. "Yes," he wrote back. "Who is she?"

❖

Black Cube's work was designed never to be discovered. But, once in a while, an operative would leave too many prints. In the spring of 2017—as the Trump administration and its supporters worked to dismantle the 2015 Iran nuclear deal—a string of peculiar inquiries reached prominent defenders of the deal. A woman identifying herself as Adriana Gavrilo, of Reuben Capital Partners, emailed Rebecca Kahl, a former program officer at the National Democratic Institute and the wife of Obama administration foreign policy advisor Colin Kahl. Gavrilo told Kahl that she was launching an initiative on education and repeatedly asked to meet to discuss the school that Kahl's daughter attended. Worried that she was "strangely a target of some sort," Kahl stopped responding.

A few weeks later, a woman named Eva Novak, of a London-based film company called Shell Productions, emailed Ann Norris, a former State Department official and the wife of Ben Rhodes, another Obama foreign policy advisor. Novak wanted Norris to consult on a movie that she described as *"All the President's Men* meets *The West Wing,"* telling the stories of government officials during times of geopolitical crisis, including "nuclear negotiations with a hostile nation." Finding Novak's request "bizarre," Norris decided not to write back at all.

Later, Freedman would leak again, helping me assemble the documents underlying the operation: Black Cube profiles of the Obama administration officials, ferreting out damaging information, detailing bogus claims that they worked with Iran lobbyists, or were getting kickbacks, and a rumor that one of them had an affair.

There were other examples. During the summer of 2017, a woman who identified herself as Diana Ilic, a London-based consultant to a European software mogul, began calling and meeting with critics of AmTrust Financial Services Inc., pressing them to make statements about their work that could be used against them. Not long after, Maja Lazarov of Caesar & Co., a London-based recruitment agency, began doing the same with employees of West Face Capital, a Canadian asset management firm.

Social media accounts tied to these names, and photos taken during the meetings, showed a familiar face, with high cheekbones framed by long blond hair.

The marks were left with the same question:

*Anna, Adriana, Eva, Diana, Maja.*

*Who are you?*

❖

Stella Penn Pechanac was born between two worlds and belonged to none. "I was a Bosnian Muslim, and my husband was a Serbian Orthodox," her mother later said. "And what was our little Steliza?" In childhood photos, the girl was not yet blond but dark: dark hair, dark eyes. She was raised in the faded sprawl of Sarajevo, amid beat-up cars and dilapidated tower blocks. That was before things got bad.

Pechanac watched it all turn to ash and blood. War began, Serbian Orthodox against Bosnian Muslim. Sarajevo was roadblocked and cordoned according to sect. At best, during the war, there was the grind of poverty and near starvation. When nothing else could be found, her mother made grass soup. Pechanac was smart, but there were few opportunities for education. At worst, it was a childhood like Guernica. Sharpshooters on rooftops made the streets a death trap. For half a year, the family moved into a bare, closet-sized basement room. When shells started landing nearby, Pechanac's parents gathered up what wounded they could, and shared the room and the thin mattress in it. "One woman died on it," Pechanac would later recall with a shrug. After the shelling, the entryway of their rundown building flooded with blood. "There were water hoses we used to clean with, and they simply washed all the blood out the door. I remember, seven years old."

About a decade before the Weinstein affair, when Pechanac was in her early twenties, she and her mother had gone back to Sarajevo to appear in a documentary about the war and their family's flight from it. Her mother wept openly, walking the streets and recalling the bloodshed. Pechanac seemed a reluctant participant. She hovered at the margin of shots, chewing gum or smoking, casting petulant glances at the camera.

Eventually, one of the filmmakers cornered the impassive young woman at the entrance to a crumbling building and asked what it was like to relive such painful memories. Another shrug. "It makes me mad that she had to go through this," she said, referring to her mother. "But personally, I haven't felt anything for a long time."

During World War II, Pechanac's grandmother had hidden and protected Jews. The State of Israel bestowed upon her the Righteous Among the Nations honorific, a novelty for a Muslim woman. As Sarajevo burned, a Jewish family returned the favor and helped to exfiltrate the Pechanacs. They settled in Jerusalem and converted from their Muslim faith to Judaism. Young Stella Pechanac adapted to a new identity and cultural context. "She doesn't feel inside patriotic like the people born in Israel," said one person who knew her well. "Always in one level, she feel like a stranger."

At eighteen, Pechanac enlisted in the Israeli Air Force. After that, she enrolled at Nissan Nativ acting school. She dreamed of Hollywood. But she found only a few fleeting acting opportunities in plays and music videos. "At all the auditions," Pechanac later observed, "they all noticed my accent, they all noticed I was different."

The job at Black Cube presented an ideal compromise. Its operatives were trained in psyops — psychological operations designed to manipulate targets. Like the best actors, they were students of body language, of the gentle tics that expose lying and vulnerability. They knew how to read them in others and how to deploy them convincingly themselves. They wore costumes and used technology straight out of spy thrillers: watch-cameras; recording pens. "She went to work in Black Cube," said the person who knew her well, "'cause she needs to be a character."

◆

As I presented them with the evidence from Sleeper, the men close to the Black Cube operation dropped their denials. They confirmed, like Boies, that Freedman was the journalist in the contract, describing him as an informal adjunct to the team. They described, in detail, Pechanac's efforts to insinuate herself into McGowan's life. McGowan had been an easy mark. "She was trusting," the deeper voice explained. "They became very good friends. I'm sure she's a bit shocked." McGowan had told Pechanac that it seemed like everyone in her life was turning out to be secretly connected to Weinstein. She even suspected her lawyers. But, "she, of course, didn't suspect us."

When I finally told McGowan what I'd learned, she reeled. "It was like the movie *Gaslight*," she told me. "Everyone lied to me all the time." For the past year, she said, "I've lived inside a mirrored fun house."

CHAPTER 49:

# *VACUUM*

*I*t wasn't just Black Cube. The calls led to more calls, and soon a dam was fracturing and the shadowy underworld of private intelligence spilling its secrets. There were the conscientious objectors feeding me information about their intelligence agencies. And there were the leaders at those firms, frantically leaking about their competitors in a bid to broaden the focus of my reporting beyond their own activities.

Documents and sources illuminated Weinstein's long relationship with Kroll and Dan Karson, the firm's chairman of Investigations and Disputes for America. One former Weinstein staffer remembered a call in the early 2010s during which Karson said, of a chauffeur who was involved in a dispute with Weinstein, "You know we can put this guy at the bottom of a lake." The staffer assumed it was a figure of speech but was uncomfortable enough to note it down. Through the years, Kroll had assisted in Weinstein's efforts to thwart reporters. Several Kroll sources said that Weinstein had assigned the firm to dig up unflattering information about David Carr, the late essayist and media reporter, as he had suspected. One of the dossiers compiled by Weinstein's private investigators noted that Carr had never included the allegations of sexual abuse in any of his coverage of Weinstein, "due to fear of HW's retaliation, according to HW."

In 2016 and 2017, Kroll and Karson had worked closely with Weinstein again. In one October 2016 email, Karson sent Weinstein eleven photographs of McGowan and Weinstein together at events in the years after he allegedly assaulted her. Weinstein's criminal defense attorney Blair Berk replied that one photo, which showed McGowan warmly talking with Weinstein, "is the money shot." As Wallace worked on the story, Kroll searched for damaging information about him and Adam Moss, his editor at *New York* magazine. "No adverse information about Adam Moss so far (no libel/defamation cases, no court records or judgments/liens/UCC, etc.)," Karson wrote in one email. Kroll also sent Weinstein criticism of Wallace's previous reporting and a detailed description of a UK libel suit filed in response to a book he wrote, which was ultimately settled out of court.

PSOPS, the firm founded by Jack Palladino and Sandra Sutherland, had assisted in the search for damaging information about reporters and accusers. One PSOPS report on McGowan had sections labeled "Lies/Exaggerations/Contradictions," "Hypocrisy," and "Potential Negative Character Wits," an apparent abbreviation of "witnesses." A subhead read "Past Lovers." Palladino sent Weinstein a detailed profile of Moss, noting, "Our research did not yield any promising avenues for the personal impeachment of Moss." PSOPS even profiled Wallace's ex-wife, in case she proved "relevant to considerations of our response strategy." The firm's work on reporters had carried forward through its dossiers on me and Jodi Kantor, of the *Times*, seeking to uncover our sources. (Some of the investigators' observations were more mundane. On Twitter, one document noted, "Kantor is NOT following Ronan Farrow." You can't have everything.)

Weinstein had also worked with K2 Intelligence, a second firm founded by Jules Kroll after he sold the firm bearing his name in the

2000s. During the Gutierrez investigation, K2 had been retained by Elkan Abramowitz, Weinstein's attorney. K2 hired Italian private investigators to dig up rumors about Gutierrez's sexual history — the Bunga Bunga parties, the prostitution claims she disputed. Current and former K2 employees, all of whom had previously worked at the district attorney's office, relayed the information about Gutierrez in calls to prosecutors. Lawyers working for Weinstein also presented a dossier of the private investigators' findings to prosecutors in a face-to-face meeting. Two K2 employees said that those contacts were part of a "revolving door" culture between the DA and high-priced private investigation firms. A spokesperson for Vance's office later said that such interactions with defense attorneys were standard procedure — and for the wealthy and connected, they were.

◆

The expanding reporting also showed Weinstein's efforts to enlist journalists in his campaign to undermine accusers. In caches of Weinstein's communications, his alliance with Dylan Howard of the *National Enquirer* was inescapable. In one December 2016 exchange, Howard sent Weinstein a list of contacts and suggested they "discuss next steps on each." After Weinstein thanked him, Howard described his efforts to obtain damaging statements about McGowan from the film producer Elizabeth Avellan. Robert Rodriguez, Avellan's ex-husband and the father of her children, had left Avellan to have a relationship with McGowan. Weinstein figured Avellan had to be disgruntled.

For some of his work on Weinstein's behalf, Howard turned to a frequent subcontractor of the *National Enquirer*, a celebrity photography service called Coleman-Rayner. For the Avellan job, Howard tapped a British reporter who was at the time a news editor at

Coleman-Rayner and who had written celebrity gossip items for the *Sun*, the *Daily Mail*, and the *Enquirer* itself.

When I reached her on the phone, Avellan told me that she remembered the incident well. The reporter "kept calling and calling and calling," she said, and also contacted others close to her. Avellan finally called back, because "I was afraid people might start calling my kids."

Avellan insisted that the call be off the record, and the reporter agreed. Though he was at the time in California, where both parties are legally required to consent to recording, he secretly taped her anyway. And so Weinstein and Howard exchanged their excited emails that winter: Howard writing "I have something AMAZING... eventually she laid into Rose pretty hard"; Weinstein replying, "This is the killer. Especially if my fingerprints r not on this." Howard assured him there were no prints, and the whole thing had been recorded.

I stayed late at *The New Yorker,* combing through the emails, a vacuum echoing nearby. It was, it would come to pass, just the tip of the iceberg when it came to the *National Enquirer* and its work on behalf of prominent men with closely guarded secrets.

◆

As we prepared to publish our report about Weinstein's army of collaborators, panic set in at the institutions named in it. In several calls, Dylan Howard evinced a mix of flattery and menace. "Careful," he said, as Weinstein had. Judd Burstein, a lawyer working with Howard, followed up with a letter describing the reporting as defamation and libel. When that didn't prevail, Howard grew angry. He said of me to two colleagues: "I'm going to get him."

Black Cube's UK-based law firm was sending threats, too,

promising to take "appropriate action against you" if we published the Black Cube documents or information from them. Inside the agency, Dr. Avi Yanus, the director, contemplated destroying the materials from the Weinstein investigation. "We wish to dispose of every document and information we possess in regards with this project," he wrote in one email. Then he pressed the agency's lawyers to seek an injunction to stop *The New Yorker* from publishing.

But we did publish, and the story reverberated like a gunshot. On one program after another, television personalities expressed disbelief. What did it say about the gulf between the powerful and the powerless that wealthy individuals could intimidate, surveil, and conceal on such a vast scale?

❖

Ostrovskiy, the private investigator, saw the story immediately. He read about Black Cube's target list, and the journalists on it, and thought back to the jobs of the past summer. He sent the story to Khaykin and asked if he'd seen it. Khaykin replied that they'd have to discuss it in person. A few days later, during a routine stakeout, Ostrovskiy asked again. Khaykin seemed irritated, wanted to get off the subject. But finally, he said, "Now you know who we work for."

Some time passed before Ostrovskiy had the chance to press the point again. It was the dead of night, and the two private investigators were on a boat in the cold waters just north of Sandy Hook, New Jersey. Khaykin loved sailing—he ran a social media account for sailing enthusiasts. The men were heading back to New York after dinner at a waterside restaurant in Atlantic Highlands. Ostrovskiy seized on the chance to bring up Black Cube again.

Khaykin fixed his hard eyes on him and said, "To me, this is like doing a mitzvah. I'm doing something good for Israel." Ostrovskiy stared back. It was not a mitzvah, and it wasn't for Israel.

"I'm scared, but it's interesting and it's exciting," Ostrovskiy said of their work for Black Cube, playing along.

"I'm the one who needs to be scared, this whole Weinstein thing was under my license," Khaykin replied. He quickly added: "It was all legal. We never broke the law." But he sounded nervous.

All through the last days of reporting, the men close to the Black Cube operation had undertaken a frantic hunt for the source who'd passed me the contracts and other documents. "We're investigating everything. All the parties involved, and what was stolen," the deeper of the two voices said. He mentioned he was enforcing a new round of polygraphs, and promised to sue anyone he caught. "We find it hard to believe that a worker would go on a suicide mission like this," the higher voice added.

"I just want to make sure you are not at risk," I wrote to Sleeper. "I will do all I can to keep you protected."

A response, quick as usual: "I do appreciate your care . . . Momentarily, I feel safe."

Just before we published, I made a last push for the source's identity. I wrote that knowing more was a matter of journalistic importance. Sleeper told me one thing that made it clear where the documents were coming from — and asked me to do one thing to keep the secret.

There was also a note about motive. "I'm an insider who is fed up with BC's false and devious ways of obtaining material illegally," Sleeper wrote. "Moreover, in this case, I truly believe HW is a sex offender and I'm ashamed as a woman for participating."

I paused, processing this, feeling another moment of hair-prickling realization. That, in the end, is what I can tell you about Sleeper, and the risks she took to uncover something vast. She was a woman and she'd had enough.

"Lets just say that I will never ever give you something that I cant back you for 100%," she wrote in one of her final messages to me. "I work in the information industry. World of espionage and endless action. Hope we can actually talk about it some day. The project I'm involved in. . . . out of this world, my dear."

# CHAPTER 50:

# *PLAYMATE*

*T*he reporting on Dylan Howard and the *Enquirer* opened up a vein. One after another, sources in and around American Media Inc. were calling, saying that Weinstein wasn't the only figure with whom the tabloid empire had worked to suppress stories.

Late that November, a lawyer, Carol Heller, wrote to me. There was more, she explained, to a report that the *Wall Street Journal* had published in the fall of 2016, about a Playboy model who'd signed over to AMI the exclusive rights to her story about a purported affair with Donald Trump — a story AMI never published. Heller told me that the woman at the heart of the mystery, a former *Playboy* Playmate of the Year named Karen McDougal, was still "too frightened" to talk. If I could get her and others around the transaction to open up, I might be able to reveal how the contract with AMI came about, and begin to unravel how the culture of nondisclosure agreements and buried stories extended beyond Hollywood and into politics.

Late that month, I was on the phone with McDougal. She told me the contract with AMI "took my rights away." It contained a clause that could allow AMI to force her into a private arbitration process and seek financial damages. McDougal was struggling to make ends meet. AMI could wipe her out. "At this point I feel I can't talk about anything without getting into trouble," she told me. Of Trump, she said, "I'm afraid to even mention his name." But as I gathered more evidence, including her contract with AMI and accounts of how it came about from others involved in the process, McDougal began to share her story.

McDougal, who grew up in a small town in Michigan and worked as a preschool teacher before beginning her modeling career, met Trump at a pool party at the Playboy Mansion. It was June 2006, and he was there to shoot an episode of his reality show *The Apprentice*. "Come on over," he said to a couple of models in corsets and bunny tails. "Wow, beautiful." The show's camera operators zoomed and panned like they were nature photographers and breasts were an endangered species. At the time of the party, Trump had been married to the Slovenian model Melania Knauss for less than two years; their son, Barron, was a few months old. But Trump seemed uninhibited by his new family obligations. McDougal remembered him being "all over" her, calling her beautiful. Then he asked for her number. The two began talking frequently and, soon after, met for dinner in a private bungalow at the Beverly Hills Hotel. "We talked for a couple hours—then, it was 'ON'! We got naked + had sex," McDougal wrote in notes about the affair that I later obtained. As McDougal got dressed and prepared to leave, Trump offered her money. "I looked at him (+ felt sad) + said, No thanks—I'm not 'that girl.'" Afterward, McDougal "went to see him every time he was in LA (which was a lot)."

Over the course of the affair, Trump flew McDougal to public events across the country but hid the fact that he paid for her travel.

"No paper trails for him," her notes read. "Every time I flew to meet him, I booked/paid for flight + hotel + he reimbursed me." During the relationship, Trump introduced McDougal to members of his family and gave her tours of his properties. In Trump Tower, McDougal wrote, Trump pointed out Melania's separate bedroom. He "said she liked her space," McDougal wrote.

In April 2007, after nine months, McDougal ended the affair. Learning more about Trump's family had brought on a creeping sense of guilt. And Trump's behavior chafed against her polite Midwestern sensibility. Once, he called McDougal's mother, who was around his age, "that old hag." On another occasion, as she and one of her girlfriends joined Trump in his limo on the night of a Miss Universe pageant, he started slinging comments about penis size and pressing McDougal's girlfriend about her experiences and preferences—asking about "small dicks" and "big dicks" and "black dick."

❖

A friend of McDougal's, Johnny Crawford, first proposed selling the story. In 2016, as they watched election-season coverage of Trump, Crawford said, "You know, if you had a physical relationship with him, that could be worth something." At his urging, McDougal wrote the notes on the affair. She didn't want to tell her story at first. But when a former friend of hers, fellow Playboy model Carrie Stevens, started posting about the affair on social media, McDougal figured she should talk before someone else did.

Crawford enlisted Jay Grdina, the ex-husband of the porn star Jenna Jameson, to help sell the story. Grdina first brokered two meetings between McDougal and JJ Rendón, a Latin American political operative who was already, by then, denying media reports that he constructed fake bases of support on social media and hacked opponents' email accounts. When he wasn't interested, Grdina turned to Keith M. Davidson, an attorney with a track record of selling salacious stories. Davidson got in touch with AMI. Pecker and Howard, in turn, alerted Michael Cohen, Trump's lawyer. Soon, Trump was on the phone with Pecker, asking for help.

In June 2016, McDougal and Howard met. Howard then made an offer: initially just $10,000 and then, after Trump won the Republican nomination, considerably more than that. On August 5, 2016, McDougal signed a limited life-story rights agreement granting AMI exclusive ownership of her account of any relationship she'd had with any "then-married man." Her retainer with Davidson made explicit that the man in question was Donald Trump. In exchange, AMI agreed to pay her $150,000. The three men involved in the deal—Davidson, Crawford, and Grdina—took 45 percent of the payment as fees, leaving McDougal with a total of $82,500. The day she signed the contract, McDougal emailed Davidson to express confusion over what she was signing up for, and how she'd have to respond to questions from reporters. "If you deny, you are safe," Davidson wrote. "We really do need to get this signed and wrapped up…" "I'm the one who took it, so it's my fault, too," McDougal told me. "But I didn't understand the full parameters of it."

As voters went to the polls on Election Day in 2016, Howard and AMI's general counsel were on the phone with McDougal and a law firm representing her, promising to boost McDougal's career and offering to employ a publicist to help her handle interviews. That publicist was Matthew Hiltzik, flack to Ivanka Trump, who had called me on Weinstein's behalf—although his services ultimately were not used. AMI responded quickly when journalists tried to interview McDougal. In May 2017, *The New Yorker*'s Jeffrey Toobin, who was writing a profile of David Pecker, asked McDougal for comment about her relationships with AMI and Trump. Howard, working with a different publicist, forwarded McDougal a draft response with the subject line "SEND THIS." In August 2017, Pecker flew McDougal to New York and the two had lunch, during which he thanked her for her loyalty.

❖

In late 2017 and early 2018, as we worked on the story, AMI's interest in enforcing the contract seemed to increase. On January 30, AMI's general counsel sent an email with the subject line "McDougal contract extension," proposing a renewal and a new magazine cover to sweeten the deal.

That February, our story ran anyway, with McDougal overcoming her fear and agreeing to speak on the record about the matter for the first time. In the years before, she had become religious and, in turn, fiercely altruistic. "Every girl who speaks is paving the way for another," she told me. Her own silence was about a consensual affair, but she could help expose a deeper and wider system of burying stories that was sometimes used to cover up more serious, even criminal, behavior.

The White House called the story "just more fake news." AMI's general counsel wrote that this report, too, was "false, and defamatory," and that I'd colluded in "a plot by McDougal and her lawyer to milk AMI for more money." Howard issued his own threats to publicly attack *The New Yorker*. AMI insisted that it had declined to print McDougal's story because it did not find it credible. It just hadn't met the *Enquirer*'s exacting journalistic standards.

# CHAPTER 51:

# *CHUPACABRA*

*B*y the time we published, I'd already heard about another transaction that might show that McDougal's contract was part of a pattern of AMI working to suppress stories for Trump. Friends and colleagues of Dylan Howard contacted me to say that Howard had boasted that he had evidence that Trump may have fathered a child with his former housekeeper in the late 1980s. Howard "would sometimes say things when drunk or high. Including telling me they would pay for stories and not publish, to protect people," one of the friends told me. "You don't forget when someone says, 'Oh, by the way. The maybe-future president has a love child.'"

In February 2018, I sat down in David Remnick's office and told him about the story. "You know what people are going to say when they find out *you're* reporting this?" he said, wonderingly. We both laughed. I knew my way around a paternity rumor.

There was no evidence that the underlying rumor about the "love child" was true. But that spring, a growing number of documents and sources made clear that AMI really had bought the rights to the dubious claim, then worked to prevent its disclosure.

◆

In late 2015, Dino Sajudin, a former Trump Tower doorman, had told AMI the story, along with the names of the supposed mother and child. For weeks, *National Enquirer* reporters pursued the matter. The tabloid retained two private investigators: Danno Hanks, who ran record searches on the family, and Michael Mancuso, a former criminal investigator, who administered a lie-detector test to Sajudin. Several of the reporters doubted Sajudin's credibility. (His ex-wife would later call him a fabulist. "He's seen the chupacabra," she said. "He's seen bigfoot.") But the former doorman passed the polygraph, testifying that high-level Trump employees, including Trump's head of security, Matthew Calamari, had told him the story.

Then, David Pecker abruptly ordered the reporters to stop. In November 2015, Sajudin signed an agreement to accept $30,000 for the exclusive rights to the information. Soon after, he met with an AMI reporter at a fast-food place in Pennsylvania and signed a further amendment, adding a $1,000,000 penalty if the ex-doorman ever disclosed the information without AMI's permission. The reporter told Sajudin he'd get his money. Sajudin, seeming pleased, said it was going to be "a very merry Christmas."

As he later did during the McDougal affair, Michael Cohen, Trump's personal attorney, had monitored the unfolding events closely. "There's no question it was done as a favor to continue to protect Trump," one former AMI employee told me. "That's black-and-white."

◆

Later, when journalists sought to report on the rumor, the *Enquirer* worked to thwart them. In the summer of 2017, two reporters at the

Associated Press, Jeff Horwitz and Jake Pearson, had reported out and filed a detailed story. As they neared publication, Howard assembled a muscular legal team and threatened to sue the AP. In July, at AMI's urging, Sally Buzbee, AP's executive editor, and her general counsel met with Howard and his team. He'd hired Weinstein's representatives: the lawyers of Boies Schiller and Lanny Davis.

The following month, Buzbee announced internally that the story wouldn't run after all. "After robust internal discussion, AP news leaders determined that the story at the time did not meet AP's rigorous sourcing requirements," Buzbee later said, defending the decision. Several other AP journalists felt the sourcing was robust and expressed shock at the decision. Horwitz left work for days and had to be persuaded by his bosses to return. For almost a year after, the story stayed dead.

◆

But the next spring, that was changing. *Enquirer* sources were beginning to talk. By early March 2018, one was close to sharing a copy of the amendment Sajudin had signed in late 2015. The source and I met at a rundown Middle Eastern restaurant in Los Angeles, where I spent hours arguing the merits of sharing the document. That night, I headed back to Jonathan's place in West Hollywood, with a printed copy in hand.

"When did you realize—" Jonathan said theatrically when I walked in, late.

"—I know, I know, that I hate you," I said. We'd done this before.

"We were gonna have dinner," he said.

"Sorry. Ran long."

"You ran long yesterday," he said, and we proceeded to fight about this. I wondered how long we could keep going like this, with me absent and consumed and stressed out. Later, with Jonathan bundled off to bed, I stepped out to meet a delivery guy. Directly across the street, a pale thirty-something-year-old man with dark, stringy hair and stubble was standing next to a car, staring. I was beginning to feel that nagging, watched feeling again.

◆

Having dealt with a lifetime of my own curiosity from the press, I didn't want to be intrusive. But in order to respect the wishes of the people involved in the rumor, I had to find out if they wanted to say anything. In mid-March, I knocked on Sajudin's door in the woods in rural Pennsylvania. "I don't talk for free," he said, then slammed the door in my face. Emails and calls to the alleged love child—who was now, of course, no longer a child at all—got no response. Late that month, I searched California's Bay Area, trying recently listed addresses. I found only one family member, who said, "I'm not supposed to talk to you." I tried a work address, too. The rumored love child was employed at (seriously) a genetic testing company.

Finally, I tried the family's home in Queens. It was small and faded, with clapboard siding. In a square of grass outside was a little shrine with a plaster Madonna. I stopped by a few times before encountering a middle-aged man I recognized as the husband of the woman who'd allegedly had the affair. He held up his hands as I approached. "She's not gonna talk to you or nobody," he said. He had a straight, uncomplicated inflection and a Latin American accent. He was convinced the rumor was untrue. The *Enquirer*'s transaction had put the family in a difficult situation. "I don't understand what they had to pay this guy for," he said. "I'm the dad."

"Got it," I said, and gave him a condoling look. I told him I was making sure they had the chance to respond if they wanted to. I said I understood how awful it could feel to have the press circling your family.

He nodded. "I understand. You're Farrow."

"Yeah."

"Oh I know."

And then he was the one with the pitying look.

◆

By early April, we'd backed up the story with the accounts of six current and former AMI employees, texts and emails from the time at which AMI struck the deal, and the amendment Sajudin had signed at the McDonald's. As it had with McDougal, the White House denied the affair, and added, "I'd refer you to AMI," which was one way to respond to a story documenting legally questionable collaboration with the company in question.

Sean Lavery, the boyish Midwesterner assigned to fact-check the story, sent a detailed memo to Howard. Less than thirty minutes later, Radar Online, an AMI website, put out a post acknowledging everything. "Ronan Farrow from *The New Yorker*," it read, "is calling our staff, and seems to think this is another example of how *The ENQUIRER*, by supposedly . . . killing stories about President Trump is a threat to national security."

Minutes later Howard was emailing. As he had with McDougal, he pled pure journalistic motivation and denied any collaboration with Trump. "You're about to sh*t all over the institution that is The New Yorker," he wrote to Remnick. "Ronan's unhealthy obsession with our publication (*and me—perhaps it's my smile?*) puts you at peril." He added, of me: "*he's about to make for terrific Enquirer fodder.*" (Dylan Howard used a lot of italics.)

With Howard's confessional Radar Online post out in the wild, the AP raced to revive its efforts. The AP went live with its resurrected draft, and we published our story at *The New Yorker*, overnight.

Not all of AMI's efforts on Trump's behalf panned out. I'd later learn of one other case in which the company looked into a matter in close concert with Trump's associates. In early 2016, an anonymous woman—"Katie Johnson" in an initial legal document, "Jane Doe" in a subsequent one—filed a lawsuit against Trump. The plaintiff claimed that, in 1994, when she was thirteen years old and newly arrived in New York City to pursue modeling work, she'd been offered money to attend parties hosted by Jeffrey Epstein, the billionaire investor, and attended by Trump. Hair-curling allegations of sexual violence followed: the lawsuit contended that the plaintiff and other minors were forced to perform sex acts on Trump and Epstein, culminating in a "savage sexual attack" by Trump; that Trump had threatened the plaintiff and her family with physical harm should she ever speak; and that both Trump and Epstein were told that the girls involved were underage.

There was truth in the general context: Epstein was close friends with Donald Trump. "I've known Jeff for fifteen years. Terrific guy," Trump told a reporter in 2002. "He's a lot of fun to be with. It is even said that he likes beautiful women as much as I do, and many of them are on the younger side. No doubt about it—Jeffrey enjoys his social life." *Miami Herald* writer Julie K. Brown later published powerful reporting on widespread allegations that Epstein sexually abused minors. In 2019, federal agents arrested him on sex trafficking charges, unraveling a plea deal that had shielded the investor. The lenient agreement had been brokered by Alexander Acosta, a secretary of labor in Trump's cabinet, when he was a prosecutor. He later resigned over the matter. Soon after, Epstein was found dead in jail, hanged in an apparent suicide.

But, as had been the case with Sajudin's claims about the love child, the anonymous rape allegation wasn't backed by convincing evidence. The initial suit, filed in California, was dismissed on procedural grounds, re-filed in New York, then dropped yet again. Norm Lubow, a former producer on *The Jerry Springer Show* and pusher of several dubious celebrity scandals, helped orchestrate the lawsuit and acted as the plaintiff's intermediary in the press. The plaintiff herself was difficult to reach. One attorney who represented her told me even he sometimes had trouble finding her. Few reporters ever made contact with her. One, Emily Shugerman, said that the woman's lawyer canceled a planned Skype or FaceTime interview several times, then replaced it with a brief phone call. Shugerman emerged as doubtful as most journalists about the story and the elusive woman at the heart of it. Possibly she was being threatened into retreat. Or possibly she was an invention of the checkered figures around her.

But one additional curiosity was never made public. According to several AMI employees and one senior associate of Trump's, Pecker, who was at the time in close contact with Trump, learned of the lawsuit shortly after it was filed. After that, Howard was on the phone with Cohen, Trump's personal attorney, assuring him that they would track down the woman with the rape allegation and see what they could do about her. "Dylan was on the phone with Cohen at all hours" about it, one of the AMI employees recalled. "It became a top priority." With Cohen monitoring the situation, Howard dispatched an AMI reporter to an address associated with one of the initial court filings. But the reporter found only a foreclosed home in the sleepy desert community of Twentynine Palms, California. A neighbor said that no one had been there since the previous fall.

There was no opportunity to buy this story. Nevertheless, in the early days after the anonymous suit, when few media outlets were touching it, AMI ran several stories shooting down the claims in the lawsuit. One of the company's headlines on the suit quoted Trump calling it "disgusting"; another went with "bogus."

In late 2016, the anonymous woman with the rape allegation resurfaced with new legal representation. Her new attorney was a professed defender of women, whom Howard would later describe as a "long-time friend": Lisa Bloom. After he learned that Bloom was working on the case, Howard contacted the attorney to warn her away from it. Eventually, Bloom announced a last-minute cancelation of a planned press conference with the plaintiff and withdrew the suit for the final time.

◆

Other outlets were reporting stories that reinforced the idea of a pact between Trump and AMI, too. From early in the reporting on McDougal, I'd heard rumors that the porn actress Stormy Daniels had signed a nondisclosure agreement barring her from talking about a sexual encounter she claimed to have had with Trump. Two months after I started talking to McDougal, the *Wall Street Journal* reported that Daniels had indeed signed such a contract, arranged directly through Michael Cohen. Not included in the *Journal*'s report was the fact that Daniels's lawyer, Keith Davidson, who had previously represented McDougal, had called Dylan Howard about the story first. Howard told Davidson that AMI was passing on the Daniels matter. Pecker had just extended himself for Trump, and was growing antsy about the potential for fallout. But Howard directed Davidson to Michael Cohen, who established a shell company to pay Daniels $130,000 in exchange for her silence. The contract used pseudonyms: Daniels was "Peggy Peterson" and Trump, "David Dennison."

"You know who's really been fucked?" Davidson later told me. "David Dennison. Who was on my high school hockey team. And he is pissed."

The stories AMI bought and buried during the election, like Sajudin's and McDougal's, along with the ones on which they engaged with Cohen more preliminarily, like those of Daniels and the anonymous accuser, raised thorny legal and political questions. Trump hadn't included any of the payments on his financial disclosure forms during the election. As we released our reporting, a nonprofit watchdog organization and a left-leaning political group filed formal complaints requesting that the Justice Department, the Office of Government Ethics, and the Federal Election Commission examine whether the payments to Daniels and McDougal violated federal election law.

Legal experts said they might have. The timing, during the election, was good circumstantial evidence that AMI's intent had been to help the campaign; the conversations with Cohen even more so. Media companies have various exemptions from campaign finance law. But that might not apply, the legal experts added, were it established that a media company was acting not in its press capacity but as an extension of a powerful person's public relations effort.

346 • CATCH AND KILL

All of the AMI employees I spoke with said that the alliance with Trump had distorted the place and its business model. "We never printed a word about Trump without his approval," said Jerry George, the former AMI senior editor. Several of the employees told me that Pecker had reaped tangible benefits. They said that people close to Trump had introduced Pecker to potential sources of funding for AMI. In the summer of 2017, Pecker visited the Oval Office and dined at the White House with a French businessman known for brokering deals with Saudi Arabia. Two months later, the businessman and Pecker met with the Saudi crown prince, Mohammed bin Salman.

Some of the employees felt that the most significant reward was AMI's steadily accumulating blackmail power over Trump. Howard bragged to friends that he was turning down television job offers because he felt his current position, and his ability to hold negative stories over people, gave him more power than any career in traditional journalism. "In theory, you would think that Trump has all the power in that relationship," Maxine Page, the AMI veteran, told me, "but in fact Pecker has the power—he has the power to run these stories. He knows where the bodies are buried." The concern had run through the conversations with McDougal, too. "Someone in a high position that controls our country, if they can influence him," she said of Trump, "it's a big deal."

The relationship between AMI and Trump was an extreme example of the media's potential to slip from independent oversight to cocktail party alliances with reporting subjects. But, for AMI, it was also familiar territory. Over the years, the company had reached deals to shelve reporting around Arnold Schwarzenegger, Sylvester Stallone, Tiger Woods, Mark Wahlberg, and too many others to count. "We had stories and we bought them knowing full well they were never going to run," George said.

One after another, the AMI employees used the same phrase to describe this practice of purchasing a story in order to bury it. It was an old term in the tabloid industry: "catch and kill."

# PART V: SEVERANCE

# CHAPTER 52:

# *CIRCLE*

*D*ylan Howard had a vindictive streak, ten people who worked with him told me. Former employees would later tell the Associated Press that he "openly described his sexual partners in the newsroom, discussed female employees' sex lives and forced women to watch or listen to pornographic material." In 2012, in response to complaints from female colleagues, AMI launched an internal inquiry, led by an outside consultant. The company maintained that the report found no "serious" wrongdoing. Its general counsel confirmed that women had lodged complaints about Howard, including one that he'd offered to create a Facebook page for a colleague's vagina. Maxine Page, the AMI veteran, said she complained on behalf of multiple other women. Liz Crokin, another former reporter, said that after she told the outside consultant investigating the matter that Howard harassed her, she believed Howard retaliated against her, assigning her menial tasks and withholding substantive ones. Howard denied all allegations of misconduct and a spokesperson said the women were "disgruntled." Howard had left AMI for Celebuzz, where he'd prompted another HR investigation, and a finding that he sexually harassed and retaliated against colleagues. He'd departed Celebuzz ahead of the finding against him and made it back to AMI, unscathed.

After my stories, several of Howard's colleagues said he appeared to be enraged. Two recalled him saying that he was going to "get" me. One warned him that this was silly, that the retaliation would be too transparent. Howard was undeterred.

For a brief, shining moment, I was an all-caps, sans serif, recurring villain in the pages of the *National Enquirer*. A few days after the doorman story broke, a first comment request arrived, about the uncle I couldn't recall having met, whom Weinstein had brought up in his legal threat letters: "The National Enquirer intends to publish a story reporting Ronan Farrow's uncle John Charles Villiers-Farrow was convicted of sexually abusing two 10-year-old boys." Shortly after that, intermediaries began sending messages aggressively soliciting "dick pics." When I failed to send any, the *Enquirer* published a complaint that I'd refused. When I responded with anything that seemed flirtatious or frank, Howard ran that, too. Howard and his colleagues reached out for comment about fabricated yarns, including one implicating me and another journalist, who'd worked on a prominent story critical of AMI, in some sort of Brazilian sex romp. (If only my life were so exciting.)

Howard and his associates were calling, emailing. These moves were rote formula. And on the recipient's side, too, there was a playbook: respond, curry favor with Howard, trade an item. The other journalist Howard targeted was engaging the *Enquirer* through a well-connected lawyer who could have a quiet conversation, broker an agreement, ensure that AMI kept the journalist's name out. But the other journalist wasn't working on ongoing reporting on the subject. I was. Acquiescing to threats from a hostile subject of reporting was exactly the response that had nearly killed the Weinstein story the year before. I did nothing, and kept reporting.

These machinations had been the least elaborate of Howard's efforts. He had also, several AMI employees said, deployed a subcontractor associated with Coleman-Rayner—the same infrastructure used to create secret recordings for Weinstein—to surveil Jonathan in Los Angeles. His home had been watched, his movements followed. Howard would "come in and be like, 'We're gonna put a tail on Ronan's boyfriend,'" one of the employees recalled. And later: "I've got someone following him, we're gonna find out where he's going." Howard said the employees' assertions were false. In the end, the employees said, Jonathan's routine had been so boring the subcontractor surveilling him had given up.

"I'm interesting!" Jonathan said, when I told him. "I am a very interesting person! I went to an escape room!"

◆

By then, the walls were closing in on AMI. Several outlets, especially the *Wall Street Journal,* were still digging into the company's transactions on Trump's behalf during the election, and the revelations were spinning up law enforcement. In April 2018, FBI agents raided Cohen's hotel and office, looking for records related to the payment to McDougal and correspondence between Cohen, Pecker, and Howard. Law enforcement bore down on Pecker and Howard. In response to my articles, they had denied everything, called the notion of catch and kill ridiculous, claimed to have had only journalistic intentions. Just a few months later, they cut a deal to avoid prosecution for a battery of potential crimes, including violations of campaign finance law, and admitted to everything. In the early days of Trump's candidacy, they conceded, Pecker had met with Cohen and another member of the campaign. "Pecker offered to help deal with negative stories about that presidential candidate's relationships with women by, among other things, assisting the campaign in identifying such stories so they could be purchased and their publication avoided," the nonprosecution agreement read. They'd caught, and they'd killed, and the intention had been to swing a presidential election.

As part of its agreement with prosecutors, AMI promised to "commit no crimes whatsoever" for three years. Within the year, the *Enquirer* was facing questions as to whether it had breached that clause. Howard threw the full weight of the publication into chasing a story about Jeff Bezos, the founder and CEO of Amazon, cheating on his wife. This time, Howard secured the dirty pictures he habitually sought. (Aside from Bezos's wife and mistress, Dylan Howard appeared to have more interest in the man's penis than any other person on the planet.) The familiar routine played out: AMI threatened to publish and pressed Bezos to cut a deal. Bezos went on the offensive. "No thank you, Mr. Pecker," he wrote in an open letter. "Rather than capitulate to extortion and blackmail, I've decided to publish exactly what they sent me, despite the personal cost and embarrassment they threaten."

In early 2019, with federal prosecutors circling whether Howard had breached the nonprosecution agreement and AMI swimming in debt, the company brokered a deal to sell the *Enquirer* and its sister outlets the *Globe* and the *National Examiner* for scrap. The purchaser, James Cohen, whose father founded the Hudson News franchise, was mostly known as a collector of art and for throwing his daughter a $1 million bat mitzvah. Questions swirled as to whether Cohen was really financing the agreement himself or there were others doing so behind the scenes. The *New York Post*, practically exploding with schadenfreude, quoted a source familiar with AMI as saying, "It looks like the whole thing could be a big circle."

❖

The walls were closing in on Howard's ally Harvey Weinstein, too. In the months after the *New York Times* and *New Yorker* stories broke, dozens of additional women accused Weinstein of sexual harassment or violence. The number grew to thirty, then sixty, then more than ninety. Some, including Canosa, filed lawsuits. Law enforcement in London,

Los Angeles, and New York circled. The day after the first *New Yorker* story broke, Sgt. Keri Thompson, a detective from the NYPD Cold Case Squad who had overseen the sting operation in the Gutierrez case years earlier, began traveling up and down the Eastern Seaboard to find Lucia Evans, who'd told me that Weinstein sexually assaulted her in his office in 2004. When the detectives found Evans, they told her that if she filed a complaint, it could help put Weinstein behind bars. Evans wanted to help. But she was scared. She realized, and the detectives conceded, that playing a role in criminal proceedings would be a bruising process. Weinstein's lawyers would play dirty. They'd throw everything they could at her. "I think everyone's self-preservation mechanism kicks in when they make a big life decision such as this," she said. "What is it going to mean to you? How is it going to affect your life, your family, your friends?" After months of sleepless nights, she decided to proceed with the complaint against Weinstein.

Early on the morning of May 25, 2018, a black SUV slid up to the entrance of the NYPD's First Precinct. As cameras flashed, Thompson and another detective, Nick DiGaudio, met Harvey Weinstein at the SUV and led him into the precinct. For the occasion of his surrender, Weinstein had been styled as a mild-mannered professor, in a black blazer and a powder-blue V-neck sweater. Under one arm, he carried a stack of books about Hollywood and Broadway. Weinstein disappeared into the building to be booked on charges of rape and a criminal sex act. When he was led out afterward, the books were gone, the hands in cuffs.

Weinstein was accompanied by his latest attorney, Benjamin Brafman, and a private detective named Herman Weisberg. Weisberg was a former NYPD detective himself, and his firm, Sage Intelligence and Security, flaunted that expertise much as the Israelis did their former Mossad status. He'd been on the Weinstein team for a while—the previous fall, before my story broke, he'd been on the McGowan beat, arriving at one meeting with Weinstein to announce that he'd uncovered a not-yet-public police inquiry into whether she'd been caught carrying drugs. "Can we leak that?" Weinstein had said, excited. Former colleagues called Weisberg a "bloodhound." He specialized in ferreting out and interrogating witnesses.

For all the symbolism of the perp walk, Weinstein posted $1 million bail that day and went home. Ankle-braceleted, he was permitted to move between his homes in New York and Connecticut. In the ensuing months, the NYPD case expanded from two women to three, adding a charge of "predatory sexual assault" from Mimi Haleyi, a former production assistant who claimed Weinstein sexually assaulted her at his apartment in 2006. But Weinstein's offensive expanded, too, its tendrils encircling those who agreed to participate in the case and those who worked on it.

In the press and to prosecutors, Brafman raged that Weinstein had friendly messages from Haleyi, including one seeking a meeting after the alleged assault. And, after Weisberg's labors, fruitful grounds emerged for discrediting DiGaudio, the detective. A peripheral witness in Lucia Evans's case claimed she'd given DiGaudio new details that he then withheld from prosecutors. DiGaudio denied it—but it was all the ammunition Brafman needed. He expressed public outrage and accused law enforcement of a conspiracy against Weinstein. DiGaudio was removed from the case. Lucia Evans's count against Weinstein was dropped. "Two things can be true," a source in the district attorney's office told me. "You can believe a survivor but consent to dismissal of her count because maintaining it would result in a weakening of the other counts, because of things that happened in the process."

Brafman attributed the move to bravura private espionage. "Whatever success I may have in the Weinstein case, Herman has played a substantial part in those accomplishments," Brafman said, explaining that Weisberg had helped "uncover materials" about "several of the important prosecution witnesses."

As Weinstein's trial began, protesters gathered outside the courthouse. They carried signs that read "Justice for survivors" and "Listen to survivors." Rose McGowan was there, and Rosanna Arquette. "We aren't going anywhere," said Arquette. In court, witnesses told their stories, including Haleyi and a former actress named Jessica Mann. Annabella Sciorra gave the jury the same wrenching account she'd provided to me. Rosie Perez took the stand to back her up. A partner at Boies Schiller testified about the deal with Black Cube, laying bare in open court the secrets Sleeper had leaked.

Weinstein's cast of lawyers kept shifting. Brafman resigned and was succeeded by Donna Rotunno, a hard-charging Chicago-based attorney who during the case boasted that she'd never been sexually assaulted "because I would never put myself in that position." But it wasn't enough. A jury convicted Weinstein of sex crimes including rape.

Weinstein's attorneys pled for leniency, itemizing his charitable activities and arguing he'd already suffered. In a letter to the judge, they wrote, "Since the New Yorker article was published in October 2017, Mr. Weinstein's life has been destroyed." The judge sentenced Weinstein to twenty-three years, close to the maximum. Ambra Gutierrez was at the courthouse that day. "I was twenty-three years old when he ruined my life," she said. "That's my number." The Department of Corrections housed Weinstein, who was complaining of chest pains, in an infirmary on Rikers Island, before moving him to his new home: Wende Correctional Facility, a maximum-security prison east of Buffalo, not far from where he'd gotten his start years before.

His most frequent visitors were men in suits: lawyers, onlookers were told, or private investigators. The now-convicted, now-former studio head had fallen as far as a man could fall, but his checks still cashed. For men like him, there would always be an army of spies. It was all Harvey Weinstein had left.

# CHAPTER 53:

# *AXIOM*

*I*t was after the love child story, and summer again, when I stumbled into the first clues about Black Cube's activities following the Weinstein job. I'd just slipped onto a hot, airless subway car when the call came in. The caller ID read "Axiom." A moment later, I got a text. "I am trying to reach you directly and privately. It's regarding a Fry Pan that's Scratch Resistant. Sometimes I cook and the black coating scares me."

I'd recently posted a social media picture of a frying pan marketed under the label "Black Cube." "Scratch resistant. May use false identities and shell companies to extract information," I'd written. ("Hahaha," Ambra Gutierrez commented drily.)

As the subway car slipped into a tunnel, I wrote back, "Can you say more about who you are?"

"I can say I do surveillance." And, later, resisting my entreaties for more information: "We will need to meet discreetly and make sure we are not followed."

A few days after, I was threading my way through the perspiring crowds of the theater district. I'd suggested we meet at the Brazilian restaurant where I got the recording from Gutierrez. I arrived on time, asked for a table for two, sat down. The phone rang with an encrypted Signal call. "Axiom" appeared on the screen again.

"Don't order," said a man's voice.

I looked around again. No one I could see.

"You are wearing the messenger bag, light blue shirt, and slightly darker jeans," he continued. He told me to leave and walk slowly.

"Walk against traffic, please."

I craned my neck around.

"Don't look around," he continued, a little annoyed. "I'll be about a half a block away, so please stop for 1–1.5 minutes at the intersections. I'm going to make sure no same people show up there from here."

As he took me on a circuitous route through Hell's Kitchen, I tried to check again. "Don't look, just walk naturally. Against traffic. It's good, keep going." He told me to stop at a basement Peruvian restaurant that lacked cell reception. "Ask for a table in the back, all the way in the back."

I did as he said. Ten minutes later, a man sat down in front of me. His hair was dark and curly, and he was a little soft around the middle. He had a thick Ukrainian accent.

"I'm a concerned party," said Igor Ostrovskiy. He slid a phone across the table. Motioned for me to swipe through the pictures on it. There was my block, my front door, my superintendent outside. And there was the Nissan, with two men inside: Ostrovskiy, dark and chubby, and Khaykin, pale and bald, with a fierce glare.

Ostrovskiy said that they were with a local private investigation firm licensed in New York. "But the work product, the final reports, Black Cube was putting their name on it."

"Why are you doing this?" I asked.

While much of the work the subcontractors did was routine—tracking cheating spouses or digging for dirt in custody cases that "might not be ethical, but it's legitimate"—their work for Black Cube was something else. Ostrovskiy told me about their efforts to track me, in person and through my phone. I thought back to the spam texts—the weather updates, and then the blitz of political surveys I got at the World Trade Center. He didn't know if either was connected, but did say he'd gotten accurate information about my location at roughly the same time that I'd received the survey texts. "I fear," Ostrovskiy told me, "that it may be illegal." He took issue with the tactics used against me. And it wasn't just me. The subcontractors were still following people for Black Cube. Ostrovskiy wanted to know why.

He read me a list of target names, and the dates and times of the operations surveilling them. At one upscale hotel restaurant after another, the subcontractors had monitored meetings between Black Cube agents and marks who appeared to be experts in technology and cybercrime. Several had expertise in aggressive new solutions for hacking and monitoring cell phones—like the Pegasus software made by the Israeli cyber intelligence firm NSO Group, which Sleeper had worried about.

Ostrovskiy said that the limited information he possessed was "designed to be traceable back to me." He was anxious that he was being surveilled. He'd even swept the area surrounding the restaurant before entering.

I was also becoming watchful. I'd asked a colleague to follow a few blocks behind, then keep an eye on the restaurant. Unjin Lee, a slight Korean American woman who just cleared five feet, wasn't much for Krav Maga, but she'd spot any tails.

Ostrovskiy and I left separately, ten minutes apart. When I got a safe distance away, Lee called. A man had appeared to follow the two of us, lagging behind as we entered, and lingering by the entrance for more than an hour.

Nothing is certain, it turns out, except death and taxes and investigation by the Southern District of New York. Federal prosecutors there had begun to circle Black Cube after my story about the spy agency in late 2017, launching an investigation out of their Complex Frauds and Cybercrime Unit. It didn't take long before the prosecutors, who were looking at Harvey Weinstein and AMI, too, were hoping to meet with me, not as a reporter but as a witness.

The calls and messages from the Southern District started coming in the days following the McDougal story in February 2018 and didn't let up in the months that followed. The inquiries came from the Southern District prosecutors themselves and from intermediaries, including Preet Bharara, the former U.S. Attorney there. They came to me and to Bertoni, *The New Yorker*'s lawyer.

A law school classmate working in law enforcement had been sending messages, too, asking to catch up. Not long after Ostrovskiy and I first met, I made my way through the heat to dinner at a small restaurant near the World Trade Center.

I was sitting at the bar, sweaty and dowdily suited, when his voice sounded. "Hi, there."

I looked up from my phone. A row of perfect teeth flashed. He was symmetrical to a catalogue-model standard. Even his name was an actor name, a pretend name, the name of the most trustworthy doctor in a 1950s suburb.

He slid closer. Another blinding smile. "Been a long time!"

Me, feeling shlubby: "I've been busy."

"Can't imagine with what."

He ordered us drinks, then we settled into a booth.

It was a lovely dinner, with much "how *is* so-and-so?" I'd

forgotten how much I'd withdrawn from my own life. Were it not for the aggressive surveillance efforts, I'd have had no social life at all.

He'd married, he said.

"How's that?"

He shrugged. "Complicated. You?"

"Good. He's great." A beat of silence. I thought about the long, tense year with Jonathan.

"But also complicated?" he asked.

"Well, long-distance is hard."

He looked at me sympathetically. "You're under a lot of pressure."

"It's not so bad now. And you must be, too."

He leaned in. The warmest smile yet, no longer appropriate for catalogues, even. "It doesn't have to be like this, you know," he said. I could feel his breath across the narrow table. "Dealing with all of this. By yourself."

He was adjusting a knife in front of him a little, running a finger up its silvered length.

"Are you talking about—"

"You should come in."

"Oh."

"Be a witness. You won't have to reveal any sources you don't want to."

I withdrew, sitting up straight. "You know you can't guarantee that."

"So?" he said. "If you're a victim, you should talk."

The personal interest seemed benign and separate from the professional entreaties. But the two dynamics jostled uncomfortably. As we stepped out into the night and said our goodbyes, he lingered for a moment during a parting hug. "Call me," he said. "If you change your mind about any of it." Then he was flashing the Crest ad smile over his shoulder, walking off into the night.

Bertoni and I turned over the dilemma. Working with law enforcement was a fraught decision for any journalistic outlet. There were obvious scenarios in which journalists should go to the cops, including any tip-off about impending physical harm to someone. But there were no easy calls in this case. It wasn't inconceivable that I'd been a victim of a crime, flowing from the phone tracking or the deceptions designed to elicit reporting material from me. But I wasn't confident that there was enough danger to myself or others to merit sitting with prosecutors and answering questions that might quickly turn to sources and reporting I'd pledged to keep secret. Protecting those sources, including Ostrovskiy, had to be my priority. And it wasn't just about me. Bertoni feared that any one conversation with law enforcement would set a dangerous precedent for *The New Yorker*. Would we as easily be able to decline inquiries about, say, a government whistle-blower, once we'd already said yes on this story?

# CHAPTER 54:

# *PEGASUS*

At first, Ostrovskiy wouldn't give me the name of his boss. But there were more than enough clues. In one of the images he'd shown me, the Nissan's license plates were even visible. I typed in the name I'd come up with and pulled up a promotional video. "I'm the guy out in the field. The action-taker," a bald man with a Russian accent said in the video. "My name is Roman Khaykin. And I'm the founder of InfoTactic Group."

A jaunty techno beat played. Over footage of buttonhole cameras, title cards promised "the best high-tech surveillance equipment." Khaykin, doing his best impression of James Bond or Ethan Hunt, darted athletically through crowds. It was beguilingly cheesy. InfoTactic was small-time, just a handful of freelancers, most of them with day jobs. Still, Khaykin, over the course of that past year working for Black Cube, had sought to push the envelope, from the phone tracking to the boasts about his ability to illicitly obtain financial records.

In the video, Khaykin was deadly serious about his skills. "When I was young and first learned how to read," he said, "I would fascinate my parents with my ability to memorize the text of my favorite book — Sherlock Holmes."

Ostrovskiy kept passing along his insights about InfoTactic's ongoing operations for Black Cube. Sometimes I'd go to the appointed location, or send colleagues who were less likely to be spotted, to keep watch from afar. The pattern was always the same: undercover Black Cube agents meeting with cybercrime and technology experts in luxe hotels.

Ostrovskiy and I would meet, too, at hole-in-the-wall restaurants we'd immediately depart in favor of jumpy conversations conducted while walking mazy routes through side streets. Once, we sat in a dim corner of a hotel lobby and spoke for half an hour before he abruptly excused himself, then came back worried, saying we had to move, fast. He suspected two men sitting nearby were following us. They looked like professionals. They'd been watching too closely. We took a cab, and then another cab. He had one taxi stop on the West Side Highway, pull over to the shoulder, and wait for any tails to go by or be exposed for slowing. A year before, I'd have thought the paranoia excessive.

Through the remainder of 2018, I continued my reporting on the world of Israeli private intelligence, keeping at Black Cube in the process. Eido Minkovsky, the genial freelancer who handled the spy agency's public relations, was a regular contact. "Ronan, baby," he'd say, when I called. "Don't divorce me," he'd write, responding evasively to my latest reporting inquiry. In January 2019, he agreed to have a drink during one of his regular stops in New York.

Several hours before that meeting, Ostrovskiy called. Black Cube had ordered Roman Khaykin and InfoTactic to find a pen capable of secretly recording audio. Ostrovskiy sent a picture of the spy pen they'd found. It was piano-black, with a silver clip: nothing you'd notice if you weren't looking for it, but it had features you could track, like a little ring of chrome at a specific height on its barrel.

Minkovsky and I had agreed to meet at a wine bar in Hell's Kitchen. I arrived to find him lounging in a corner with a Cheshire cat grin. Minkovsky ordered a cocktail, led with his usual flattery offensive. Then he announced that he was going to take notes on my reporting questions. He produced, from his jacket pocket, a black pen with a silver clip.

"Funny, I have the same one," I said.

His grin faltered. "It's a special pen," he said. "From Minkovsky Industries."

I asked Minkovsky if he was recording. He looked injured. He informed Zorella, the Black Cube founder, of any meetings, of course. He had to—he was polygraphed periodically. But: "Ronan, I would never, ever record."

Later, Minkovsky would maintain that the pen he'd taken out was perfectly innocent, and that he wasn't aware of any other. But on my way out of the meeting that night, I texted Ostrovskiy, "Do you know who that pen was delivered to?"—and he replied with a string of pictures, all showing Minkovsky, just before we met, standing on a corner, accepting delivery of the spy pen.

A few days later the spy pen appeared to resurface in Black Cube's latest operation. A middle-aged man with a neat white beard, who identified himself as Michel Lambert, sat down for lunch with John Scott-Railton, a researcher for the watchdog group Citizen Lab. Lambert had said he worked for the Paris-based agricultural technology firm CPW-Consulting, and asked to meet about Scott-Railton's doctoral research on using kite-mounted cameras to create maps, which is a thing, apparently.

But as food arrived, Lambert's interests strayed. Citizen Lab, which tracks state-backed efforts to hack and surveil journalists, had recently reported that NSO Group's Pegasus software compromised an iPhone belonging to a friend of the journalist Jamal Khashoggi, not long before Saudi operatives cut Khashoggi to pieces with a bone saw. The investigation had prompted sharp criticism of NSO Group, which denied that its software was used to target Khashoggi but also refused to answer questions about whether the software had been sold to the Saudi government. Lambert wanted to know about Citizen Lab's work on NSO Group. He asked whether there was any "racist element" to the focus on an Israeli group. He pressed Scott-Railton about his views on the Holocaust. As they spoke, Lambert took out a black pen with a silver clip and a chrome ring on its barrel. He laid it just so on a legal pad in front of him, tip pointed at Scott-Railton.

The script was familiar. In the operations in which Stella Penn Pechanac had been involved, targeting employees of West Face Capital and critics of AmTrust Financial Services, Black Cube agents had also solicited anti-Semitic statements. But this time, the mark was wise to it: suspecting subterfuge, Scott-Railton had decked himself out with recording devices. He'd been taping the whole time.

It was a spy vs. spy confrontation of sorts — and each had brought his own tail as backup. Raphael Satter, an Associated Press journalist with whom Scott-Railton had been working, arrived with a camera and started questioning the man who was not named Michel Lambert after all. The Black Cube agent's cover had been blown. From a table nearby, Ostrovskiy had been watching and photographing the meeting, too. Khaykin, who had been there earlier and then departed, started calling, apoplectic. "Our guy got burned!" he said. "Get to the lobby immediately! He needs to get out."

The Black Cube agent ducked out of a service entrance. Ostrovskiy picked up the agent and his luggage, then drove around, trying to shake potential tails. As they drove, the agent placed frantic calls, trying to book the first possible flight out of New York. On his luggage was a tag bearing the name "ALMOG" and a home address in Israel. This name was real: the agent was Aharon Almog-Assouline, a retired Israeli security official later reported to have been involved in a string of Black Cube operations.

Black Cube and NSO Group would later deny any connection to the operation against Citizen Lab. But in many of the meetings Ostrovskiy had described to me over the preceding months, Almog-Assouline had been there, appearing to target figures who criticized NSO Group and argued that its software was being used to hunt journalists.

Black Cube was furious about the botched operation. The agency ordered that everyone with knowledge of the matter be polygraphed immediately. Ostrovskiy called, worried that it was only a matter of time before he was exposed. He wanted to talk, and not just to a reporter. He had knowledge of espionage operations, by agents closely linked to a foreign government, on American soil. He had already tried the FBI, only to be passed between skeptical agents who finally hung up. He asked if I had a better contact in law enforcement. I called Bertoni. He was still adamant about keeping direct engagement with prosecutors to a minimum. But he agreed that there was nothing wrong with informing a source about how to get to the authorities.

The last time I discussed the matter with my old classmate was at another restaurant in the Financial District. I stepped messily out of a downpour. He, neatly dry, flashed another perfect smile and ordered drinks.

"You should think about it," he said again. On the table, his hand was a hairsbreadth from mine. "You don't have to deal with all this alone."

I turned over how it would feel. Then I withdrew my hand by a few inches. I said I wouldn't talk, but I had sources who might. I asked for the right contact to give them.

Soon after, I sent Ostrovskiy a name at the Southern District of New York. Ostrovskiy got a lawyer—John Tye, the same whistle-blower attorney I consulted—and began the process of volunteering to be a witness.

# CHAPTER 55:

# *MELTING*

*A*t NBC News, the year after the Weinstein story was fraught. In late November 2017, Savannah Guthrie, wearing a floral-print black dress fit for a morning TV funeral, announced that Matt Lauer had been fired overnight. A "detailed complaint from a colleague about inappropriate sexual behavior in the workplace" had come in less than forty-eight hours before. She said she was "heartbroken," calling Lauer "my dear, dear friend" and emphasizing that he was "loved by many, many people here."

Guthrie read a statement from Andy Lack that suggested management was shocked about Lauer, too. The unnamed colleague had lodged "the first complaint about his behavior in the over twenty years he's been at NBC News." The network moved quickly to reinforce that idea in the wider press.

After the announcement, Oppenheim gathered members of the investigative unit in the conference room on the fourth floor. He said that, while the behavior alleged by the unnamed colleague was "unacceptable," the breach was of professional, not criminal, standards of conduct. "Some of the behavior took place in the workplace. And Matt Lauer is Matt Lauer," he said. "So there's obviously a power differential there." But, Oppenheim emphasized, the network employees who spoke with the unnamed colleague "did not report her using words like 'criminal' or 'assault.'" Soon, articles to which NBC's communications team contributed were conveying the same message. When the network collaborated with *People* magazine on a cover story announcing Hoda Kotb as Lauer's replacement—"Hoda & Savannah: 'Our Hearts Were Broken,'" read the headline—this party line would become more explicit. "Multiple sources describe the cause for termination as an affair that violated NBC's terms of employment," that article read. "Sources initially told The Post that Lauer had been accused of sexual assault," Page Six reported, "but later said it was inappropriate sexual behavior." Outlets in contact with NBC at the time said the network made no attempt to alter the characterizations of the matter as an affair.

Oppenheim also echoed Lack's suggestion that the network had been unaware of any complaints about Lauer until two days before, when the unnamed colleague came forward. The statement struck several journalists present as strange. *Variety* and the *New York Times* had both been working on articles accusing Lauer of serial sexual misconduct for weeks, calling numerous people at the network in the process. And many in the building had heard of complaints about Lauer long before that. At the meeting with Oppenheim, McHugh spoke up again: "Prior to Monday, a lot of us have heard rumors of stuff about Matt...let's just say that. Prior to Monday, was NBC aware of any allegations of sexual misconduct against Matt?"

"No," Oppenheim said. "We went back and looked, and, as we said in the statement, there has not been an allegation made internally in twenty years" in "any place where there would be a record of such a thing." The qualifying language was significant: that there would be no formal HR records about a figure of Lauer's importance was practically an assumption. Weinstein had also been adamant that there were no "formal" records of sexual misconduct allegations in his file, either. So had Bill O'Reilly at Fox News. But that wasn't the question. McHugh hadn't asked about formal records—he'd asked whether NBC had been "aware." And on this, Oppenheim was less clear. "We all read the *New York Post* and walk past supermarket checkout stands and see the *National Enquirer*," he said. "There's not a lot you can do with that, especially when the parties involved are saying this is *National Enquirer* nonsense."

Oppenheim was right: Lauer, AMI's employees and internal records would later reveal, had been of great interest to the *Enquirer* all through 2017 and 2018. One email exchange within the tabloid even contained the résumé of the anonymous colleague whose accusations precipitated the firing.

Not long after, Greenberg called McHugh into his office for what McHugh suspected was an effort to determine whether he was talking to the press. McHugh said that he was disquieted by what he was learning about NBC's in-house problems, and the bearing they might have had on our Weinstein coverage. "That's what people are talking about, they're all saying that—"

"That they were covering up Matt Lauer," Greenberg said.

"Yeah," McHugh replied.

"You really think they were aware of a problem with Matt Lauer?" Greenberg said.

McHugh looked him in the eye and said, "I do."

Over the following months, the message that no one at NBC knew about Lauer became a steady drumbeat. In May 2018, NBC-Universal announced the final results of an internal investigation: "We found no evidence indicating that any NBC News or Today show leadership, News HR or others in positions of authority in the News Division received any complaints about Lauer's workplace behavior prior to Nov. 27, 2017," the self-report concluded. The network had resisted calls for an independent investigation, both within the company and in the press. Outside lawyers were enlisted to review the results after the fact, but the research was conducted entirely by Kim Harris's team, including Stephanie Franco, the company's senior vice president for employment law. The day the internal report was announced, Oppenheim and Harris called another crisis meeting with the investigative unit. The assembled journalists erupted with skeptical questions. McHugh was again among them. "Has NBC ever paid an employee who presented information on Matt to sign a nondisclosure agreement?" he asked. Harris blinked. "Umm," she said, "no."

Then he asked if there had been any settlements in the last "six or seven years" with any employees related to harassment in general. More hesitation. "Not that I'm aware of," Harris said finally.

At one point in the meeting, Harris appeared to grow impatient with the journalists' calls for an independent review. "It feels like having an outside voice, whether they came to the same conclusions or not, would make it go away quicker," said one woman in the room. "It's so frustrating."

"Well, if the *press* would stop covering it, it will go away," Harris said.

There was a pause, then still another investigative journalist said, "But we *are* the press."

From the beginning, other outlets were publishing reporting at odds with Oppenheim's and Harris's characterizations of what the network knew. Hours after NBC announced Lauer's termination, *Variety* asserted that "several women...complained to executives at the network about Lauer's behavior, which fell on deaf ears given the lucrative advertising surrounding *Today*." The publication suggested that the complaints about Lauer were an open secret. He had given one colleague a sex toy, with an explicit note about how he hoped to use it on her. He'd played "fuck/marry/kill" games on open mics during commercial breaks. Clips of a similar tenor began to surface, including one of Lauer in 2006, seeming to tell Meredith Vieira, "Keep bending over like that. It's a nice view." At a 2008 private Friars Club roast of Lauer, Katie Couric had performed a David Letterman–style top ten list that included a reference to a sex act between Lauer and Ann Curry, and Jeff Zucker, then the head of NBCUniversal, did a bit about Lauer's wife forcing him to sleep on the couch because of his indiscretions. Donald Trump, then the host of *The Celebrity Apprentice*, had attended. "The whole theme was that he does the show and then he has sex with people, with employees," Joe Scarborough said on air. "So was this whispered behind closed doors? No. It was shouted from the mountaintops and everybody laughed about it."

Several junior *Today* employees said Lauer had been brazen in pursuing sexual encounters with them in the office. Addie Collins, a former production assistant, told me that Lauer had aggressively, almost obsessively, hit on her in 2000, when she was twenty-four years old. She'd kept many of the notes he'd sent her over work email or in the software used to maintain show rundowns. "NOW YOU'RE KILLING ME...YOU LOOK GREAT TODAY! A BIT TOUGH TO CONCENTRATE," read a typical one. Because of Lauer's power in their workplace, Collins told me she'd found it difficult to decline when he started ordering her to his dressing room, or even, on one occasion, to a bathroom stall, for sexual favors. She'd consented, but it had made her feel sick, afraid for her job, afraid of retaliation. Though she couldn't prove it, she suspected Lauer later contributed to her missing out on professional opportunities.

Some of the women claimed their office encounters with Lauer had not been consensual. One former NBC employee told the *New York Times* that, in 2001, Lauer summoned her to his office, then pressed the button on his desk that, like those in many executive offices at 30 Rock, remotely shut his door. She said she'd felt helpless as he'd pulled down her pants, bent her over a chair, and had sex with her. She passed out. Lauer's assistant took her to a nurse.

Over the course of 2018, I'd learn of seven claims of sexual misconduct raised by women who worked with Lauer. Most of the women could point to documents or other people they'd told to back up their accounts. Several said they had told colleagues, and believed the network knew about the problem.

◆

I was also beginning to learn of a pattern surrounding women with complaints. In the years after 2011 or 2012 — the time frame in which Harris claimed NBC hadn't settled with any employees over harassment issues — the network in fact brokered nondisclosure agreements with at least seven women who experienced alleged harassment or discrimination within the company. The agreements also required the women to waive their right to bring suit. In most cases, the women received substantial payouts that parties involved in the transactions said were disproportionate to any conventional compensation for departing the company. When Harris said she was unaware of any harassment settlements, she appeared to be capitalizing on a technicality: many of the payouts were what the network referred to as "enhanced severance," offered to the women as they left their jobs. But individuals involved—including on the company's side—disputed that characterization, saying the agreements were designed to restrain women with allegations from speaking.

Several of the women who signed the nondisclosure agreements had complaints that were unrelated to Lauer, about other men in leadership positions within NBC News. Two settlements, reached in the first few years of the period Harris described, were with women who experienced alleged harassment from two senior executives who subsequently left the company. "Everyone knew why they were let go, internally," said one member of NBC's leadership who was closely involved in the departure of both men. NBC also brokered the 2017 agreement with the woman who accused Corvo—the *Dateline* producer who oversaw the review of the Weinstein story—of sexually harassing her.

But other pacts called into question the network's claim that it had known nothing about women's allegations against Lauer.

One on-air personality, who signed a nondisclosure agreement in 2012, said that NBC sought the deal after she showed colleagues messages that she took to be propositions, from both Lauer and one of the senior executives who later departed the company. Colleagues recalled both men making lewd remarks about the on-air personality over open mics during broadcasts. "I was like a hanging piece of meat," she said. "I would walk into work with a knot in my stomach. I would come home and cry." After she declined the advances, she felt she received fewer assignments. "I got punished," she said. "My career took a sharp nosedive." She decided not to make a formal report because she doubted the efficacy of the company's HR department and feared further harm to her career. She did, however, begin to tell colleagues, and to plan her departure from the company.

When NBC proposed the agreement as she departed, she recalled her agent saying, "I've never seen this before in my life. They want you to sign an NDA," adding, "You must have something huge on them." The agent told me that he recalled the exchange too. The contract, which I later reviewed, waived the on-air personality's right to sue. It barred her from making negative statements about NBC-Universal, "except as may be required for bona fide news reporting." It was on NBC News letterhead, signed by her and the executive she said harassed her.

◆

Another settlement with a woman who disclosed a serious allegation about Lauer within the company was reached in 2013. A few months after the Lauer story broke, I took a seat next to Ann Curry, his former co-anchor, at an Italian restaurant in Greenwich Village. She sat on a bar stool next to me, face graven with concern. She told me that complaints about Lauer verbally harassing women in the office were well known in her day—and that once, in 2010, a colleague had pulled her into an empty office and broken down, saying Lauer had exposed himself and propositioned her. "It was as close as you could get to a woman just *melting* in front of you in pain," Curry said.

Later, I'd learn the woman's identity: Melissa Lonner, the *Today* producer who met with me after she left to work in radio. As Lonner told the story to colleagues, she and Lauer had been at a work event at 30 Rock the evening before she broke down in front of Curry. Lauer had asked her to leave the event to see him in his office, which she took to be a professional inquiry. When they arrived, he closed the door behind them.

She recalled standing expectantly and telling Lauer, "I thought you had to chat." Lauer told her to sit on his couch and began to make small talk. He joked about how much he disliked work cocktail parties like the one they'd just attended. Then, she told the colleagues, he unzipped his pants and exposed his erect penis.

Lonner was separated from her husband but still married. Born in the slums of Bangkok, she'd worked hard to reach her professional role at the time. She remembered reeling in response to Lauer's advance, laughing nervously, trying to extricate herself by cracking a joke about not wanting to be intimate in an office where "everyone else has done it."

Lonner recalled Lauer saying that he knew she wanted it, and, in response to the joke about his office dalliances, that he figured she liked it dirty, and that the encounter would "be a first for you." Then, by her account, he became angry, saying, "Melissa, you're a fucking tease. This is not good. You led me on."

Sources close to Lauer told me he disputed her account of events, saying that he recalled making a joking lewd gesture but not exposing himself or propositioning her. But Lonner, visibly distraught, began recounting her claim in detail the next day, and told it consistently in the years after. She begged Curry and another on-air personality not to report her name, saying she knew Lauer would destroy her career. But Curry did tell two senior executives at the company that they needed to do something about Lauer. "I told them that they had a problem in him. That he had a problem with women. That they had to keep an eye on him." And then, as far as Curry ever heard, nothing happened.

Lonner told the colleagues that she was miserable afterward. Lauer didn't talk to her for weeks. Afraid that she'd be fired, she began looking for other jobs. But when she got an offer at CNN, something strange happened: several NBC News executives called her into their offices for meetings and delivered the same message. Each said that Lauer had insisted that she stay. "I don't know what's going on between you and him," one told her, "But I need to keep him happy."

She stayed at the network. Several years later, as her contract was about to end, she was fired anyway. She told the colleagues she was never given a reason why. A lawyer she consulted noted that the delayed departure prevented her from raising harassment claims due to their statutes of limitations. As Lonner left NBC News, her agent called to report something unusual: in addition to standard nondisclosure and nondisparagement clauses, the network was offering her a six-figure sum in exchange for signing a release of rights. "I've never seen that before," the agent told her. "You must know where all the skeletons are." Lonner's understanding was that the primary intention of the payout was to prevent her from talking to the press.

Despite the fact that Lonner was a behind-the-scenes figure, tabloid items surfaced about her, claiming she was difficult to work with. Lonner told friends that she believed she'd been smeared because of her refusal of Lauer's overture.

When I asked Lonner about NBC, she told me she was unable to comment on her time there. NBC disputed the idea that Lonner's payout was related to her complaint about Lauer. But the network appeared to harbor some awareness of the connection. In 2018, as a *Daily Beast* reporter named Lachlan Cartwright pursued a story about NBC's purported pattern of settlements with sexual harassment victims, Stephanie Franco, the senior employment lawyer at NBC-Universal, contacted Lonner's lawyer to remind her of the existence, and enforceability, of her pact. NBC's legal team would later say that the call was in response to a query from Lonner's attorney, and provided notice of Lonner's release of legal claims, rather than any nondisclosure provision.

The settlements continued in the years after. In 2017, the senior member of the *Today* show team I'd seen crying on set a year before received a seven-figure payout in exchange for signing a nondisclosure agreement. In communications that I reviewed surrounding the contract, attorneys emphasized that the promise of silence was the primary objective, not an incidental provision. As her contract with the network ended, she'd raised harassment and discrimination concerns, though the network said that the payout was unrelated to any specific complaint. She had also mentioned Lauer and sexual harassment to one senior vice president — though she didn't share with them the material I later reviewed that showed Lauer had left voicemails and sent texts that she saw as passes at her. When he took her responses as a cold shoulder, she felt he'd retaliated against her, spreading negative rumors in the office.

## CHAPTER 56:

# *ZDOROVIE*

**T**he complaint that prompted Lauer's firing ended in the same way—with a payout, and a nondisclosure agreement. When we first spoke, Brooke Nevils, the unnamed colleague whose story NBC leadership and the press had deemed a consensual affair, doubted she'd ever be able to go public. As I stepped out of hard rain into her New York apartment, she kept an eye over my shoulder until she locked us in. "I just live in terror," she said. "And after your story about the spies, I got even more scared. I knew who I was up against. And the shady shit they did."

She was in her early thirties, but with a gangly, adolescent quality. "Tall, awkward, and flat-chested," she said with a laugh. In her apartment, art and books were everywhere. As in a Murakami novel, *cats* were everywhere. Nevils had six, until that morning, when one had to be put down due to kidney failure.

She told me this with the affectless delivery of someone who had been through too much. Over the course of the past two years, Nevils had attempted suicide. She'd been hospitalized for post-traumatic stress disorder, descended into heavy drinking, pulled herself back. She'd lost fourteen pounds, and gone to doctors twenty-one times in a single ten-month period. "I've lost everything I cared about," she said. "My job. My goals."

Nevils was raised in the suburbs of Chesterfield, Missouri. Grade-school report cards said she spoke up a lot, smiled a lot, had a sharp sense of humor. Her dad was a Marine in Vietnam, earned a PhD in marketing, and became a civilian contractor for the Pentagon. Her mother, a TWA flight attendant, died of a heart attack a little over a year before our meeting. Nevils told me that her mother was "just that kind of a person that wanted the world to be better."

Nevils had wanted to be a journalist since she was thirteen and learned that Hemingway wrote for the *Kansas City Star*. "You go into journalism because you believe in the truth. That people's stories matter." She frowned. Rain drummed at the windows. "I believed we were the good guys." After college at Johns Hopkins, she interned at a few newspapers. In 2008, she got her dream job as an NBC page — the network's career development program. Over the following years, she worked her way up from giving tours to helping with big stories and staffing big stars.

In 2014, she was doing just that, working for Meredith Vieira — a personal hero of hers, on whose career she hoped to model her own. When Vieira got tapped to cover the Olympics in 2014, the two headed off to Sochi, a coastal resort city in Russia. At the end of one of their long work days, Vieira and Nevils hit the bar at the luxury hotel where the NBC team was staying. They laughed and gossiped over martinis. It was late, midnight maybe, when Lauer walked in and scanned the bar for familiar faces. "I had always been so intimidated by him. He really was kind of a bully at work. Had we not been in such a happy mood..." She trailed off. But the women *were* in a happy mood. And they'd been drinking. She patted the low seat next to her, invited Lauer to join.

Sitting down next to her, Lauer surveyed the martinis and said: "You know, what I really like is a nice cold vodka." He ordered shots of Beluga vodka. Nevils had six. "Na zdorovie!" Lauer cried— literally, to health. When Lauer took out his iPhone and started snapping pictures, Nevils felt some worry seep into the fun. Lauer was known for jokingly putting after-hours photos of colleagues on air, part of the prankster culture he presided over at *Today*. Nevils felt drunk, and worried she looked it in the photos.

After they parted ways—Lauer to his room, the women to theirs, higher up in the hotel—Vieira grinned and produced Lauer's official press credential that granted him access to the events they were covering. Vieira and Lauer had a teasing, sibling-like rapport. This was the latest in a long history of mutual pranks. The women called Lauer and asked, between fits of tipsy laughter, if he was missing anything. Nevils recalled Lauer asking if she had looked for *her* credential lately. He had it.

Nevils went to Lauer's room, a massive suite with wide views of the Black Sea, to retrieve her credential. She found him still professionally attired, and the two had an uneventful exchange about the credential heist. Nevils noticed his fancy stationery, with "Matthew Todd Lauer" in raised navy ink, and thought about scrawling "sucks" underneath as another drunk prank, but decided against it. Lauer was at times formal and high-handed with junior staff like her. She'd been watching him on television since she was thirteen years old. She worried she'd get in trouble.

Nevils went back upstairs and, as she and Vieira said their good nights, texted one to Lauer, too, with a joking reference to the trouble the women were having drunkenly fitting their key cards into their doors. A few minutes later, as Nevils was brushing her teeth, her work

BlackBerry buzzed. A message from Lauer's work email suggested that she should come back downstairs. She replied that she'd only come if she could delete the photos of her looking drunk at the bar. He told her the offer expired in ten minutes. Later, sources close to Lauer told me that he considered her concern about the photos to be a thin pretext, and her messages to be come-ons. Nevils said that she found the idea of flirting with Lauer unthinkable. She had intended the messages to be playful, in line with his rapport with her and Vieira throughout the night. In retrospect, she considered going into a man's room at night, by herself, unwise. She said that she was drunk, didn't consider the implications deeply, and had no reason to suspect Lauer would be anything but friendly based on prior experience. "He always treated me like a little sister," she said. "I had been to his room many times." She didn't put herself together before heading down. She was still dressed for work, in maroon jeans from Uniqlo, a baggy green sweater from Target, and one of the Nike Sochi Olympics jackets that had been handed out to NBC staff. She hadn't shaved her legs for weeks. She said that she assumed she'd be right back up.

In her apartment, years later, Nevils tried not to cry, and did so anyway. "I do this PTSD therapy, right? Every week, a different thing messes me up. I just get so angry how this one thing derailed my life."

When Nevils arrived at his door, Lauer had changed into a tee shirt and boxers. As he pushed her against the door and began to kiss her, she became aware of how drunk she was. She recalled the room spinning. "I thought I was going to throw up," she said. "I kept thinking, I'm gonna throw up on Matt Lauer." She said that she felt acutely embarrassed about her baggy clothes and unshaved legs.

Not long into the encounter, she recalled Lauer pushing her onto the bed, flipping her over, and asking if she liked anal sex. She said that she declined several times, replying, at one point, "No, that's not my thing." Nevils said that she was still in the midst of telling him she wasn't interested when he "just did it." Lauer, she said, didn't use lubricant. The encounter was excruciatingly painful. "It hurt so bad. I remember thinking, Is this normal?" She told me that she stopped saying no, but wept silently into a pillow.

After Lauer finished, Nevils recalled him asking if she liked it.

"Yes," she said, mechanically. She felt humiliated and in pain. She told him that she needed to delete the drunk photos of her, and he gave her his phone to let her do so.

"Did you tell Meredith anything?" she remembered him asking.

"No," she said.

"Don't," he told her. Nevils wondered if it was advice or a warning.

Back in her room, she threw up. She took off her pants, passed out. When she woke up, blood was everywhere, soaked through her underwear, soaked through her sheets. "It hurt to walk, it hurt to sit." She was afraid to google the problem on her work devices. Later, she was afraid to get tested for sexually transmitted diseases — what would her boyfriend of five years say? She bled for days.

Lauer would later release a statement saying, "we performed oral sex on each other, we had vaginal sex, and we had anal sex," and maintaining that Nevils's allegation that any of it was nonconsensual "is categorically false, ignores the facts, and defies common sense." Nevils said that, regardless of Lauer's interpretation of their exchanges before and after, what transpired in his room was not consensual. "It was nonconsensual in the sense that I was too drunk to consent," she said. "It was nonconsensual in that I said, multiple times, that I didn't want to have anal sex."

The next day, Lauer emailed her a joke about her not writing or calling. Nevils told him everything was fine. She told me that she was terrified she'd angered him, a concern that deepened as he appeared to ignore her for the remainder of the trip. When she finally worked up the nerve to call him, he said they could talk back in New York.

On their return, she said that Lauer would ask her to his palatial Upper East Side apartment, where they had two sexual encounters, and to his office, where they had more. Sources close to Lauer emphasized that she sometimes initiated contact. What is not in dispute is that Nevils, like several of the women I'd spoken to, had several further sexual encounters with the man she said assaulted her. "This is the thing I blame myself most for," she said. "It was completely transactional. It was not a relationship." Nevils told friends at the time that she felt trapped. Lauer's position of authority — over both her and her boyfriend, whose brother worked for Lauer — made her feel unable to say no. She said that, in the first weeks after the alleged assault, she attempted to convey that she was comfortable and even enthusiastic about the encounters. She even tried to convince herself of the same. She readily admitted that her communications with Lauer might have appeared friendly and obliging.

But she also said she lived in terror of Lauer jeopardizing her career and that the encounters caused anguish and shame that eventually prompted her to break up with her boyfriend. She said that she successfully avoided the encounters for several months. But ultimately, she found she had to interact with Lauer for professional reasons. In September 2014, when Vieira was decorating her talk show set with photos from colleagues, Lauer's assistant told Nevils to come to Lauer to collect his pictures. At 9:30 a.m., in the little secondary office over the *Today* show studio where he and I had sometimes met, he pointed at an electronic photo frame Savannah Guthrie had given him, set on a deep ledge in front of the window. "It's on there," he told her. She had to bend over the ledge to reach it. She said that, as she shuffled through the photos and emailed them to herself, he grabbed her hips and fingered her. She told me that she was just trying to do her job. "I just went numb. In my internal narrative I failed because I didn't say no." Nevils bruises easily. Lauer left dark purple marks where he'd forced her legs open. Crying, she ran to the new guy she'd started seeing, a producer who was working in the control room that morning, and told him what had happened.

That November, she volunteered to put together a goodbye video for her ex-boyfriend, who was leaving a job at the network. Such videos were a common gesture for departing employees, and usually featured well-wishes from talent. When she asked Lauer for his, he told her to come to his office to record it herself. When she arrived, she said, he told her to go down on him. "I was really upset. I felt terrible," she told me. "I was trying to do this nice thing, and I had to give Matt a blow job to get him to film a goodbye video. I just felt sick." She recalled asking, "Why do you do this?" and Lauer replying, "Because it's fun."

The sexual encounters stopped after that. She said that once, a month later, as she was grappling with depression and felt fearful about where she stood with him, she sent him a text asking if he was in New York. He replied saying he was not.

Nevils told "like a million people" about Lauer. She told her inner circle of friends. She told colleagues and superiors at NBC. As in so many of the stories I'd reported on, Nevils told some of them a partial story, skipping over some details. But she was never inconsistent, and she made the seriousness of what had happened clear. When she moved to a new job within the company, working as a producer for Peacock Productions, she reported it to one of her new bosses there. She felt they should know, in case it became public and she became a liability. This was no secret.

And then, for several years, nothing happened. She didn't know about the pattern of harassment allegations within the company, or the payouts and other appeasements that had concealed them. She didn't know that control of Peacock Productions, specifically, had once been handed over to Corvo's accuser.

◆

"If the Weinstein accusers hadn't talked to you, I never would have said a word," Nevils told me. "I saw myself in those stories. And when you see the worst part of your life in the pages of *The New Yorker*, it changes your life." As the momentum around the Weinstein story accelerated, colleagues started asking Nevils questions about Lauer. Over drinks, one *Today* show colleague inquired about how much Nevils appeared to have changed. Nevils, previously as confident and outspoken as her grade-school report cards had projected, had withdrawn. She'd passed up work opportunities, fearing her experiences with Lauer would come up if she stuck her neck out. She started drinking heavily. After years of orienting her life around long-term committed relationships, she fell in and out of them.

Nevils told the *Today* show colleague everything. "This is not your fault," Nevils remembered the colleague saying, bursting into tears. "And trust me, you're not alone." The colleague had her own experience with Lauer, and professional fallout from it afterward. The colleague told Nevils she had to tell Vieira. And soon Nevils was at Vieira's apartment, recounting the whole story again. "It's Matt, isn't it?" Vieira asked, at the outset of the conversation. "I was thinking about it and he was the only one who had enough power over you to do that." Vieira was distraught. She blamed herself for not doing more to protect Nevils, and feared there were more victims. "Think of all the other women I've gotten jobs there," Vieira said. Nevils just kept apologizing.

Both women knew how far the network would go to shield its top talent. But Nevils felt she had to do something to protect other women. Vieira said if she was going to do anything, she should file a formal report with NBC's office of human resources. And that's how, in November 2017, Nevils found a lawyer, and wound up sitting with him opposite two women from NBCUniversal, telling the whole story.

She asked for, and was promised, anonymity. But she left out nothing. She disclosed the ongoing contact afterward but made it clear it was no affair. She described the incident in detail, making it clear that she'd been too drunk to consent and that she'd said no to Lauer's request for anal sex repeatedly. She was still early in her process of reliving the trauma—she didn't use the word "rape" that day. But she described one, unambiguously. Her attorney, Ari Wilkenfeld, paused the proceedings at one point to reiterate that the interaction was not consensual. One of the representatives from NBC replied that they understood, though later the network would say that it had reached no official conclusion on the matter. Stephanie Franco, the NBCUniversal lawyer who had placed the call reminding Lonner's attorney of the enforceability of her settlement, was present for the meeting.

At work a few days later, when Nevils learned that Lack and Oppenheim were emphasizing that the incident hadn't been "criminal" or an "assault," she left her desk, walked to the nearest bathroom, and threw up. Her distress deepened as articles to which NBC's communications team contributed began labeling the incident an "affair." Angry letters began flooding her attorney's office. "Shame on you for throwing your cunt at a married man," read one.

Nevils's work life became torture. She was made to sit in the same meetings as everyone else, discussing the news, and in all of them, colleagues loyal to Lauer cast doubt on the claims, and judgment on her. In a *Dateline* staff meeting, Lester Holt asked skeptically, "Does the punishment fit the crime?" Soon, colleagues were averting their eyes in the hallways. After the items characterizing the relationship as an affair, her boyfriend at the time became sharply less supportive, asking her, "How could you?" NBC management had turned her into a pariah. "You need to know that I was raped," she told a friend. "And NBC lied about it."

The network appeared to be doing little to protect Nevils's identity. Lack announced that the incident had taken place in Sochi, narrowing the potential complainants to a small group of women on that trip with close proximity to Lauer. A member of the communications staff identified Nevils by name in conversations with colleagues. Sources familiar with the matter later said that Kornblau had warned that member of his team not to do so. Wilkenfeld publicly accused NBC of outing Nevils. "They know exactly what they've done and they need to stop," he said.

Nevils hadn't initially asked for money. She'd wanted to do right by other women, then carry on with a job she loved. But as public scrutiny of the story and of Nevils mounted, NBC offered her one year's salary to depart and sign a nondisclosure agreement. Nevils felt her reputation had been damaged. She was grappling with losing both the job she loved and the possibility of finding future employment. She threatened to sue the network, and a protracted and punishing negotiation commenced. Sources familiar with the talks said that lawyers working with the network argued that Nevils's distress flowed from her mother's death and was unrelated to the alleged assault. In the end, her lawyer told her not to mention grief to her therapist, fearing NBC might subpoena her therapy records. The network would later deny that it made the threat or raised her mother's death. As the negotiations stretched over the course of 2018, Nevils took medical leave. Eventually, she was hospitalized for posttraumatic stress and alcohol abuse.

In the end, NBC wanted the problem gone. It offered Nevils a growing settlement sum — seven figures, finally, in exchange for her silence. The network proposed a script she would have to read, suggesting that she had left to pursue other endeavors, that she was treated well, and that NBC News was a positive example of how to handle sexual harassment. The sources familiar with the talks said that the network initially sought to include a clause that would have prevented Nevils from talking to other Lauer accusers, but Nevils pushed back. The network later denied they'd pressed for the provision.

Lawyers closed ranks and pushed Nevils to take the offer, as they had with Gutierrez and so many other women. For Comcast, the sum was a rounding error. For Nevils, it was a matter of survival. She surveyed the professional future she had lost, and the damage she felt the network had done to her reputation, and felt she didn't have a choice. NBC took the extraordinary step of having not only Nevils but also her lawyer and others close to her sign away their right to ever speak about the network.

## CHAPTER 57:

# *SPIKE*

*T*he allegations about Lauer weren't the only ones emerging. From the first days after the Weinstein story broke, NBC had been buffeted by allegations about men in its upper echelons. Shortly after the first *New Yorker* story about Weinstein, the network fired Mark Halperin, MSNBC and NBC News's most prominent political analyst, after five women told CNN he had been harassing or assaulting women in the workplace — grabbing, exposing himself, rubbing an erection against one woman — dating back to his days at ABC more than a decade earlier.

Days later, NBC fired Matt Zimmerman, the senior vice president of booking at the *Today* show and a close confidant of Lauer's, for sleeping with two underlings. Less than a month after the Lauer story broke, multiple outlets reported that the network had paid an assistant producer $40,000 in 1999, after she raised a verbal harassment allegation against Chris Matthews, one of MSNBC's biggest stars.

More news followed. There had been the large-scale payout to David Corvo's accuser during his involvement in the Weinstein story. And there was a more startling claim that shook me personally:

three women had accused Tom Brokaw of unwanted advances, many years earlier. These weren't claims of assault. But coworkers, at times young ones, beginning their careers, as he was at the apex of his, said he'd propositioned them and that they'd felt frightened. Brokaw was furious, heartbroken, denied it all.

Practically alone among the prominent figures of NBC News, Brokaw had objected to the killing of the Weinstein story. He'd told me how he'd protested to the network's leadership. In one email to me, he called the killing of the story "NBC's self inflicted wound." But both things could be true. Tom Brokaw, a principled defender of a tough story, had also once been part of a network news culture that made women feel uncomfortable and unsafe, and left little room for accountability around its larger-than-life stars.

Six, and then twelve, and then dozens of current and former employees gave me a similar account of a permissive atmosphere when it came to harassment by prominent men at the network. Several of the employees said that they believed the years-long pattern of settlements had allowed the behavior to continue. Some said that the problems had deepened under Andy Lack's leadership. When Lack began his first tenure as president of NBC News, in the nineties, "it was a fundamental shift of, all of a sudden, a tolerance for abusive behavior, whether it was sexually harassing or it was just verbally abusive," Linda Vester, who raised the first complaint about Brokaw, told me. "Degrading, humiliating talk, mainly to women. And that became the climate under Andy Lack. It was just—it was very stark."

All of the employees said that they were concerned about the effect the pattern of complaints and settlements had on the network's coverage. That knock-on effect, said Vester, was one of Lack's trademarks. "He would spike stories about women," she told me. "And this happened routinely."

❖

NBC was embattled. Over the course of 2018, investigative stories in the *Washington Post*, *Esquire*, and the *Daily Beast* described a culture of harassment at the network. As the *Post* prepared to report that Ann Curry had told NBC executives about Lauer sexually harassing women, Stephanie Franco, the same NBCUniversal employment attorney who had attended the meeting with Nevils, called Curry. Franco, as Curry recalled the conversation, wanted to know what she was telling the press. "It was really a call to try to intimidate me," Curry said. "That was my impression." Dismayed at what she took to be a focus on silencing her rather than addressing the sexual harassment problem at the network, she became direct. "You need to be taking care of these women," Curry told Franco. "This is your job. You should be making sure these women are protected from this guy."

"I try to do that when they let me do it," Franco said. Later, the internal report on Lauer would cite the call to Curry as part of its research. Curry said Franco made no mention of a report, and asked no questions about sexual harassment at the network.

Several of the current and former employees recalled other instances in which the network appeared to be working to forestall disclosures. In one case, NBC hired as a paid contributor a reporter who had, until just before the hiring, been making calls to women at the network, inquiring about harassment. One of the women the reporter had contacted texted me: "Coverup."

❖

No publication had circled the sexual harassment claims at the network, and the allegations against Lauer, more closely than the *National Enquirer*. Over the years, the tabloid had pursued Lauer's accusers. In 2006, when Addie Collins was working as a local anchor in West Virginia, she came home to a stakeout: a reporter from the *Enquirer* approached, peppering her with questions about Lauer. After his firing, the tabloid focused on Nevils, whose name was not yet public. It was her résumé that had been attached to internal emails at AMI that I later reviewed. Soon after she registered her complaint, the *Enquirer* began calling Nevils's colleagues and, eventually, Nevils herself.

In May 2018, after the meeting in which Oppenheim and Harris tried to explain the internal investigation of Lauer to a skeptical investigative unit, William Arkin, one respected member of that unit, called me, troubled. He said that two sources, one connected to Lauer, the other within NBC, had told him that Weinstein had made it known to the network that he was aware of Lauer's behavior and capable of revealing it. Two sources at AMI later told me they'd heard the same thing. NBC denied any threat was communicated.

But there was no doubt that the allegations against Lauer, and NBC's wider use of nondisclosure agreements with women who experienced harassment, were under threat of exposure during our reporting. That precarious culture of secrecy made NBC more vulnerable to Harvey Weinstein's intimidation and enticement, delivered through lawyers, and intermediaries, and calls to Lack and Griffin and Oppenheim and Roberts and Meyer that the network initially concealed. That pattern of nondisclosure agreements and ongoing threats to enforce them was playing out as the network acquiesced to Weinstein's argument that his own similar pacts were ironclad and couldn't be reported on. And, as Weinstein huddled with Dylan Howard, all these secrets had been under threat. The *Enquirer* had pulled Lauer's file, and called one NBC employee after another with questions about him, and begun to run articles that threatened the future of the star anchor, who had become synonymous with the network's value.

# CHAPTER 58

# *LAUNDER*

**R**ich McHugh spent the year grappling with fallout from the story, too. In his meeting with Oppenheim, he'd declined to yield to the network president's characterizations of the reporting, and watched Oppenheim grow agitated and curse at him, and wondered what the implications would be for his future. As he continued to speak up in the group meetings, McHugh said, "I was basically put on watch." HR began to call, offering him a raise to stay and — he felt this, after the meeting with Oppenheim — sign onto the party line. On the other hand, the network reminded him that his contract was about to run out.

"No one knows my name," he told me, sitting at the corner diner near my place on the Upper West Side. "They can say whatever they want about me. They can keep me from getting a job."

"Do what's best for your girls," I said.

McHugh shook his head. "I don't know if I can." Bringing up the family was no use — it was the man's conscientiousness about the world his daughters were stepping into that had prompted these fits of principle in the first place.

In the end, he decided he couldn't take the money. "I sat in the meetings while they lied to the rest of the people," McHugh said. "Had to bite my tongue. And then decided not to."

A year after he was ordered to stand down on the Weinstein reporting, McHugh resigned. Then he gave an interview to the *New York Times*, saying that the reporting had been killed at "the very highest levels of NBC," that he'd been ordered to stop taking calls about the story, and that the network had lied about what happened.

❖

Mark Kornblau and the NBC News public relations machine went apoplectic. Lack, resisting calls for independent review as he had in Lauer's case, released to the press another self-report. I sat in one of the glassed-in offices at *The New Yorker*, and read his memo, and wasn't sure what to make of it. Later, the network would acknowledge that it had conducted no fact-checking on the memo. Within hours of its release, many of the sources discussed in it had made public statements disputing its contents.

"Farrow never had a victim or witness willing to be identified," the memo said repeatedly. This was not true of any point in the life span of the story at NBC. "Ambra had always been willing to allow Farrow to identify her by name and use the recording of her, and I had filmed an interview in silhouette," Nestor wrote in a furious statement she released to the press shortly after the Lack memo went out. "After Rose McGowan pulled out of the story, realizing that the story was in peril of not being made public at all, Farrow and I discussed and I had tentatively offered either to attach my name to the interview in silhouette or potentially even reshoot the interview with my face visible. However, they were not interested in this interview." Gutierrez added: "I was as available to Ronan before he left nbc as I was after he left. Nothing about me has ever waivered." Rose

McGowan gave a statement to Megyn Kelly's program, reiterating that she'd been on the record for months.

The memo contained a long tract in which Lack and the communications team attempted to undercut and dismantle the credibility of the sources. They dismissed Abby Ex's recollections of Weinstein's meetings designed for sexual entrapment by saying that "her account was based on suspicion alone." Ex, too, released a statement saying this wasn't true. "That is factually incorrect," she wrote. "Harvey asked ME, many times, to join these meetings, to which I refused. But I was a witness to them, and in fact, was a first-hand witness to physical and verbal abuse at his hands as well, all of which Ronan has on camera from my interview." The memo suggested that Dennis Rice, the marketing executive, hadn't been referring to Weinstein and that my use of his quotes had been misleading. In fact, Rice's statements had been designed to give him plausible deniability in the event that he faced retaliation, and he'd approved of how his quotes were used. Rice told a reporter that McHugh and I "didn't take anything out of context. I always knew what I was saying on camera would end up in a story about Harvey." *The New Yorker* had later used these accounts without incident.

Lack's memo was a "misleading and incorrect account," Ex wrote, expressing bewilderment at the network's effort to attack and expose sources without consulting them. "To see this memo leaked to the press with the sources listed, even without our names, and without the full and honest picture of the reporting, feels like the opposite of honest and direct."

The memo copped — for the first time, contradicting earlier communiqués to the press — to Weinstein's "numerous" calls and emails to Lack, Griffin, and Oppenheim. It painted a portrait of those conversations at odds with the records I'd later uncover, and the accounts of those who had stayed on the line while they played out. It made no mention of Griffin's assurances to Weinstein, or of the warm rapport implied by a bottle of Grey Goose.

Several investigative reporters at the network said they found the memo's focus on picking apart the work-in-progress reporting baffling. A number of television journalists I consulted agreed that the audio, in and of itself, was worthy of air. But McHugh and I hadn't argued that the story was finalized at NBC, or that it didn't have room to grow and come to fuller fruition, as it did in just a few weeks at *The New Yorker*. The problem, rather, was that we received a hard order to stop that development. Lack's memo made no mention of Greenberg ordering me to cancel an interview, blaming Oppenheim. It omitted McHugh being told to stand down, and Oppenheim being the first to suggest sending the reporting out the door to a print outlet. "It's immaterial," one veteran correspondent recalled telling Oppenheim and Greenberg, in response to their protestations about how much we'd had. "I know what it looks like when we're trying to bring a story to air and I know what it looks like when we're not." The correspondent said that "privately, the internal narrative is, we blew it."

The memo was greeted with similar skepticism in the press. On the network's own air, Megyn Kelly questioned NBC's self-reporting, joining the calls for independent oversight. Soon she'd be gone, too—fired after another conflagration over a racially insensitive remark. For the network, the firing had the added benefit of cutting off what several sources around Lack said were mounting tensions over Kelly's focus on Weinstein and Lauer.

◆

The memo was only one in a series of steps designed to rewrite the history of the story at the network. NBC also hired Ed Sussman, a

"Wikipedia whitewasher," to unbraid references to Oppenheim, Weinstein, and Lauer on the crowdsourced encyclopedia. The Lauer matter, Sussman wrote, justifying one edit, "should be handled seperately." He spun the material in NBC's favor, sometimes weaving in errors. In one edit, he proposed that the month between the Weinstein story being greenlit and running at *The New Yorker* be revised to "several months." Other times, he simply removed all mention of the controversies.

"This is one of the most blatant and naked exercises of hard corporate spin that I have encountered in WP and I have encountered a lot," one veteran Wikipedia editor complained. But Sussman often prevailed: he reasserted his changes again and again, with a doggedness that unpaid editors could not match. And he deployed a network of friendly accounts to launder his changes and make sure they stuck. Several Wikipedia pages, including Oppenheim's, were stripped of evidence of the killing of the Weinstein story. It was almost as if it had never happened.

# CHAPTER 59:

# *BLACKLIST*

After the first *New Yorker* story, I faced a dilemma similar to McHugh's. For a time, I did as I'd uneasily promised during the argument with Oppenheim and Kornblau, and dodged questions about the story's history at NBC. On CBS, Stephen Colbert looked at me narrowly as I said I didn't want the story to be about me and changed the subject. "Part of this story is the story not being told for so long," he said. "And you experienced the story not being told."

My sister called at the height of the evasive interviews. "You're covering for them," she said.

"I'm not lying," I replied.

"No. You're omitting. It's dishonest."

The low points between us flickered back to me. I remembered the hard years, after I'd told her to shut up about her own allegation: walking into her room after she came back from the hospital; seeing her pull a long sleeve over the ladder of blood-red em-dashes on her forearm; saying I was sorry, and that I wished I could have done more.

Throughout that fall, the network followed up on Oppenheim's text dangling a new deal. "You should counter however aggressively you need," he added. Griffin called my agents and said, "I'm his guy. What do we have to do?" Before the claims about him surfaced, Brokaw emailed after my media appearances to tell me, "You've handled this perfectly. Now the future....." He called, saying the network had asked him to convince me to come back. "I realize the offer might have to be over the top, but you should consider it. It's still a great place to do journalism." He said he felt confident the network would agree to a statement acknowledging what had gone wrong and a new set of guidelines to prevent editorial interference. I still just wanted my job back. And I believed in the values NBC News represented at its best. I convinced myself that maybe the killing of the Weinstein story was a one-off, not a sign of deeper ills. I said I'd hear the network out, and told my agents the same.

But with McHugh's refusals to compromise, and with each source who called to allege a pattern of harassment and settlements at the network, it got harder to go along to get along. From the early days after the Weinstein story broke, I'd been talking to a group of sources who described serial misconduct at CBS: an executive who was said to sleep with underlings and harass and assault others; a pattern of payouts to silence women; dozens of employees describing how the cover-up was distorting a news outlet's priorities. In the end, I didn't think I could report out the allegations against Leslie Moonves and the other CBS executives while shutting up about the pervasive claims streaming out of 30 Rockefeller Plaza.

I told my agents to drop negotiations.

The reprisal was decisive. With each of the AMI stories over the following months, I was invited to appear on MSNBC and NBC shows at all hours—and then, suddenly, uninvited. On-air personalities called upset, one near tears, to say I'd been unbooked over their objections, on direct orders from Griffin. A senior executive at the network later said Lack had issued an edict too. "These people are insidious," one anchor wrote. "I'm so angry." Then the executives were reaching out, saying they knew I had a book coming out—I'd managed to finish the foreign policy book I'd ignored for so long—and they'd be happy to consider having me back on air to promote it, if I'd come in and reach a formal agreement about not rehashing the past. I called Maddow, who listened, and said no one tells her how to run her show. And so it came to pass that, all through the two years after the Weinstein story, I appeared on her show, and never again on any other NBC or MSNBC program. Later, as I finished work on this book, NBC's litigation department began contacting the publisher, Hachette.

❖

The last conversation I had with Noah Oppenheim in the aftermath of the story was a call he made. I spoke to him while pacing the strange safe house in Chelsea, Jonathan listening in the background. "I've become the poster boy for this," Oppenheim told me. The backfire from his and Kornblau's dissembling statements to media reporters had flared into the political zeitgeist. On Fox News a few days earlier, Tucker Carlson had sat in front of a picture of Oppenheim and called for his resignation. "Let's be clear. NBC is lying," Carlson said. "Many powerful people knew what Harvey Weinstein was doing and not only ignored his crimes but actively took his side against his many victims. It's a long list but at the very top of that list is NBC News." He appeared to relish the chance to attack a mainstream outlet, Hollywood liberals, and a sexual predator all at once. "News executives are not allowed to tell lies," he said, as if he'd never met one.

As I paced, Oppenheim said, "You know, I just got a call this morning from NBC Global Security saying they need to send a police car to my house because of all the online death threats." He sounded angry, not afraid. "I've got three young kids who are wondering why there are cops out front." I said I was sorry to hear it. I meant it.

"Even if you think that NBC was either cowardly or acted inappropriately or whatever, which you're entitled to feel, I hope that you would realize the way this has become personalized and hung on *me* is not fair or accurate," he added. "Even if you believe that there is a villain in this, that the villain is not *me*."

He was agitated, talking over me. Everyone, it seemed, had some culpability for his predicament except him. When I told him media reporters were telling me their criticism was a result of Kornblau's blanketing the press with false claims, he wailed: "Kornblau works for Andy! He works for the news group! He doesn't work for me! He *doesn't work for me!*" And then: "I can't tell him what to do. I can try and I have tried." When he said he'd never threatened me, I reminded him that Susan Weiner had explicitly done so, on his orders. He shouted: "Susan Weiner is *Andy's* lawyer! These are not people who work for me!" Later, others involved disputed that characterization of Oppenheim's authority as president of NBC News.

"You keep saying you're the one who takes the hit and it wasn't you. So where does it come from?" I asked finally.

"My boss! Okay? I have a boss. I don't run NBC News exclusively," he said, then seemed to catch himself. "You know, *everyone* was involved in this decision. You can speculate what Kim Harris's motives are, you can speculate what Andy's motives are, you can speculate what my motives are. All I can tell you is at the end of the day, they felt like, you know, there was a *consensus about the organization's comfort level moving forward.*"

He reminded me, twice, that he'd revived my career after my show was canceled. That we'd been friends. He hoped we could get a beer and laugh about it all in a few months. I struggled to understand what he was asking for. Gradually, he let it out. "I'm just making a plea," he said. "If the opportunity ever does present itself to you to say that maybe *I'm* not the villain in all this, I would be grateful."

And there it was, at the end of his arguments: an unwillingness not just to take responsibility but to admit that responsibility might, in some place, in someone's hands, exist. It was a *consensus about the organization's comfort level moving forward* that stopped the reporting. It was a *consensus about the organization's comfort level moving forward* that bowed to lawyers and threats; that hemmed and hawed and parsed and shrugged; that sat on multiple credible allegations of sexual misconduct and disregarded a recorded admission of guilt. That anodyne phrase, that language of indifference without ownership, upheld so much silence in so many places. It was *a consensus about the organization's comfort level moving forward* that protected Harvey Weinstein and men like him; that yawned and gaped and enveloped law firms and PR shops and executive suites and industries; that swallowed women whole.

Noah Oppenheim was not the villain.

◆

"I do not think you will be getting a beer with Noah Oppenheim in a few months," Jonathan deadpanned later. It was a sunlit afternoon, back at his place in Los Angeles.

"No more morning TV, I guess," I replied. I was, increasingly, realizing I'd be spending the next year chasing leads about CBS and NBC.

"I'll take care of you, baby," he said. "I'll keep you in finery and smoothies."

He hugged me around the middle like a kid hugging a stuffed animal. I laughed, put a hand on his. It had been a long year, for me and for us, but we hung in there.

Later, when I decided some of that reporting would make its way into a book, I'd send him a draft, and put in a question, right on this page: "Marriage?" On the moon or even here on earth. He read the draft, and found the proposal here, and said, "Sure."

❖

The first time I saw my sister Dylan after the stories began to break, she gave me a hug, too. We were at her cottage in the countryside, near my mother and several other siblings, under a blanket of snow—a universe apart from the tempest of unfolding reporting. Dylan's two-year-old daughter, looking uncannily like her mother—wearing one of her mother's old onesies even—cooed for something, waving her arms. My sister handed her a pacifier with a little stuffed monkey attached to it, and we watched her bound off on wobbly legs.

I shuffled through mental images of Dylan and me during our own onesie years, and those that followed: dressed up for school plays, waiting for the bus, constructing a magic kingdom together that no one could touch. I remembered us, as we positioned those pewter kings and dragons, and a grown-up voice sounded, calling her away. Her startled look, too frightened. Her asking, if anything bad ever happened to her, whether I'd be there. And me making a promise.

In the countryside with her daughter running around, she told me she was proud of the reporting. She was grateful for it. And here she trailed off.

"No story for you," I said. When she'd spoken, as a child and again several years before all of this, she felt people had looked the other way.

"Right," she replied.

It was a time of newfound accountability. But for every story being heard, countless others weren't. Dylan was frustrated. She, like many of the sources who had suffered at the hands of the unaccountably powerful and whose stories now filled my in-box, was angry. And not long after, she joined the others — in industry after industry — and told the world she was frustrated too. She invited a TV crew into the cottage in the countryside, and they made the place as bright as an operating room. A news anchor beckoned her over, and Dylan took a deep breath, and stepped into the light — and this time, people were listening.

◆

It was dusk when I filed into David Remnick's office at *The New Yorker*. I found him flipping through a document. "Oh!" I said, reddening a little. "That was for me." I'd asked a colleague to print it and leave it for me to pick up. Notes, not a handout. Remnick's assistant had brought it over to him instead.

"It's interesting," he said. A sly smile, a little mischief.

We took seats near a big window with views of the Hudson. Remnick had been gracious, dispensing advice as I grappled with what to do next. He thought of me as a "TV guy," perhaps a little too obsessed with seeing my face onscreen. And maybe I was. "You don't want to keep doing this forever, do you?" he asked, gesturing toward the magazine's offices around us. But I realized I did.

I pointed at the notes. The next wave of potential stories. Some were about sexual violence. There was the developing reporting around New York Attorney General Eric Schneiderman, about whom *New Yorker* writer Jane Mayer and I would eventually publish four allegations of physical abuse, prompting him to step down. There was the investigation into CBS, which would swell to include twelve claims of assault and harassment against Leslie Moonves, prompting his resignation—the first in this new era by a Fortune 500 CEO over such claims—as well as changes within CBS's board and news division. Other leads were about different forms of corruption: waste and fraud and cover-ups in media and government. Some you have seen, some you have not.

He looked at the document again, handed it back to me.

"Too much?" I asked. Outside of the window next to us, the sky was changing.

Remnick looked at me. "I was going to say we have our work cut out for us."

In the months that followed, I wasn't sure those plans would include the claims about harassment at NBC. At the network, everything was in its place: the Wikipedia articles had been scrubbed; the self-reports declared definitive. The people who would claim otherwise had been paid, and remained too frightened to risk their non-disclosure agreements. The men of NBC News had put in the last word about Brooke Nevils, who had an affair, who hadn't been assaulted, about whom the company had known nothing.

Only not quite. In early 2019, I returned to Nevils, and sat in her book-lined living room again. This time, I brought Lavery, the *New Yorker* fact-checker. Afternoon light streamed through the windows.

Cats, white and black and gray, encircled Nevils. Among them was a new kitten, taking the place of the one she'd lost before.

Nevils was leafing through letters her late mother sent her. Meticulous notes, in dreaming, swooping cursive, a mother's love for her daughter leaping off the yellowing pages. "My dearest darling daughter," one read. "Each time a door closes, another opens."

Nevils felt she'd ruined her life by not shutting up. And she was increasingly convinced it was the right thing to do. "All the women before feel I am their fault," she said. "And if there were women after me, I feel that is my fault." She told me she was willing to take another risk—to tell her story again, for the sake of those women yet to come.

As I prepared to leave, she looked me in the eye and repeated her answer to all my questions about the network. "I am obliged to tell you that I cannot disparage Andy Lack, or Noah Oppenheim, or any other employee of NBC News."

I nodded. As I watched, a smile just began to turn the edges of her lips.

In the end, the courage of women can't be stamped out. And stories—the big ones, the true ones—can be caught but never killed.

# EPILOGUE

*N*ot long after the meeting with Nevils, Igor Ostrovskiy and I reunited at a French bistro on the Upper West Side. Sun fell through the window behind him over our little table. He looked exhausted, like he hadn't slept in days. I asked him what brought it all on, this crazy high-wire act of leaking information to me through the months.

"I like to be able to read the news and not think somebody's holding a gun to the reporter's head deciding what they write," he said. "Coming from a society where the news was controlled by those in power, I never, ever want to allow this to happen to the country that gave me and my wife and my son a chance."

Turns out, his wife had just had a baby. A first-generation American boy.

"I happened to be at this intersection where we were following reporters whose stories I read, who I thought were doing something honest and good for society. If somebody wants to attack that, that's attacking my country. That's attacking my home."

I studied him. How strange, this speech, from the man who spent a summer following me, trying to stop my reporting.

Once he'd refused to take the polygraph for Black Cube, the Info-Tactic jobs had stopped coming. Now he was hanging out his own shingle, Ostro Intelligence. He'd still be a private investigator, but there'd be a public service angle, he announced, proud and earnest, meaning it and wanting me to know he meant it. Maybe he could help groups like Citizen Lab. "Moving forward, I'm going to try to be more involved with this kind of stuff, to better society, to seek out these kind of actors, try to expose them," he said. "You know, the press is as much part of our democracy as Congress or the executive branch or the judicial branch. It has to keep things in check. And when the powerful control the press, or make the press useless, if the people can't trust the press, the people lose. And the powerful can do what they want."

Ostrovskiy flicked through pictures on his phone, a far-off smile on his face. A mother, flushed and exhausted after birth. A new son coming home. A father imagining how good a man he could become for his family. A blue-gray cat with clever, lamplike eyes, peering wonderingly at the new arrival.

The cat's name, by the way, was Spy.

◆

"The last part of the Harvey Weinstein story, the part that's being told right now, is the story of how the story got told at all," Rachel Maddow said, under the lights again, over the lucite desk again. "Accusations that people in positions of authority in this building may have been complicit in some way in shielding those guys from accountability?" she said, referring to Weinstein and Lauer, "Those accusations are very, very hard to stomach. And I can tell you that inside this building, this issue, the Weinstein story, having to leave the building in order to get told? And combine that with another previous gigantic story on a related subject, the *Access Hollywood* tape Billy Bush story, also having to leave this building to get told? The amount of consternation this has caused among the rank-and-file people who work here would be almost impossible for me to overstate."

It was late 2019. Since I'd disclosed the pattern of secret settlements within NBC and detailed the killing of the Weinstein story, NBC had denied it all. The story just hadn't been worthy of air. The women's settlements had been coincidental. Steve Burke — the CEO of NBCUniversal, who had told colleagues so casually about killing the Weinstein story — had protected Andy Lack and Noah Oppenheim, reportedly re-upping Oppenheim's contract in advance of the publication of this book.

Journalists at the network made renewed calls for independent investigations. Days before, Chris Hayes had addressed the issue sharply, noting how little time had elapsed between my departing NBC with the story and *The New Yorker* publishing it. "The path of least resistance is always there," he'd said. "Beckoning seductively with an entirely plausible cover story — 'you've got bigger fish to fry, this isn't the hill to die on, the story isn't ready.' But of course, it's the very ease of that path that makes it the enemy to the kind of work that we, as journalists, are supposed to do."

On her show that evening, Maddow cut down one of her network's denials. "As to whether or not Ronan Farrow was told to hit pause on any new reporting at a time when NBC didn't think there was enough to go to air with, we have independently confirmed that NBC News did that. That did happen. He was told to pause his reporting," she continued. Of the network's report on what it had known about Lauer — the one rendered by the legal team that was simultaneously enforcing nondisclosure provisions related to Lauer — she added, "I'll tell you, there has been consternation even inside this building, inside MSNBC and NBC News, that that matter was handled with an internal investigation, with the company, in effect, investigating itself rather than hiring an external firm to do it . . . As far as we can tell, there has never been an independent investigation of that."

That night, NBC issued a series of new statements. It was now "profoundly disappointed" about its decision not to air the Weinstein story. As to the settlements the company said didn't exist, "Any former NBC News employee who believes that they cannot disclose their experience with sexual harassment as a result of a confidentiality or non-disparagement provision in the separation agreement should contact NBCUniversal and we will release them from that perceived obligation." It was a hand wave. The women with the most serious allegations wondered why the network had opaquely required those seeking release from a "perceived obligation" to make contact to negotiate that release. Others tried to do so with little effect. Calling a number provided by the network reached a front desk assistant who "had absolutely no idea what I was talking about," one source wrote to me. A protracted attempt to explain led to a transfer to a legal office. "Unsurprisingly, that call went directly to voicemail. Once there, the message was that the box was full, please call back...I guess NBCUniversal thinks if they deflect and delay enough, the problem will go away."

But the problem wasn't going away. Investigators with the New York Attorney General's office began asking current and former staffers about harassment at the network. As Maddow and I spoke, NBC's digital journalists were preparing to unionize, in part in protest of the disclosures in this book. "Recent weeks have highlighted serious questions as to how NBC News has handled incidents of sexual misconduct in the workplace as well as the opaque processes and procedures for reporting on and exposing powerful predators," their announcement would read. "NBC News repeatedly refused calls for an independent review on both counts despite numerous such requests from staff. This lack of transparency and NBC News' troubling trend of passing on stories which investigate the powerful ultimately harm our credibility as journalists." Protesters demonstrated outside of the network's headquarters, demanding leadership change, waving signs that read "SURVIVORS DEMAND JUSTICE AT NBC." Weeks later, it was reported that Burke would step down early. Not long after that, Andy Lack was gone too.

The reporting — the Weinstein story and the ones that came

after — had "changed how we understand sexual predation by very, very powerful men in this country," Maddow said that night. Her eyes flickered to the side, to a brightly lit set in studio 3A of 30 Rockefeller Plaza, inside the Comcast building, which had once been the GE building, which had once been the RCA building. "And how we understand the vast resources they can bring, even on powerful institutions, to shield themselves from accountability."

◆

Through the end of that year and into the next, AMI slashed spending and cut staff. Prosecutors continued to assess whether David Pecker and Dylan Howard had breached AMI's nonprosecution agreement. A year after the sale of the *National Enquirer* was announced, the deal still hadn't closed.

Howard had become increasingly sulky about the scrutiny. After a journalist with Australia's *60 Minutes* approached him in AMI's lobby ("Can we talk about the work you've been doing for your friend Harvey Weinstein?" the reporter asked) Howard had sued the show for trespassing, resulting in a settlement. That fall, during a party Howard threw for a book he was releasing — attended by several Real Housewives and held at a venue a press report later described as "sexy-trashy" — another reporter tried to question him about continuing fallout from the Bezos imbroglio, including a lawsuit from Bezos's mistress's brother (long story). Howard poked at the other man's chest. "I'll talk about *Be*-zos as much as I fucking want," Howard hissed, leaning in. "I have audiotapes, kay? I have audiotapes." He'd spent the ensuing months hiring lawyers around the world to threaten bookstores and stop them from stocking this book. (Amazon briefly halted, then reinstated, sales in Australia. Bookstore owners there told the Associated Press that they'd disregarded the legal threats. "There's no way it would have got the publicity that it's got if it hadn't been for the attempt to ban it," said one, whose copies had sold out.) In early 2020, when *The Hollywood Reporter* disclosed Celebuzz's finding that Howard had sexually harassed colleagues there, he threatened, without apparent irony, to expose the *Reporter's* ties to Harvey Weinstein.

Not long after that, Howard was ousted from his role at AMI. "We are texting each other and wish we could host a party to mark the end of an era," one colleague said. "An awful era."

In their salad days, Pecker and Howard had maintained a database of which headlines sold and which didn't. Several employees invoked a perennial favorite to describe the atmosphere at AMI after its collaborations with Weinstein and Trump: these were, they said, the company's "Sad Last Days."

Soon after Harvey Weinstein was sentenced and taken into custody, a doctor arrived to perform a medical exam. "I'm too sick to be here," Weinstein said, as the exam got underway. "That's not really true," replied the doctor. Weinstein was thinner, older, more hunched than before. He'd graduated from a walker he'd relied on during his trial to a wheelchair. He continued to suffer cardiac issues. But he looked the doctor in the eye and said, with a little of his old bravado, "It's okay. I'm gonna get out of here with my appeal. I had very good lawyers. But now? Now I have the best lawyers."

Weinstein would likely spend the rest of his days behind bars. Outside, authorities in Los Angeles and London were building additional criminal cases. Inside, he told himself and anyone who would listen a different story. "The movie I make when I get out of here is gonna be better than *Pulp Fiction*," he said, poring over a script. One day, he handed a note to a uniformed officer guarding him. "Can you take this to the front desk?" Weinstein asked, as if he were back at the Peninsula, as if he might ever be.

The officer replied: "What front desk?"

# ACKNOWLEDGMENTS

*Catch and Kill* was exhaustively vetted by Sean Lavery, a senior fact-checker at *The New Yorker*, who has also worked on many of my investigations for the magazine. Without his steady judgment and lack of work-life balance, this book would not have been possible. Noor Ibrahim and Lindsay Gellman, my impeccable researchers, put in long hours. The brilliant and tireless Unjin Lee managed and assisted that research team, counseled me during stressful low points, and performed light countersurveillance duties. She is still planning to learn Krav Maga.

I hope *Catch and Kill* serves as a tribute to other journalists I admire. Without their labors, powerful people would never be held accountable. I am grateful, every day, for the peerless team at *The New Yorker* that rescued the Weinstein story and continues to stand behind one difficult investigation after another.

I don't know how to thank David Remnick. The fact that he did so right by the stories, and by me, changed my outlook on journalism and life. You know that clip where Oprah Winfrey says of Gayle King, "She is the mother I never had. She is the sister everybody would want. She is the friend that everybody deserves. I don't know a better person"? That's David Remnick. Esther Fein, a wonderful journalist and David Remnick's wife, is impossibly kind. Deirdre

Foley-Mendelssohn, my editor, is a singular talent with an unerring moral compass. She is responsible for the voice of our *New Yorker* stories and somehow found time to give exacting notes on this book through work and travel and a pregnancy. David Rohde is my fearless collaborator. I find unconvincing his claims that he is not, as described in these pages, an angel. He and Michael Luo have both been important defenders of the reporting.

Fabio Bertoni is a badass lawyer who approached the thorny legal challenges and threats we faced with integrity and common sense. It's easy for lawyers to say no. The best media lawyers give advice on how to get to yes carefully and fairly. Natalie Raabe, *The New Yorker*'s head of communications, went to the barricades to defend our stories against some pretty efficient spin machines. There are many others, including Peter Canby, the magazine's head of fact-checking, E. Tammy Kim, the checker who worked so diligently on the first Weinstein story, along with Fergus McIntosh, who also helped me untangle Black Cube and AMI. Natalie Meade scrutinized follow-up stories. They all ensured the reporting was precise, accurate, and fair. Other senior editors at the magazine, including Pam McCarthy and Dorothy Wickenden, have been kind and generous. Roger Angell graciously, if unknowingly, allowed me to use his desk. I love *The New Yorker*—and the people there, who inspire me to be a better journalist.

Thanks also to everyone I've worked with at HBO, including Richard Plepler, Casey Bloys, Bob Greenblatt, Nancy Abraham, and Lisa Heller, who supported my reporting at every turn (even when book leave lasted longer than science thought possible).

I also owe a debt of gratitude to the many reporters and publications who helped break ground relevant to this book. Thank you to the journalists who pursued the Weinstein story, and then shared their insights with me, when they didn't know me and didn't have to but for their sense of principle. Ken Auletta is a prince among men and the history of the Weinstein story would be different without his work. Ben Wallace was similarly generous. Janice Min and Matt Belloni and Kim Masters were too. And admiration to Jodi Kantor and Megan Twohey, whose powerful stories made me feel less alone and taught me to type faster.

Thank you to the reporters who shed light on the AMI story, including Jeff Horwitz and Jake Pearson of the Associated Press and Joe Palazzolo and Michael Rothfeld of the *Wall Street Journal*. Thank you to Shachar Alterman of *Uvda*, the documentarian Ella Alterman, Adam Ciralsky of *Vanity Fair*, Raphael Satter of the Associated Press, John Scott-Railton of Citizen Lab, and Adam Entous, my colleague at *The New Yorker*, for their help with the Black Cube reporting.

Thank you to those who exposed allegations of abuse at NBC News, including Ramin Setoodeh and Elizabeth Wagmeister of *Variety*, Sarah Ellison of the *Washington Post*, and Lachlan Cartwright of the *Daily Beast*—who doggedly pursued the pattern of settlements.

Thank you to the journalists and producers of NBC News who continue to chase important stories and believe in the place's promise and principles. Before the intercession of executives, the Weinstein story was well supported by Rich McHugh's and my colleagues. I am so grateful to Anna Schechter, Tracy Connor, William Arkin, Cynthia McFadden, Stephanie Gosk, and many others on the investigative unit. Rachel Maddow was a voice of principle. Phoebe Curran, an associate producer, helped conduct research in the story's early days.

Rich McHugh did the right thing, even when it was the worst thing for himself, every time. Without his fierce ethics and the sense of mission in his bones, not to mention the righteous indignation of his wife Danie, we would have been lost. He's a hero and he lives in New Jersey.

Most importantly, I thank the sources. I am inspired by those who exposed unethical and at times illegal conduct from the inside. Sleeper's courage broke through a wall of lies and helped victims of deception and gaslighting. Igor Ostrovskiy put principle and patriotism before self-protection at every turn, first by informing me, and then by agreeing to put his name in this book. Thank you also to John Tye for supporting him in that process and for being helpful as I navigated my own security concerns. The list of conscientious objectors includes many employees of Miramax and the Weinstein Company, of NBC News and AMI, of the Manhattan District Attorney's Office, the NYPD, and the Southern District of New York. Most of them, I can't name. A few to whom I owe a debt of gratitude: Abby Ex, Dede Nickerson, Dennis Rice, and Irwin Reiter.

I am especially grateful to the women who risked so much to reveal important and difficult truths. Rosanna Arquette overcame her fears to help with the Weinstein story, then stayed in the fight, urging source after source to come forward. She has been indispensable to my follow-up stories about Weinstein, my investigation of CBS, and to other reporting that still hasn't seen the light of day.

Ambra Gutierrez is a source for the ages, with the courage of a jewel thief. Her story in these pages speaks for itself. Emily Nestor is as compassionate and steadfast a person as I've encountered. Before the story was a sure thing, she stood by it. And she's continued to stand by it, in the face of continuing attempts to discredit her and the other sources.

We are better for the fact that there are too many others to mention them all. But here are some: Ally Canosa, Annabella Sciorra, Asia Argento, Brooke Nevils, Daryl Hannah, Emma de Caunes, Jane Wallace, Jennifer Laird, Jessica Barth, Karen McDougal, Lauren

O'Connor, Lucia Evans, Melissa Lonner, Mira Sorvino, Rose McGowan, Rowena Chiu, Sophie Dix, and Zelda Perkins.

Tough stories don't get told without editors and publishers being willing to weather the storm. Thank you to Vanessa Mobley, the editor of every writer's dreams and an unwavering ally in getting this book right. Thank you to Sabrina Callahan and Elizabeth Garriga for their efforts defending the message of this book. I also depended on Mike Noon, our hardworking production editor, on Janet Byrne, our meticulous copyeditor, and on Gregg Kulick, our talented designer, who was collaborative and gracious about my backseat driving. Liz McNamara and Carol Fein Ross further defended the reporting with their legal vetting. And the legendary Lynn Nesbit, my literary agent and dear friend, stood by me during the long journey of the Weinstein story and through the writing of this book.

I learned through press reports that Hachette, as it supported this book through a protracted reporting and fact-checking process, had secretly acquired Woody Allen's memoir after other major publishers refused to do so. It concealed the acquisition from me and its own employees while we were working on this book — documenting how powerful men, including Woody Allen, avoid accountability for sexual abuse. Hachette reportedly agreed to an unorthodox arrangement whereby it ceded traditional publisher's oversight and input. We now know, as the book ultimately found another publisher, that Hachette planned to publish a book filled with ugly, demonstrably false attacks on me and my family while reaping the financial rewards of our partnership. Fact-checking would have caught many of these inaccuracies and allowed my sister to respond to any denial or mischaracterization of the abuse she suffered at the hands of Woody Allen — a credible allegation, maintained for almost three decades, backed up by contemporaneous accounts and evidence. But even if Hachette didn't wish to fact check a memoir, basic legal vetting should have raised serious red flags, and that's an understatement. Thank you to the numerous Hachette employees who staged a walk-out—in New York, and then Boston, men and women, one after another—protesting an evident conflict of interest given the company's existing relationship with me, and arguing passionately that books purporting to be nonfiction, that attempt to refute or downplay credible allegations of abuse, should be afforded some degree of care and due diligence prior to publication.

Finally, thank you to my family. My mother, who stood by a survivor of abuse in the face of smearing and blacklisting and intimidation, constantly inspires me to be a better person. My sister Dylan's courage kept me going and helped me understand the unfathomable—and she provided the interior illustrations in *Catch and Kill*. My sister Quincy, whose wedding I missed while closing the Weinstein story, was so understanding. I'm sorry, Quincy!

Jonathan already got a dedication and he's quoted throughout these pages. How much more attention does he need?

# NOTES

## CHAPTER 1

5 **published an article:** David A. Fahrenthold, "Trump Recorded Having Extremely Lewd Conversation About Women in 2005," *Washington Post,* October 8, 2016.

6 **Donald Trump held forth about grabbing women "by the pussy":** Billy Bush's *Access Hollywood* tape with Donald Trump, 2005.

6 **"How do you feel about your butt?":** Billy Bush interview with Jennifer Lopez, *Access Hollywood,* 2002.

6 **sat on it:** Jack Shafer, "Why Did NBC News Sit on the Trump Tape for So Long?" *Politico Magazine,* October 10, 2016.

6 **Leaked accounts presented differing timelines:** "NBC Planned to Use Trump Audio to Influence Debate, Election," TMZ, October 12, 2016.

6 **"The executive was unaware":** Paul Farhi, "NBC Waited for Green Light from Lawyers Before Airing Trump Video," *Washington Post,* October 8, 2016.

7 **"Get to Know Billy" video:** "Get to Know Billy Bush — from Billy Himself, As His Parents Send Special Wishes," *Today* show, August 22, 2016.

7 **"Pending further review of the matter":** "Here's How the *Today* show Addressed Billy Bush's Suspension On-Air," *Entertainment Tonight,* October 10, 2016.

7 **against the head of that network:** Michael M. Grynbaum and John Koblin, "Gretchen Carlson of Fox News Files Harassment Suit Against Roger Ailes," *New York Times,* July 6, 2016.

7 **women in at least fifteen cities staged sit-ins and marches:** Edward Helmore, "Anti-Trump Protests Continue Across US as 10,000 March in New York," *Guardian,* November 12, 2016.

8 **A hashtag:** Emanuella Grinberg, "These Tweets Show Why Women Don't Report Sexual Assault," CNN, October 13, 2016.

8   "time for some goddamned honesty": Rose McGowan quoted in Gene Maddaus, "Rose McGowan Says a Studio Executive Raped Her," *Variety*, October 14, 2016.


# CHAPTER 2

9   helping to reinvent the model for independent films: Ronan Farrow, "From Aggressive Overtures to Sexual Assault: Harvey Weinstein's Accusers Tell Their Stories," *The New Yorker*, October 10, 2017. Reporting from this article also referenced in subsequent chapters.

9   he had been thanked more than almost anyone else: Catherine Shoard, "They Know Him as God, but You Can Call Him Harvey Weinstein," *Guardian*, February 23, 2012.

9   "sex movie": Ken Auletta, "Beauty and the Beast," *The New Yorker,* December 8, 2002.

10   "'Denny the Hustler' did not take no for an answer": Harvey Weinstein quoted in Margaret Sullivan, "At 18, Harvey Weinstein Penned Tales of an Aggressive Creep. It Sure Sounds Familiar Now," *Washington Post*, October 17, 2017.

10   hundreds of millions of dollars: Edward Jay Epstein, "The Great Illusionist," *Slate*, October 10, 2005.

11   "The wall just shook": Donna Gigliotti quoted in Ken Auletta, "Beauty and the Beast," *The New Yorker,* December 8, 2002.

11   at a cocktail party for William J. Bratton: Leena Kim, "A Night Out with NYC's Former Police Commissioner," *Town & Country*, October 30, 2016.

11   laughing with Jay-Z: Ashley Lee, "Weinstein Co. Sets Exclusive Film and TV First-Look Deal with Jay Z," *Hollywood Reporter*, September 29, 2016.

11   "About to forward some creative": Harvey Weinstein quoted in Zaid Jilani, "Harvey Weinstein Urged Clinton Campaign to Silence Sanders's Black Lives Matter Message," *Intercept*, October 7, 2016.

11   raised hundreds of thousands of dollars: Ashley Lee, "Harvey Weinstein, Jordan Roth Set Star-Studded Broadway Fundraiser for Hillary Clinton," *Hollywood Reporter*, September 30, 2016.

12   Sara Bareilles sat bathed in purple light: Robert Viagas, "Highlights of Monday's All-Star Hillary Clinton Broadway Fundraiser," *Playbill*, October 18, 2016.

12   "Harvey Weinstein, the Comeback Kid": Stephen Galloway, "Harvey Weinstein, the Comeback Kid," *Hollywood Reporter*, September 19, 2016.

12   represented Al Gore: James B. Stewart, "David Boies Pleads Not Guilty," *New York Times*, September 21, 2018.

12   "They r strategists and say your firm have used them": Email from Harvey Weinstein, October 16, 2016.

13 **"highly experienced and trained in Israel's elite military"**: Black Cube website homepage, "What makes us unique," under "Cutting-Edge Analytical Skills."

## CHAPTER 3

16 **taken on a sensitive assignment**: Joe Palazzolo, Michael Rothfeld and Lukas I. Alpert, "National Enquirer Shielded Donald Trump From Playboy Model's Affair Allegation," *Wall Street Journal*, November 4, 2016.

17 **Illicitly obtaining medical records**: "Cedars Sinai Fires Six over Patient Privacy Breaches After Kardashian Gives Birth," Associated Press, July 13, 2013.

18 **"The guy's a personal friend of mine"**: David Pecker quoted in Jeffrey Toobin, "The *National Enquirer*'s Fervor for Trump," *The New Yorker*, June 26, 2017.

18 **killed perhaps ten fully reported stories**: Maxwell Strachan, "David Pecker's DARKEST TRUMP SECRETS: A National Enquirer Insider Tells All!" *HuffPost*, August 24, 2018.

19 **revelation about Trump**: Jack Shafer, "Pravda on the Checkout Line," *Politico Magazine*, January/February 2017.

19 **contact with Alex Jones**: "One of your biggest fans is Dylan Howard. He listens to you every day," wrote Lenny Dykstra, the former baseball player who went on to be charged, variously, with indecent exposure, cocaine possession, and grand theft auto (the last of these resulting in a felony conviction). Dykstra copied Howard and Jones, and the two men discussed meeting. Email from Lenny Dykstra to Alex Jones, October 10, 2015.

19 **struck a production deal**: "The Weinstein Company Partnering with American Media, Inc. to Produce Radar Online Talk Show," *My New York Eye*, January 5, 2015.

20 **claimed a studio head had sexually harassed her**: Ramin Setoodeh, "Ashley Judd Reveals Sexual Harassment by Studio Mogul," *Variety*, October 6, 2015.

20 **"is RECORDED"**: Email from Dylan Howard to Harvey Weinstein, December 7, 2016.

## CHAPTER 4

21 **local television in West Virginia**: Jared Hunt, "*Today* Show Host Left $65 in W.Va.," *Charleston Gazette-Mail*, October 19, 2012.

21 **by helicopter to and from his house**: Emily Smith, "NBC Pays for Matt Lauer's Helicopter Rides to Work," Page Six, *New York Post*, September 3, 2014.

22 **"Ronan Farrow Goes from Anchor's Desk to Cubicle"**: Ian Mohr, "Ronan Farrow Goes from Anchor's Desk to Cubicle," Page Six, *New York Post*, December 14, 2016.

25 **"started talking to some undergraduate girls"**: Noah Oppenheim quoted in Mike Fleming Jr., "Rising Star *Jackie* Screenwriter Noah Oppenheim Also Runs NBC's *Today*? How Did That Happen?" *Deadline*, September 16, 2016.

26 **holiday gifts**: "Oppenheim to Lauer: 'There Is No Summer House,'" Today.com, October 16, 2007.

26 **"got antsy"**: Noah Oppenheim quoted in Mike Fleming Jr., "Rising Star *Jackie* Screenwriter Noah Oppenheim Also Runs NBC's *Today*? How Did That Happen?" *Deadline*, September 16, 2016.

26 **"Steven Spielberg in his office"**: Noah Oppenheim quoted in Mike Fleming Jr., "Rising Star *Jackie* Screenwriter Noah Oppenheim Also Runs NBC's *Today*? How Did That Happen?" *Deadline,* September 16, 2016.

27 **ultimately reported in the *Atlantic***: Alex French and Maximillion Potter, "Nobody Is Going to Believe You," the *Atlantic,* January 23, 2019.

# CHAPTER 5

29 **making headway**: Email from Avi Yanus to Christopher Boies, November 25, 2016.

29 **had quickly covered the last payment, for Phase 2A**: Email from Avi Yanus to Christopher Boies, November 28, 2016.

30 **there she was, at Kandahar Air Field**: PJF Military Collection, Alamy.com stock photo, photo of Rose McGowan and U.S. Navy Petty Officer 2nd Class Jennifer L. Smolinski, an intelligence specialist with Naval Construction Regiment 22, at Kandahar Air Field, Afghanistan, March 29, 2010.

30 **"a stylized bombshell"**: Rose McGowan, BRAVE (New York: HarperCollins, 2018), 154.

33 **"through a network of attorneys and subcontractors"**: Andy Thibault, "How Straight-Shooting State's Attorney Frank Maco Got Mixed Up in the Woody-Mia Mess," *Connecticut Magazine*, April 1, 1997.

33 **"That kind of silence"**: Ronan Farrow, "My Father, Woody Allen, and the Danger of Questions Unasked," *Hollywood Reporter,* May 11, 2016.

# CHAPTER 6

37 **"I am haunted"**: Richard Greenberg, "Desperation Up Close," *Dateline NBC* blog, updated January 23, 2004.

41 **"hold hands and jump"**: Jennifer Senior (@JenSeniorNY) on Twitter, March 30, 2015.

41 **did a feature about him**: David Carr, "The Emperor Miramaximus," *New York*, December 3, 2001.

## CHAPTER 7

44 **"rock-chick swagger"**: Bill Carter, "NBC News President Rouses the Network," *New York Times*, August 24, 2014.

46 **Children of God Cult**: Michael Phillips, "'Brave': Rose McGowan's Memoir Details Cult Life, Weinstein Assault and Hollywood's Abuse of Women," *Chicago Tribune*, February 6, 2018.

## CHAPTER 8

52 **publicly threatened**: Michael Schulman, "Shakeup at the Oscars," *The New Yorker*, February 19, 2017; and Jesse David Fox, "A Brief History of Harvey Weinstein's Oscar Campaign Tactics," *Vulture*, January 29, 2018.

52 **"Ferrari-driving tenpercenter"**: Variety Staff, "Partners Get Chewed in UTA's Family Feud," *Variety*, January 15, 1995.

52 **"afraid of being sued and more afraid of losing advertising"**: Gavin Polone, "Gavin Polone on Bill Cosby and Hollywood's Culture of Payoffs, Rape and Secrecy (Guest Column)," *Hollywood Reporter*, December 4, 2014.

54 **"Bunga Bunga" party**: Danika Fears and Maria Wiesner, "Model who accused Weinstein of molestation has sued before," Page Six, *New York Post,* March 31, 2015.

## CHAPTER 9

59 **the district attorney's office announced**: James C. McKinley Jr., "Harvey Weinstein Won't Face Charges After Groping Report," *New York Times,* April 10, 2015.

60 **had contributed $26,450 to Vance's campaigns**: Jay Cassano and David Sirota, "Manhattan DA Vance Took $10,000 From Head Of Law Firm On Trump Defense Team, Dropped Case," *International Business Times,* October 10, 2017.

61 **He would give $10,000 to Vance's reelection campaign**: David Sirota and Jay Cassano, "Harvey Weinstein's Lawyer Gave $10,000 To Manhattan DA After He Declined To File Sexual Assault Charges," *International Business Times,* October 5, 2017.

## CHAPTER 11

70 **New York City and Toledo**: Rebecca Dana, "Slyer Than Fox," *New Republic*, March 25, 2013.

71 **"Dylan's obvious credibility"**: Email from Lisa Bloom to Ronan Farrow, March 14, 2014.

71  "I see this every day": Lisa Bloom on *Ronan Farrow Daily*, MSNBC, February 27, 2015.

71  "women are smeared": Lisa Bloom on *Ronan Farrow Daily,* MSNBC, February 27, 2015.


## CHAPTER 12

76  shutting down the gossip news site Gawker: Jason Zengerle, "Charles Harder, the Lawyer Who Killed Gawker, Isn't Done Yet," *GQ,* November 17, 2016.


## CHAPTER 13

83  "feel 'raped' ": Ken Auletta, "Beauty and the Beast," *The New Yorker,* December 8, 2002.

84  a charitable project called Women in Focus: Email from Diana Filip to Ronan Farrow, July 31, 2017.

85  The email from Reuben Capital Partners was signed by Diana Filip: Email from Diana Filip, forwarded by Lacy Lynch to Rose McGowan, April 10, 2017.

85  "info I have compiled so far on Ronan Farrow": Email from Sara Ness to Harvey Weinstein, April 11, 2017.

86  Nick and Nora Charles: Nora Gallagher, "Hart and Hart May Be Prime-Time Private Eyes but Jack & Sandra Are for Real," *People Magazine*, October 8, 1979.

86  Clinton hired Palladino: Michael Isikoff, "Clinton Team Works to Deflect Allegations on Nominee's Private Life," *Washington Post*, July 26, 1992.

86  earned the nickname "the President's Dick": Jane Mayer, "Dept. of Snooping," *The New Yorker*, February 16, 1998.

86  "boundaries of the envelope": Jack Palladino quoted in Seth Rosenfeld, "Watching the Detective," *San Francisco Chronicle*, January 31, 1999.


## CHAPTER 14

91  their most ardent defender: Manuel Roig-Franzia, "Lanny Davis, the Ultimate Clinton Loyalist, Is Now Michael Cohen's Lawyer. But Don't Call It Revenge," *Washington Post*, August 23, 2018.

91  Davis cashed in: Christina Wilkie, "Lanny Davis Wins Lobbying Fees Lawsuit Against Equatorial Guinea," *HuffPost*, August 27, 2013.

92  "game-changing intelligence": Email to Christopher Boies from Avi Yanus, April 24, 2017.

94 **a few commercials:** Phyllis Furman, "Proud as a Peacock," *New York Daily News*, March 1, 1998.

94 **been credited with a turnaround:** "The Peripatetic News Career of Andrew Lack," *New York Times*, June 9, 2015.

96 **"the disclosure of high quality intelligence":** Email to Christopher Boies from Avi Yanus, May 5, 2017.

## CHAPTER 15

98 **"a great deal of information":** Email from Seth Freedman to Benjamin Wallace, February 8, 2017.

## CHAPTER 16

106 **Weinstein applauded:** Anna Palmer, Jake Sherman, and Daniel Lippman, *Politico Playbook*, June 7, 2017.

108 **"further unwanted advances":** LinkedIn message from Irwin Reiter to Emily Nestor, December 30, 2014.

109 **"if you were my daughter":** LinkedIn message from Irwin Reiter to Emily Nestor, October 14, 2016.

## CHAPTER 17

112 **He attached an invoice for $600,000:** Email from Avi Yanus to Christopher Boies, June 6, 2017.

112 **"update about the status of the payment":** Email from Avi Yanus to Christopher Boies, June 12, 2017.

113 **"thoroughly reviewed our findings again":** Email from Avi Yanus to Christopher Boies, June 18, 2017.

113 **"hasn't solved his problem completely":** Email from Black Cube project manager, June 23, 2017.

## CHAPTER 18

120 **"are you still writing about NDAs?":** Text from Lisa Bloom, July 13, 2017.

122 **detailed dossier:** "Confidential memo to counsel Re: Jodi Kantor/Ronan Farrow Twitter Contacts and Potential Sources," PSOPS report, July 18, 2017.

125 **"Relevance: Cameraman that is working with Ronan Farrow":** "JB Rutagarama," Black Cube profile, 2017.

# CHAPTER 19

128 **"From my very first time left alone with Harvey"**: Zelda Perkins quoted in Ronan Farrow, "Harvey Weinstein's Secret Settlements," *The New Yorker*, November 21, 2017. Reporting from this article also referenced in other chapters.

132 **trying to rescue it**: Peter Kafka, "Why Did Three Sites Pass on a Story About an Amazon Exec Before It Landed at The Information?" *Recode*, September 12, 2017.

133 **"pro-female male"**: Email from Diana Filip to Rose McGowan, July 24, 2017.

# CHAPTER 22

152 **"invaluable addition to our activities"**: Email from Diana Filip to Ronan Farrow, July 31, 2017.

# CHAPTER 23

154 **"delighted to know that you are close to completing your book project"**: Letter from Hillary Clinton, July 20, 2017.

# CHAPTER 24

165 **had sent lewd texts to coworkers**: Yashar Ali, "Fox News Host Sent Unsolicited Lewd Text Messages To Colleagues, Sources Say," *HuffPost*, August 4, 2017.

166 **inaugural Truthteller Award**: *Hollywood Reporter* Staff, "Jay Z, Harvey Weinstein to Receive Inaugural Truthteller Award from L.A. Press Club," *Hollywood Reporter*, June 2, 2017.

# CHAPTER 26

173 **He'd been generous with**: Jon Campbell, "Who Got Harvey Weinstein's Campaign Cash and Who Gave It Away," *Democrat and Chronicle*, October 9, 2017.

174 **hosted a book party**: Emily Smith, "George Pataki Fetes His Daughter's New Book," Page Six, *New York Post*, March 9, 2016.

# CHAPTER 28

186 **"Reading 'Clit Notes'"**: Noah Oppenheim, "Reading 'Clit Notes,'" *Harvard Crimson*, April 3, 1998.

186 **"Transgender Absurd"**: Noah Oppenheim, "Transgender Absurd," *Harvard Crimson*, February 24, 1997.

186 **"impassioned adversaries"**: Noah Oppenheim, "Remembering Harvard," *Harvard Crimson*, May 22, 2000.

186 **"more deserving of protected space"**: Noah Oppenheim, "Considering 'Women's Issues' at Harvard," *Harvard Crimson*, December 17, 1999.

187 **"appease female sensibilities"**: Noah Oppenheim, "The Postures of Punch Season," *Harvard Crimson*, October 9, 1998.

## CHAPTER 29

197 **"we have some experience"**: Email from David Remnick to Ronan Farrow, August 9, 2017.

203 **"I hope such a meeting could be arranged"**: Email from Diana Filip to John Ksar, August 11, 2017.

## CHAPTER 30

206 **the *Wall Street Journal* reporter who ultimately broke the story**: Dorothy Rabinowitz, "Juanita Broaddrick Meets the Press," *Wall Street Journal*, Updated February 19, 1999.

206 **"whenever you go to the pool, you must let me know"**: David Corvo quoted in Lachlan Cartwright and Maxwell Tani, "Accused Sexual Harassers Thrived Under NBC News Chief Andy Lack," *Daily Beast*, September 21, 2018.

206 **"I love warm weather, but are you going to a school event dressed like that?"**: David Corvo quoted in Lachlan Cartwright and Maxwell Tani, "Accused Sexual Harassers Thrived Under NBC News Chief Andy Lack," *Daily Beast*, September 21, 2018.

212 **"agitated, distressed, not happy"**: Sam Anson's testimony in *The People of the State of New York v. Harvey Weinstein,* Ind. Nos. 2335-18, 2673-19, New York Supreme Court, January 24, 2020.

212 **"The red flags"**: Elizabeth Wagmeister, "Private Investigator Testifies Harvey Weinstein Asked Him to Look into 'Red Flag List' of Women," *Variety,* January 24, 2020.

## CHAPTER 31

214 **a substantial payout to sign a binding nondisclosure agreement**: Lachlan Cartwright and Maxwell Tani, "Accused Sexual Harassers Thrived Under NBC News Chief Andy Lack," *Daily Beast*, September 21, 2018.

216 "We can't move forward with anything": Text message from Noah Oppenheim to Ronan Farrow, August 17, 2017.

219 "not on behalf of or with the blessing of NBC": Text message from Noah Oppenheim to Ronan Farrow, August 21, 2017.

## CHAPTER 32

225 "I'm sure I'm not on Matt Lauer's Christmas card": Jeffrey Toobin, unpublished interview for "The National Enquirer's Fervor for Trump," *The New Yorker,* June 26, 2017.

225 "NBC Gives Sleazy Lauer One More Chance": "NBC Gives Sleazy Lauer One More Chance," *National Enquirer,* December 19, 2016.

225 "Hey Matt, That's Not Your Wife!": "Hey Matt, That's Not Your Wife!" *National Enquirer,* September 25, 2017.

## CHAPTER 33

226 "Are you available for a call now?": Email from Harvey Weinstein to David Pecker, September 28, 2017.

226 "I am in Saudi Arabia on business": Email from David Pecker to Harvey Weinstein, September 28, 2017.

226 *Rolling Stone* magazine: Email from Harvey Weinstein to David Pecker, September 28, 2017.

226 "I can reduce costs": Email from David Pecker to Harvey Weinstein, September 28, 2017.

227 "dedicated 'Hillary channels'": Email from Deborah Turness to Harvey Weinstein, September 20, 2017.

227 "I wanted to talk to you about Universal doing our home video": Email from Harvey Weinstein to Ron Meyer, September 27, 2017.

227 "I would love to make this work": Email from Ron Meyer to Harvey Weinstein, September 27, 2017.

227 a term sheet was drafted: Email from David Glasser to Harvey Weinstein, September 27, 2017.

227 two home entertainment executives: Email from David Glasser to Harvey Weinstein, September 27, 2017.

227 "I look forward to us being in business together": Email from Ron Meyer to Harvey Weinstein, October 2, 2017.

231 "opposite sides of the fence"; "appreciate the well-wishes!": Email exchange between Harvey Weinstein and Noah Oppenheim, September 25, 2017.

232 **"Noah Oppenheim received a bottle of Grey Goose"**: Email to Weinstein staff, September 25, 2017. (A source familiar with Oppenheim said that "if" Weinstein sent the Grey Goose, Oppenheim would not have drunk it, and an assistant would have regifted it.)

## CHAPTER 34

234 **"I think he is absolutely pursuing the story"**: Email from Bryan Lourd to Harvey Weinstein, September 26, 2017.

234 **Copies of a letter started arriving at the offices of CAA**: Letter from Harder Mirell & Abrams, September 29, 2017.

237 **her first memo to Weinstein**: Jodie Kantor and Megan Twohey, *She Said* (New York: Penguin Publishing Group, 2019), 100-104.

## CHAPTER 35

240 **"the Miramax smear campaign"**: Peter Jackson quoted in Molly Redden, "Peter Jackson: I Blacklisted Ashley Judd and Mira Sorvino Under Pressure from Weinstein," *Guardian*, December 16, 2017.

242 **could have, should have, done more**: Jodi Kantor, "Tarantino on Weinstein: 'I Knew Enough to Do More Than I Did,'" *New York Times,* October 19, 2017.

242 **By then, Black Cube had already circulated another profile**: "Rosanna (Lisa) Arquette," Black Cube profile, 2017.

243 **"this could be great for Jay Z"**: Email from Harvey Weinstein to David Glasser, September 27, 2017.

243 **and that she was just playing along**: Megan Twohey, Jodi Kantor, Susan Dominus, Jim Rutenberg, and Steve Eder, "Weinstein's Complicity Machine," *New York Times*, December 5, 2017.

## CHAPTER 36

247 **a financial settlement with an actor**: Yohana Desta, "Asia Argento Accuser Jimmy Bennett Details Alleged Assault in Difficult First TV Interview," *Vanity Fair*, September 25, 2018.

247 **"sexually attacking"**: Dino-Ray Ramos, "Asia Argento Claims Jimmy Bennett 'Sexually Attacked Her', Launches 'Phase Two' Of #MeToo Movement," *Deadline*, September 5, 2018.

249 **publicly apologized for hearing without really listening**: Lisa O'Carroll, "Colin Firth Expresses Shame at Failing to Act on Weinstein Allegation," *Guardian*, October 13, 2017.

# CHAPTER 37

252 **"The balance of power":** Lauren O'Connor quoted in Jodi Kantor and Meghan Twohey, "Harvey Weinstein Paid Off Sexual Harassment Accusers for Decades," *New York Times*, October 5, 2017.

253 **"I didn't make the call":** Claire Forlani quoted in Ashley Lee, "Claire Forlani on Harvey Weinstein Encounters: 'I Escaped Five Times,'" *Hollywood Reporter*, October 12, 2017.

253 **"I am hosting and cooking tearing my hair":** Email from Meryl Streep to Ronan Farrow, September 28, 2017.

254 **six women would accuse Ratner:** Amy Kaufman and Daniel Miller, "Six Women Accuse Filmmaker Brett Ratner of Sexual Harassment or Misconduct," *Los Angeles Times*, November 1, 2017.

# CHAPTER 38

259 **"the New York Times are going to be posting their article today":** Email from Harvey Weinstein to Dylan Howard, September 22, 2017.

259 **a *Times* breaking news alert:** Megan Twohey, "Tumult After AIDS Fund-Raiser Supports Harvey Weinstein Production," *New York Times*, September 23, 2017.

# CHAPTER 39

263 **"We demand that you refrain from publishing this story":** Letter from Harder Mirell & Abrams, October 2, 2017.

264 **"meet him in front of the NY Times Building":** Email from Harvey Weinstein's office to Dylan Howard, October 4, 2017.

266 **"without any merit whatsoever":** Email from Fabio Bertoni to Charles Harder, October 4, 2017.

267 **Kim Masters ran a story for the *Hollywood Reporter*:** Kim Masters and Chris Gardner, "Harvey Weinstein Lawyers Battling N.Y. Times, New Yorker Over Potentially Explosive Stories," *Hollywood Reporter*, October 4, 2017.

267 ***Variety* ran its version a few minutes later:** Brent Lang, Gene Maddaus and Ramin Setoodeh, "Harvey Weinstein Lawyers Up for Bombshell New York Times, New Yorker Stories," *Variety*, October 4, 2017.

# CHAPTER 40

268 **women in cities around the world:** Adam Ciralsky, " 'Harvey's Concern Was Who Did Him In': Inside Harvey Weinstein's Frantic Final Days," *Vanity Fair*, January 18, 2018.

271 **"old dinosaur learning new ways":** Lisa Bloom (@LisaBloom) on Twitter, October 5, 2017.

271 **"I'm using the term *workplace misconduct*":** Lisa Bloom quoted in Nicole Pelletiere, "Harvey Weinstein's Advisor, Lisa Bloom, Speaks Out: 'There Was Misconduct,' " ABC News, October 6, 2017.

271 **"Lisa Bloom to tutor me":** Statement from Harvey Weinstein to the *New York Times*, October 5, 2017.

# CHAPTER 41

274 **there had been a cover-up:** Shawn Tully, "How a Handful of Billionaires Kept Their Friend Harvey Weinstein in Power," *Fortune*, November 19, 2017.

274 **"I could use some support":** Email from Harvey Weinstein to Brian Roberts, October 6, 2017.

275 **founded by Roberts's father:** Ellen Mayers, "How Comcast Founder Ralph Roberts Changed Cable," *Christian Science Monitor,* June 19, 2015.

275 **unshakable power:** Tara Lachapelle, "Comcast's Roberts, CEO for Life, Doesn't Have to Explain," *Bloomberg*, June 11, 2018.

275 **Burke worked at Disney:** Jeff Leeds, "Ex-Disney Exec Burke Knows His New Prey," *Los Angeles Times*, February 12, 2004.

277 **dominated by Weinstein's rebuttals:** Yashar Ali, "At NBC News, the Harvey Weinstein Scandal Barely Exists," *HuffPost*, October 6, 2017.

277 **didn't mention Weinstein once:** Dave Itzkoff, "SNL Prepped Jokes About Harvey Weinstein, Then Shelved Them," *New York Times*, October 8, 2017.

# CHAPTER 42

283 **her plans to discredit accusers:** Megan Twohey and Johanna Barr, "Lisa Bloom, Lawyer Advising Harvey Weinstein, Resigns Amid Criticism From Board Members," *New York Times*, October 7, 2017.

# CHAPTER 43

289 **"Speaking of media complicity":** Jake Tapper (@jaketapper) on Twitter, October 10, 2017.

289 **"nowhere close to what ultimately ran":** Lloyd Grove, "How NBC 'Killed' Ronan Farrow's Weinstein Exposé," *Daily Beast*, October 11, 2017.

291 **"a long chase":** The *Rachel Maddow Show*, October 10, 2017.

## CHAPTER 44

295 "it was the moment when Mark knew the truth": Rielle Hunter, *What Really Happened: John Edwards, Our Daughter, and Me* (Dallas, TX; BenBella Books, 2012), loc 139 of 3387, Kindle.

295 just hadn't asked the right questions: Joe Johns and Ted Metzger, "Aide Recalls Bizarre Conversation with Edwards Mistress," CNN, May 4, 2012.

296 latest reframing: The *Today* show with Matt Lauer, Hoda Kotb, and Savannah Guthrie, October 11, 2017.

297 "You're damn right": David Remnick on *CBS Sunday Morning*, November 26, 2017.

298 warned Clinton team members: Megan Twohey, Jodi Kantor, Susan Dominus, Jim Rutenberg, and Steve Eder, "Weinstein's Complicity Machine," *New York Times*, December 5, 2017.

298 "Harvey's a rapist and this is going to come out": Lena Dunham quoted in Megan Twohey, Jodi Kantor, Susan Dominus, Jim Rutenberg, and Steve Eder, "Weinstein's Complicity Machine," *New York Times*, December 5, 2017.

298 "shocked and appalled": Jeremy Barr, "Hillary Clinton Says She's "Shocked and Appalled" by Harvey Weinstein Claims," *Hollywood Reporter*, October 10, 2017.

299 "avoid 'a witch hunt atmosphere'": "Harvey Weinstein a Sad, Sick Man — Woody Allen," BBC News, October 16, 2017.

299 right-wing guerrilla artist: Rory Carroll, "Rightwing Artist Put Up Meryl Streep 'She Knew' Posters as Revenge for Trump," *Guardian*, December 20, 2017.

299 "Not everybody knew": Meryl Streep quoted in Emma Dibdin, "Meryl Streep Speaks Out Against Harvey Weinstein Following Sexual Harassment Allegations," *Elle*, October 9, 2017.

## CHAPTER 45

301 "wanted to tell you how brave I think you are": Email from Diana Filip to Rose McGowan, October 10, 2017.

301 "And I just wanted to get off the phone": Annabella Sciorra quoted in Ronan Farrow, "Weighing the Costs of Speaking Out About Harvey Weinstein," *The New Yorker*, October 27, 2017. Reporting from this article also referenced in other chapters.

## CHAPTER 46

308 a colorful profile: Miriam Shaviv, "IDF Vet Turned Author Teases UK with Mossad Alter Ego," *Times of Israel*, February 8, 2013.

308 *Dead Cat Bounce:* Seth Freedman, *Dead Cat Bounce* (United Kingdom, London: Cutting Edge Press, 2013), loc 17 of 3658, Kindle.

309 **who conducted the interviews, and why:** Mark Townsend, "Rose McGowan: "Hollywood Blacklisted Me Because I Got Raped," *Guardian*, October 14, 2017.

311 **a ready pipeline of trained operatives:** Adam Entous and Ronan Farrow, "Private Massod for Hire," *The New Yorker*, February 11, 2019.

311 **veterans of a secret Israeli intelligence unit:** Haaretz staff, "Ex-Mossad Chief Ephraim Halevy Joins Spy Firm Black Cube," *Haaretz,* November 11, 2018.

311 **once pitched Black Cube's services:** Adam Entous and Ronan Farrow, "Private Massod for Hire," *The New Yorker*, February 11, 2019.

311 **more than a hundred operatives, speaking thirty languages:** Yuval Hirshorn, "Inside Black Cube — the 'Mossad' of the Business World," *Forbes Israel,* June 9, 2018.

311 **"the exclusive supplier to major organizations and government ministries":** Hadas Magen, "Black Cube — a "Mossad-style" Business Intelligence Co," *Globes*, April 2, 2017.

313 **"new information concerning the HW&BC affair":** Email from Sleeper1973, October 31, 2017.


## CHAPTER 47

314 **That last arrangement:** Agreement between Boies Schiller Flexner LLP and Black Cube, July 11, 2017.

315 **two Black Cube operatives were jailed in Romania:** Yuval Hirshorn, "Inside Black Cube — the 'Mossad' of the Business World," *Forbes Israel,* June 9, 2018.

316 **"it's complicated":** Email from David Boies to Ronan Farrow, November 4, 2017.

318 **"via a girl named 'Ana'":** Email from Sleeper1973 to Ronan Farrow, November 1, 2017.


## CHAPTER 48

320 **peculiar inquiries reached prominent defenders of the deal:** Ronan Farrow, "Israeli Operatives Who Aided Harvey Weinstein Collected Information on Former Obama Administration Officials," *The New Yorker*, May 6, 2018.

321 **their work that could be used against them:** Mark Maremont, "Mysterious Strangers Dog Controversial Insurer's Critics," *Wall Street Journal*, August 29, 2017.

321 **Maja Lazarov:** Mark Maremont, Jacquie McNish and Rob Copeland, "Former Israeli Actress Alleged to Be Operative for Corporate-Investigation Firm," *Wall Street Journal*, November 16, 2017.

321 **a Canadian asset management firm:** Matthew Goldstein and William K. Rashbaum, "Deception and Ruses Fill the Toolkit of Investigators Used by Weinstein," *New York Times,* November 15, 2017.

322 **a documentary about the war:** *The Woman from Sarajevo* (2007, dir. Ella Alterman).

323 **watch-cameras; recording pens:** Yuval Hirshorn, "Inside Black Cube — the 'Mossad' of the Business World," *Forbes Israel,* June 9, 2018.

324 **"I've lived inside a mirrored fun house":** Rose McGowan quoted in Ronan Farrow, "Harvey Weinstein's Army of Spies," *The New Yorker,* November 6, 2017. Reporting from this article also referenced in other chapters.

# CHAPTER 49

326 **"due to fear of HW's retaliation, according to HW":** "Confidential memo to counsel, Re: Jodi Kantor/Ronan Farrow Twitter Contacts and Potential Sources," PSOPS report, July 18, 2017.

326 **eleven photographs:** Email from Dan Karson to Harvey Weinstein, October 22, 2016.

326 **"is the money shot":** Email from Blair Berk to Harvey Weinstein, October 23, 2016.

326 **"No adverse information":** Email from Dan Karson to Harvey Weinstein, October 13, 2016.

326 **criticism of Wallace's previous reporting:** Email from Dan Karson to Harvey Weinstein, October 13, 2016.

326 **in response to a book he wrote:** Email from Dan Karson to Harvey Weinstein, October 23, 2016.

326 **"Lies/Exaggerations/Contradictions":** "Confidential memo to counsel, Re: Weinstein Inquiry, Re: Rose Arianna McGowan," PSOPS report, November 8, 2016.

326 **"personal impeachment of Moss":** "Confidential memo to counsel, Re: Weinstein Inquiry, Re: Adam Wender Moss," PSOPS report, December 21, 2016.

326 **"relevant to considerations of our response strategy":** "Confidential memo to counsel, Re: Weinstein Inquiry," PSOPS report, November 11, 2016.

326 **"Kantor is NOT following Ronan Farrow":** "Confidential memo to counsel, Re: Jodi Kantor/Ronan Farrow Twitter Contacts and Potential Sources," PSOPS report, July 18, 2017.

327 **suggested they "discuss next steps on each":** Email from Dylan Howard to Harvey Weinstein, December 7, 2016.

328 **"AMAZING...eventually she laid into Rose pretty hard":** Email from Dylan Howard to Harvey Weinstein, December 7, 2016.

328 **"This is the killer. Especially if my fingerprints r not on this":** Email from Harvey Weinstein to Dylan Howard, December 6, 2016.

329 **"appropriate action against you"**: Email from Black Cube's UK-based law firm to Ronan Farrow, November 2, 2017.

329 **"We wish to dispose of every document and information we possess"**: Email from Avi Yanus, October 31, 2017.

331 **"out of this world, my dear"**: Email from Sleeper1973 to Ronan Farrow, November 2, 2017.


# CHAPTER 50

333 **"I'm afraid to even mention his name"**: Karen McDougal quoted in Ronan Farrow, "Donald Trump, a Playboy Model, and a System for Concealing Infidelity," *The New Yorker*, February 16, 2018. Reporting from this article also referenced in other chapters.

334 **hacked opponents' email accounts**: Jordan Robertson, Michael Riley, and Andrew Willis, "How to Hack an Election," *Bloomberg Businessweek*, March 31, 2016.

335 **selling salacious stories**: Beth Reinhard and Emma Brown, "The Ex-Playmate and the Latin American Political Operative: An Untold Episode in the Push to Profit from an Alleged Affair with Trump," *Washington Post*, May 28, 2018.

335 **asking for help**: Joe Palazzolo, Nicole Hong, Michael Rothfeld, Rebecca Davis O'Brien, and Rebecca Ballhaus, "Donald Trump Played Central Role in Hush Payoffs to Stormy Daniels and Karen McDougal," *Wall Street Journal*, November 9, 2018.

335 **"If you deny, you are safe"**: Email from Keith Davidson to Karen McDougal, August 5, 2016.

335 **That publicist was Matthew Hiltzik**: Cameron Joseph, "*Enquirer* Gave Trump's Alleged Mistress a Trump Family Associate to Run Her PR," *Talking Points Memo*, March 27, 2018.

336 **"SEND THIS"**: Email from Dylan Howard to Karen McDougal, June 23, 2017.

336 **"McDougal contract extension"**: Email from AMI general counsel, January 30, 2018.

336 **"just more fake news"**: Ronan Farrow, "Donald Trump, a Playboy Model, and a System for Concealing Infidelity," *The New Yorker*, February 16, 2018.


# CHAPTER 51

338 **Dino Sajudin, a former Trump Tower doorman, had told AMI the story**: Ronan Farrow, "The National Enquirer, a Trump Rumor, and Another Secret Payment to Buy Silence," *The New Yorker*, April 12, 2018. Reporting from this article also referenced in other chapters.

338 **"He's seen the chupacabra"**: Nikki Benfatto quoted in Edgar Sandoval and Rich Schapiro, "Ex-Wife of Former Trump Building Doorman Who Claimed the President Has a Love Child Says He's a Liar," *New York Daily News*, April 12, 2018.

339 **Horwitz left work for days**: Michael Calderone, "How a Trump 'Love Child' Rumor Roiled the Media," *Politico,* April 12, 2018.

341 **a post acknowledging everything**: "Prez Love Child Shocker! Ex-Trump Worker Peddling Rumor Donald Has Illegitimate Child," RadarOnline.com, April 11, 2018.

342 *"terrific Enquirer fodder"*: Email from Dylan Howard to David Remnick, April 11, 2018.

342 **resurrected draft**: Jake Pearson and Jeff Horwitz, "$30,000 Rumor? Tabloid Paid For, Spiked, Salacious Trump Tip," Associated Press, April 12, 2018.

342 **Hair-curling allegations of sexual violence followed**: *Katie Johnson v. Donald J. Trump and Jeffrey E. Epstein*, Case 5:16-cv-00797-DMG-KS, United States District Court Central District of California, complaint filed on April 26, 2016 and *Jane Doe v. Donald J. Trump and Jeffrey E. Epstein*, Case 1:16-cv-04642, United States District Court Southern District of New York, complaint filed on June 20, 2016.

342 **close friends with Donald Trump**: Landon Thomas Jr., "Jeffrey Epstein: International Moneyman of Mystery," *New York*, October 28, 2002.

343 **widespread allegations that Epstein sexually abused minors**: Julie K. Brown, "How a Future Trump Cabinet Member Gave a Serial Sex Abuser the Deal of a Lifetime," *Miami Herald*, November 28, 2018.

343 **plaintiff's intermediary in the press**: Jon Swaine, "Rape Lawsuits Against Donald Trump Linked to Former TV Producer," *Guardian*, July 7, 2016.

343 **emerged as doubtful as most journalists**: Emily Shugerman, "I Talked to the Woman Accusing Donald Trump of Rape," *Revelist*, July 13, 2016.

344 **AMI ran several stories shooting down the claims in the lawsuit**: "Trump Sued by Teen 'Sex Slave' for Alleged 'Rape'—Donald Blasts 'Disgusting' Suit," RadarOnline.com, April 28, 2016; and "Case Dismissed! Judge Trashes Bogus Donald Trump Rape Lawsuit," RadarOnline.com, May 2, 2016.

344 **arranged directly through Michael Cohen**: Michael Rothfeld and Joe Palazzolo, "Trump Lawyer Arranged $130,000 Payment for Adult-Film Star's Silence," *Wall Street Journal*, Updated January 12, 2018.

345 **filed formal complaints**: Greg Price, "McDougal Payment from American Media Was Trump Campaign Contribution, Watchdog Group Claims to FEC," *Newsweek*, February 19, 2018.

346 **Pecker visited the Oval Office**: Jim Rutenberg, Kate Kelly, Jessica Silver-Greenberg, and Mike McIntire, "Wooing Saudi Business, Tabloid Mogul Had a Powerful Friend: Trump," *New York Times*, March 29, 2018.

# CHAPTER 52

351 **"pornographic material"**: Jake Pearson and Jeff Horwitz, "AP Exclusive: Top Gossip Editor Accused of Sexual Misconduct," Associated Press, December 5, 2017.

351 **Celebuzz, where he'd prompted another HR investigation**: Gary Baum, "Dylan Howard's Hollywood Reboot: Why Are So Many A-Listers Working With a Tabloid Henchman?" *Hollywood Reporter,* February 3, 2020.

352 **"The National Enquirer intends to publish a story"**: Email from AMI, April 17, 2018.

353 **looking for records**: Michael D. Shear, Matt Apuzzo, and Sharon LaFraniere, "Raids on Trump's Lawyer Sought Records of Payments to Women," *New York Times,* April 10, 2018.

353 **"identifying such stories so they could be purchased and their publication avoided"**: Letter from the United States Attorney for the Southern District of New York to American Media Inc., September 20, 2018.

354 **"Rather than capitulate"**: Jeff Bezos, "No Thank You, Mr. Pecker." Medium. com, February 7, 2019.

354 **whether Howard had breached**: Devlin Barrett, Matt Zapotosky, and Cleve R. Wootson Jr., "Federal Prosecutors Reviewing Bezos's Extortion Claim Against *National Enquirer,*" Sources Say," *Washington Post,* February 8, 2019.

354 **a $1 million bat mitzvah**: Edmund Lee, "*National Enquirer* to Be Sold to James Cohen, Heir to Hudson News Founder," *New York Times,* April 18, 2019.

354 **more than ninety**: Ronan Farrow, "'I Haven't Exhaled in So Long': Surviving Harvey Weinstein," *The New Yorker,* February 25, 2020.

356 **Former colleagues called Weisberg**: Lachlan Cartwright and Pervaiz Shallwani, "Weinstein's Secret Weapon Is a 'Bloodhound' NYPD Detective Turned Private Eye," *Daily Beast,* November 12, 2018.

356 **sexually assaulted her at his apartment in 2006**: Elizabeth Wagmeister, "Former Weinstein Production Assistant Shares Graphic Account of Sexual Assault," *Variety,* October 24, 2017.

356 **friendly messages from Haleyi**: Jan Ransom, "Weinstein Releases Emails Suggesting Long Relationship With Accuser," *New York Times,* August 3, 2018.

356 **all the ammunition Brafman needed**: Tarpley Hitt and Pervaiz Shallwani, "Harvey Weinstein Bombshell: Detective Didn't Tell D.A. About Witness Who Said Sex-Assault Accuser Consented," *Daily Beast,* October 11, 2018.

357 **"Whatever success I may have"**: Benjamin Brafman quoted in Lachlan Cartwright and Pervaiz Shallwani, "Weinstein's Secret Weapon Is a 'Bloodhound' NYPD Detective Turned Private Eye," *Daily Beast,* November 12, 2018.

356 **Weisberg had helped "uncover materials":** Benjamin Brafman quoted in Lachlan Cartwright and Pervaiz Shallwani, "Weinstein's Secret Weapon Is a 'Bloodhound' NYPD Detective Turned Private Eye," *Daily Beast*, November 12, 2018.

357 **They carried signs:** Lauren Aratani, "Harvey Weinstein Accusers Gather in Solidarity to Mark Start of Trial," *Guardian*, January 7, 2020.

357 **"because I would never put myself in that position":** Megan Twohey interviews Donna Rotunno on *The Daily*, hosted by Michael Barbaro, *New York Times*, February 7, 2020.

357 **"Mr. Weinstein's life has been destroyed":** Letter from Damon M. Cheronis, Donna Rotunno, and Arthur Aidala to Judge James M. Burke, March 9, 2020.

357 **"I was twenty-three years old when he ruined my life":** Ambra Gutierrez quoted in Ted Johnson, "Hollywood Reacts to Harvey Weinstein Sentencing," *Deadline,* March 11, 2020.

## CHAPTER 53

361 **launching an investigation out of their Complex Frauds and Cybercrime Unit:** Alan Feuer, "Federal Prosecutors Investigate Weinstein's Ties to Israeli Firm," *New York Times*, September 6, 2018.

## CHAPTER 54

364 **promotional video:** Infotactic group promotional video, posted to the Infotactic group Facebook and Youtube accounts, March 3, 2018.

367 **Lambert's interests strayed:** Raphael Satter, "APNewsBreak: Undercover Agents Target Cybersecurity Watchdog," Associated Press, January 26, 2019.

367 **NSO Group's Pegasus software compromised an iPhone:** Miles Kenyon, "Dubious Denials & Scripted Spin," Citizen Lab, April 1, 2019.

367 **solicited anti-Semitic statements:** Ross Marowits, "West Face Accuses Israeli Intelligence Firm of Covertly Targeting Employees," *Financial Post*, November 29, 2017.

368 **Aharon Almog-Assouline, a retired Israeli security official:** Raphael Satter and Aron Heller, "Court Filing Links Spy Exposed by AP to Israel's Black Cube," Associated Press, February 27, 2019.

## CHAPTER 55

371 **"an affair that violated NBC's terms of employment":** Charlotte Triggs and Michele Corriston, "Hoda Kotb and Savannah Guthrie Are Today's New Anchor Team," People.com, January 2, 2018.

371 "but later said it was inappropriate sexual behavior": Emily Smith and Yaron Steinbuch, "Matt Lauer Allegedly Sexually Harassed Staffer During Olympics," Page Six, *New York Post*, November 29, 2017.

372 "We found no evidence": Claire Atkinson, "NBCUniversal Report Finds Managers Were Unaware of Matt Lauer's Sexual Misconduct," NBC News, May 9, 2018.

373 resisted calls for an independent investigation: Maxwell Tani, "Insiders Doubt NBC Did a Thorough Job on Its #MeToo Probe," *Daily Beast*, May 11, 2018, and David Usborne, "The Peacock Patriarchy," *Esquire,* August 5, 2018.

374 the complaints about Lauer were an open secret: Ramin Setoodeh and Elizabeth Wagmeister, "Matt Lauer Accused of Sexual Harassment by Multiple Women," *Variety*, November 29, 2017.

374 "Keep bending over like that": Matt Lauer quoted in David Usborne, "The Peacock Patriarchy," *Esquire*, August 5, 2018.

374 "It was shouted from the mountaintops": Joe Scarborough quoted in David Usborne, "The Peacock Patriarchy," *Esquire*, August 5, 2018.

374 "NOW YOU'RE KILLING ME": Ramin Setoodeh, "Inside Matt Lauer's Secret Relationship with a Today Production Assistant (EXCLUSIVE)," *Variety*, December 14, 2017.

375 he'd pulled down her pants, bent her over a chair, and had sex with her: Ellen Gabler, Jim Rutenberg, Michael M. Grynbaum and Rachel Abrams, "NBC Fires Matt Lauer, the Face of *Today*," *New York Times*, November 29, 2017.

# CHAPTER 56

385 "we performed oral sex on each other": Matt Lauer statement quoted in Maane Khatchatourian, "Matt Lauer Denies 'False and Salacious' Rape Allegation, Says Affair Was 'Consensual'," *Variety*, October 9, 2019.

390 "They know exactly what they've done": Ari Wilkenfeld quoted in Elizabeth Wagmeister, "Matt Lauer Accuser's Attorney Says NBC Has Failed His Client During Today Interview," *Variety*, December 15, 2017.

# CHAPTER 57

392 fired Mark Halperin: Oliver Darcy, "Five Women Accuse Journalist and *Game Change* Co-Author Mark Halperin of Sexual Harassment," CNNMoney website, October 26, 2017.

392 Days later, NBC fired Matt Zimmerman: *Variety* Staff, "NBC News Fires Talent Booker Following Harassment Claims," *Variety*, November 14, 2017.

392 **a verbal harassment allegation against Chris Matthews:** Erin Nyren, "Female Staffer Who Accused Chris Matthews of Sexual Harassment Received Severance from NBC," *Variety,* December 17, 2017.

393 **three women had accused Tom Brokaw of unwanted advances:** Emily Stewart, "Tom Brokaw Is Accused of Sexual Harassment. He Says He's Been 'Ambushed,'" Vox, Updated May 1, 2018.

393 **said he'd propositioned them and that they'd felt frightened:** Elizabeth Wagmeister and Ramin Setoodeh, "Tom Brokaw Accused of Sexual Harassment By Former NBC Anchor," *Variety,* April 26, 2018.

393 **furious, heartbroken, denied it all:** Marisa Guthrie, "Tom Brokaw Rips 'Sensational' Accuser Claims: I Was 'Ambushed and Then Perp Walked,'" *Hollywood Reporter,* April 27, 2018.

393 **"NBC's self inflicted wound":** Email from Tom Brokaw to Ronan Farrow, January 11, 2018.

394 **the *Washington Post*:** Sarah Ellison, "NBC News Faces Skepticism in Remedying In-House Sexual Harassment," *Washington Post*, April 26, 2018.

394 ***Esquire*:** David Usborne, "The Peacock Patriarchy," *Esquire*, August 5, 2018.

394 ***Daily Beast*:** Lachlan Cartwright and Maxwell Tani, "Accused Sexual Harassers Thrived Under NBC News Chief Andy Lack," *Daily Beast*, September 21, 2018.

394 **Franco said:** Maxwell Tani, "Insiders Doubt NBC Did a Thorough Job on Its #MeToo Probe," *Daily Beast*, May 11, 2018. (NBC News later maintained that the outreach to Curry was part of its official research for its internal report on Lauer. In a statement to the *Daily Beast*, it said, "As soon as we learned about Ann Curry's comments to *The Washington Post*, which we considered relevant to our investigation, a senior NBCUniversal employment lawyer on the investigation team reached out to her directly and they had a conversation on April 25, 2018.")

# CHAPTER 58

397 **saying that the reporting had been killed:** John Koblin, "Ronan Farrow's Ex-Producer Says NBC Impeded Weinstein Reporting," *New York Times,* August 30, 2018.

397 **"Farrow never had a victim":** Internal memo from Andy Lack, "Facts on the NBC News Investigation of Harvey Weinstein," September 3, 2018.

397 **"they were not interested in this interview":** Emily Nestor quoted in Abid Rahman, "Weinstein Accuser Emily Nestor Backs Ronan Farrow in Row with 'Shameful' NBC," *Hollywood Reporter*, September 3, 2018.

397 **"Nothing about me has ever waivered":** Ambra Battilana (@AmbraBattilana) on Twitter, September 4, 2018.

398 "didn't take anything out of context": former senior Miramax executive quoted by Yashar Ali (@Yashar) on Twitter, September 4, 2018.

398 "misleading and incorrect account": Abby Ex (@abbylynnex) on Twitter, September 4, 2018.

400 "should be handled seperately": Ed Sussman, proposed edit to NBC News Wikipedia page, "Talk:NBC News," Wikipedia, February 14, 2018.

400 a network of friendly accounts: Ashley Feinberg, "Facebook, Axios and NBC Paid This Guy to Whitewash Wikipedia Pages," *HuffPost*, March 14, 2019.


## CHAPTER 59

402 "Now the future….": Email from Tom Brokaw to Ronan Farrow, October 13, 2017.

403 "Many powerful people knew what Harvey Weinstein was doing": *Tucker Carlson Tonight,* Fox News, October 11, 2017.


## EPILOGUE

414 "Those accusations are very, very hard to stomach": *The Rachel Maddow Show,* October 25, 2019.

415 re-upping Oppenheim's contract: Joe Flint and Benjamin Mullin, "NBC News Chief Signed New Deal as Weinstein, Lauer Allegations Brewed, *Wall Street Journal,* October 22, 2019.

415 "The path of least resistance is always there": *All In with Chris Hayes,* October 14, 2019.

416 "Unsurprisingly, that call went directly to voicemail": Email to Ronan Farrow, November 7, 2019.

416 NBC's digital journalists were preparing to unionize: J. Clara Chan, "NBC News Digital Staff Form Union Following Network's Handling of Sexual Harassment Accusations," *The Wrap,* October 30, 2019.

416 Protesters demonstrated outside of the network's headquarters: Mackenzie Nichols, "NBC News Sexual Misconduct Controversy Draws Small Protest Outside 30 Rock," *Variety,* October 23, 2019.

416 It was reported that Burke would step down early: Rosie Perper, "NBCUniversal CEO Steve Burke Expected to Step Down in 2020, According to New Report," *Business Insider,* December 13, 2019.

416 Andy Lack was gone too: David Folkenflik, "NBC News Chief Andrew Lack Out After Tenure Marked By Scandal," NPR.org, May 4, 2020.

417 AMI slashed spending: Oli Coleman, "American Media Inc. Slashes Staff Ranks, Pay during Corona Downturn," Page Six, *New York Post,* March 30, 2020.

417 **"Can we talk about the work you've been doing for your friend Harvey Wein-stein?"**: Liam Bartlett, "Army of Spies," Australia's *60 Minutes*, 2018.

417 **"I'll talk about *Be*-zos as much as I fucking want"**: Dylan Howard quoted in Simon van Zuylen-Wood, "Bad Romance," *Columbia Journalism Review*, 2019.

417 **Bookstore owners there told the Associated Press**: Rod McGuirk, "Farrow Books Sells Across Australia Despite Legal Threat," Associated Press, October 17, 2019.

418 **Celebuzz's finding that Howard had sexually harassed colleagues there**: Gary Baum, "Dylan Howard's Hollywood Reboot: Why Are So Many A-Listers Working With a Tabloid Henchman?" *Hollywood Reporter*, February 3, 2020.

418 **"An awful era"**: Lachlan Cartwright and Lloyd Grove, "'Radioactive' National Enquirer Alum Dylan Howard Ousted by AMI," *Daily Beast*, April 6, 2020.

# *INDEX*

# *ABOUT THE AUTHOR*

**R**onan Farrow is a contributing writer for *The New Yorker,* where his investigative reporting has won the Pulitzer Prize for public service, the National Magazine Award, and the George Polk Award, among other honors. He previously worked as an anchor and investigative reporter at MSNBC and NBC News, with his print commentary and reporting appearing in publications including the *Wall Street Journal,* the *Los Angeles Times,* and the *Washington Post.* Before his career in journalism, he served as a State Department official in Afghanistan and Pakistan. Farrow has been named one of *Time* magazine's 100 Most Influential People and one of *GQ*'s Men of the Year. He is a graduate of Yale Law School and a member of the New York Bar. He holds a PhD in political science from Oxford University, where he studied as a Rhodes Scholar. Farrow is also the author of the *New York Times* bestseller *War on Peace: The End of Diplomacy and the Decline of American Influence* and he hosts *The Catch and Kill Podcast,* featuring additional reporting and interviews to accompany this book. The podcast, a Peabody Award finalist, has been downloaded more than eight million times and is available in fine apps everywhere. He lives in New York.